FEMMES FATALES

FEMMES FATALES

Feminism, Film Theory, Psychoanalysis

Mary Ann Doane

ROUTLEDGE · NEW YORK AND LONDON

For Bob and Jo Ann

Published in 1991 by

Routledge
An imprint of Routledge, Chapman and Hall, Inc.
29 West 35 Street
New York, NY 10001

Published in Great Britain by

Routledge
11 New Fetter Lane
London EC4P 4EE

Library of Congress Cataloging in Publication Data

Doane, Mary Ann.
    Femmes fatales : feminism, film theory, and psychoanalysis / Mary
Ann Doane.
        p.   cm.
    Includes bibliographical references and index.
    ISBN 0-415-90319-X. — ISBN 0-415-90320-3 (pbk.)
    1. Femmes fatales in motion pictures. 2. Sex in motion pictures.
3. Feminism and motion pictures.   I. Title.
PN1995.9F44D6   1991
791.43′652042—dc20   91-3659

British Library Cataloguing in Publication data also available

Table of Contents

III. THE BODY OF THE AVANT-GARDE

IV. AT THE EDGES OF PSYCHOANALYSIS

Acknowledgments

This book was written over a number of years and many people have offered valuable criticism, support, and encouragement. Because much of my writing derives from my teaching, I would first like to thank my students at Brown University and The University of Iowa for their sustained curiosity and brilliance, which proved to be contagious. I would also like to thank those who contributed quite materially to the production of these essays by organizing the conferences where they were first presented. Those colleagues who gave particularly helpful advice on certain sections of the book are thanked individually at the beginning of the footnote section of these essays. Peggy Phelan and Linda Williams read an early version of the manuscript and I took their rigorous criticisms (as well as their strong encouragement) very much to heart, although I may not have been entirely adequate to resolving the problems they so astutely pinpointed. The members of a feminist reading group at Brown—Christina Crosby, Coppélia Kahn, Karen Newman, and Ellen Rooney—read and intensively interrogated a number of the essays. Leora Tannenbaum, Ruth Santos, and Virginia Polselli gave crucial support in the preparation of the manuscript. I would especially like to thank Joan Copjec, Naomi Schor, and Elizabeth Weed for sharing with me their knowledge, skills, and dedication to feminist theory. Finally, special thanks go to Phil Rosen for offering clarity, sanity, and lucidity when it was most needed.

A number of the essays included here have been published elsewhere, in earlier versions, in the following journals and anthologies:

"Film and the Masquerade: Theorising the Female Spectator," *Screen* 23.3–4 (1982), by permission of Oxford University Press and the John Logie Baird Centre.

"Masquerade Reconsidered: Further Thoughts on the Female Spectator," *Discourse* 11.1 (1988–89).

"Veiling Over Desire: Close-ups of the Woman," *Feminism and Psychoanalysis*, ed. Richard Feldstein and Judith Roof. Copyright (c) 1989 by Cornell University. Reprinted with permission of Cornell University Press.

"Remembering Women: Psychical and Historical Constructions in Film Theory," *Psychoanalysis and Cinema*, ed. E. Ann Kaplan (New York: Routledge, 1990).

"*Gilda*: Epistemology as Striptease," *Camera Obscura* 11 (Fall 1983).

"The Abstraction of a Lady: *La Signora di tutti*," *Cinema Journal* 28.1 (1988), copyright (c) 1988 by the Board of Trustees of the University of Illinois.

"The Erotic Barter: *Pandora's Box* (1929)," *The Films of G. W. Pabst: An Extraterritorial Cinema*, ed. Eric Rentschler. Copyright (c) 1990 by Rutgers, The State University. Reprinted with permission of Rutgers University Press.

"Woman's Stake: Filming the Female Body," *October* 17 (Summer 1981).

"The Retreat of Signs and the Failure of Words: Leslie Thornton's *Adynata*," *Millenium Film Journal* 16/17/18 (Fall/Winter 1986–87).

"'When the direction of the force acting on the body is changed': The Moving Image," *Wide Angle* 7.1–2 (1985).

I am grateful for permission to reprint these essays here.

Deadly Women, Epistemology, and Film Theory

The femme fatale is the figure of a certain discursive unease, a potential epistemological trauma. For her most striking characteristic, perhaps, is the fact that she never really is what she seems to be. She harbors a threat which is not entirely legible, predictable, or manageable. In thus transforming the threat of the woman into a secret, something which must be aggressively revealed, unmasked, discovered, the figure is fully compatible with the epistemological drive of narrative, the hermeneutic structuration of the classical text. Sexuality becomes the site of questions about what can and cannot be known. This imbrication of knowledge and sexuality, of epistemophilia and scopophilia, has crucial implications for the representation of sexual difference in a variety of discourses—literature, philosophy, psychoanalysis, the cinema. Both cinematic and theoretical claims to truth about women rely to a striking extent on judgments about vision and its stability or instability. Although her origins are literary and pictorial, the femme fatale has a special relevance in cinematic representation, particularly that of Hollywood insofar as it appeals to the visible as the ground of its production of truth.

The femme fatale emerges as a central figure in the nineteenth century, in the texts of writers such as Théophile Gautier and Charles Baudelaire and painters such as Gustave Moreau and Dante Gabriel Rossetti. If, as Christine Buci-Glucksmann points out, the archaeology of modernity is "haunted by the feminine," the femme fatale is one of its most persistent incarnations.[1] She is associated with the styles of Decadence, Symbolism, and Art Nouveau as well as with the attention to decoration and excessive detail linked to a persistent and popular Orientalism (in the constant return, for instance, to the figures of Salome and Cleopatra). Her appearance marks the confluence of modernity, urbanization, Freudian psychoanalysis and new technologies of production and reproduction (photography, the cinema) born of the Industrial Revolution. The femme fatale is a clear indication of the extent of the fears and anxieties prompted by shifts in the understanding of sexual difference in the late nineteenth century. As Buci-Glucksmann argues, this is the moment when the male seems to lose access to the body, which the woman then comes to *overrepresent*. The "working body" is "confiscated by the alienation of machines" and "submitted to industrialization and urbanization." At the same time, in a compensatory gesture, the woman is made to inhere even more closely to the body. The feminine body is insistently allegorized and mythified as excess in art, literature, philosophy. It becomes the "veritable formal correlative" of an increasingly instrumentalized reason in a technological society.[2] Consequently, it is appropriate that the femme fatale is represented as the antithesis of the maternal—sterile or barren, she produces nothing in a society which fetishizes production.[3] It is not surprising that the cinema, born under the mark of such a modernity as a technology of representation, should offer a hospitable home for the femme fatale. She persistently appears there in a number of reincarnations: the vamp of the Scandinavian and American silent cinemas, the *diva* of the Italian film, the femme fatale of film noir of the 1940s.

In what does the deadliness of the femme fatale consist and why is she so insistently a figure of fascination in the texts of modernity? Her power is of a peculiar sort insofar as it is usually not subject to her conscious will, hence appearing to blur the opposition between passivity and activity. She is an ambivalent figure because she is not the subject of power but its *carrier* (the connotations of disease are appropriate here). Indeed, if the femme fatale overrepresents the body it is because she is attributed with a body which is itself given agency independently of consciousness. In a sense, she has power *despite herself*. The evacuation of intention from her operations is fully consistent with the epistemological recognition accorded to the newly born psychoanalytic concept of the unconscious. The femme fatale is an articulation of fears surrounding the loss of stability and centrality of the self, the "I," the ego. These anxieties appear quite explicitly in the process of her representation as castration anxiety. Virginia Allen has associated the femme fatale with "that moment of abandonment in the sex act" and the ensuing "loss of self-awareness."[4] The power accorded to the femme fatale is a function of fears linked to the notions of uncontrollable drives, the fading of subjectivity, and the loss of conscious agency—all themes of the emergent theories of psychoanalysis. But the femme fatale is situated as evil and is frequently punished or killed. Her textual eradication involves a desperate reassertion of control on the part of the threatened male subject. Hence, it would be a mistake to see her as some kind of heroine of modernity. She is not the subject of feminism but a symptom of

Conclusion

male gaze

male fears about feminism. Nevertheless, the representation—like any representation—is not totally under the control of its producers and, once disseminated, comes to take on a life of its own.

This book is not really *about* the femme fatale (although I would like to write that book someday). Instead, the femme fatale acts as a kind of signpost or emblem for many of the issues and concerns addressed in the essays collected here. From the early "*Gilda*: Epistemology as Striptease" (1983) to the quite recently written "Dark Continents: Epistemologies of Racial and Sexual Difference in Psychoanalysis and the Cinema" (1990), these essays, written in many different contexts spanning almost a decade, repeatedly return to questions of the imbrication of knowledge and sexuality and their impact on feminism in a variety of discourses—philosophy, psychoanalysis, the cinema. The emphasis on procedures of masquerade and veiling is an attempt to analyze the extent to which these discourses ally women with deception, secretiveness, a kind of anti-knowledge or, on the other hand, situate them as privileged conduits to a—necessarily complex and even devious—truth. Many of these essays explore the discursive unease, the epistemological trauma associated with the femme fatale and attempt to exploit some of the figure's more disruptive connotations. Because the femme fatale's representation is so dependent upon perceptual ambiguity and ideas about the limits of vision in relation to knowledge, her incarnation in the cinema is a particularly telling one. Because she seems to confound power, subjectivity, and agency with the very lack of these attributes, her relevance to feminist discourses is critical. Since feminisms are forced to search out symbols from a lexicon that does not yet exist, their acceptance of the femme fatale as a sign of strength in an unwritten history must also and simultaneously involve an understanding and assessment of all the epistemological baggage she carries along with her.

But to suggest that these essays were written to promote—or even inadvertently all promote—the understanding of the femme fatale would be to bind them together in a false coherence and unity. There is a strong temptation to find retrospectively a consistency and coherence—perhaps, more importantly, a direction—in one's own work, making an author the least reliable historian of her own ideas. The inconsistencies and contradictions which inevitably mark the passage from one essay to another are a function of the fact that the essays were written at different historical moments, as responses to changing debates and evolving theoretical paradigms. Even within the space of nine years (1981-1990), feminist theory (which is the crucial reference point for all of the essays) has witnessed a number of ruptures, displacements of emphasis, internal antagonisms, and shifting alliances as well as a confrontation with its own assumptions (about race or class) to which it had largely been blind. Indeed, it is something of a misnomer to use the term "feminism" since this implies a monolithic position which the sheer variety of feminisms belies. It is a period which also observed the emergence of new entities—postmodernism, cultural studies—which attempted to restructure the terrain of theoretical work.

On the whole, I think it is fair to say that the form these essays take, the various approaches which characterize them, mark them as the inheritance of the intense methodological consciousness of film and literary theory in the 1970s. This hyperawareness of position and method was an effect of the structuralist, semiotic, and poststructuralist movements which generated the most exciting and intellectually radical cultural work of this period. However, my training as a film student somewhat complicated my relation to these movements. For, while structuralism and poststructuralism were stressing an attention to theoretical frameworks and methods, the emerging discipline of film studies was constantly impelled to justify the status of its own object, the value of analyzing the cinema. Struggling to establish its own legitimacy, film studies was confronted with relentless oppositions between high art and mass culture, single-authored works and collective industrial productions, art and mechanical reproduction. Debates in the field of literature about structuralism and poststructuralism took a specific form precisely because they were waged in the context of well-established departments of English, French, or, to a lesser extent, Comparative Literature, many with lengthy histories and deeply embedded traditions of literary criticism and history which were threatened by the new theory. The institutional positioning of film studies was less stable. Dispersed across a wide variety of departments—Communications, Theater, English, Speech, Art—film studies was constantly made aware of its own institutional fragility.

This had at least two effects which I believe have had a major impact on my own thinking. First, because carving out a space within the institution meant legitimizing film as an object of study, theories of cinematic specificity (such as those of Christian Metz, Raymond Bellour, and Jean-Louis Baudry) became extremely attractive. It was crucial to define film as autonomous and hence necessitating its own modes of analysis (film was *not* a subset of literature). When I was a graduate student in the late 1970s, to claim that someone adopted a (much maligned) *literary* approach to film was to suggest that he/she had recourse to thematic, character, or plot analysis—in other words, that the approach was easily and unproblematically transferable from literature to film without regard for the material specificity of either medium. This was already, however, an out-of-date notion of what constituted literary criticism which, with its conceptualization of *literariness*, shared many of the same concerns about specificity. Nevertheless, the identity of literature and its academic credentials—its right to inhabit a space in the institution—were solidly established in comparison with film. To ensure that film did not become a subset of the study of literature, it was crucial to articulate its difference and to work out a method or methods of analysis which were adequate to its special properties. Hence, debates flourished over the use of viewing equipment designed to slow down or stop the movement of film and allow for close, shot-by-shot or even frame-by-frame analysis. The use of the still as a unit of film analysis caused controversy due to the fact that it is an entity which is not a part of the actual phenomenological experience of a film, which is constantly an effect of movement, however minute. The use of terms which had unique relevance for the film medium—the shot/reverse shot, continuity editing, off-screen space, the 180 degree rule, the point-of-view shot—became pervasive and grounded any appeals to semiotic or poststructuralist theory for their explanatory power.[5] This desire to expose and analyze the technological underside of film bears witness to a belief, which I share, in the critical historical difference of the film medium and its impact on conceptualizations of art and representation in general. As the essays collected here demonstrate, my work has consistently been characterized by a close attention to the formal and technical substructure which supports filmic narrative and which lends it its unique spectatorial effects. The notion of an orchestration of the gaze has a literal resonance in film which it could never have in literature. This approach is testimony to the decisive importance of Walter Benjamin's formulations in "The Work of Art in the Age of Mechanical Reproduction" about the impact of technology on perception and about changing modes of spectatorship in modernity.[6]

The second effect of the institutional fragility of film studies in the 1970s had to do with the degree of openness or receptivity to the new theories and methodologies of structuralism, semiotics, and poststructuralism. Because film studies lacked the solidly ensconced traditions of literary studies and the institutional values accompanying them, it faced less resistance to the incorporation of these non- and even anti-traditional approaches (which is not to suggest that this resistance was entirely absent). In fact, it was much easier for younger scholars in a younger field to embrace the new theories wholeheartedly. This was true of feminism as well, which very quickly became central to the field of film studies as a whole in the United States. If feminism in film analysis was ever truly marginalized, from the vantage point of the 1990s that marginalization would seem to occupy only a brief historical moment. Feminist film theory certainly had and continues to have its opponents and detractors, but it is difficult to imagine a graduate course of studies in film which would not include the cardinal texts of the feminist approach. Indeed, what feminist film theory has to fear much more than the effects of marginalization is a certain orthodoxy and institutionalization.[7] Similarly, the relative ease of entry of semiotics and poststructuralism into the field also risked encouraging a facile or mechanistic "application" of these methodologies to film analysis. In this context, it has always seemed important to me to demonstrate the complexity of these encounters and to resist notions that theory functioned as a grid or map. These theories, instead, provided a different framework of questions and procedures which at times could be productively aligned with the questions of film analysis and at other times collided with its assumptions in particularly telling ways. The peculiar intellectual history characterizing film studies and its institutional positioning have had an effect on the mode of address adopted in the essays collected here. Most of the essays are addressed not to "outsiders" who might need to be convinced of the appropriateness of a semiotic approach to film, but to those who share certain assumptions about the theoretical status of film as an object, about the difficulties of any unproblematic notion of referentiality, and about the necessity of under-standing the ideological effects of the medium. They attempt to push further, to refine questions which may have been too hastily formulated. There are advantages and disadvantages to this approach. It has become increasingly clear to me, for instance, that in the earlier essays in particular, I conceived of the audience as far too small and intellectually homogeneous. Even when the audience was quite small, it turned out to be remarkably heterogeneous.

The emphasis upon cinematic specificity in film studies was somewhat tempered by an equally strong interdisciplinary imperative. As a graduate student at Iowa, I was encouraged to take courses in philosophy, linguistics, comparative literature, theater, English, art history, and mass communica-tions as well as film. Lacking both an established canon as well as orthodox methods, film students often searched for critical tools in other disciplines. But, beyond this rationalization, the object—film itself—seems to demand an interdisciplinary approach. Film is a significant site for the confluence of representational traditions associated with literature, art, theater, and music. In any event, within this context, I would not want to underestimate my debt to literary studies and the particularly exciting developments which took place within it in the 1970s. Literary theory was the locus of questions which extended far beyond literature, engaging feminism, psychoanalysis and its attendant theories of subjectivity, ideological analysis, and linguis-tics. Nevertheless, there are critical differences in the ways in which the two fields—film studies and literary theory—aligned themselves with respect to the various theoretical paradigms. For instance, feminist literary criticism has been haunted for over a decade by the opposition between "French Feminist" approaches and "Anglo-American" feminism. This polarization generally indicates the seemingly unbridgeable gap between continental theories of signification and sexuality inflected by a long speculative philosophical tradition and the pragmatism and empiricism which are said to characterize American intellectual history. Feminist film theory felt the impact of this polarization, but its issues and concerns were also somewhat peripheral to the reigning arguments between French and American feminisms.[8] This was due in large measure to the greater influence in film studies of the British assimilation of continental theory, filtered through the journal *Screen* after its 1971 editorial rupture, and, later, the feminist journal *m/f*. The major reference points of this approach were Louis Althusser and Jacques Lacan and the most influential feminists for American film theorists during this period were British—Juliet Mitchell, Jacqueline Rose, Laura Mulvey, Rosalind Coward. In film, Rose and Mulvey together with Pam Cook and Claire Johnston provided the terms and debates which were to have a profound effect upon the course of feminist film theory. A crucial turning point in my own thinking came in the mid-1970s when, in a search for materials in Larry Edmunds Cinema Bookstore in Los Angeles for an "Images of Women in Film" course I was teaching, I picked up a pamphlet entitled *Notes on Women's Cinema* (1973) edited by Claire Johnston.[9]

Much of this theory was heavily invested in exploring the possible contributions of psychoanalysis not only to an understanding of the "cinematic signifier" as Metz would have it[10] but to the inscription of sexual difference within the cinema as well. A theory of the unconscious was perceived as absolutely crucial to the comprehension of the cinema as the realm of fantasy and desire and the activator of mechanisms of voyeurism and fetishism. Laura Mulvey's "Visual Pleasure and Narrative Cinema" (1975) provided a paradigm which every feminist film critic henceforth felt obliged to confront precisely because it seemed to demonstrate the "perfect fit" between the concepts and scenarios of psychoanalysis—the Oedipus complex, scopophilia, castration, fetishism, identification—and the cinematic imaging and narrativization of sexual difference. Much of my own work has been shaped by the conviction that psychoanalysis was a particularly appropriate methodology for deciphering the psychical operations of the cinema and its impact upon the spectator. But this belief always existed in an uneasy tension with the simultaneous conviction that psychoanalysis was most significantly about the limits and instability of such knowledge, about the decenteredness of the investigative position itself as the effect of the unconscious. Psychoanalysis—both Freudian and Lacanian—always

implicitly or explicitly interrogated the effectivity of language and its adequation to its object. The theoretical concepts of psychoanalysis can be
thought only through its connection with a practice, through its emphasis
upon intersubjectivity and the frequently destabilizing relation to the other.
This necessarily complicates any notion of a "perfect fit."

When my work is unproblematically labeled "psychoanalytic," there is,
I think, a failure to register the wariness in my relation to psychoanalysis
which is legible in the earliest essays. That relation might be described as
one of attraction-repulsion. Psychoanalysis is clearly the most powerful
theory of the psyche and subjectivity we have and it is impossible to
ignore its influence. On the other hand, its epistemological quandaries are
frequently linked with a problematic inscription of sexual difference which
makes psychoanalysis one of the most blatantly symptomatic of cultural
productions. The contradictory construction here is revealing—symptoms
are rarely "blatant." Yet, psychoanalysis enhances the legibility of the
ideological effects of Western culture's construction of femininity. When
I argue, for instance, in "Film and the Masquerade" (1982), that Freud's
theory of castration anxiety and fetishism relies on positing a distinction
between the immediacy of knowledge (in relation to vision) in the little girl
and its delay or distancing in the little boy, it is not in order to demonstrate
that Freud is "right." Rather, his statements about female subjectivity are
symptomatic of a larger cultural configuration. Psychoanalysis offers itself
as a particularly rich and productive site for the examination of these cultural
conventions because it relentlessly pursues their logic, hence revealing the
assumptions that support that logic. I have never felt an obligation to be
"faithful" to the texts of Freud and Lacan—indeed, I am amazed at the
extent and the rigidity of the orthodoxy which has grown up around Lacanian psychoanalysis. Such an orthodoxy would seem to be antithetical to the
psychoanalytic project. Psychoanalysis has an institutional basis but, as
Michel de Certeau points out, "Every institution gives a position. It does
not give legitimation."[11] The ambivalence of my relation to psychoanalysis
becomes most manifest here in the section entitled "At the Edges of Psychoanalysis," but it is also present in earlier essays such as "Veiling Over
Desire," "Remembering Women," and "'When the direction of the
force . . . .'." I continue to find psychoanalysis intellectually irresistible but,
at the same time, am convinced of the necessity of maintaining a distance
which involves analyzing its historical position and effects.

Hence, psychoanalysis has been crucial for the development of feminist
film theory but in different ways, for different theorists. There are also
forms of feminist film criticism which are violently opposed to any appeal
to psychoanalysis. As mentioned earlier, it is highly misleading to use the

term "feminism" in the singular. Nevertheless, I would want to make the claim that feminism as a rubric historically *enabled* the discourses presented in these essays, whether one wishes to refer to feminist theory or theories, the feminist movement or movements. Over the past decade, during which these essays were all written, feminism has witnessed internal conflicts and ruptures and radically changed the framework of its own questions. Many of these shifts and mutations have been attempts to ward off what Nancy K. Miller has referred to as "the temptations of a feminist reuniversaliza-tion."[12] The term "woman," because it erases differences of race, class, sexual preference, national identity, and historical context, has become for many feminists untenable.[13] Criticisms by those who have been margin-alized in relation to white middle-class feminism—women of color, lesbi-ans, Third World women, working-class women—have forced a reassess-ment of the terms used and the types of questions posed. In film studies, the work of Teresa de Lauretis and Jane Gaines has persistently pointed to a narrowness in the conceptualization of "women" in feminist film criticism.[14]

Yet, as Isaac Julien and Kobena Mercer have pointed out, the phrase "race, class and gender" has become something of a *mantra*, ritualistically chanted as though its sheer articulation could resolve a host of problems.[15] The pressing question is how to do this—how to acknowledge and analyze a multiplicity of differences and articulate their extraordinarily complex relation to each other, without reducing the specificity of different modes of oppression. It is easier to point out the gaps, the forms of neglect than to remedy them because it is not simply a question of addition. Considerations of class difference, sexual preference, or racial difference ought to restructure the entire framework of analysis and the questions it sustains. Feminist theory's emphasis upon sexuality as a site of oppression has been and continues to be crucial, but it is also clear that the focus on sexuality can blind the analyst to other realities of discrimination and differentiation.[16] A discourse which refuses to substantialize or essentialize "woman" is not immune from such criticisms. Even in its negativity in relation to all "identities," anti-essentialist feminist theory has concentrated its efforts on a history of negation which is largely white or Eurocentric.

The forms of differentiation which appear to be neglected within contem-porary feminist theory are not only posited as synchronic (racial, class differences) but diachronic (differences of historical context) as well. This critique is partially a function of the feminist use of the term "patriarchy" in not only a global but an ahistorical manner. The call to "historicize" is addressed to feminists but also, in a parallel fashion, to a number of different theoretical enterprises: structuralist, semiotic, poststructuralist. Inheriting

Ferdinand de Saussure's emphasis upon the synchronic, these approaches have been stigmatized for their systematicity and abstraction. To a great extent, the demand to take the notion of historicity seriously has been significant and productive. Unfortunately, it has also often been formulated in terms which pit history against theory (this problem is discussed more extensively in Chapter Four, "Remembering Women: Psychical and Historical Constructions in Film Theory"). The general trend now is toward the local, the particular, the specific, the non-generalizable or the non-totalizable. This tendency is a reaction-formation against something referred to, quite globally, as "Theory." The burgeoning field of cultural studies participates, to a certain extent, in this process of fragmentation, favoring the case studies of local issues or problems and sustaining an eclecticism of methodologies which do not, in themselves, define cultural studies. It is crucial to recognize some of the counterproductive aspects of this enterprise. Part of the impulse of the theoretical approaches of the 1970s (particularly ideological analysis and psychoanalytically informed ideological analysis) was to counter the effects of tendencies in contemporary society toward increasing fragmentation, specialization, individualism, and positivism. This could only be done by establishing a framework or frameworks within which interconnections between seemingly isolated components of society—i.e. art and politics, sexuality and representation, language and ideology—could become visible and analyzable. The fear of abstraction, the fear of "Theory," threatens to transform the analysis of culture into another aspect of that culture's relentless drive toward compartmentalization.

The essays collected here all take seriously the significance of the process of abstraction. Forms of abstraction are crucial to thought itself and are not necessarily in conflict with the "real." Our abstractions are our realities. We live them every day. A collection of essays is, however, quite different from a book. Each considers a different issue or problem and was generated in a specific context for a particular purpose—some were written for conferences organized around a special topic, or for special issues of journals, or as a response to dilemmas I perceived within the field at a certain moment. The essay as such is a unique form, with its own distinct properties. The first definition of "essay" given in the Oxford English Dictionary is "the action or process of trying or testing." An essay is a trial, an attempt, a tentative endeavor. Unlike the book, the essay is an intellectual foray with limited parameters and no claims to being definitive or exhaustive (with these terms' suggestions of "wearing out" knowledge). In many ways, it is a less intimidating form than a book. Because the essay leaves questions open, because it tends to respond to "timely" concerns, it also appears as more historically bound. Although I have resisted any temptation to "update" the essays or to erase the historical traces of the context of their production, I have not arranged them in chronological order. A chronological ordering might suggest that one could witness in their unfolding a coherent development or progression of ideas and attitudes over time. I do not think this is the case. Rather, the essays are collected in sections according to their topics and their affinities with one another. Nevertheless, I would like to pause here and say something about the specific context within which each essay was written.

All of the sections except the final one, "At the Edges of Psychoanalysis," bind together essays written at quite different times, for quite different purposes. The first essay in "Theoretical Excursions," "Film and the Masquerade" (1982) was written originally for a conference at Yale organized by Miriam Hansen and Donald Crafton. Its genesis was simultaneous with the planning and research of my first book, *The Desire to Desire: The Woman's Film of the 1940s* (Indiana UP, 1987). This is evident both in the choice of examples and in the form of the questions posed about female spectatorship. Yet, at a more fundamental level, the essay grapples with the dilemma of the female subject and her positioning within a system and logic of differentiation which seems to exclude her. The strategies of the masquerade article are a kind of litmus test of the compelling strength of poststructuralist and psychoanalytic theories of subjectivity and, simultaneously, of the desire to move beyond them. Perhaps the best way of describing my thinking at that time (and this is relevant to the writing of "Woman's Stake: Filming the Female Body" as well) would be to say that I felt intellectually trapped but, at the same time, could not help admiring the form and structure, the specific architecture, of my cage. I do not believe that the concept of masquerade was capable of effecting a complete escape, but it did stretch the understanding of certain processes of imaging women and pose significant questions to that theory. Because that essay provoked a very large number of responses—both positive and negative—that I had not anticipated, I gladly accepted the invitation from Kathleen Woodward to write a reconsideration or "afterthoughts" article, somewhat on the model of Laura Mulvey's "Afterthoughts" piece on her visual pleasure essay. "Masquerade Reconsidered: Further Thoughts on the Female Spectator" (1988–89) appeared in a special issue of *Discourse* devoted to the concept of masquerade. Among the many critiques of my original masquerade essay, Tania Modleski's seemed most productive in its return to the problem of the joke, hence raising issues of reading and readability which are a focus of my response.

"Veiling Over Desire: Close-Ups of the Woman" continues the analysis of masking and veiling in their relation to vision and deception. Written specifically for a conference on Feminism and Psychoanalysis held at Normal, Illinois in May 1986, it was also partially generated by a course I taught that spring entitled "Philosophical and Theoretical Constructions of the Feminine." The attempt here is to decipher the tropological functions of the veil in the cinema, psychoanalysis, and philosophy. The final essay in this section, "Remembering Women: Psychical and Historical Constructions in Film Theory" was written for an Australian Screen Studies Association conference in Sydney (December 1986). Its reception at that conference illuminated, for me, the significance of national differences in the development and institutionalization of feminist film theory. The impulse in writing the essay was to confront some of the difficulties and dangers in the demand to historicize—a demand threatening to polarize irremediably theory and history. It does so through an examination of the concept of memory and its place within psychoanalytic theory.

The second section, "Femmes Fatales," is constituted by three close analyses of specific films centering on the figure of the femme fatale in differing guises (the extent of her passivity or activity varies greatly from film to film). "*Gilda*: Epistemology as Striptease" (1983) is the earliest essay in this triptych and confronts the classic femme fatale of film noir, demonstrating the way in which she becomes "the other side of knowledge as it is conceived within a phallocentric logic" or "an epistemological trouble." The other two essays deal respectively with Max Ophuls's *La Signora di tutti* (1934) and G.W. Pabst's *Pandora's Box* (1929). They were written somewhat later (1988 and 1989) and are both concerned with the unique function of the femme fatale within modernism. Here, the femme fatale incarnates the peculiar conceptualizations of history, temporality, and technology in modernity.

Although most of my work has dealt with the classical Hollywood cinema or, at the very least, with narrative cinema inflected by Hollywood, I have also attempted to theorize the inscription of the female body in a cinema which defines itself as outside and against Hollywood—the films of the avant-garde. In such a context, the question of the body and the mode of its imaging becomes crucial. "Woman's Stake: Filming the Female Body" (1981) was inspired by a simple question: how is it possible for a feminist filmmaking practice to represent a female body which has been overcoded, overwritten, overconstructed within mainstream culture and, in particular, mainstream cinema? Serious consideration of this question seemed to be blocked at the time by energy-consuming debates between essentialists and anti-essentialists. "Woman's Stake" was an attempt to move "beyond" the impasse of the essentialism/anti-essentialism opposition in order to rethink the relation between body and psyche which is a fundamental support of the psychoanalytic approach. Arguments about essentialism continue to dominate much of the discourse of feminist theory.[17] The continued relevance—indeed necessity—of an analysis of the body and its discursive and political logic is demonstrated in other ways as well. In Chapter Eleven, "Dark Continents," I cite a statement by Henry Louis Gates, Jr. about the biological foundation of racial difference versus that of sexual difference: "Race is the ultimate trope of difference because it is so very arbitrary in its application. The biological criteria used to determine 'difference' in sex simply do not hold when applied to 'race.' "[18] Even for a theorist so acutely aware of the social construction of difference, there is a certain obviousness about the biology of sexual difference—as though the body were immediately readable in this respect and in this respect alone. Such statements point to the intransigence of the body wherever sexual difference is concerned and the continued importance of a feminist reassessment of its role.

The feminist avant-garde has contributed strongly to a rethinking and reinscription of the female body and Leslie Thornton's film *Adynata* is an especially good example of an attempt to explore the articulation of racial and sexual difference. Chapter Nine, written in 1986, is an analysis of *Adynata*'s critique of Orientalism as a form of continuous and excessive misreading. The final essay in this section, "'When the direction of the force acting on the body is changed': The Moving Image," was written for a conference in 1982 at Milwaukee's Center for Twentieth Century Studies which was devoted to the avant-garde. The essay analyzes the "laws" connecting vision, space, and the body in three different discourses—avant-garde cinema, psychoanalysis, and experimental psychology.

The essays in the final section were both written specifically for this collection. They are "at the edges of psychoanalysis" because they either explore areas which psychoanalysis is accused of being incapable of dealing with (racial difference) or investigate the difficulties in setting limits to the psychoanalytic enterprise. "Dark Continents: Epistemologies of Racial and Sexual Difference in Psychoanalysis and the Cinema" is an analysis of the articulation of racial difference and sexual difference both in the texts of psychoanalysis (Freud, Fanon) and in the cinema (in films such as Griffith's *Birth of a Nation* [1915] and Sirk's *Imitation of Life* [1959]). Freud's trope of woman as dark continent is a particularly telling symptom of the white woman's fundamental and problematic role in the articulation of race and sexuality. The essay on sublimation is an inquiry into the viability of that concept in psychoanalytic approaches to questions of aesthetics. My conclusion is that the notion of sublimation attempts in vain to maintain the distinctions it sets out to confirm, that it is ultimately a failed concept. But in the process of its collapse, sublimation points to potential alternatives for activating psychoanalysis in textual analysis. This section is testimony to my belief that psychoanalysis is most useful for feminism when it is intensively interrogated.

The femme fatale as *embodied*, as an actual figure, slips in and out of the discourse of this collection, her presence most conspicuous in the essays about films where she appears. But her function of articulating questions of knowledge and sexuality, of vision and epistemological reliability, is of concern throughout the book. Feminist film theory must be especially sensitive to issues of iconography, of vision and its relation to forms of knowing, because femininity in modernity has become very much a question of hypervisibility. As soon as the relation between vision and knowledge becomes unstable or deceptive, the potential for a disruption of the given sexual logic appears. Perhaps this disruptiveness can define, for feminist theory, the deadliness of the femme fatale.

I. Theoretical Excursions

CHAPTER ONE

Film and the Masquerade: Theorizing the Female Spectator

I. HEADS IN HIEROGLYPHIC BONNETS

In his lecture on "Femininity," Freud forcefully inscribes the absence of the female spectator of theory in his notorious statement, ". . . to those of you who are women this will not apply—you are yourselves the problem. . . ."[1] Simultaneous with this exclusion operated upon the female members of his audience, he invokes, as a rather strange prop, a poem by Heine. Introduced by Freud's claim concerning the importance and elusiveness of his topic—"Throughout history people have knocked their heads against the riddle of the nature of femininity . . ."—are four lines of Heine's poem:

Heads in hieroglyphic bonnets,
Heads in turbans and black birettas,
Heads in wigs and thousand other
Wretched, sweating heads of humans . . .[2]

The effects of the appeal to this poem are subject to the work of overdetermination Freud isolated in the text of the dream. The sheer proliferation of heads and hats (and hence, through a metonymic slippage, minds), which are presumed to have confronted this intimidating riddle before Freud, confers on his discourse the weight of an intellectual history, of a tradition of interrogation. Furthermore, the image of hieroglyphics strengthens the association made between femininity and the enigmatic, the undecipherable, that which is "other." And yet Freud practices a slight deception here, concealing what is elided by removing the lines from their context, castrating, as it were, the stanza. For the question over which Heine's heads brood is not the same as Freud's—it is not "What is Woman?," but instead, ". . . what signifies Man?" The quote is taken from the seventh section (entitled "Questions") of the second cycle of *The North Sea*. The full stanza, presented as the words of "a young man. / His breast full of sorrow, his head full of doubt," reads as follows:

> O solve me the riddle of life,
> The teasingly time-old riddle,
> Over which many heads already have brooded,
> Heads in hats of hieroglyphics,
> Turbaned heads and heads in black skull-caps,
> Heads in perrukes and a thousand other
> Poor, perspiring human heads—
> Tell me, what signifies Man?
> Whence does he come? Whither does he go?
> Who lives up there upon golden stars?[3]

The question in Freud's text is thus a disguise and a displacement of that other question, which in the pre-text is both humanistic and theological. The claim to investigate an otherness is a pretense, haunted by the mirror-effect by means of which the question of the woman reflects only the man's own ontological doubts. Yet what interests me most in this intertextual misrepresentation is that the riddle of femininity is initiated from the beginning in Freud's text as a question in masquerade. But I will return to the issue of masquerade later.

More pertinently, as far as the cinema is concerned, it is not accidental that Freud's eviction of the female spectator/auditor is copresent with the invocation of a hieroglyphic language. The woman, the enigma, the hieroglyphic, the picture, the image—the metonymic chain connects with another: the cinema, the theater of pictures, a writing in images of the woman but not *for* her. For she *is* the problem. The semantic valence attributed to a hieroglyphic language is two-edged. In fact, there is a sense in which the term is inhabited by a contradiction. On the one hand, the hieroglyphic is summoned, particularly when it merges with a discourse on the woman, to connote an indecipherable language, a signifying system which denies its own function by failing to signify anything to the uninitiated, to those who do not hold the key. In this sense, the hieroglyphic, like the woman, harbors a mystery, an inaccessible though desirable otherness. On the other hand, the hieroglyphic is the most readable of languages. Its immediacy, its accessibility are functions of its status as a *pictorial* language, a writing in images. For the image is theorized in terms of a certain *closeness,* the lack of a distance or gap between sign and referent. Given its iconic characteristics, the relationship between signifier and signified is

understood as less arbitrary in imagistic systems of representation than in language "proper." The intimacy of signifier and signified in the iconic sign negates the distance which defines phonetic language. And it is the absence of this crucial distance or gap which also, simultaneously, specifies both the hieroglyphic and the female. This is precisely why Freud evicted the woman from his lecture on femininity. Too close to herself, entangled in her own enigma, she could not step back, could not achieve the necessary distance of a second look.[4]

Thus, while the hieroglyphic is an indecipherable or at least enigmatic language, it is also and at the same time potentially the most universally understandable, comprehensible, appropriable of signs.[5] And the woman shares this contradictory status. But it is here that the analogy slips. For hieroglyphic languages are *not* perfectly iconic. They would not achieve the status of languages if they were—due to what Todorov and Ducrot refer to as a certain non-generalizability of the iconic sign:

> Now it is the impossibility of generalizing this principle of representation that has introduced even into fundamentally morphemographic writing systems such as Chinese, Egyptian, and Sumerian, the phonographic principle. We might almost conclude that every logography (the graphic system of language notation) grows out of *the impossibility of a generalized iconic representation*; proper nouns and abstract notions (including inflections) are then the ones that will be noted phonetically.[6]

The iconic system of representation is inherently deficient—it cannot disengage itself from the "real," from the concrete; it lacks the gap necessary for generalizability (for Saussure, this is the idea that, "Signs which are arbitrary realize better than others the ideal of the semiotic process"). The woman, too, is defined by such an insufficiency. My insistence upon the congruence between certain theories of the image and theories of femininity is an attempt to dissect the *episteme* which assigns to the woman a special place in cinematic representation while denying her access to that system.

The cinematic apparatus inherits a theory of the image which is not conceived outside of sexual specifications. And historically, there has always been a certain imbrication of the cinematic image and the representation of the woman. The woman's relation to the camera and the scopic regime is quite different from that of the male. As Noël Burch points out, the early silent cinema, through its insistent inscription of scenarios of voyeurism, conceives of its spectator's viewing pleasure in terms of that of the Peeping Tom, behind the screen, reduplicating the spectator's position in relation to the woman as screen.[7] Spectatorial desire, in contemporary

film theory, is generally delineated as either voyeurism or fetishism, as precisely a pleasure in seeing what is prohibited in relation to the female body. The image orchestrates a gaze, a limit, and its pleasurable transgression. The woman's beauty, her very desirability, becomes a function of certain practices of imaging—framing, lighting, camera movement, angle. She is thus, as Laura Mulvey has pointed out, more closely associated with the surface of the image than its illusory depths, its constructed three-dimensional space which the man is destined to inhabit and hence control.[8] In *Now Voyager* (1942), for instance, a single image signals the momentous transformation of the Bette Davis character from ugly spinster aunt to glamorous single woman. Charles Affron describes the specifically cinematic aspect of this operation as a "stroke of genius":

> The radical shadow bisecting the face in white/dark/white strata creates a visual phenomenon quite distinct from the makeup transformation of lipstick and plucked eyebrows. . . . This shot does not reveal what we commonly call acting, especially after the most recent exhibition of that activity, but the sense of face belongs to a plastique pertinent to the camera. The viewer is allowed a different perceptual referent, a chance to come down from the nerve-jarring, first sequence and to use his eyes anew.[9]

A "plastique pertinent to the camera" constitutes the woman not only as the image of desire but as the desirous image—one which the devoted cinéphile can cherish and embrace. To "have" the cinema is, in some sense, to "have" the woman. But *Now Voyager* is, in Affron's terms, a "tear-jerker," in others, a "woman's picture," i.e. a film purportedly produced for a female audience. What, then, of the female spectator? What can one say about her desire in relation to this process of imaging? It would seem that what the cinematic institution has in common with Freud's gesture is the eviction of the female spectator from a discourse purportedly about her (the cinema, psychoanalysis)—one which, in fact, narrativizes her again and again.

II. A LASS BUT NOT A LACK

Theories of female spectatorship are thus rare, and when they are produced, seem inevitably to confront certain blockages in conceptualization. The difficulties in thinking female spectatorship demand consideration. After all, even if it is admitted that the woman is frequently the object of the voyeuristic or fetishistic gaze in the cinema, what is there to prevent her from reversing the relation and appropriating the gaze for her own

pleasure? Precisely the fact that the reversal itself remains locked within the same logic. The male striptease, the gigolo—both inevitably signify the mechanism of reversal itself, constituting themselves as aberrations whose acknowledgment simply reinforces the dominant system of aligning sexual difference with a subject/object dichotomy. And an essential attribute of that dominant system is the matching of male subjectivity with the agency of the look.

The supportive binary opposition at work here is not only that utilized by Laura Mulvey—an opposition between passivity and activity, but perhaps more importantly, an opposition between proximity and distance in relation to the image.[10] It is in this sense that the very logic behind the structure of the gaze demands a sexual division. While the distance between image and signified (or even referent) is theorized as minimal, if not non-existent, that between the film and the spectator must be maintained, even measured. One need only think of Noël Burch's mapping of spectatorship as a perfect distance from the screen (two times the width of the image)—a point in space from which the filmic discourse is most accessible.[11]

But the most explicit representation of this opposition between proximity and distance is contained in Christian Metz's analysis of voyeuristic desire in terms of a kind of social hierarchy of the senses: "It is no accident that the main socially acceptable arts are based on the senses at a distance, and that those which depend on the senses of contact are often regarded as 'minor' arts ($-$ culinary arts, art of perfumes, etc.)."[12] The voyeur, according to Metz, must maintain a distance between himself and the image—the cinéphile *needs* the gap which represents for him the very distance between desire and its object. In this sense, voyeurism is theorized as a type of meta-desire:

> If it is true of all desire that it depends on the infinite pursuit of its absent object, voyeuristic desire, along with certain forms of sadism, is the only desire whose principle of distance symbolically and spatially evokes this fundamental rent.[13]

Yet even this status as meta-desire does not fully characterize the cinema for it is a feature shared by other arts as well (painting, theater, opera, etc.). Metz thus adds another reinscription of this necessary distance. What specifies the cinema is a further re-duplication of the lack which prompts desire. The cinema is characterized by an illusory sensory plenitude (there is "so much to see") and yet haunted by the absence of those very objects which are there to be seen. Absence is an absolute and irrecoverable distance. In other words, Noël Burch is quite right in aligning spectatorial desire with a certain spatial configuration. The viewer must not sit either too close or too far from the screen. The result of both would be the same—he would lose the image of his desire.

It is precisely this opposition between proximity and distance, control of the image and its loss, which locates the possibilities of spectatorship within the problematic of sexual difference. For the female spectator there is a certain overpresence of the image—she *is* the image. Given the closeness of this relationship, the female spectator's desire can be described only in terms of a kind of narcissism—the female look demands a becoming. It thus appears to negate the very distance or gap specified by Metz and Burch as the essential precondition for voyeurism. From this perspective, it is important to note the constant recurrence of the motif of proximity in feminist theories (especially those labeled "new French feminisms") which purport to describe a feminine specificity. For Luce Irigaray, female anatomy is readable as a constant relation of the self to itself, as an autoeroticism based on the embrace of the two lips which allow the woman to touch herself without mediation. Furthermore, the very notion of property, and hence possession of something which can be constituted as other, is antithetical to the woman: "*Nearness* however, is not foreign to woman, a nearness so close that any identification of one or the other, and therefore any form of property, is impossible. Woman enjoys a closeness with the other that is *so near she cannot possess it any more than she can possess herself.*"[14] Or, in the case of female madness or delirium, ". . . women do not manage to articulate their madness: they suffer it directly in their body . . . ."[15] The distance necessary to detach the signifiers of madness from the body in the construction of even a discourse which exceeds the boundaries of sense is lacking. In the words of Hélène Cixous, "More so than men who are coaxed toward social success, toward sublimation, women are body."[16]

This theme of the overwhelming presence-to-itself of the female body is elaborated by Sarah Kofman and Michèle Montrelay as well. Kofman describes how Freudian psychoanalysis outlines a scenario whereby the subject's passage from the mother to the father is simultaneous with a passage from the senses to reason, nostalgia for the mother henceforth signifying a longing for a different positioning in relation to the sensory or the somatic, and the degree of civilization measured by the very distance from the body.[17] Similarly, Montrelay argues that while the male has the possibility of displacing the first object of desire (the mother), the female must become that object of desire:

> Recovering herself as maternal body (and also as phallus), the woman can no longer repress, "lose," the first stake of representation . . . . From now on,

anxiety, tied to the presence of this body, can only be insistent, continuous. This body, so close, which she has to occupy, is an object in excess which must be "lost," that is to say, repressed, in order to be symbolized.[18]

This body so close, so excessive, prevents the woman from assuming a position similar to the man's in relation to signifying systems. For she is haunted by the loss of a loss, the lack of that lack so essential for the realization of the ideals of semiotic systems.

Female specificity is thus theorized in terms of spatial proximity. In opposition to this "closeness" to the body, a spatial distance in the male's relation to his body rapidly becomes a temporal distance in the service of knowledge. This is presented quite explicitly in Freud's analysis of the construction of the "subject supposed to know." The knowledge involved here is a knowledge of sexual difference as it is organized in relation to the structure of the look, turning on the visibility of the penis. For the little girl in Freud's description seeing and knowing are simultaneous—there is no temporal gap between them. In "Some Psychological Consequences of the Anatomical Distinction Between the Sexes," Freud claims that the girl, upon seeing the penis for the first time, "makes her judgement and her decision in a flash. She has seen it and knows that she is without it and wants to have it."[19] In the lecture on "Femininity" Freud repeats this gesture, merging perception and intellection: "They [girls] at once notice the difference and, it must be admitted, its significance too."[20]

The little boy, on the other hand, does not share this immediacy of under-standing. When he first sees the woman's genitals he "begins by showing irresolution and lack of interest; he sees nothing or disowns what he has seen, he softens it down or looks about for expedients for bringing it into line with his expectations."[21] A second event, the threat of castration, is necessary to prompt a rereading of the image, endowing it with a meaning in relation to the boy's own subjectivity. It is in the distance between the look and the threat that the boy's relation to knowledge of sexual difference is formulated. The boy, unlike the girl in Freud's description, is capable of a re-vision of earlier events, a retrospective understanding which invests the events with a signifi-cance which is in no way linked to an immediacy of sight. This gap between the visible and the knowable, the very possibility of disowning what is seen, prepares the ground for fetishism. In a sense, the male spectator is destined to be a fetishist, balancing knowledge and belief.

The female, on the other hand, must find it extremely difficult, if not impossible, to assume the position of fetishist. That body which is so close continually reminds her of the castration which cannot be "fetishized away." The lack of a distance between seeing and understanding, the mode of judging "in a flash," is conducive to what might be termed an "over-identification" with the image. The association of tears and "wet wasted afternoons" (in Molly Haskell's words)[22] with genres specified as feminine (the soap opera, the "woman's picture") points very precisely to this type of over-identification, this abolition of a distance, in short, this inability to fetishize. The woman is constructed differently in relation to processes of looking. For Irigaray, this dichotomy between distance and proximity is described as the fact that:

> The masculine can partly look at itself, speculate about itself, represent itself and describe itself for what it is, whilst the feminine can try to speak to itself through a new language, but cannot describe itself from outside or in formal terms, except by identifying itself with the masculine, thus by losing itself.[23]

Irigaray goes even further: the woman always has a problematic relation to the visible, to form, to structures of seeing. She is much more comfortable with, closer to, the sense of touch.

The pervasiveness, in theories of the feminine, of descriptions of such a claustrophobic closeness, a deficiency in relation to structures of seeing and the visible, must clearly have consequences for attempts to theorize female spectatorship. And, in fact, the result is a tendency to view the female spectator as the site of an oscillation between a feminine position and a masculine position, invoking the metaphor of the transvestite. Given the structures of cinematic narrative, the woman who identifies with a female character must adopt a passive or masochistic position, while identification with the active hero necessarily entails an acceptance of what Laura Mulvey refers to as a certain "masculinization" of spectatorship.

> . . . as desire is given cultural materiality in a text, for women (from childhood onwards) trans-sex identification is a *habit* that very easily becomes *second Nature*. However, this Nature does not sit easily and shifts restlessly in its borrowed transvestite clothes.[24]

The transvestite wears clothes which signify a different sexuality, a sexuality which, for the woman, allows a mastery over the image and the very possibility of attaching the gaze to desire. Clothes make the man, as they say. Perhaps this explains the ease with which women can slip into male clothing. As both Freud and Cixous point out, the woman seems to be *more* bisexual than the man. A scene from Cukor's *Adam's Rib* (1949) graphically demonstrates this ease of female transvestism. As Katherine Hepburn asks the jury to imagine the sex role reversal of the three major characters involved in the case, there are three dissolves linking each of the characters successively to shots in which they are dressed in the clothes of the opposite sex. What characterizes the sequence is the marked facility of the transformation of the two women into men in contradistinction to a certain resistance in the case of the man. The acceptability of the female reversal is quite distinctly opposed to the male reversal which seems capable of representation only in terms of farce. Male transvestism is an occasion for laughter; female transvestism only another occasion for desire.

Thus, while the male is locked into sexual identity, the female can at least pretend that she is other—in fact, sexual mobility would seem to be a distinguishing feature of femininity in its cultural construction. Hence, transvestism would be fully recuperable. The idea seems to be this: it is understandable that women would want to be men, for everyone wants to be elsewhere than in the feminine position. What is not understandable within the given terms is why a woman might flaunt her femininity, produce herself as an excess of femininity, in other words, foreground the masquerade. Masquerade is not as recuperable as transvestism precisely because it constitutes an acknowledgment that it is femininity itself which is constructed as mask—as the decorative layer which conceals a non-identity. For Joan Riviere, the first to theorize the concept, the masquerade of femininity is a kind of reaction-formation against the woman's trans-sex identification, her transvestism. After assuming the position of the subject of discourse rather than its object, the intellectual woman whom Riviere analyzes felt compelled to compensate for this theft of masculinity by overdoing the gestures of feminine flirtation.

> Womanliness therefore could be assumed and worn as a mask, both to hide the possession of masculinity and to avert the reprisals expected if she was found to possess it—much as a thief will turn out his pockets and ask to be searched to prove that he has not the stolen goods. The reader may now ask how I define womanliness or where I draw the line between genuine womanliness and the "masquerade." My suggestion is not, however, that there is any such difference; whether radical or superficial, they are the same thing.[25]

The masquerade, in flaunting femininity, holds it at a distance. Womanliness is a mask which can be worn or removed. The masquerade's resistance to patriarchal positioning would therefore lie in its denial of the production of femininity as closeness, as presence-to-itself, as, precisely, imagistic. The transvestite adopts the sexuality of the other—the woman becomes a man in order to attain the necessary distance from the image. Masquerade, on the other hand, involves a realignment of femininity, the recovery, or more accurately, simulation, of the missing gap or distance. To masquerade is to manufacture a lack in the form of a certain distance between oneself and one's image. If, as Moustafa Safouan points out, ". . . to wish to include in oneself as an object the cause of the desire of the Other is a formula for the structure of hysteria,"[26] then masquerade is anti-hysterical for it works to effect a separation between the cause of desire and oneself. In Montrelay's words, "the woman uses her own body as a disguise."[27]

The very fact that we can speak of a woman "using" her sex or "using" her body for particular gains is highly significant—it is not that a man cannot use his body in this way but that he doesn't have to. The masquerade doubles representation; it is constituted by a hyperbolization of the accoutrements of femininity. *A propos* of a recent performance by Marlene Dietrich, Silvia Bovenschen claims, ". . . we are watching a woman demonstrate the representation of a woman's body."[28] This type of masquerade, an excess of femininity, is aligned with the *femme fatale* and, as Montrelay explains, is necessarily regarded by men as evil incarnate: "It is this evil which scandalizes whenever woman plays out her sex in order to evade the word and the law. Each time she subverts a law or a word which relies on the predominantly masculine structure of the look."[29] By destabilizing the image, the masquerade confounds this masculine structure of the look. It effects a defamiliarization of female iconography. Nevertheless, the preceding account simply specifies masquerade as a type of representation which carries a threat, disarticulating male systems of viewing. Yet, it specifies nothing with respect to female spectatorship. What might it mean to masquerade as spectator? To assume the mask in order to see in a different way?

III. "MEN SELDOM MAKE PASSES AT GIRLS WHO WEAR GLASSES"

The first scene in *Now Voyager* depicts the Bette Davis character as repressed, unattractive, and undesirable or, in her own words, as the spinster aunt of the family. ("Every family has one.") She has heavy eyebrows, keeps her hair bound tightly in a bun, and wears glasses, a drab dress, and heavy shoes. By the time of the shot discussed earlier, signaling her transformation into beauty, the glasses have disappeared, along with the other signifiers of unattractiveness. Between these two moments there is a scene in which the doctor who cures her actually confiscates her glasses (as a part of the cure). The woman who wears glasses constitutes one of the most intense visual clichés of the cinema.

The image is a heavily marked condensation of motifs concerned with repressed sexuality, knowledge, visibility and vision, intellectuality, and desire. The woman with glasses signifies simultaneously intellectuality and undesirability; but the moment she removes her glasses (a moment which, it seems, must almost always be *shown* and which is itself linked with a certain sensual quality), she is transformed into spectacle, the very picture of desire. Now, it must be remembered that the cliché is a heavily loaded moment of signification, a social knot of meaning. It is characterized by an effect of ease and naturalness. Yet, the cliché has a binding power so strong that it indicates a precise moment of ideological danger or threat—in this case, the woman's appropriation of the gaze. Glasses worn by a woman in the cinema do not generally signify a deficiency in seeing but an active looking, or even simply the fact of seeing as opposed to being seen. The intellectual woman looks and analyzes, and in usurping the gaze she poses a threat to an entire system of representation. It is as if the woman had forcefully moved to the other side of the specular. The overdetermination of the image of the woman with glasses, its status as ıa cliché, is a crucial aspect of the cinematic alignment of structures of seeing and being seen with sexual difference. The cliché, in assuming an immediacy of understanding, acts as a mechanism for the naturalization of sexual difference.

But the figure of the woman with glasses is only an extreme moment of a more generalized logic. There is always a certain excessiveness, a difficulty associated with women who appropriate the gaze, who insist upon looking. Linda Williams has demonstrated how, in the genre of the horror film, the woman's active looking is ultimately punished. And what she sees, the monster, is only a mirror of herself—both woman and monster are freakish in their difference—defined by either "too much" or "too little."[30] Just as the dominant narrative cinema repetitively inscribes scenarios of voyeurism, internalizing or narrativizing the film-spectator relationship (in films like *Psycho* [1960], *Rear Window* [1954], *Peeping Tom* [1960]), taboos in seeing are insistently formulated in relation to the female spectator as well. The man with binoculars is countered by the woman with glasses. The gaze must be dissociated from mastery. In *Leave Her to Heaven* (John Stahl, 1945), the female protagonist's (Gene Tierney's) excessive desire and overpossessiveness are signaled from the very beginning of the film by her intense and sustained stare at the major male character, a stranger she first encounters on a train. The discomfort her look causes is graphically depicted. The Gene Tierney character is ultimately revealed to be the epitome of evil—killing her husband's crippled younger brother, her unborn child, and ultimately herself in an attempt to brand her cousin as a murderess in order to insure her husband's future fidelity. In *Humoresque* (Jean Negulesco, 1946), Joan Crawford's problematic status is a result of her continual attempts to assume the position of spectator—fixing John Garfield with her gaze. Her transformation from spectator to spectacle is signified repetitively by the gesture of removing her glasses. Rosa, the character played by Bette Davis in *Beyond the Forest* (King Vidor, 1949) walks to the station every day simply to *watch* the train departing for Chicago. Her fascination with the train is a fascination with its phallic power to transport her to "another place." This character is also specified as having a "good eye"—she can shoot, both pool and guns. In all three films the woman is constructed as the site of an excessive and dangerous desire. This desire mobilizes extreme efforts of containment and unveils the sadistic aspect of narrative. In all three films the woman dies. As Claire Johnston points out, death is the "location of all impossible signs,"[31] and the films demonstrate that the woman as subject of the gaze is clearly an impossible sign. There is a perverse rewriting of this logic of the gaze in *Dark Victory* (Edmund Goulding, 1939), where the woman's story achieves heroic and tragic proportions not only in blindness, but in a blindness which mimes sight—when the woman pretends to be able to see.

IV. OUT OF THE CINEMA AND INTO THE STREETS: THE CENSORSHIP OF THE FEMALE GAZE

This process of narrativizing the negation of the female gaze in the classical Hollywood cinema finds its perfect encapsulation in a still photograph taken in 1948 by Robert Doisneau, *"Un Regard Oblique."* Just as the Hollywood narratives discussed above purport to center a female protagonist, the photograph appears to give a certain prominence to a woman's look. Yet, both the title of the photograph and its organization of space indicate that the real site of scopophilic power is on the margins of the frame. The man is not centered; in fact, he occupies a very narrow space on the extreme right of the picture. Nevertheless, it is his gaze which defines the problematic of the photograph; it is his gaze which effectively erases that of the woman. Indeed, as subject of the gaze, the woman looks intently. But not only is the object of her look concealed from the spectator, her gaze is encased by the two poles defining the masculine axis of vision. Fascinated by nothing visible—a blankness or void for the spectator—unanchored by a "sight" (there is nothing "proper" to her vision—save, perhaps, the mirror), the female gaze is left free-floating, vulnerable to

Figure 1.1 *"Un Regard Oblique."* **Photograph by Robert Doisneau.
The Metropolitan Museum of Art, Warner Communications Inc.
Purchase Fund, 1981 (1981.1199)**

subjection. The faint reflection in the shop window of only the frame of
the picture at which she is looking serves merely to rearticulate, *en abyme,*
the emptiness of her gaze, the absence of her desire in representation.

On the other hand, the object of the male gaze is fully present, there for
the spectator. The fetishistic representation of the nude female body, fully
in view, insures a masculinization of the spectatorial position. The woman's
look is literally outside the triangle which traces a complicity between the
man, the nude, and the spectator. The feminine presence in the photograph,
despite a diegetic centering of the female subject of the gaze, is taken over
by the picture as object. And, as if to doubly "frame" her in the act of
looking, the painting situates its female figure as a spectator (although it is
not clear whether she is looking at herself in a mirror or peering through a
door or window). While this drama of seeing is played out at the surface
of the photograph, its deep space is activated by several young boys, out-
of-focus, in front of a belt shop. The opposition out-of-focus/in-focus

reinforces the supposed clarity accorded to the representation of the woman's "non-vision." Furthermore, since this out-of-focus area constitutes the precise literal center of the image, it also demonstrates how the photograph makes figurative the operation of centering—draining the actual center point of significance in order to deposit meaning on the margins. The male gaze is centered, in control—although it is exercised from the periphery.

The spectator's pleasure is thus produced through the framing/negation of the female gaze. The woman is there as the butt of a joke—a "dirty joke" which, as Freud has demonstrated, is always constructed at the expense of a woman. In order for a dirty joke to emerge in its specificity in Freud's description, the object of desire—the woman—must be absent and a third person (another man) must be present as witness to the joke—"so that gradually, in place of the woman, the onlooker, now the listener, becomes the person to whom the smut is addressed . . . ."[32] The terms of the photograph's address as joke once again insure a masculinization of the place of the spectator. The operation of the dirty joke is also inextricably linked by Freud to scopophilia and the exposure of the female body:

> Smut is like an exposure of the sexually different person to whom it is directed. By the utterance of the obscene words it compels the person who is assailed to imagine the part of the body or the procedure in question and shows her that the assailant is himself imagining it. It cannot be doubted that the desire to see what is sexual exposed is the original motive of smut.[33]

From this perspective, the photograph lays bare the very mechanics of the joke through its depiction of sexual exposure and a surreptitious act of seeing (and desiring). Freud's description of the joke-work appears to constitute a perfect analysis of the photograph's orchestration of the gaze. There is a "voice-off" of the photographic discourse, however—a component of the image which is beyond the frame of this little scenario of voyeurism. On the far left-hand side of the photograph, behind the wall holding the painting of the nude, is the barely detectable painting of a woman imaged differently, in darkness—*out of sight* for the male, blocked by his fetish. Yet, to point to this almost invisible alternative in imaging is also only to reveal once again the analyst's own perpetual desire to find a not-seen that might break the hold of representation. Or to laugh last.

There is a sense in which the photograph's delineation of a sexual politics of looking is almost uncanny. But, to counteract the very possibility of such a perception, the language of the art critic effects a naturalization of this joke on the woman. The art-critical reception of the picture emphasizes a natural but at the same time "imaginative" relation between photography and life, ultimately subordinating any formal relations to a referential ground: "Doisneau's lines move from right to left, directed by the man's glance; the woman's gaze creates a line of energy like a hole in space . . . . The creation of these relationships from life itself is imagination in photography."[34] "Life itself," then, presents the material for an "artistic" organization of vision along the lines of sexual difference. Furthermore, the critic would have us believe that chance events and arbitrary clicks of the shutter cannot be the agents of a generalized sexism because they are particular, unique—"Kertész and Doisneau depend entirely upon our recognition that they were present at the instant of the unique intersection of events."[35] Realism seems always to reside in the streets and, indeed, the out-of-focus boy across the street, at the center of the photograph, appears to act as a guarantee of the "chance" nature of the event, its arbitrariness, in short—its realism. Thus, in the discourse of the art critic the photograph, in capturing a moment, does not construct it; the camera finds a naturally given series of subject and object positions. What the critic does not consider are the conditions of reception of photography as an art form, its situation within a much larger network of representation. What is it that makes the photograph not only readable but pleasurable—at the expense of the woman? The critic does not ask what makes the photograph a negotiable item in a market of signification.

V. THE MISSING LOOK

The photograph displays insistently, in microcosm, the structure of the cinematic inscription of a sexual differentiation in modes of looking. Its process of framing the female gaze repeats that of the cinematic narratives described above, from *Leave Her to Heaven* to *Dark Victory*. Films play out scenarios of looking in order to outline the terms of their own under-standing. And given the divergence between masculine and feminine sce-narios, those terms would seem to be explicitly negotiated as markers of sexual difference. Both the theory of the image and its apparatus, the cinema, produce a position for the female spectator—a position which is ultimately untenable because it lacks the attribute of distance so necessary for an adequate reading of the image. The entire elaboration of femininity as a closeness, a nearness, as present-to-itself is not the definition of an essence but the delineation of a *place* culturally assigned to the woman. Above and beyond a simple adoption of the masculine position in relation to the cinematic sign, the female spectator is given two options: the maso-chism of over-identification or the narcissism entailed in becoming one's own object of desire, in assuming the image in the most radical way. The effectivity of masquerade lies precisely in its potential to manufacture a distance from the image, to generate a problematic within which the image is manipulable, producible, and readable by the woman. Doisneau's photograph is not readable by the female spectator—it can give her pleasure only in masochism. In order to "get" the joke, she must once again assume the position of transvestite.

It is quite tempting to foreclose entirely the possibility of female spectatorship, to repeat at the level of theory the gesture of the photograph, given the history of a cinema which relies so heavily on voyeurism, fetishism, and identification with an ego ideal conceivable only in masculine terms. And, in fact, there has been a tendency to theorize femininity and hence the feminine gaze as repressed, and in its repression somehow irretrievable, the enigma constituted by Freud's question. Yet, as Michel Foucault has demonstrated, the repressive hypothesis on its own entails a very limited and simplistic notion of the working of power.[36] The "no" of the father, the prohibition, is its only technique. In theories of repression there is no sense of the productiveness and positivity of power. Femininity is produced very precisely as a position within a network of power relations. And the growing insistence upon the elaboration of a theory of female spectatorship is indicative of the crucial necessity of understanding that position in order to dislocate it.

CHAPTER TWO

Masquerade Reconsidered: Further Thoughts on the Female Spectator

I

There is a type of violence in my 1982 essay, "Film and the Masquerade: Theorizing the Female Spectator,"[1] which is a result of the attempt (which fails in many respects) to tear the concept of masquerade out of its conventional context. Generally, masquerade is employed not to illuminate the agency usually associated with spectatorship, but to designate a mode of being for the other—the sheer objectification or reification of representation. When she masquerades, Joan Riviere's famous patient renounces her status as the subject of speech (as a lecturer, as an intellectual woman with a certain amount of power), and becomes the very image of femininity in order to compensate for her "lapse" into subjectivity (i.e. masculinity in Riviere's analysis) and to attract the male gaze. Masquerade would hence appear to be the very antithesis of spectatorship/subjectivity. And, indeed, my earlier essay continually oscillates between a consideration of the vicissitudes of female spectatorship in the cinema and the filmic representation of women looking (and performing a masquerade, as in the examples of Marlene Dietrich and the femme fatale).

The essay deviates in another way from the psychoanalytic discussion of masquerade initiated by Riviere. For Riviere, as well as Lacan and Irigaray who take up the concept within their work, masquerade specifies a norm of femininity—not a way out, a "destabilization" of the image, as I argued, or a "defamiliarization of female iconography."[2] But it is a curious norm, which indicates through its very contradictions the difficulty of *any* concept of femininity in a patriarchal society. In Riviere's analysis, "normal" femininity is a masquerade, but masquerade, as in the case of her female patient, is pathological. That female patient, like Riviere herself, was an intellectual whose skill and professionalism were recognized by her colleagues. But in order to compensate for the supposed masculinity of such a role, the patient would assume the exaggerated aspects of femininity, flirting with her colleagues after each of her professional performances. The focal point of Riviere's analysis is the following, frequently cited, passage.

> Womanliness therefore could be assumed and worn as a mask, both to hide the possession of masculinity and to avert the reprisals expected if she was found to possess it—much as a thief will turn out his pockets and ask to be searched to prove that he has not the stolen goods. The reader may now ask how I define womanliness or where I draw the line between genuine womanliness and the 'masquerade.' My suggestion is not, however, that there is any such difference; whether radical or superficial, they are the same thing.[3]

In this description, femininity is in actuality non-existent—it serves only as a disguise to conceal the woman's appropriation of masculinity and as a deception designed to placate a potentially vengeful father figure. Masculinity is not hers; it is a form of "theft" if she purports to speak from a position of authority.

The theme of "stolen goods" or "stolen property" is a recurrent one in Riviere's essay and invokes memories of Freud's alignment of femininity and criminality in his essay on narcissism.[4] The "stolen property" is, of course, the phallus, and the female subject has no fear of "turning out her pockets" and "asking to be searched," for the phallus is an object which will never be found. Riviere thus reinscribes the thematics of lack and the dialectic of the phallus in the determination of sexual difference. There is no femininity precisely because it is a concept which turns on the definition of masculinity, seemingly supporting Freud's contention that there is only one libido and it is masculine. Femininity, in this description, is a reaction-formation against the illicit assumption of masculinity. Hollow in itself, without substance, femininity can only be sustained by its accoutrements, decorative veils, and inessential gestures. For Lacan, "the fact that femininity takes refuge in this mask . . . has the strange consequence that, in the human being, virile display itself appears as feminine."[5]

It is significant that Riviere's patient suffers these attacks of normalized-yet-pathological masquerade after speaking performances. Riviere can only conceptualize the woman as subject of discourse in relation to a masculine role. As one who speaks, who enters and appropriates a language regulated by absence and difference, she must also wield the phallus as signifier of lack. In language, she is phallicized, a thief. In this sense, Riviere's analysis seems to anticipate the Lacanian articulation of sexual difference and linguistic difference, without a theory of language. Less theoretically, but still compellingly, Riviere specifies a certain feminine anxiety in relation to language.

The first two sections of my essay, "Film and the Masquerade," were designed as an exploration of the theory of language which supports Lacanian psychoanalysis and the way in which it has been articulated with the problematic of sexual difference. This theory is above all a theory of lack, of distance, of separation. For Saussure, the "ideal of the semiotic process" is grounded upon the very distance between signifier and signified, their arbitrary relation. Language is haunted by the difference, lack, and absence which constitute its most efficient mechanism. In her attempt to produce an alternative feminist reading of Hitchcock's films, Tania Modleski interrogates this semiotic theory: "One might, as I shall do in the chapters that follow, question the very 'ideals' of the 'semiotic systems' invoked by Doane—and, in particular, the ideal of 'distance,' or what in Brechtian theory is called 'distanciation.' "[6] Now, I am quite sure that Saussure did not have Brechtian distanciation in mind when he analyzed the distance between signifier and signified—they are not at all equivalent. There is a certain, very dangerous, slippage between levels here. Saussure's "distance" is the very condition of language; Brecht's "distanciation" is a radical political strategy in representation. Modleski, although she may believe that she is questioning the "ideals of semiotic systems," does not produce an alternative theory of language in which the signifier would embrace the signified, but moves immediately to the levels of distanciation and identification.[7]

This is a crucial point because the problem is not so much the theory of language itself as the way in which it is articulated with sexual difference. In the work of Lacan, as well as in that of the women writers who extend his analysis, Irigaray and Montrelay, women are deprived of the distance required by language—femininity is closeness, nearness, "wrapped in its own contiguity."[8] My point in the essay was not that this is an adequate definition of femininity but that it is a *persistent* one both in various theories of discourse informed by psychoanalysis and in the cinema itself (particularly in its alignment of the female spectator with genres such as the "weepie" or tearjerker). These discourses assign to the woman a *position*, a *place* within a patriarchal culture. Certainly the position is unreal—in the sense that it does not specify all behaviors or particular differences of individual women. But an admission of its unreality does not constitute a denial of its forcefulness, its effectivity.

Saussure is not the only theorist to have felt the necessity of designating the linguistic function as distance or separation.[9] For Jacques Derrida, the specificity of language, as exemplified by the structure of writing, is the very violence of the separation from presence and immediacy.[10] Julia Kristeva takes the process a step further by equating that violent separation with castration: "Castration is, in sum, the imaginary construction of a radical operation which constitutes the symbolic field and all beings inscribed therein. This operation constitutes signs and syntax; that is, language, as a *separation* from a presumed state of nature. . . ."[11] For neither theorist is the operation of separation or distance a neutral one. Instead, this idea of a radical break, a violence, or a sacrifice is invested with anguish, anxiety, and an intense sense of loss. In the midst of this very insistent theorization of the necessary violence of separation and distance, it is interesting to note that the discourses of psychoanalytic theory (and its feminist extensions) together with the cinema feel the absolute necessity of situating femininity outside of this violence, in the realm of sheer proximity and an overwhelming presence-to-itself. Clearly this indicates a compensatory move in the face of such violence, a form of reassurance for a threatened subjectivity—a way of using sexual difference to make up for the sheer pain of the entry into language. These theories do not assume that something valuable—i.e. nature as ground—is *really* lost. Distance, differentiation, absence can also be accepted and affirmed. But, historically, this has not been the case. What is the status of this longing for presence and plenitude? Is it inevitable, essential, psychical, historical? Can it be dealt with in some other way, without invoking the drama of sexual differentiation and hierarchization?

One could also pose the question of the precise relation between sexual difference and linguistic difference in Lacanian theory. Is it a temporal one—are the recognitions of the two forms of difference simultaneous, coincident? And, if so, what are the implications of this? One might also hypothesize a cause-effect relation in which recognition of sexual difference catapults one into language, although this is rarely if ever explicitly articulated in the theory. Or, is the relation between the two one of analogy: is sexuality *like* language insofar as it is irrevocably divorced from any ground or referent (the "natural" instincts)? The exact nature of the relation is never specified but often it seems to me that it is a poetic one in which sexual difference somehow infuses and animates the understanding of linguistic difference. Lévi-Strauss's early attempt to construct an analogy between the exchange of women and the exchange of words ends in a tribute to the "affective richness, ardour and mystery"[12] of the relations between the sexes (which has been lost in the realm of human communication). Sexual differentiation becomes a way of dramatizing the entry into language. But it is a drama whose effects for female subjectivity are extremely disadvantageous, if not disastrous and which points, perhaps, to the limits of the usefulness of psychoanalytic theory for feminism. For, if linguistic difference and sexual difference are merged in a way which allows them no relative autonomy, the theory indeed becomes totalizing, leaving no room for feminist strategy.

Patrice Petro claims that the discourse of distance and differentiation is in itself a "male epistemology."[13] I do not believe that this is the case. What we are dealing with is an epistemology—that is, a theory of language and hence of knowledge—which is collapsed onto a theory of sexual difference that throws the epistemology into a phallocentric arena. But I would certainly hesitate to counter it with anything claiming to be a "female epistemology," with a theory which valorized closeness, nearness, or presence (and which therefore assumed that these qualities are essential female attributes). For the epistemology seems to me to have a certain force and explanatory power. Furthermore, it helps to delineate, with a great deal of persuasiveness, the positions, identities, and relations to power which accompany given cultural understandings of sexual difference. To embrace and affirm the definition of femininity as closeness, immediacy, or proximity-to-self is to accept one's own disempowerment in the cultural arena, to accept the idea that women are outside of language. To investigate this idea as an idea, with a certain cultural effectivity, is another matter altogether.

To claim that femininity is a function of the mask is to dismantle the question of essentialism before it can even be posed. In a theory which stipulates a claustrophobic closeness of the woman in relation to her own body, the concept of masquerade suggests a "glitch" in the system. What I was searching for, in the 1982 essay, was a contradiction internal to the psychoanalytic account of femininity. Masquerade seems to provide that contradiction insofar as it attributes to the woman the distance, alienation, and divisiveness of self (which is constitutive of subjectivity in psychoanalysis) rather than the closeness and excessive presence which are the logical outcome of the psychoanalytic drama of sexualized linguistic difference. The theorization of femininity as masquerade is a way of appropriating this necessary distance or gap, in the operation of semiotic systems, of deploying it for women, of reading femininity differently. Here it is crucial to point to the constant slippage in Riviere's discourse between "normal" femininity and pathology—the former appearing inherently unstable. Femininity is fundamentally, for Riviere, the play of masks. Yet, there is no censure involved in claiming that the woman hides behind the mask when the mask is all there is—it conceals only an absence of "pure" or "real" femininity. Indeed, the assumption of a mask conveys more of the "truth" of sexuality, in Lacanian psychoanalysis, than any recourse to "being" or "essence." For Lacan, masks are the proper sphere of sexuality and this emphasis upon "appearing" has "the effect that the ideal or typical manifestations of behavior in both sexes, up to and including the act of sexual copulation, are entirely propelled into comedy."[14]

Nevertheless, there remain significant difficulties and drawbacks in the concept of masquerade. Because its first appearance in psychoanalytic texts specifies it as a reaction-formation designed to counter the possession of masculinity, it makes femininity dependent upon masculinity for its very definition. Thus, although it may not secure a feminine "essence," it does presuppose a system and a logic dictated by a masculine position, once again subordinating femininity. Secondly, masquerade is not theorized by Riviere as a joyful or affirmative play but as an anxiety-ridden compensatory gesture, as a position which is potentially disturbing, uncomfortable, and inconsistent, as well as psychically painful for the woman. It is socially "inappropriate" behavior. This invocation of social *propriety* cannot be dismissed as merely a moralistic condemnation. For, as much as Lacan might want to situate sexuality in the realm of appearance, comedy, and the mask, to attribute a certain emptiness to the concepts of masculinity and femininity, these are concepts and identities which have enormous socio-political implications and which are linked to relations of power. In this same article, Riviere analyzes another intellectual woman, a university lecturer in "an abstruse subject which seldom attracts women" who, in her flippancy and lack of seriousness, exhibits the need "to treat the situation of displaying her masculinity to men as a 'game,' as something *not real*, as a 'joke' " (215). With respect to this woman, Stephen Heath claims that "she returns masculinity to them [her male audience] as equally unreal, another act, a charade of power. But then masculinity is real in its effects, femininity too, the charade is *in* power . . . this woman's life is marked by power and effects, is caught up in the definitions of masculinity/femininity, the identifications of the man and the woman."[15] Perhaps this is why Joan Riviere's masquerading patient (the one who is the primary focus of the analysis) obsessively turns around and reinscribes her sexuality, born as it is of power and its effects, within another field of power relations—that of race. Riviere's patient has a number of sexual fantasies linking blacks, sexuality, power, and degradation—fantasies which are rarely, if ever, discussed in the critical accounts of Riviere's concept of masquerade. The patient had spent her childhood and youth "in the Southern states of America" and her sexual fantasies at that time were bound up with fears and desires circulating around images of the sexuality of black men and their relation to white women (212-13). Riviere, consistent with her general neglect of the problem of power and resistance in sexual relations, does not locate race as a pertinent feature in her analysis of the fantasies.

Hence, the concept of masquerade, in terms of both its historical inscription in Riviere's text and its subsequent activation by Lacan, is by no means unproblematic. Furthermore, in my 1982 essay there is a pronounced difficulty in aligning the notion of masquerade with that of female spectatorship. This is partially due to the curious blend of activity and passivity in masquerade (Riviere's patient actively strives to produce herself as the passive image of male attention) and the corresponding blurring of the opposition between production and reception. On the face of it, masquerade would seem to facilitate an understanding of the woman's status as spectacle rather than spectator. At the time, however, masquerade seemed to provide a feminine counter to the concept of fetishism which had dominated discussion of (male) spectatorship. Both concepts theorize subjectivity as constituted both spatially and temporally by a gap or distance; but fetishism does so through a scenario which is dependent upon the presence-in-absence of the phallus. While masquerade, as noted above, is also haunted by a masculine standard, masculinity as measure is not internal to the concept itself (the masquerade designates the distance between the woman and the image of femininity; the fetish is the substitute maternal *phallus*). Rather, in masquerade, masculinity is present as the context provoking the patient's reaction-formation.

II

It is masquerade more generally conceived as designating the impossibility of a stable feminine position which seemed to align it with female spectatorship and its vicissitudes, pointing to problems which are still extremely insistent and have to do with issues of reading and readability, of pleasure, and of feminist interpretation. Beyond the concept of masquerade itself, my 1982 essay struggled with the difficulty of theorizing female spectatorship. Its primary object in this regard, however, was the troubled and troubling representation of women seeing—hence, the emphasis upon the 1948 photograph by Robert Doisneau, *"Un Regard Oblique,"* which would seem, at first glance, to be very much about the woman's vision. My analysis of this photograph has recently been criticized by Tania Modleski and, with respect to the question of the limits and constraints of reading, it might be helpful to return to this feminist discussion of the joke and to continue the interrogation. For the joke is the textual instance which often seems most coercive in its production of reading effects. In the 1982 essay, I analyzed Doisneau's *"Un Regard Oblique"* as a kind of dirty joke at the expense of the woman. The photograph depicts a man and a woman standing in front of the plate glass window of what is apparently an art gallery. While the woman stares at a painting whose content is hidden from the spectator, the man, from the margin of the photograph, looks across her and beyond to another painting, of a female nude, concentrating attention on his own voyeuristic desire and negating that of the woman. Briefly, I argued that, in line with Freud's analysis of the dirty joke, the photograph insures a complicity between the man and the presumably male spectator, operating to exclude the woman and that "Doisneau's photograph is not readable by the female spectator—it can give her pleasure only in masochism. In order to 'get' the joke, she must once again assume the position of transvestite."[16]

In her book on Hitchcock, which contains a powerful reading of *Blackmail* (1929), Modleski criticizes this analysis.

> There seems to me in Doane's formulation a major confusion between the notion of "getting," or reading, a joke and the idea of receiving pleasure from it. While it may be true that in order to derive pleasure from the joke, a woman must be masochistic . . . , surely a woman (*as* woman) may at least "get" the joke even if she doesn't appreciate it, just as, say, a Black may comprehend a racist joke without adopting the guise of a white person or assuming the position of a masochist. It even seems reasonable to suppose that the oppressed person may see more deeply into the joke than the oppressor is often able or willing to do. . . . Surely, Doane herself in her analysis, or "reading," of the joke is speaking neither as a masochist nor as a man (a transvestite) but as a woman who deeply understands the experience of women's oppression under patriarchy—and not only understands it, but quite rightly resents it. (26–27)

Modleski goes on to explain that the woman's inability to laugh at or obtain pleasure from the dirty joke is hardly a loss and that, in any event, there are other types of pleasure open to her—e.g. that of analysis. Now the last impression that I would want to promote is that I lack a sense of humor. Meaghan Morris refers to "that most terrifying of media bogeys, that dreaded figure who looms so large in our language that women toil untold hours over their prose to writer her off—the humorless feminist."[17] But I would still maintain that the dirty joke does operate as the structural exclusion of the woman. Modleski's analysis depends upon a slippage between the terms "getting" and "reading" (or sometimes "comprehending"). But they are not at all the same. It's all a matter of timing. Everyone knows that you cannot explain a joke to someone effectively if they have not understood (read correctly, comprehended) it the first time. If you get the joke at the moment of its transmission, fine, but if you don't, you will never get it. You may understand its mechanisms but you will never get it. The term "getting" suggests that the effect of the joke must be instantaneous, that comprehension and the induced affect (i.e. laughter, pleasure) must be simultaneous. The one who "gets" the joke automatically, unthinkingly, colludes in the maintenance of the systems of sexual oppression which support its meaning. Sometimes, when I am subject to a strong desire to laugh and hence "belong" to an audience, or when I am tired, watching late night television, and off my guard, I will find myself laughing at a sexist joke. I "find myself," I am beside myself, I am other. I am, precisely, off guard, and texts, especially jokes (as Freud recognized) do have a certain psychical force. Our desire to laugh must not blind us to the still pervasive ideological ordering of the sexual. In the 1982 essay, I was able to "see more deeply" (as Modleski puts it) into Doisneau's joke than Doisneau, but only *in a second moment*—a moment made possible by feminist theory. There is a difference between the critical act and the act of reception. I was able to read the Doisneau joke, without really getting it, due to the historicity of the feminist enterprise.

It is all a question of timing. Feminist critical theory must be attentive to both the temporality of reading and the historicity of reading. What has to be acknowledged is that there are, in fact, constraints on reading, constraints on spectatorship. Social constraints, sexual constraints, historical constraints. If there were no constraints, there would be no problem, no need for feminist criticism. The difficulty is to hold on, simultaneously, to the notion that there are constraints and to the notion that there are gaps, outlets, blind spots, excesses in the image—to keep both in tension. The questions asked by one type of feminist criticism, today, confronting a text, attempting to re-read it, to produce a feminist interpretation, are different from the questions raised by an analysis attempting to delineate the terms of address of a film, its assumptions about a quite historically specific audience. Modleski is quite anxious (understandably) to read *Blackmail* differently—to counter a patriarchal critical tradition which assigns to the woman a clear sexual guilt. But how we produce that reading is certainly as important as the product itself. Modleski raises the issue of the Doisneau photograph and the joke in order to construct an analogy between its reading and that of *Blackmail*, which through its activation of the figure of the jester appears to situate itself as an elaborate joke on the woman. But Modleski argues that the joke is not constructed at the expense of the woman. Instead, Hitchcock is on her side. She does so by focusing on (and demonstrating that Hitchcock focuses on) the subjectivity of the central female character, Alice. For instance, with reference to the scene of the rape in the artist's studio, Modleski claims,

> Since the scene is presented more or less "objectively"—or, if anything, slightly emphasizes Alice's reactions—a feminist interpretation is available

to the female spectator without her necessarily having to adopt the position of "resisting viewer" (to paraphrase Judith Fetterley). (24)

Throughout the analysis, Modleski's concern is with the extent to which the film creates sympathy for or identification with the female character. But this is not the problem. Numerous films in the Hollywood cinema hinge upon the creation of "sympathy for and identification with" the female character (the "weepies" are notorious for precisely this) but this does not insure the availability of a feminist interpretation to the female spectator. Modleski assumes all too quickly that the terms "feminist" and "feminine" are equivalent. The sexual politics of a film is not necessarily a function of the extent to which it adheres to either a male or a female character. It is one thing to note the importance of contradictions within the text which are a result of the extreme pressure it applies to a politics of sexuality, rape, and guilt (another way of pointing, once again, to the fact that Hitchcock's text is a limit text), and another thing to align its feminist proclivities with the subjectivity of an individual female character. The concept of subjectivity must be more broadly understood. As Gertrud Koch maintains,

> The aesthetically most advanced films resist any facile reading, not only because they operate with complex aesthetic codes but also because they anticipate an expanded and radicalized notion of subjectivity. What is achieved in a number of these films is a type of subjectivity that transcends any abstract subject-object dichotomy; what is at stake is no longer the redemption of woman as subject over against the male conception of woman as object.[18]

The stakes are greater and involve the very transformation of current understandings of subjectivity.

Nevertheless, at this historical moment within feminism there is a strong desire to read differently if not to receive differently—even if this entails a violence against the set norms of criticism, a rewriting of the critical questions. The pressures are great—the pressure to find pleasure, the pressure to laugh, the pressure not to feel excluded from the textual field of a dominant mass culture. Yet, feminist criticism must continually and insistently focus *its* gaze on the enormous problems posed by a feminist aesthetics and by the concept of subjectivity as it is articulated with representation. And it cannot lose sight of the critical advantages gained, for feminism, by rethinking subjectivity outside of the context of a liberal humanism. Feminist film theory and criticism have forcefully demonstrated the extent to which aesthetic structures organize and orchestrate psychical investments defined by their very tenacity. Doisneau's photograph *is* a joke which is funny only at the expense of the woman, but it is not the only way of visualizing female spectatorship. Riviere's patient, looking out at her own male audience, with impropriety, throws the image of their own sexuality back to them as "game," as "joke," investing it, too, with the instability and the emptiness of masquerade. Heath refers to this as a "strong social-political, feminist joke" in the manner of Virginia Woolf in *Three Guineas*.[19] As long as she is not caught in her own act. As long as she does not forget that the masquerades of femininity and masculinity are not totally unreal or totally a joke but have a social effectivity we cannot ignore. We still need to tell our own jokes, but hopefully they will be different ones. *Structurally* different ones.

CHAPTER THREE

Veiling Over Desire:
Close-ups of the Woman

Psychoanalysis has consistently adopted a stance of suspicion in relation to the realm of the visible, intimately bound as it would seem to be to the register of consciousness. The psychical layer Freud designated perception-consciousness is frequently deceived, caught from behind by unconscious forces which evade its gaze and which are far more determinant in the constitution of subjectivity. Stephen Heath goes so far as to specify the birth of psychoanalysis as a rejection of vision as a mode of organizing and apprehending psychical phenomena. Freud's most important move, from this perspective, lies in the displacement from the "look" to the "voice," from the visible to language. Charcot analyzed hysteria with the aid of a series of photographs depicting women in various stages of the disease. For Heath, this series of photographs is a pre-figuration of the cinema—a cinema which is thus placed ineluctably on the side of the pre-Freudian. Freud rejected the photographic techniques of Charcot in favor of the analytic session in which contact with the patient was achieved through speech, association, interpretation of linguistic lapses. According to Heath,

> Charcot sees, Freud hears . . . Psychoanalysis is the anti-visible; significant in this respect, moreover, are Freud's distrust of projects for rendering analysis on the screen and, conversely, the powerful social desire to bring that same analysis into sight, the fascination of so many films with psychoanalysis.[1]

The visible and its relation to knowledge are problematized in psychoanalysis, ensured in the cinema, polarizing the two discourses. In much of film theory, psychoanalysis becomes the superior, intelligent discourse of which cinema is the symptom, the guilty mechanism of that cultural constitution and reconstitution of subjectivity as imaginary coherence and security.

On the other hand, the fascination with psychoanalysis on the part of film theory is linked to the centrality and strength of its reliance on scenarios of vision: the primal scene, the "look" at the mother's (castrated) body, the mirror stage. Psychoanalytic theory would appear to be dependent upon the activation of scenarios with visual, auditory, and narrative dimensions. Yet, the visible in no way acts as a guarantee of epistemological certitude. Insofar as it is consistently described as a lure, a trap, or a snare, vision dramatizes the dangers of privileging consciousness. In Lacan's analysis of the eye and the gaze, the gaze takes on an unconscious dimension and is significant in that it "escapes from the grasp of that form of vision that is satisfied with itself in imagining itself as consciousness."[2] There is a hole in the visible. What consciousness and the cinema both fail to acknowledge in their lust for plenitude is that the visible is always lacking. This failure is then subject to formulation by psychoanalysis as the elision of castration. According to Lacan, "To go from perception to science is a perspective that seems to be self-evident . . . But it is a way that analytic experience must rectify, because it avoids the abyss of castration."[3] This abyss is most evident, of course, in the scenario whereby castration anxiety is generated as an effect of the look at the woman—a scenario in which what is involved is the perception of an absence rather than a presence, a negative perception or, in effect, a non-perception. For what the subject confronts is the woman's "nothing-to-see." At first glance, then, sexual differentiation in psychoanalysis seems to hinge on the visibility or invisibility of the sexual organs, the phallus taking on prominence because it is most easily seen. Yet, the phallus actually becomes important only insofar as it might be absent, it might disappear. It assumes meaning only in relation to castration. Vision remains precarious. As Jacqueline Rose points out, the phallus must be understood in its relation to vision as a "seeming" or an "appearing" rather than as an essential value: "The phallus thus indicates the reduction of difference to an instance of visible perception, a *seeming* value . . . And if Lacan states that the symbolic usage of the phallus stems from its visibility (something for which he was often criticized), it is only in so far as the order of the visible, the apparent, the seeming is the object of his attack. In fact he constantly refused any crude identification of the phallus with the order of the visible or real."[4]

Such a position seems to justify situating psychoanalysis as a metalanguage with respect to the cinema which forces its spectator to consent to the lure of the visible. For the classical cinema is the opposite of psychoanalysis in that it depends on the axiom that the visible equals the knowable, that truth resides in the image. Yet, while it is clear from the foregoing arguments that psychoanalysis does not trust the visible, denies its appeal to certitude, and does not, in effect, believe in love at first sight, neither does the cinema at all moments. An investigation of these moments of slippage between vision and epistemological certitude in the cinema can illuminate something of the complexity of the relations between truth, vision, and the woman sustained by patriarchy. For the subtextual theme recurrent in filmic texts, which resists the dominant theme whereby vision is constantly ratified, is that appearances can be deceiving. And surely they are most apt to deceive when they involve a woman. The seductive power attributed to the figure of the femme fatale in film noir exemplifies the disparity between seeming and being, the deception, instability, and unpredictability associated with the woman. While the organization of vision in the cinema pivots around the representation of the woman—she is always aligned with the quality of to-be-looked-at-ness—it is also the case that in her attraction to the male subject she confounds the relation between the visible and the knowable.

A site where the classical film acknowledges the precariousness of vision and simultaneously seeks to isolate and hence contain it is the close-up of the woman, more particularly, the *veiled* woman. For the veil functions to visualize (and hence stabilize) the instability, the precariousness of sexuality.[5] At some level of the cultural ordering of the psychical, the horror or threat of that precariousness (of both sexuality and the visible) is attenuated by attributing it to the woman, over and against the purported stability and identity of the male. The veil is the mark of that precariousness. Clearly, one can trace a poetics or theoretics of the veil in the texts of literature, psychoanalysis, and philosophy as well as the cinema, but in the cinema it is most materially a question of what can and cannot be seen. Only the cinema need give the uncertainty and instability of vision visible form. Ultimately, however, the cinematic activation of the veil serves to demonstrate that doubting the visible is not enough. Psychoanalysis' distrust of the visible is not a guarantee of its use-value for feminism, of an alternative and non-complicit conceptualization of sexual difference. In fact, a psychoanalytic discourse, a philosophical discourse, and a cinematic discourse are more likely to converge at certain points in attaching the precariousness of vision (in its relation to truth) to the figure of the woman or the idea of the feminine—or to make it ineluctably bound up with sexual difference.

Despite the perhaps apocryphal Billy Bitzer story in which D. W. Griffith's purported discovery of the close-up is resisted as a violent fragmentation of the human body ("We pay for the whole actor, Mr. Griffith. We want to see *all* of him"),[6] the close-up has become crucial in the organization of cinematic narrative. And with the formation of a star system heavily dependent upon the maintenance of the aura, the close-up became an important means of establishing the recognizability of each star. At moments it almost seems as though all the fetishism of the cinema were condensed onto the image of the face, the female face in particular. Barthes describes this phenomenon in relation to the face of Garbo: "Garbo still belongs to that moment in cinema when capturing the human face still plunged audiences into the deepest ecstasy, when one literally lost oneself in a human image as one would in a philtre, when the face represented a kind of absolute state of the flesh, which could be neither reached nor renounced."[7] The scale of the close-up transforms the face into an instance of the gigantic, the monstrous: it overwhelms. In the dystopia of *Blade Runner* (1982), a giant video close-up of an Oriental woman oversees, haunts the Los Angeles of the future. The face, usually the mark of individuality, becomes tantamount to a theorem in its generalizability. In the close-up, it is truly bigger than life. The face is that bodily part not accessible to the subject's own gaze (or accessible only as a virtual image in a mirror)—hence its over-representation as *the* instance of subjectivity.[8] But the face is not taken in at a glance—it already problematizes the notion of a pure surface since it points to an interior, a depth. The face is the most *readable* space of the body. Susan Stewart traces the process by means of which the face becomes a text.

> If the surface is the location of the body's meaning, it is because that surface is invisible to the body itself. And if the face reveals a depth and profundity which the body itself is not capable of, it is because the eyes and to some degree the mouth are openings onto fathomlessness. Behind the appearance of eyes and mouth lies the interior stripped of appearances . . . The face is a type of "deep" text, a text whose meaning is complicated by change and by a constant series of alterations between a reader and an author who is strangely disembodied, neither present nor absent, found in neither part nor whole, but, in fact, *created* by this reading. Because of this convention of interpretation, it is not surprising that we find that one of the great *topoi* of Western literature has been the notion of the face as book.[9]

The face, more than any other bodily part, is *for* the other. It is the most articulate sector of the body, but it is mute without the other's reading. In the cinema, this is evidenced in the pause, the meaningful moment of the close-up, *for the spectator*, the scale of the close-up corresponding less than other shots to the dictates of perspectival realism. And this being-for-the-gaze-of-the-other is, of course, most adequate as a description of the female subject, locked within the mirror of narcissism. Stewart suggests why it is the woman who most frequently inhabits the close-up in various discourses of the image.

> Because it is invisible, the face becomes gigantic with meaning and significance. . . . The face becomes a text, a space which must be "read" and

interpreted in order to exist. The body of a woman, particularly constituted by the mirror and thus particularly subject to an existence constrained by the nexus of external images, is spoken by her face, by the articulation of another's reading. Apprehending the image becomes a mode of possession. We are surrounded by the image of the woman's face, the obsession of the portrait and the cover girl alike. The face is what belongs to the other; it is unavailable to the woman herself.[10]

Lacan also refers to this idealist "*belong to me* aspect of representations, so reminiscent of property."[11] From this perspective it is not at all surprising that the generalized social exchange of women should manifest itself in the cinematic institution as a proliferation of close-ups of the woman— established as the possession of the gaze of a man through glance-object editing.

What is most intriguing here, however, is the frequency with which the face of the woman in the close-up is masked, barred, shadowed, or veiled, introducing a supplementary surface between the camera or spectator and the contents of the image. When attempting to decipher the rationale of the veil, it is crucial to acknowledge that it has at least several different functions. The veil serves as a form of protection—against light, heat, and, of course, the gaze. To "take the veil" is to become a nun, to seclude oneself in a convent. Most prominently, perhaps, the veil's work would seem to be that of concealing, of hiding a secret. Garbo, as a well-known instance, has recourse to the veil in order to conceal an aging and disintegrating beauty. In Helma Sanders-Brahms's *Germany Pale Mother* (1980), an idyllic mother-daughter relationship is broken by the postwar return of the father, and the resulting neurosis of the mother is evidenced by a paralysis of one side of her face which she desperately attempts to conceal. Here, the veil is used to hide the scar of historicity, etched upon the woman's face as a hysterical symptom. In Fritz Lang's *Secret Beyond the Door* (1948), a marginal female character uses a scarf to veil a facial scar obtained when she saved the male protagonist's son from a fire. The existence of the scar acts as a reminder of the deed and is used by the woman to maintain an emotional hold over the man. At a certain point in the film, however, she is caught without the veil and it is revealed that she has no scar (its disappearance, she guiltily explains, is a result of plastic surgery obtained years before). The veil in this instance functions to hide an absence, to conceal the fact that the woman has nothing to conceal, to maintain a debt, and thus to incite desire.

Yet, in all these instances of concealing, covering, hiding, or disguising, the veil is characterized by its opacity, its ability to fully block the gaze.

When it is activated in the service of the representation of the seductive power of femininity, on the other hand, it simultaneously conceals and reveals, provoking the gaze. The question of whether the veil facilitates vision or blocks it can receive only a highly ambivalent answer inasmuch as the veil, in its translucence, both allows and disallows vision. In the cinema, the magnification of the erotic becomes simultaneous with the activation of objects, veils, nets, streamers, etc., which intercept the space between the camera and the woman, forming a *second screen*. Such a screen is no longer the ground of the image but its filter. This is particularly the case in the films of directors who are explicitly and insistently associated with the photography or the narrativization of the woman—directors such as Max Ophuls and Josef von Sternberg. In the first image of Marlene Dietrich as Concha Perez in Sternberg's *The Devil Is A Woman* (1935), the sight of her face is doubly obscured by a filigreed mask which surrounds her eyes and an elaborate tufted veil which encages the head (figure 3.1). The disguise is partially motivated by the fact that the mise-en-scène is that of the carnival, authorizing as well the masking of the figure of her potential lover in the reverse shot (figure 3.2). He, however, has a supplemental, political motivation for concealing his face, hiding his identity in order to avoid detection (he is very vaguely situated as a "revolutionary" who is sought by the police). But his disguise does not change throughout the film; it at least has the attribute of stability, anchored as it is by the desire to hide. The various disguises, masks, and veils of the Marlene Dietrich character, on the other hand, take on the arbitrariness of the signifier in their apparent lack of any motivation beyond that of pure exhibitionism, pure show. The tropes of the mask, fan, and veil are here the marks of a dangerous deception or duplicity attached to the feminine (figures 3.3, 3.4, 3.5, 3.6, 3.7). In *Dishonored* (1931), Dietrich assumes a masquerade when she works as a spy for her country—this is an honorable disguise—but in the beginning of the film when she is literally found in the streets and at the end when she reverts to the status of prostitute, she is veiled. And the excess and incongruity of the veiled woman is condensed onto her gesture of lifting the veil to apply lipstick as she faces a firing squad.

In Sternberg's films, politics is generally an afterthought, but it is always there, lurking in the background, articulating a discourse of femininity with a discourse of power. In *The Scarlet Empress* (1934), a seductive, provocative femininity is the pure distillation of power in the figure of Catherine the Great. In a scene with a powerfully situated priest who offers her political aid, Catherine claims, "I have weapons that are far more powerful than any political machine" and this statement is followed by the gesture of raising a veil to her face so that only the eyes are visible (figure

Figure 3.1

Figure 3.2

3.8). In a subsequent scene, Catherine's antagonistic idiot husband has her surrounded by his Hessian troops and uses his own sword to play dangerously with the bodice of her dress. Her response is to take the veil of the earlier scene and push it over his sword (figure 3.9). In this and other scenes, the politico-military realm is baffled by femininity. The film produces a fantasy of power in which femininity conquers the sword and becomes the

Figure 3.3

Figure 3.4

Figure 3.5

Figure 3.6

Figure 3.7

foil to the phallus. Yet, the limits of that alleged feminine power are also represented by the iconography of the veil. In a scene in which Marlene Dietrich once again appears to demonstrate her control over the male, she literally plays with the veil (figure 3.10) as she instructs one duped male lover to travel down a secret passage from her bedroom in order to admit his rival. But in the course of the scene, the camera moves closer and closer

Figure 3.8

Figure 3.9

to Dietrich, she gradually lies back on the bed, and the veil covers the screen (figures 3.11, 3.12, 3.13). The film traces a movement from a moment where the woman controls thc vcil, moves in and out of its folds in order to lure the male, to a tableau where her very stillness mimics her death in representation, her image entirely subsumed by the veil.

Apart from any intradiegetic motivation, the woman is veiled in an appeal

Figure 3.10

Figure 3.11

to the gaze of the spectator. And the veil incarnates contradictory desires—the desire to bring her closer and the desire to distance her. Its structure is clearly complicit with the tendency to specify the woman's position in relation to knowledge as that of the enigma. Freud described female sexuality as "still veiled in an impenetrable obscurity."[12] In the discourse of metaphysics, the function of the veil is to make truth profound, to ensure

Figure 3.12

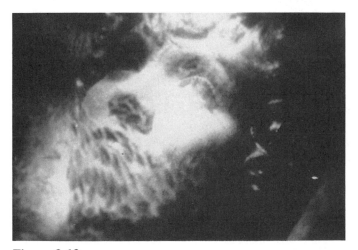

Figure 3.13

that there is a depth which lurks behind the surface of things. The veil acts as a trope that allows one to evade the superficial, to complicate the surface by disallowing its self-sufficiency. But what the veil in the cinema makes appear to be profound is, in fact, a surface. The function of the veil here is to transform the surface of the face into a depth, an end in itself. While the face in Stewart's analysis is a kind of "deep text," revealing a "depth and profundity which the body itself is not capable of," the addition of a veil as secondary or surplus surface results in the annihilation of that depth which hides behind the face. The veil, in a curious dialectic of depth and surface, reduces all to a surface which is more or less removed, more or less accessible. It is not a privileged depth, interiority, or psychology of the woman which is inaccessible but her sexualized, eroticized, and perfected surface, the embodiment of pure form. Thus, the woman comes to confound the topology of Western metaphysics, its organization of space and hierarchization of depth and surface in their relation to truth. This process has not gone unrecognized. In a temporary deviation from this discussion of the cinema, I would like to explore some of the ramifications of this confused topology in certain texts of philosophy and psychoanalysis.

Nietzsche's attempt to dismantle a philosophy of truth and to undermine the security of knowing produced what is perhaps the most striking analysis of the veil—an analysis which coincides with the beginning of a sustained philosophical attack on metaphysics. And the woman figures prominently there. Furthermore, two recent texts, by Derrida (*Spurs*) and Irigaray ("Veiled Lips"), return to Nietzsche's text in order to extricate a logistics of the veil. Nietzsche both reinscribes and criticizes philosophy's tropological system linking the woman, truth, and the veil. In his writing there is quite definitely a sense in which the movement of truth resembles the veiled gesture of feminine modesty. The veil produces the differentiation between surface and depth required by truth but it also presupposes the necessity of concealing and hence the moral opposition between decent and indecent. Nietzsche extends the metaphor of clothing in the preface to the second edition of *The Gay Science*: "We no longer believe that truth remains truth when the veils are withdrawn; we have lived too much to believe this. Today we consider it a matter of decency not to wish to see everything naked, or to be present at everything, or to understand and 'know' everything."[13] By securing truth's position as a question of decency vs. indecency as it concerns the clothed or unclothed state of the body, Nietzsche aligns it more surely with the figure of the woman—a woman who refuses to or cannot or ought not be known. In preparation for this disclaimer of the desire to know (i.e. to unveil) the truth, Nietzsche alludes to a poem by Schiller entitled "The Veiled Statue at Saïs" in which a young man, "impelled by a burning thirst for knowledge," travels to Egypt and confronts a veiled statue of Isis.[14] He is told that the veil conceals the very form of truth, but also that there is a divine decree prohibiting its disturbance. The youth transgresses, pulls aside the veil and looks. Yet, the sight of truth—head-on—induces death. There is no "other space" to counterpose to Plato's cave. The philosophical gaze must be blocked, indirect, difficult. Reminiscent of the structure of fetishism in which the gaze finds itself consistently displaced in relation to the horror of absence, this gaze also aligns or misaligns itself with the body of a woman, in this case, Isis, the sorrowing wife and eternal mother.

Nietzsche's claim to philosophical superiority in this preface rests on his attempt to differentiate between the "we" ("we, artists") of the passage and "those Egyptian youths who endanger temples by night, embrace statues, and want by all means to unveil, uncover, and put into a bright light whatever is kept concealed for good reasons" (38). On the contrary, Nietzsche allies himself with the Greeks who knew how to "stop courageously at the surface, the fold, the skin, to adore appearance, to believe in forms, tones, words, in the whole Olympus of appearance. Those Greeks were superficial—*out of profundity*" (38). The real does not lurk behind the surface: it resides on that surface or exists as a play of surfaces. In this valorization of the surface, Nietzsche elaborates an anti-hermeneutics whose ultimate aim is the collapse of the oppositions surface/depth, appearance/reality. Nietzsche would like to distance himself from the enterprise of metaphysics.

Yet, this demolition of the dichotomy of surface and depth in relation to truth does not signify the definitive loss of the category of deception. As one of Nietzsche's commentators, Eric Blondel (who characterizes Nietzsche's "ontology" as "feminine" or "gynecological") points out, in his philosophy

> the notion of a truth *beyond* appearance, underneath or behind the veil, is rendered null and void. It is certainly true that life deceives us with her ambiguous apparitions: but she deceives us not because she conceals an essence or a reality beneath appearances, but because she has *no* essence and would only like to make us think that she does. Her "essence" is to appear.[15]

Deception, from this point of view, is not defined as the non-coincidence or incompatibility of surface and depth (appearance and the truth), but as the very posing of the question of truth and its hiding place—the gesture indicating truth's existence. Deception, far from distorting truth, operates a double negation by, as Derrida will point out in another context, concealing the secret that there is no secret. Furthermore, it is not accidental that in the quote from Blondel the pronoun "she" plays such a major role in delineating the operation of this mode of deception. For in Nietzsche's view, woman epitomizes the pretense of essence. Her great talent lies in the area of deception or dissimulation, in what would appear to be the very opposite of truth: in giving herself, as Nietzsche says in *The Gay Science*, she "gives herself for" (317), that is, plays a part, produces herself as spectacle. In *Beyond Good and Evil* Nietzsche compares her to the actor who dons a mask for every occasion and whose "essence" is ultimately subsumed by the mask. Confronted with the demands of a vocal feminist movement, Nietzsche seeks shelter in the idea that woman does not *want* truth, reinforcing her association with dissimulation.

> We may in the end reserve a healthy suspicion whether woman really *wants* enlightenment about herself—whether she *can* will it—
> Unless a woman seeks a new adornment for herself that way—I do think adorning herself is part of the Eternal-Feminine?—she surely wants to inspire fear of herself—perhaps she seeks mastery. But she does not *want* truth—her great art is the lie, her highest concern is mere appearance and beauty.[16]

The desire to know can only be a new piece of clothing for the woman, a new surface, something with which to play at seduction. Only this will make feminism palatable for Nietzsche.

Deception and dissimulation are hence not negative categories in Nietzsche's work, since they align themselves with the work of the anti-metaphysical philosopher. Nevertheless, they also place the woman as the privileged exemplar of instability. Luce Irigaray criticizes Nietzsche for situating femininity as "the simulacrum which introduces the false into the true."

> So she who is always mobile renders him the possibility of movement in remaining, for him, the persistence of his being. Truth or appearances, according to his desire of the moment, his appetite of the instant. Truth and appearances and reality, power . . . she is—by virtue of her inexhaustible aptitude for mimicry—the living support of all the staging/production of the world. Variously veiled according to the epochs of history.[17]

Derrida is more generous to Nietzsche, claiming that his alliance of the woman with the artist or the actor represents an instance of his determined anti-essentialism. In this sense, she becomes the ruin of philosophy, an activity which Derrida can only approve: "There is no such thing as the essence of woman because woman averts, she is averted of herself . . . And the philosophical discourse, blinded, founders on these shoals and is hurled down these depthless depths to its ruin. There is no such thing as the truth of woman, but it is because of that abyssal divergence of the truth, because that untruth is 'truth.' Woman is but one name for that untruth of truth."[18] Woman is truth only insofar as it diverges from itself, is not reducible to the evidence of self-presence, multiplies its surfaces, and produces frames within frames. Always "averting," it is anything but straightforward. Just like a woman. For Derrida, woman incarnates the mise-en-abyme structure of truth.

This deception attributed to the woman does not, however, connote hypocrisy on her part. Her dissembling is not a conscious strategy. She has no knowledge of it or access to it as an operation. And this unconsciousness of the woman, her blindness to her own work, is absolutely necessary in order to allow and maintain the man's idealization of her, his perfection of her as an object. According to Nietzsche,

> Given the tremendous subtlety of woman's instinct, modesty remains by no means conscious hypocrisy: she divines that it is precisely an actual naive modesty that most seduces a man and impels him to overestimate her. Therefore woman is naive—from the subtlety of her instinct, which advises her of the utility of innocence. A deliberate *closing of one's eyes to oneself*— Wherever dissembling produces a stronger effect when it is unconscious, it *becomes* unconscious.[19]

The philosopher-voyeur sees quite well that the woman "closes her eyes to herself." She does not *know* that she is deceiving or *plan* to deceive; conscious deception would be repellent to the man and quite dangerous. Rather, she intuits or "divines" what the man needs—a belief in her innocence—and she *becomes* innocent. Closing her eyes to herself she becomes the pure construct of a philosophical gaze. Becoming unconscious of any knowledge she might have concerning truth as dissimulation, as surface, she becomes instead its representation, its idea. As Derrida points out, "It is impossible to resist looking for her" (71). Woman is situated as the substrate of representation itself, its unconscious material.

In this way, Nietzsche deprives the woman of subjectivity. Or, it could be said that women attain subjectivity only when they become old, and the recurrent image of the old woman in Nietzsche's work corroborates his own philosophy. For the old woman knows more than the metaphysicians: "I am afraid that old women are more skeptical in their most secret heart of hearts than any man: they consider the superficiality of existence its essence, and all virtue and profundity is to them merely a veil over this 'truth,' a very welcome veil over a pudendum—in other words, a matter of decency and shame, and no more than that."[20] A woman is granted knowledge when she is old enough to become a man—which is to say, old enough to lose her dissembling appearance, her seductive power. And even then, it is a kind of "old wives" knowledge, not, properly speaking, philosophical. For the most part, the figure of the woman is the projection of Nietzsche's own epistemological desires, his will to *embody* the difficulties, the impossibilities of what remains a tantalizing Truth. This is how the woman comes to represent a variety of often contradictory notions: truth, dissimulation, superficiality, even "calm." Overcome in *The Gay Science* by the philosophical tumult of ideas, Nietzsche envisages the woman as a sail floating in the calm distance: "When a man stands in the midst of his own noise, in the midst of his own surf of plans and projects, then he is apt also to see quiet, magical beings gliding past him and to long for their happiness and seclusion: *women*" (124). But if one gets too close to the sailboat, the magical silence is broken by the chattering, babble, and incoherency of the woman: "The magic and the most powerful effect of women is, in philosophical language, action at a distance, *actio in distans*; but this requires first of all and above all—*distance*" (124). Proximity reduces her (its) value. She (it) can seduce only from a distance. Or behind a veil. Nietzsche here gives us the mise-en-scène of the philosophical hypostatization of Woman.

Woman as a truth which is difficult to win, as semblance, as the mistress of the lie and dissimulation or seductive deceiver, as residing in the realm of appearances—there is no doubt that Nietzsche invokes "worn" metaphors in the service of an anti-traditional, anti-metaphysical discourse, in an attempt to collapse the opposition between appearance and reality and, consequently, that he revalues the notions of "appearance," "surface," "dissimulation." But the worn metaphors carry with them a problematic haze of associations and the revaluation of the woman-image is not always distinguishable from an idealization. One is forced to pose the question: Why is it the woman who must represent either truth or its fading, its disappearance—especially in relation to an erotics of the veil?

The veil poses difficulties for both Nietzsche and Derrida insofar as it drags along its metaphysical baggage, but neither of them will reject the trope altogether. According to Derrida, Nietzsche recognized the fragile structure of truth in its relation to the veil and both refuse to perform either the gesture of veiling or that of unveiling. Derrida prefers the image of *suspending* the veil:

> "Truth" can only be a surface. But the blushing movement of that truth which is not suspended in quotation marks casts a modest veil over such a surface. And only through such a veil which thus falls over it could "truth" become truth, profound, indecent, desirable. But should that veil be suspended, or even fall a bit differently, there would no longer be any truth, only "truth"— written in quotation marks. (59)

To suspend means to hang from a single point of support in space, to interrupt, to defer. The woman perpetually defers the question of truth. It remains, precisely, suspended. In *Spurs*, the term "woman" functions as a point of comparison to style, writing, inscription, particularly inasmuch as the notion of "writing" in Derrida's work always signifies the undoing of metaphysical oppositions. The attempt is clearly to introduce a division between any question of the woman and an ontological question. Nevertheless, it is still the woman who figures the very resistance to the ontological question.[21]

> The question of the woman suspends the decidable opposition of true and non-true and inaugurates the regime of quotation marks which is to be enforced for every concept belonging to the system of philosophical decidability. The hermeneutic project which postulates a true sense of text is disqualified under this regime. (107)

In a quite Nietzschean gesture, Derrida takes up and employs the worn-out tropes of femininity—instability, indecisiveness, dissimulation—and yet injects them with a new and more positive value for the sake of his philosophical operation. The woman is used to destabilize the hierarchy of values of metaphysics and the eroticism of such an operation is not lost. The voyeurism continues: "It is impossible to resist looking for her."

Nietzsche manipulates and works within the problematic wherein the woman is a trope of truth. Yet, believing in truth is, from his point of view, a common mistake of philosophers. The woman, on the other hand, who represents truth, has no use for it herself. Derrida reiterates this idea in claiming that the philosopher must emulate the woman, who does not believe in truth or castration. He locates three types of proposition about the woman in Nietzsche's text. In the first, the woman is a figure of falsehood, against which the man measures his own phallogocentric truth. Here, she is castrated. In the second proposition, she is the figure of truth, but plays with it at a distance through a guile and naiveté which nevertheless ratify truth. Here, she is castrating. In the first two types of proposition in Nietzsche's text, the woman is "censured, debased and despised." Only the third type of proposition is conceived outside the bind of castration. Here, the woman is an "affirmative power, a dissimulatress, an artist, a dionysiac" (97). Derrida succinctly outlines the desire of Nietzsche: "He was, he dreaded this castrated woman. He was, he dreaded this castrating woman. He was, he loved this affirming woman" (101). And Derrida would like to be Nietzsche being the woman. According to Irigaray, "Ascribing his

[Derrida's] own project to her, he rises from the abyss—or the *abyme*."[22] Woman-truth, woman-lie, woman-affirmation—it is quite striking that the woman comes to represent all these things, as though affirmation, the most highly treasured category, could somehow not be *thought* except in and through the figure of the woman. She enables the philosophical operation, becomes its support.

In Derrida's text, the woman no longer figures the veiled movement of truth but the suspended veil of undecidability. She comes to represent the limit to the relevance of the hermeneutic question. Derrida's skepticism about that question, about the project of interpretation in general, is focused in his consideration of Nietzsche's marginal unpublished note, "I have forgotten my umbrella." For its secret, its hidden meaning beneath the veil of a surface, may be that it has no secret. The note is therefore like the woman insofar as "it might only be pretending to be simulating some hidden truth within its folds. Its limit is not only stipulated by its structure but is in fact intimately confused with it. The hermeneut cannot but be provoked and disconcerted by its play" (133). The woman becomes even more tantalizing, desirable, and like the umbrella, something you do not want to forget. The veil ensures that this is not a question of visibility, of the visible as a guarantee or measure of certitude. For, as Derrida admits, "Nietzsche himself did not see his way too clearly there" (101). Nevertheless, he managed. In both Nietzsche's and Derrida's texts, the woman becomes the site of a certain philosophical reinvestment—this time in the attempt to deconstruct truth. She remains the fetish of philosophy.

From this point of view, Lacan's appeal to the trope of the veil might seem more desirable for feminist theory inasmuch as it hovers around not the woman but questions of representation and the phallus. Yet, it is still contaminated a little by the problematic of truth and deception or fraud. The veil is the privileged content of the trompe l'oeil constituted by painting: it fools or deceives the human subject. In the story of Zeuxis and Parrhasios invoked by Lacan, Zeuxis, challenged by his rival, Parrhasios, produces a painting of grapes which attracts birds who attempt to pick at them. But when Zeuxis demands that Parrhasios draw aside the veil which covers his painting, he is startled to find that the veil itself is painted. Lacan uses the story to establish a distinction between the "natural function of the lure" (the painted grapes) and that of trompe l'oeil (the painted veil): "If one wishes to deceive a man, what one presents to him is the painting of a veil, that is to say, something that incites him to ask what is behind it."[23] This painting elicits the desire to touch, to transgress the barrier of representation and to posit its "beyond" or "depth," prompted by the extent to which the surface posits something "other." Plato's objection to painting is therefore not based on its illusion of equaling its object but on the fact that the "*trompe-l'oeil*" of painting pretends to be something other than what it is" (112). Lacan's analysis of the story constitutes a complication of vision, marking it with absence so that the picture takes on the mechanism of language.

In the process, vision is destabilized; it becomes less sure, precisely because it is subject to desire. Parrhasios's painting demonstrates that "what was at issue was certainly deceiving the eye (*tromper l'oeil*). A triumph of the gaze over the eye" (103). *Gaze* here signifies the excess of desire over geometral vision or vision as the representation of space through perspective. In the geometral relation of perspective, the subject is centered as the master of representation; visual space is mapped and controlled. The gaze, on the other hand, indicates that the "I," no longer master of what it sees, is grasped, solicited, by the depth of field (that which is beyond). Zeuxis, subject to desire, seeks to know what is beyond the surface/veil. The trick is that the surface is all there is to be seen. There is dissimulation or deception here but, as in Nietzsche's text, it does not consist of a distortion of the truth behind appearances but a mere gesture toward that "beyond."[24] And while, according to Nietzsche, it is the woman who exemplifies the instability of the visual and the pretense of essence, in Lacan's analysis it is representation—the picture—which pretends to be something other than what it is.

However, this theoretical move is not, in fact, a desexualization of the dialectic of appearance and reality, the veil and the beyond. For behind the veil lurks the phallus. The gaze and desire are in tandem because the field of the visible always registers (is always inhabited by) a lack: "The subject is presented as other than he is, and what one shows him is not what he wishes to see" (104). The gaze is hence the *objet a* in the scopic dimension. Symbolic of lack, it is clearly inscribed in a phallic order. Furthermore, in Lacan's work the veil itself is, most strikingly, reserved for the phallus. Torn from the woman's face, it is located elsewhere. I am thinking, of course, of the often quoted statement in which Lacan claims that "the phallus can play its role only when veiled." For Rose, this appeal to a procedure of veiling is evidence of Lacan's demotion of the realm of the visible: "He constantly refused any crude identification of the phallus with the order of the visible or real and he referred it instead to that function of 'veiling.' "[25] The disorganization of the field of perception—its destabilization—is attributed not to the woman but to the phallus. Now it is certainly possible to develop the argument that the phallus is not a masculine category, that it is a signifier and not equivalent to the penis (the consistent strategy of those who argue that Lacanian psychoanalysis is useful for feminism), and therefore that we are not confronted with a situation in which the psychoanalyst snatches the veil from the woman in order to conceal his own private parts. Far from being exhausted by its masculine status, the phallus would appear to be to some degree feminized in Lacan's text. The woman's relation to the phallus is that of "being" rather than "having" and the mother is sometimes "phallic." Or one could subscribe to Jane Gallop's analysis of the grammatical categories of gender and note that the phallus, in a slip of the type, is modified by "la" rather than "le" or that "voile" as Lacan uses it, is both feminine (as "sail") or masculine (as "veil"). For, in "The Agency of the Letter in the Unconscious," Nietzsche's sailboat in the distance glides through Lacan's text and becomes the privileged example of metonymy: "thirty sails." As Gallop points out, " 'Voile' for 'sail' is derived from 'voile' for 'veil' and it may be just this sort of slippage between a masculine and a feminine term that is at play in Lacan's notion of the phallus, which is a latent phallus, a metonymic, maternal, feminine phallus."[26]

But even Gallop acknowledges that "the masculinity of the phallic signifier serves well as an emblem of the confusion between phallus and male which inheres in language, in our symbolic order,"[27] and concludes her reading of "The Meaning of the Phallus" with a return to the penis (the knot). It might be useful, then, to turn our attention to an examination of what the role of the phallus is and therefore why the veil is necessary. The phallus takes on meaning in relation to the differential function of language and the corresponding structure of signifier/signified. The entire sentence reads, "All these propositions merely veil over the fact that the phallus can only play its role as veiled, that is, as in itself the sign of the latency with which everything signifiable is struck as soon as it is raised (*aufgehoben*) to the function of the signifier."[28] The veil over the phallus points to the necessity of a division between the latency of the signifiable and the patency—the materiality—of the signifier, a splitting in language as well as a splitting of subjectivity. The phallus, as the signifier with no signified, indicates the perpetual deferral of meaning, its failure to coagulate. Behind the veil, which must remain in place, lies a series of linked terms: lack, the gaze, the *objet a*, the phallus. There is no doubt that Lacan attempts to disrupt the spatialization of the classical philosophical dialectic between surface and depth, appearance and being. The "beyond" is a function of desire and hence de-essentialized, but not entirely negated. Rather, the surface/depth dichotomy is reformulated as a splitting, a fracture, necessitated by the subject's relation to language and the unconscious. If there is a truth in Lacanian psychoanalysis it is a truth of language and the contribution of language to the constitution of subjectivity. But it is a truth which, like Nietzsche's, is particularly evasive, slippery. For that which is latent—the signifiable—is also always deferred, out of reach, subject to a metonymic displacement. Like a woman, the phallus—in a perpetual demonstration of the inadequacy of language with respect to meaning—plays its role only when veiled. Neither the woman nor the phallus seems to be capable of completely escaping the problematic of truth, even if it is defined in its very inaccessibility, in its resistance to the purely visible, or as belonging to the order of language. Whether or not the phallus is feminized, truth, in the Lacanian text, insofar as it concerns a question of veiling, is usurped for the phallus, no longer figured explicitly through the woman, who nevertheless comes to represent an absolute and unattainable state of *jouissance*. Both Derrida and Lacan envy the woman they have constructed.

There is, at one point in *The Gay Science*, a reference to a female figure who might disturb or disconcert this phallocentric staging of truth (or its destabilization) and representation with respect to procedures of veiling and unveiling. It is a reference Nietzsche does not develop. He writes, "Perhaps truth is a woman who has reasons for not letting us see her reasons? Perhaps her name is—to speak Greek—*Baubo*?"[29] There is nothing more about Baubo, only this vague reference to her name in relation to truth and what it allows or disallows in the realm of vision. The translator and editor, Walter Kaufmann, adds, however, a footnote which transforms Nietzsche's citation into something of a dirty joke: "*Baubo*: A primitive and obscene female demon; according to the *Oxford Classical Dictionary*, originally a personification of the female genitals." In Greek mythology, Baubo is a minor character in the story of Demeter, the goddess of fertility, whose daughter Kore (renamed Persephone after the abduction) was stolen and raped by Hades, Lord of the Underworld. Demeter fled Olympus and wandered throughout the world for years, in the guise of an old woman, searching for her daughter. One day, as she was resting in the shade of a tree in Eleusis, Baubo offered her a drink of barley-water and mint. In her grief, Demeter refused the drink and, in response, Baubo lifted her skirts to reveal her pudenda. A drawing of a boy's face (Iacchus—a mystic name for Dionysus) appeared on the lower part of her body, and Baubo, with a gesture of her hand, made it seem to grimace, provoking Demeter to laugh, breaking her mourning. The laughter freed Demeter, and she accepted the drink from Baubo. Afterward, she managed to free her daughter Persephone from the underworld for three-fourths of the year. In the remaining one-fourth, when Persephone resides with her husband in the underworld, Demeter's sadness is reflected in the coldness and barrenness of the earth.

In Peter Wollen's brief but fascinating analysis of the myth, Baubo's exhibitionism is interpreted as a potential alternative to the castrating display of the Medusa: "[Baubo's] display is to another woman and its effect is to provoke laughter and to end grief and mourning (brought about by mother-daughter separation at the hands of a man, Pluto) . . . Demeter is shown the 'Truth,' but is it just a joke? It is not shameful, not horrifying, but funny, comical, laughable." The laugh, outside the semantic and "on the edge of language," breaks the hold of a phallogocentric grammar.[30] Sarah Kofman also interprets Baubo as a figure who resides outside the regime of phallocentrism, undermining its logic. Through a number of links, including the inscription of Dionysus's face on Baubo's body, Kofman makes the claim that Baubo is a feminine double of Dionysus. And Dionysus, nude but also the god of masks, "erases the opposition of veiled and non-veiled, masculine and feminine, fetishism and castration."[31] Both Wollen and Kofman point out that the story of Baubo is told in the texts of the early church fathers. Kofman observes that these texts are censored and qualified with obscurities, seemingly confirming the notion that Baubo exemplifies the marginalization of the woman's story as well as the woman's genitals within a patriarchal discourse.[32]

The myth of Baubo finds an interesting—and similarly porno-graphic—echo in Lacan's work. Lacan is fascinated with anamorphosis and its inverted use of perspective. In *The Four Fundamental Concepts*, he makes it the center point of a large part of his analysis of the gaze and claims that it is evocative of that which "geometral researches into perspective allow to escape from vision" (87). Anamorphosis gives a glimpse of this excess; its fascination is a fascination with the annihilation of the subject. But the scenario he constructs to illustrate anamorphosis, immediately before the better-known analysis of Holbein's painting, *The Ambassadors*, is rather strange, almost fantastical, and, like the myth of Baubo, invokes a notion of body-writing:

> How is it that nobody has ever thought of connecting this [anamorphosis] with . . . the effect of an erection? Imagine a tattoo traced on the sexual organ *ad hoc* in the state of repose and assuming its, if I may say so, developed form in another state. How can we not see here, immanent in the geometral dimension . . . something symbolic of the function of the lack, of the appearance of the phallic ghost? (87–88)

The preferred space of inscription for anamorphosis becomes the phallic organ. The apparently alternative conceptualization of the female genitals in Baubo's story is here recuperated, revamped. For the male subject's body allows him to do it better. Lacan, envious of the woman, appropriates her picture-making activity, her body-writing, and inscribes it on the phallus. After all, anamorphosis would seem to prefer a masculine space, as in the Holbein painting.

Yet, Lacan has to go to certain contortions in order to write on the penis/ phallus. When the metaphor of writing is invoked, the phallus is usually conceptualized as the tool which writes, the pen, rather than the surface of writing. Lacan seems to be uncomfortable with the specification of the penis/phallus as mere ground, space for inscription (a traditionally "femi- nine" characterization). Perhaps this is why the reference to the phallic organ as the site of anamorphosis is so brief, laconic, and almost immedi- ately displaced by the analysis of the Holbein painting. Here the phallus is no longer the ground for anamorphosis but its central figure. The phallus is *in* the picture—the picture no longer *on* the phallus. Such a move allays any fears about the complete feminization of the phallus, particularly since the mise-en-scène of the Holbein painting is so insistently masculine.

The male theorist's relation to the woman, in general, seems to oscillate between fear and envy of the feminine. Lacan attributes to the phallus qualities formerly specified as feminine—veiled, it connotes visual instabil- ity, deception. The phallus symbolizes the failure of meaning, the fact that it is mere semblance. If "the status of the phallus is a fraud,"[33] as Rose points out, it is fraudulent in much the same way that woman represents untruth or dissimulation in Nietzsche's text. Lacan reverses the usual terms of sexual difference in relation to the visual field. In Nietzsche the precari- ousness of vision is incarnated in the woman, while the man is a point of stability (in relation to the will to know, to philosophize, if not in relation to knowledge itself—Derrida's "It is impossible to resist looking for her"). In Lacan, the necessary destabilization or deception of the visual is a function of the phallus, while the woman, in some sense, comes to represent the immediacy and security of the visible. This immediacy is a result of the *jouissance* attributed to her:

> As for Saint Theresa—you only have to go and look at Bernini's statue in Rome to understand immediately that she's coming, there is no doubt about it. And what is her *jouissance*, her *coming* from? It is clear that the essential testimony of the mystics is that they are experiencing it but know nothing about it.[34]

As Stephen Heath points out, the "more" of the woman's *jouissance* in Lacan's work compensates for the absence which she represents in relation to the scenario of castration.[35]

And one could add that the price to be paid for visual immediacy and the "more" of *jouissance* is the absence of knowledge. Lacan explains that while the woman is "not all" in relation to the phallic function and "excluded by the nature of things which is the nature of words," she nevertheless has a supplementary *jouissance*.

> There is a *jouissance* proper to her, to this "her" which does not exist and which signifies nothing. There is a *jouissance* proper to her and of which she herself may know nothing, except that she experiences it—that much she does know. . . . As I have said, the woman can love in the man only the way in which he faces the knowledge he souls for. But as for the knowledge by which he is, we can only ask this question if we grant that there is something, *jouissance*, which makes it impossible to tell whether the woman can say anything about it—whether she can say what she knows of it.[36]

Jouissance presupposes a non-knowledge or even an anti-knowledge. It is linked to the realm of the mystics and hence, at the very least, divorces the register of knowledge from the register of discourse. The woman cannot say what she knows; that knowledge may exist but it always resides elsewhere. Since psychoanalysis, however, is in itself a form of anti-epistemology insofar as the unconscious subverts the possibility of a stable knowledge, the woman here becomes emblematic of the subject who is duped by the unconscious, of the non-knowledge of the subject. It is almost as though there were an obligatory blind spot as far as the woman is concerned which is compensated for by an *over*-sight, a compulsion to see her, to image her, to make her revelatory of something.

Nietzsche's woman, closing her eyes to herself, and Lacan's woman, who doesn't know (who has *jouissance* without knowledge), have something in common. Yet, knowledge, like truth, is a peculiar term in the work of both Nietzsche and Lacan. The subject's position outside of knowledge is not necessarily to be lamented. In these theories, therefore, it is a question not so much of depriving the woman of subjectivity (a term psychoanalysis problematizes in any event), as of making her a privileged trope, a site of theoretical excess, an exemplar of the philosophical enterprise. In Derrida's work, this is manifest in his positioning of the woman as affirmative and Dionysiac, the figure of undecidability, and the point of impasse of the hermeneutic question. Clearly, Lacan's theoretical assumptions about subjectivity and his strategic moves distance him significantly from Derrida's deconstructive efforts, and their differences should not be minimized. But Lacan's phallocentrism and Derrida's anti-phallocentrism (or hymenism) ultimately occupy the same discursive register as far as the fate of the woman is concerned. Is there that much difference between the affirmation beyond castration of the Derridean woman and the *jouissance* of the Lacanic woman? *Affirmation* and *jouissance* both indicate a certain "beyond" in their respective theories, a beyond which seems to represent, interestingly, the very limit of what is theorizable.

The theoretical limit is tantalizing, seductive in its very inaccessibility. But the term which seems to most adequately describe the relation of the philosopher/psychoanalyst to the woman here is envy. And it is Lacan who gives us a clue to a possible deciphering of this envy. The scenario he invokes in order to depict envy as a way of looking is that of the child at the mother's breast.

> The most exemplary *invidia*, for us analysts, is the one I found long ago in Augustine, in which he sums up his entire fate, namely, that of the little child seeing his brother at his mother's breast, looking at him *amare conspectu*, with a bitter look, which seems to tear him to pieces and has on himself the effect of a poison.

Lacan claims that this envy has nothing to do with the child's desire for what the brother has—the milk or the breast or the mother as possessions. In this sense, it differs from jealousy. Rather,

> such is true envy—the envy that makes the subject pale before the image of a completeness closed upon itself, before the idea that the *petit a*, the separated *a* from which he is hanging, may be for another the possession that gives satisfaction, *Befriedigung*.[37]

Lacan initially interprets the envy as that of brother for brother—male subject for the apparently total gratification and contentment of another male subject. But the fact that it is an "image of a completeness closed upon itself" which prompts the envy would seem to suggest instead that it is the woman—the mother—who is the object of the envy. For in psychoanalytic theory the woman is depicted, in her narcissistic self-sufficiency, as the being who most fully embodies a "completeness closed upon itself." In effect, what the male subject of theory here envies is the woman whom he has constructed as inhabiting a space outside his own theory—nevertheless supporting that theory through her very absence. "You only have to go and look" to see that she is not of this world. As Lacan himself points out, the Latin *invidia*—envy—is derived from *videre*, to see. What we witness here is the displacement of vision's truth to the realm of theoretical vision. The psychoanalyst sees immediately that to see the woman is to envy her, to recognize that what she represents is desirable.

Figure 3.14

Figure 3.15

The "seeing" is often on the side of the theory which hopes to disengage itself from the visible, from the seeing/seen nexus.

The idea that the visible is a point of crisis seems to be conveniently forgotten when theory contemplates its own limits. On the whole, however, Lacan's analysis of vision, hovering around the "phallic ghost" and lack, does seem to emphasize the precariousness of vision, as Rose suggests.

Figure 3.16

Figure 3.17

But it is not always necessary to be able to see or to be able to see clearly in order to maintain the given symbolics of a patriarchally ordered sexual difference. Distrusting the visible or geometral optics and valorizing ana-morphosis for its departure from a pictorial realism or its annihilation of the centered subject of perspective do not suffice. This insufficiency is, once more, demonstrated by the function of the veil, where the philosophical and

Figure 3.18

the cinematic organization of vision in relation to desire appear to coincide. The veil's curious dialectic of vision and obscurity, of closeness and distance, is evidenced, again, in Sternberg's work which, in its sheer concentration upon the surface of the image, recapitulates many of the themes and difficulties of the philosophical discourse. Although Sternberg is fond of interposing veils, screens, and streamers between the camera and Marlene Dietrich, he would also like to get as close to her as possible. Early in *The Scarlet Empress*, in her marriage scene, Catherine appears predictably enough in a wedding gown (figure 3.14). What is not predictable, however, is the insistence of the camera upon positioning itself closer and closer to her face as the scene progresses, until the very texture of the veil becomes marked (figures 3.15, 3.16, 3.17). An even more striking instance of this tactic occurs later in the film. Catherine has just given birth to a baby boy, heir to the throne. She lies in a bed surrounded by veils and is presented with a gift, a necklace, from the queen (figure 3.18). Again, as she examines the necklace the camera reduces its distance from her (figures 3.19, 3.20). As Sternberg's camera gets closer to the woman, she almost disappears, the outline of her face grows indistinct, and her place is taken by the surface or texture of the image, the screen.

As the camera increases its proximity to the veil, the veil and the screen it becomes seem to become the objects of desire. The veil mimics the grain of the film, the material substrate of the medium, and becomes the screen as surface of division, separation, and hence solicited transgression. In

Figure 3.19

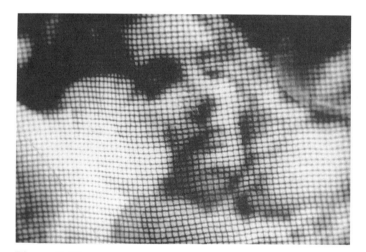

Figure 3.20

mimicking the grain of the film, this gesture *might* be viewed as deconstructive par excellence, for it indicates the woman's status as the substrate of representation. The woman is revealed as no longer simply the privileged object of the gaze in the cinema but the support of the cinematic image. Yet, I would argue that the marking of the image in this way, the foregrounding of the grain, the positioning of the woman as screen—all of this merely

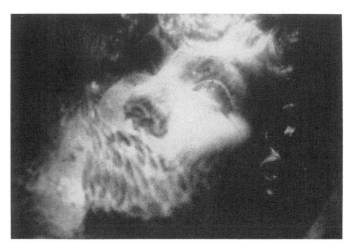

Figure 3.21

heightens the eroticism, makes her more desirable, stimulates the envy of
the filmmaker ("Marlene is me," Sternberg once said). The image of
Dietrich indicates that even when the woman is no longer fully visible, she
is the support of its seduction of the spectator, its provocation. And I think
one could ask similar kinds of questions about the desire of the philosopher
or the psychoanalyst who appeals to the woman as a form of theoretical
proof—the desire to reveal her status as support, substrate of truth/untruth
or representation, and simultaneously to maintain her "operation," because
she can indeed be so representative of so many things even if she doesn't
understand them herself. The question is why the woman must always carry
the burden of the philosophical demonstration, why she must be the one to
figure truth, dissimulation, *jouissance*, untruth, the abyss, etc., why she
is the support of these tropological systems—even and especially anti-
metaphysical or anti-humanistic systems.

It is not surprising that the confused topology of Western metaphysics
finds a perfect site for its inscription in a classical cinema which organizes
its appeals to scopophilia around the figure of the woman as distanced
surface. That topology takes on the burden of defusing the philosophical
insecurity associated with the instabilities, the contradictions, and the limits
of its own discourse—defusing them by projecting that instability in relation
to truth onto the woman.[38] It is at once more striking and more disconcerting,
however, that the anti-humanist and anti-metaphysical discourses associated with poststructuralism are inexorably drawn to the same necessity of

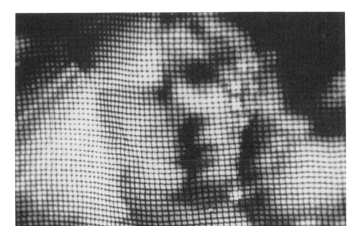

Figure 3.22

troping the woman (although here she is revalued and becomes the signifier of what is most desirable in theory—or at its limits).

It might be useful to imagine what Dietrich's return look might be, from behind the veil (figures 3.21, 3.22). Usually, the placement of a veil over a woman's face works to localize and hence contain dissimulation, to keep it from contaminating the male subject. But how can we imagine, conceive her look back? Everything would become woven, narrativized, dissimulation. Derrida envies that look. He loses himself in her eyes. It would be preferable to disentangle the woman and the veil, to tell another story. As soon as the dichotomy between the visible as guarantee and the visible as inherently destabilized, between truth and appearance, is mapped onto sexual difference, the woman is idealized, whether as undecidability or *jouissance*. The necessary incompletion or failure of the attempt to leave behind the terms of such a problematic is revealed in the symptomatic role of the woman, who takes up the slack and becomes the object of a desire which reflects the lack that haunts theory. What I have attempted to suggest here is how we might begin to understand the philosophical and psychoanalytical envy of the woman through examination of a desire which always only seems more visible in the cinema.

CHAPTER FOUR

Remembering Women:
Psychical and Historical
Constructions in Film Theory

Max Ophuls's 1934 film, *La Signora di tutti*, makes uncannily explicit many of the most crucial themes of contemporary feminist film theory.[1] Its protagonist, Gaby Doriot (Isa Miranda), as the star of the film within the film, also entitled *La Signora di tutti*, is indeed "Everybody's Lady"—she is the signifier of a generalized desire. The film demonstrates the intimate relation between the woman and the specifically cinematic and delineates the role of the cinema as a machine for the generation of desire. There are two aspects of this film which make it a crucial reference for the considerations of this essay. First, it is extremely self-reflexive insofar as it consistently analyzes the cinematic construction of the woman. The relation between the basis of her attraction and the technologically produced images and sounds of the cinema is emphasized through the intertwining of two narratives: one concerning her fatal fascination and its effects on the men who surround her; the other treating her rise to cinematic stardom. There is a sense in which the two narratives are essentially the same. The lure of Gaby Doriot is the lure of the cinema. Second, the narrative of *La Signora* is mobilized by a denial of the amnesia subtending Gaby's function as pure image. Her cinematic presence (as star, as the epitome of the woman who belongs to everyone) is based on the repression of her own history and its refabrication according to the discursive requirements of fandom. The narrative itself is formulated as a flashback, allegedly from Gaby's point of view. But, as in many films which are organized around a woman's act of remembering, Gaby's memory is forced, medically induced by the anaesthesia she is given on the operating table at the beginning of the film.[2] The cinematic abstraction of the woman is represented as in tension with the complex articulation of memory, history, and narrative.

Female trauma is also overdetermined by the cinema as an apparatus in

Augusto Genina's 1930 *Prix de Beauté*. Here, an ordinary middle-class woman, Lucienne (Louise Brooks), is transformed into the ideal Woman by winning a series of beauty pageants by means of which she becomes, successively, Miss France and Miss Europe. Lucienne's unimaginative and possessive fiancé, André, prohibits her exhibitionism, warning her to "not even dream" of entering the beauty contest. When she does so surreptitiously and wins, he forces her to choose between her newfound fame and himself. At first capitulating to his demands, Lucienne eventually tires of her monotonous existence as a housewife and leaves André to accept a movie contract. Desolate and jealous, he follows her and, during a preview of her screen test in the studio's projection room, he shoots Lucienne as she watches, enraptured, her own image. In the beginning of the film, the diegetic emphasis upon the huge machinery of the press where André works as a typesetter underscores the technological nature of the two photographic images Lucienne submits to the beauty contest. These two images anticipate her trajectory from anonymous Parisian girl, whose meaning is bound up with the contingent events of her life—visits to the beach, work, the carnival, etc.—to international film celebrity. In her death scene, there is once again a diegetic fixation upon the machinery—this time that of the cinema—for the production of images. The scene is prefaced by shots of the projector and its preparation for the screening. The flickering light from the screen is reflected on Lucienne's face, revealing not only her fascination with her own representation but the uncanny merger of the "real" woman with her image. After she is shot by André, cut-aways to the projector's unrelenting movement—ceaselessly insisting that Lucienne continues to live, to move, on the screen—appear to mock the idea of her mortality. Her dead face is lit and framed by her celluloid image and her abstraction is complete. André, who, up until this moment in the film has been oblivious to Lucienne's photographic or cinematic presence, is suddenly caught, intrigued by the image in which she continues to sing the same song she had sung to him earlier in the film. Defined throughout the narrative primarily by his overzealous possessiveness, André finally submits to the logic of mechanical reproduction, to the cinematic dialectic which insists—despite all evidence to the contrary—that "this image is for you—and you alone." Like Gaby Doriot, "Everybody's Lady," Lucienne and her image belong to everyone and at the same time to no one in particular. The abstraction of that image lies in its detachment from any origin, from any historical grounding—in short, in its exchangeability. *La Signora di tutti* and *Prix de Beauté* share this alignment of feminine desirability with the cinematic apparatus. Furthermore, in each film the woman is singled out, made simultaneously unique and yet the very embodiment of a universal axiom of femininity. This necessitates a process whereby the protagonist is clearly differentiated from other women. In *Prix*, it is the beauty contest which isolates Lucienne from the mass of ordinary women (in a film where the claustrophobia induced by the modern urban crowd is continually marked in the mise-en-scène). In *La Signora*, a male character tells Gaby at one point, "You're not like the other girls. I wish I had met you before." Gaby represents the woman in general, but is like none of them in particular.

There is a disorienting contradiction at work here. Gaby becomes the image of Woman because no other—ordinary—woman is like her. The image is characterized by a lack of resemblance. Nevertheless, she somehow represents all women through her incarnation as a generalized femininity, an abstraction or ideal of femininity. The monolithic category of Woman here is not even an alleged average or distillate of concrete women but their abstraction, their *subtraction* (in its etymological sense, abstraction is a "drawing away from"). Not like other women, Gaby becomes Woman. Both *La Signora di tutti* and *Prix de Beauté* chronicle the expropriation of the woman's look and voice and the consequent transformation of the woman into Woman—a position inaccessible to women.[3] This is not only the process of the narrative trajectories of *La Signora di tutti* and *Prix de Beauté* but of the cinematic institution as well—in its narratives, its star system, its spectacle. But further, it specifies something of the process of feminist film theory which, in a way, mimics the cinematic construction of the Woman, reinscribing her abstraction. It is not only the apparatus which produces Woman but apparatus theory, in strange complicity with its object.

This attachment to the figure of a generalizable Woman as the product of the apparatus indicates why, for many, feminist film theory seems to have reached an impasse, a certain blockage in its theorization.[4] For the often totalizing nature of its analysis of patriarchy leaves little room for resistance or for the elaboration of an alternative filmmaking practice which would not be defined only negatively, as a counter-cinema. In focusing upon the task of delineating in great detail the attributes of the woman as effect of the apparatus, feminist film theory participates in the abstraction of women. The concept "Woman" effaces the differences between women in specific socio-historical contexts, between women defined precisely as historical subjects rather than as *a* psychical subject (or non-subject). Hence, Teresa de Lauretis's attempt to specify the task of feminist film theory leads, through a series of hypergeneralizations of femininity, to the historical as the privileged term.

> This is where the specificity of a feminist theory may be sought: not in femininity as a privileged nearness to nature, the body, or the unconscious,

an essence which inheres in women but to which males too now lay a claim;
not in a female tradition simply understood as private, marginal and yet intact,
outside of history but fully there to be discovered or recovered; not, finally,
in the chinks and cracks of masculinity, the fissures of male identity or the
repressed of phallic discourse; but rather in that political, theoretical, self-
analyzing practice by which the relations of the subject in social reality can
be rearticulated from the historical experience of women.[5]

The appeal to history made here is shared by other feminist theorists
(including E. Ann Kaplan, Annette Kuhn)[6] who, in different contexts, also
call for a dismantling of the hegemony of *the* theorization of *the* woman
through an attention to the concrete specificities of history. This is not a
naive appeal to history (all agree that history must be theorized), but it is
an invocation of history designed to counter certain excesses of theory
(especially psychoanalytic theory) and the impasse resulting from those
excesses. History is envisaged as a "way out."

Psychoanalysis has been activated in feminist film theory primarily in
order to dissect and analyze the spectator's psychical investment in the
film. But to accomplish this, theory had to posit a vast synchrony of the
cinema—the cinema happens all at once (as, precisely, an apparatus) and
its image of woman is always subservient to voyeuristic and fetishistic
impulses. In this context, woman=lack=the cinematic image. Within such
a problematic, resistance can only be conceptualized through the idea of
"reading against the grain," as leakage or excess—something which
emerges between the cracks as the by-product of another process. Such a
definition of resistance is merely another acknowledgment of the totalizing
aspect of the apparatus.

The desire to add the dimension of diachrony, to historicize, is one way
of dismantling the pessimism of apparatus theory. For it opens up the
possibility of an escape from its alleged determinism and hence the possibility of change or transformation through attention to the concreteness and
specificity of the socio-historical situation. The ever-present danger here is
in the temptation to use the gesture of historicizing as a covert means of
dismissing theory which is then opposed to the "real" of the particular
historical conjunction where we can somehow unproblematically observe,
once again—free from the restrictions of a theoretical framework—what
women actually did or even how their representations reflected something
of the "real" of their situation. Perhaps we need to look more closely at
what "theory" is or might be and what "history" denotes in opposition to
that term—for it is "history" which promises to find a way around the
theoretical impasse. For that reason, what I would like to do here is isolate

and examine two moments in the archaeology of that impasse: 1) the elaboration of apparatus theory as a specific reading and reduction of the object of psychoanalytic theory and the aim of a metapsychology; 2) the appeal to history as an "outside" of psychoanalysis, a realm beyond memory and subjectivity which nevertheless seems to guarantee the dispersal of a monolithic, theorized subjectivity. My reading of these two moments will be situated within the purview of psychoanalysis. For psychoanalysis has its own theory of theory or speculation (linking it to paranoia and delirium) and its own pursuit of history (acted out primarily in the case histories and in the theory of transference).

The apparent exhaustion of psychoanalytic film theory, its impasse, is closely linked to its activation of the metaphor of the apparatus or *dispositif*. In two essays, "Ideological Effects of the Basic Cinematographic Apparatus" and "The Apparatus: Metapsychological Approaches to the Impression of Reality in the Cinema," Jean-Louis Baudry outlined the problematic whereby the cinema becomes a machine with a certain arrangement, a disposition.[7] His theses concerning the positioning of the spectator as the transcendental gaze of the camera and the screen's operation as the Lacanian mirror were taken up and expanded by theorists such as Christian Metz and Stephen Heath. Feminist film theory inherits many of the assumptions of this mode of theorizing—its transference onto psychoanalysis is mediated by apparatus theory.

Freud uses the term "psychical apparatus" to emphasize certain attributes of the psyche—"its capacity to transmit and transform a specific energy and its subdivision into systems or agencies."[8] The apparatus specifies a series of relations: relations between spaces, operations, temporalities. The psyche is not a monolithic block but must, instead, be conceptualized as a dynamism of parts, a differential machine. This is why Freud tends to choose as metaphors for the psychical apparatus objects which constitute combinatories of specific elements—the microscope, the camera, the telescope, the early model of a network of neurons and their facilitations, the mystic writing pad. Although Freud activates the analogy of the apparatus in order to conceptualize a certain chronology and its effects as well as the notion of psychical locality, optical instruments such as the microscope and the telescope lend themselves more readily to the description of a spatial arrangement. In response to G. T. Fechner's idea that "the scene of action of dreams is different from that of waking ideational life," Freud states,

> What is presented to us in these words is the idea of *psychical locality* . . . I propose simply to follow the suggestion that we should picture the instrument which carries out our mental functions as resembling a compound microscope

or a photographic apparatus, or something of the kind. On that basis, psychical locality will correspond to a point inside the apparatus at which one of the preliminary stages of an image comes into being. In the microscope and telescope, as we know, these occur in part at ideal points, regions in which no tangible component of the apparatus is situated. . . . Accordingly, we will picture the mental apparatus as a compound instrument, to the components of which we will give the name of "agencies," or (for the sake of greater clarity) "systems." It is to be anticipated, in the next place, that these systems may perhaps stand in a regular spatial relation to one another, in the same kind of way in which the various systems of lenses in a telescope are arranged behind one another.[9]

Baudry is, of course, attracted to the analogies of the telescope and photographic apparatus precisely because they are *optical* metaphors comparable to the cinematic apparatus. To the spatial arrangement of lenses in the telescope corresponds the spatial disposition of projector, spectator/camera, and screen.

The decisive rupture effected by the concept of the apparatus with respect to previous film theories lies in its engagement with the issue of realism. In Baudry's analysis, the impression of reality is a subject-effect and has nothing to do with the possibility of a comparison between representation and the real. In the scenario of Plato's cave, invoked by Baudry to buttress his claim that the cinema is the machine of idealism, the prisoners are chained since birth, habituated to their cinema, and have nothing with which to compare the shadows cast on the wall of the cave. As in Freud's theory of hallucination, reality is given all at once or not at all—it is not attained by degrees or gradual approximations as in theories of adaptation. Jean Laplanche points out, *"The hallucination is or is not*, and when it is, it is absolutely useless to imagine a procedure allowing one to demonstrate to the hallucinator that he is wrong."[10] Yet, there is an illusion at work here, both in Plato's scenario of the cave and in Baudry's scenario of the cinema. For Plato, whether the prisoners are aware of it or not, the shadows are merely copies of copies of the Idea, which is the only Real. For Baudry, the illusion is located in the deception of the apparatus which conceals its own idealist operation. Hence, when Baudry defines the apparatus it is as a unique spatial arrangement which explains the production of "truth," giving the analyst knowledge of a differentiation between real and illusion.

For we are dealing here with an apparatus, with a metaphorical relationship between places or a relationship between metaphorical places, with a topography, the knowledge of which defines for both philosopher and analyst the degree of relationship to truth or to description, or to illusion, and the need for an ethical point of view.[11]

And what Baudry produces by means of the analogy of the apparatus is precisely an ethical point of view—the cinema, the toy of idealism and of a 2000 year-old desire on the part of man (sic) to represent his own psyche to himself, dupes its spectator. In psychoanalytic film theory, the cinema seems inevitably to become the perfect machine for the incarnation or institutionalization of the wrong idea—here it is Platonic idealism; in Metz and Comolli, it is a Bazinian phenomenology.[12]

It is not surprising, given the definition of the apparatus as a topography, that the duping of the spectator should be coincident with the conceptualization of that spectator as a point in space, a site. Through its reinscription of Renaissance perspective, the apparatus positions the spectator, on this side of the screen, as the mirror of the vanishing point on the other side. Both points stabilize the representational logic, producing its readability, which is coincident with the notions of unity, coherency, and mastery. The cinema, according to Baudry, "constitutes the 'subject' by the illusory delimitation of a central location. . . ."[13] From the point of view of psychoanalytic theory this is, of course, an ideologically complicit fiction of the "self"—the result of a denial of the actual division, instability, and precarious nature of subjectivity. The cinema as an institution would thus insure that the Freudian/Lacanian theory of subjectivity be repressed, excluded from its operation. (Ideology here would truly be a kind of "false unconsciousness.")

This insistently spatial logic of apparatus theory has rigidly restricted the way in which vision has been understood as a psychical process within film theory. The gaze, emanating from a given point in this configuration, is the possession of the camera, and through identification with that camera, the spectating subject. Hence, it is not at all surprising that this gaze should be further characterized, in the work of Metz, Mulvey, and others, as precisely controlled in the service of voyeurism and fetishism—its subject male, its object female. Joan Copjec strongly criticizes this particular implementation of the theory of the apparatus and its corresponding description of the gaze.

> My question is not whether or not the gaze is male, for I know that it certainly is. While it is clearly important to remark on a certain social ordering which rakishly tilts the axis of seeing so that privilege piles up on the side of the male, it is a slip, and enormously problematic to posit something like a gaze, an idealized point from which the film can be looked at. Defined in this way,

at this moment, such a gaze can only be male. My question is prior to this other; I would ask, instead, if there is a gaze . . . It is legitimate to ask whether it is the cinerama [Copjec's term to denote the combination of panoptic and cinematic] or the cineramic *argument* which positions the subject through an identification with an anonymous gaze. What does it mean to say that the subject so identifies himself? It means the abolition of the alterity of the Other—the discursive apparatus—the elimination of difference. It means the construction of a coherent subject and of an all-male prison. This is an argument offered by obsession; it covers over the desire in the Other with the Other's demand, averts attention from the gaze and focuses on the eye.[14]

The obsessiveness of the argument is linked to its espousal of the idea of a perfect machine. The problem with the theory of the cinematic apparatus is that the apparatus always works. It never breaks down, is never subject to failure. This is what Copjec refers to as the "delirium of clinical perfection." The infallibility of the apparatus in this account is a function of the limitation of subjectivity to a single locale—the gaze of the spectator/camera. Since there is no otherness, no difference, no subjectivity associated with the discourse, its readability is always insured in advance. That readability becomes its most important psychical effect.

I would agree with Copjec that apparatus theory here operates a specific reduction of Lacan's theory of the gaze, particularly insofar as it is always articulated with the concept of desire. Furthermore, the gaze is in no way the possession of a subject. Rather, Lacan effects a separation between the gaze and the subject—the gaze is outside: ". . . in the scopic field, the gaze is outside, I am looked at, that is to say, I am a picture . . . the gaze is the instrument through which . . . I am *photo-graphed*."[15] The term "gaze" always signals in Lacan's text the excess of desire over geometral vision (vision as the representation of space through perspective). And the subject's desire is the desire of the Other—it is characterized by its alterity. In film theory, the gaze has become substantialized, directed—we speak of the gaze of the camera, the gaze of the spectator. By associating the gaze with lack, with the small object a, with, in effect, nothing, Lacan de-essentializes it. The gaze is beyond appearance but beyond appearance, "there is nothing in itself."[16]

Baudry's apparatus theory, critical as it may be of idealism's dichotomy between surface and depth, appearance and reality, reinscribes the dichotomy through a recourse to Plato's allegory of the cave. Idealism is the only guide to the spectator's apprehension of the image. Lacan, on the other hand, constructs an anti-idealist discourse on the gaze. The gaze indicates the necessity of a gesture pointing beyond the veil (the inescapability, in other words, of desire)—but beyond the veil there is nothing. He produces a sustained critique of the reduction of vision to geometral perspective. Because geometral perspective involves the mapping of space, not sight, it is an understanding of vision which is accessible to a blind man, as Diderot demonstrates. What is specific to vision escapes this delineation. While in the geometral relation, vision is calculated as an effect of light deployed in a straight line, the gaze indicates the dispersal of light—its irradiation, refraction, diffusion, scintillation. In the geometral mapping of vision, the subject is centered as the master of representation; through the gaze the "I" is grasped by the depth of field, by the "beyond" which endlessly solicits desire. Perspective guarantees the maintenance of the subject and its place. Alternatively, in perspective's own aberration—anamorphosis—one gets a glimpse of the fascination of the gaze as the annihilation of the subject. In Holbein's painting, *The Ambassadors*, what lures the subject is the distorted image of its own death—the skull whose readability is a function of the subject's decentering.

The gaze is always in excess—it is that which cannot be mapped, diagrammed, but only, perhaps, suggested in the impossible topological figures Lacan appeals to in his later work. For it is that which escapes the vision of a consciousness allegedly in control:

> In our relation to things, in so far as this relation is constituted by the way of vision, and ordered in the figures of representation, something slips, passes, is transmitted, from stage to stage, and is always to some degree eluded in it—that is what we call the gaze.[17]

The apparatus, as the exemplary model of cinematic representation, is incapable of theorizing this slippage, bound as it is to the construct of geometral perspective. It cannot accommodate the notion of desire as a disorganizing force in the field of perception. What is specific to Lacan's gaze is not the maintenance of the subject but its dispersal, its loss of stable boundaries. The gaze situated outside, the subject necessarily becomes a part of the picture, assimilated by its own surroundings. Differentiation is lost and, with it, subjectivity as a category. Here, Lacan is drawn to Roger Caillois's surrealist theory of mimicry in insects and its implications for human psychical processes. Certain insects do not come to resemble their surroundings through any defensive or adaptive procedure. Rather, becoming *like* one's environment involves succumbing to a "real *temptation by space*."[18] The lure is that of depersonalization, a lack of differentiation manifested in the form of a kind of death drive. The subject is, above all, *displaced* with respect to the usual coordinates of consciousness: ". . . the organism is no longer the origin of the coordinates, but one point among others; it is dispossessed of its privilege and literally *no longer knows where to place itself.*"[19]

The spectator of apparatus theory would seem to be diametrically opposed to this displaced subject who gives in to an overwhelming desire to become a picture, and hence to lose any mastery to which it might have laid claim. For the spectator of the apparatus is quite clearly and unambiguously placed as a controlling gaze, whether the control is illusory or not—it knows precisely where to place itself. And such an illusion requires a geometrical configuration, a mapping and, above all, a distance between subject and picture. However, Baudry has not entirely neglected the annihilation of subjectivity attendant upon processes of looking. In fact, the second essay on the apparatus could be said to revolve around the fascination and corresponding regression of a spectator who loses himself. This is the pre-Oedipal spectator of the cinema whose relation to the image is that of the dreamer or the hallucinator, who persistently confuses representation and perception, giving in to the temptation of space. Across the two essays by Baudry, there are, in effect, two subjects of the apparatus which would seem to be in conflict.

On the one hand, the first article, "Ideological Effects," theorizes the impression of reality in the cinema from the point of view of the image and its construction. The Renaissance perspective of that image insures the positioning of the subject as point of control. This spectator, prey to the illusions of the ego, is a post-Oedipal subject. In this way, the cinema acts as an ideological instrument for the perpetuation of a subject situated as a stable, transcendental gaze. The second essay, "The Apparatus," on the other hand, in its attempt to explicate the power and fascination of the cinema, posits a pre-Oedipal subject, a subject who regresses to the point where differentiation and distance are no longer feasible. This is the effect of the "more-than-real" which Baudry allies with both the cinema and the dream. The subject is not the unified origin of its own dream—or even an onlooker. Rather, the dream envelopes the subject just as the child is enveloped by its world. This description of the cinematic effect as dream is quite close to Lacan's delineation of the dream and its relation to the gaze. In the dream "it shows"—which is to say, the unconscious exhibits itself—and to that extent, "some form of 'sliding away' of the subject is apparent." The subject is not fully present or fully in control of the field of the visible: ". . . in the final resort, our position in the dream is profoundly that of someone who does not see. The subject does not see where it is leading, he follows."[20]

From the point of view of apparatus theory, then, the subject is both there and not there, maintained and annihilated. There is a certain tension between the positioning of the subject as point, control, unity (which requires distance) and the temptation of space, of losing oneself in a process of de-individualization and the corresponding annihilation of subjectivity. One might object that there is no contradiction here at all—that the constitution of the subject is always accompanied by its dismantling, that the subject must always undergo a process of placing and displacement. But what I am interested in isolating here is the apparent necessity of specifying the second subject—the one who ceaselessly witnesses its own annihilation— as a non-ideological subject. That which escapes geometral vision would also seem to escape both ideology and history in order to designate the "real" of the psychical. In this respect, Baudry's re-writing of Plato's allegory of the cave is particularly symptomatic. He can activate a 2000-year-old scenario in the analysis of the cinema precisely because the psychical force he examines is characterized as ahistorical. Desire in the cinema becomes, specifically, *Man's* desire—his desire to represent to himself the working of his own psyche. What we are faced with is another theory of Man, another essentializing gesture.

Hence, apparatus theory seems to be caught in something of a bind. It can activate an ideological analysis of the cinema at the cost of reducing vision to geometric perspective and theorizing history as a trap. The spectator is stuck at that ideal point of illusory mastery. Conversely, it can take into account other aspects of the gaze—its excess, its annihilation of subjectivity—only by, paradoxically, rigidifying that gaze, situating it outside of time as psychical essence. This is an alternative which is particularly alarming from the point of view of feminist theory. For the first reading of the ideological implications of the cinematic ordering of vision reproduces the totalizing tendency discussed earlier and hence reinforces the theoretical impasse. The second, while certainly more "faithful" to Lacanian theory, works only by assuming the autonomy of the realm of the psychical—its freedom from both historical and ideological determinations. Lacan's gaze cannot be used to analyze sexual difference because it allows no differential analysis of mastery and subjection—everyone is subjected to a gaze which is outside.

Yet, before fully accepting the notion of a theoretical impasse, it might be helpful to interrogate the idea of theory itself. What is it that theory hopes to accomplish? What is its function? And, more specifically, what is the role of theory and its relation to its object in psychoanalysis? Apparatus theory rests on the assumption that what psychoanalysis lends to film theory is a kind of map, or even a cognitive machine. Psychoanalysis is the science of the unconscious; the cinema clearly appeals to the unconscious; therefore, psychoanalysis must be able to give us the laws of its discursive formulation. The map can simply be laid over the new terrain. The desire of the analyst, which would require the replacement of the notion of the cognitive machine by that of the encounter, is rarely taken into account. Yet, psychoanalysis itself proposes the fragility of any theoretical construct, its affinity with paranoia and delirium, and hence the problematic status of knowledge and of he who purports to know. In other words, psychoanalysis must be contaminated by its own theorized and simultaneously untheorizable object—the unconscious. For the unconscious is by definition resistant to the coherence and rationality of conscious meaning, of the systematicity associated with theory. The unconscious is characterized by its alterity. As Freud pointed out with respect to the dream, "To explain a thing means to trace it back to something already known, and there is at the present time no established psychological knowledge under which we could subsume what the psychological explanation of dreams enables us to infer as a basis for their explanation."[21] This destabilization of theory with respect to its object has frequently been noted. Samuel Weber describes psychoanalytic theory as "the struggle to wrest meaning from a process that entails the deliberate dislocation of meaning."[22] In its striving after unity and totality, theory (i.e. systematic thinking) is comparable to an animistic form of thinking which dictates that everything is meaningful, explicable—nothing can remain outside the limits of the system. In this sense, theory is narcissistic, organizing reality as the image of the ego's own psychical organization.

> The pursuit of meaning; the activity of construction, synthesis; unification; the incapacity to admit anything irreducibly alien, to leave any residue unexplained—all this indicates the struggle of the ego to establish and to maintain an identity that is all the more precarious and vulnerable to the extent that it depends on what it must exclude. In short, speculative, systematic thinking draws its force from the effort of the ego to appropriate an exteriority of which, as Freud will later put it, it is only the "organized part."[23]

The theorist is not dissociable from the other which he hopes to define and theory betrays its links with speculation and its etymological affiliations—specular, speculum; it functions as a form of mirror image.

This is why François Roustang argues that psychoanalysis is not a science insofar as a science generally presupposes the foreclosure of the subject. Theory organizes the fantasies, dreams, and desires of the theorist and to deny this is to remain perpetually in a transferential relation with a "subject supposed to know." Hence it is also to deny one's own fantasies and desires and their potential activation within theory. From this point of view, theory is a process of continual revision which always bears the traces of its

historical moment. The contradictions in Freud's text, the constant changes
in his conceptual framework, are not accidental but an acknowledgment of
theory's inevitable failure in the face of the alterity of the unconscious.
Hence, the apparatus cannot be a cognitive machine or the concept which
fits its object as in much film theory. According to Roustang, "the hypotheti-
cal and conjectural character of the apparatus is an integral part of the
discourse"[24] and, with reference to Freud's style in *The Interpretation of
Dreams*, "The psychical apparatus that Freud constructs in the course of
chapter 7 is chapter 7 itself."[25] The object is indissociable from the theoretical style.

Consequently, Roustang finds the whole question of the transmissibility
of psychoanalytic theory, its institutionalization, and its tendencies toward
dogma and orthodoxy extremely problematic. The work of theory is the
practice of analysis, the encounter between analyst and analysand which
inevitably produces the surprise, the destabilization of the given theories—
the constant shock of otherness we associate with the unconscious. It is a
process of reading and encounter. Psychoanalytic theory has its own peculiar temporalization: ". . . there is no analytic theory *in advance* on which
one can lean, but rather a possibility of theorization in *deferred action*,
which, although necessary, is never guaranteed."[26] Psychoanalysis is,
above all, a form of listening in the intersubjective relation.

> If analytic practice is to be effective, it is only insofar as the peculiarity of the
> theory is abandoned in favor of a peculiarity that cannot at first be theorized.
> What counts in such cases is not the desire for the father, but the relationship
> to him which is revealed by some tiny unbearable memory. When something
> like this emerges through an association, what is important is not the verifica-
> tion of the theory, but the intensity of an incomprehensible particularity.[27]

The issue in analysis becomes how to grasp the history indicated by the
resistance associated with "some tiny unbearable memory"—how to understand that history without reducing it. There is certainly no immediacy
presupposed in this form of historical understanding—theory is crucial even
if it makes its appearance only through deferred action. Psychoanalysis is
a mode of writing history which fully acknowledges—and attempts to
theorize—the resistance of its own material. The validity of psychoanalysis
would hence be linked to the style of its confrontation with history. Instead
of atemporalizing psychical operations, as Baudry's analysis does, it is
crucial to *saturate* them with temporality—to demonstrate that the psyche
is constructed in, through, and as a history.

Thus, psychoanalysis would seem inevitably to propose the articulation of theory and history rather than their polarization. In film theory this aspect of psychoanalysis is too frequently ignored in favor of a static, inflexible theorization of an apparatus which is always in place, always functioning. Here, Baudry's comparison of the cinema with the psychical mechanism of hallucination is symptomatic. For hallucination, in Freud's work, signals a retreat from an intersubjective relation which is inevitably marked by failure. Freud's persistent attempts to theorize resistance, transference, the terminability or interminability of analysis, on the other hand, indicate the crucial importance of coming to grips with that failure of intersubjectivity. The construction in analysis, its force as a fiction, is the evidence of the subjectivity of the historian, her desire—which will inevitably miss its mark. Film history is, precisely, a problem of memory—an institutionalized memory of what would otherwise remain an incomprehensible particularity.

And Freud appealed to the apparatus primarily as a support for his attempts to theorize memory. In an early letter to Wilhelm Fliess concerning the psychical apparatus, Freud wrote:

> I am working on the assumption that our psychical mechanism has come about by a process of stratification: the material present in the shape of memory-traces is from time to time subjected to a rearrangement in accordance with fresh circumstances—is, as it were, transcribed. Thus what is essentially new in my theory is the thesis that memory is present not once but several times over, that it is registered in various species of "signs."[28]

Memory is a palimpsest—the sum total of its various rewritings through time. The "event" which is remembered is never really accessible as such.[29] Indeed, it would be more accurate to point out that there is no single event which could be isolated as a psychical determinant. Things "happen" in the history of the individual but memory resides in the reverberations between events. Trauma has no real existence as such but is a function of representation. What Freud refers to as "deferred action" (*Nachträglichkeit*) is a working over, through time, of the implications of one event as its reading feels the impact of other events. Thus, memory does not *grasp* an event, accurately or inaccurately, but subjects it to a process of inscription and reinscription.

The insistence upon the metaphor of inscription requires that Freud abandon the optical tropes he had used earlier—the microscope, the telescope, the camera. And it is not accidental that they were replaced by the "Mystic Writing Pad," the only apparatus in which unlimited receptive capacity and the retention of permanent traces—i.e. memory—are not mutually exclusive. Film retains permanent traces but can continue to receive fresh impressions (in the same space of celluloid) only at the cost of an absolute unreadability. In fact, film annihilates memory in the measure to which it adheres to presence—everything takes place in the present tense. Freud's fantasy about the Mystic Writing Pad, on the other hand, was that by virtue of its discontinuous method of functioning (mirroring that of the system Perception-Consciousness), it could indicate that which "lies at the bottom of the origin of the concept of time."[30] Freud's dream of a representative apparatus which would explain our subjective experience of temporality and demonstrate how memory is the transcription and retranscription of an event would seem to be particularly *inappropriate* for the cinema. Perhaps this apparatus is more suggestive of how we might think, not about film, but about film history as a continual process of retranscription of our memory of the cinema—a memory which is "present not once but several times over, that . . . is registered in various species of 'signs.' "

There are, of course, crucial differences between the terms "memory" and "history"—differences which are frequently invoked in order to distinguish between the disciplines of psychoanalysis and history as well. While "history" generally refers to the social complexity of a past which transcends the individual, "memory" is always resolutely linked to the "I"—these are "my" memories, they belong to no one else; they form the basis of my particular psychical history. The historian's account does include memories but it also brings into play other types of evidence as well and aims at the construction of a collective, social text.[31] Nevertheless, Freud's excursions into the realm of what might be termed a "collective memory" (the most influential of which are *Totem and Taboo* and *Moses and Monotheism*) are symptomatic of the constant desire to articulate the notions of individual memory and individual psychical history with a symbolic order of representations. The theory of subjectivity, particularly as it is linked to language, is not reducible to a theory of individuality, despite the fact that its formulation is dependent upon the encounter with individual discourses. Furthermore, to deny any link between memory and history is to desubjectivize history totally, to presume that its account has the status of a purely objective science. While it might seem paradoxical to say that I remember someone else's past, there is a sense in which, when I read or construct a history, I do precisely that. And although I certainly do want to acknowledge the limits of psychoanalysis, its specificity and divergence from history as an enterprise, this essay is predicated on the belief that a great deal can be gained by noting their similarities and points of coincidence. Psychoanalysis is, in some sense, the construction of a history, and history, in its turn, an act of remembering.

Psychoanalysis and historiography are both predicated on a relation to the past and an implicit theory of temporality. In psychoanalysis, the past is aggressive—it returns, it haunts, it sometimes dominates the present. In historiography, the past is static, inert—qualities which make it, in effect, more knowable. While, as Michel de Certeau points out, there are crucial similarities between the two—both attribute to the past an explanatory value and utilize narrative as their preferred form of organizing discourse—there are two different "strategies of time" involved here.[32] For psychoanalysis, the past and the present are fully imbricated, locked in a struggle in which "forgetting" is no longer a simple accident but a defensive weapon aimed against the past. In de Certeau's words, the past "resurfaces, it troubles, it turns the present's feeling of being 'at home' into an illusion."[33] Historiography, on the other hand, solidifies its notions about knowledge, power, and "objectivity" by effecting a "clean break" between the past and the present. The past is spatially isolated—it exists in museums and archives which neutralize, sanitize its psychical impact. The forms of relation between past and present posited in psychoanalysis are those of imbrication, repetition, substitution; in historiography, they are succession, correlation, disjunction.[34] De Certeau is convinced that it is precisely these differences, together with psychoanalysis' insistence upon the vital interconnections between past and present, which make possible a "renewal" of historiography through its encounter with psychoanalysis. Looking at psychoanalysis as a form of historiographical endeavor also promises a revitalization of our understanding of its theoretical implications.

Freud's role as historian is perhaps most visible in the essay, "Constructions in Analysis," in which he claims that the task of the analyst is "to make out what has been forgotten from the traces which it has left behind or, more correctly, to *construct* it."[35] In this sense the analyst's work is like that of the archaeologist who reconstructs, from the vestiges or surviving remains, the shape of a building or even a city. But there is one major difference: the archaeologist is often confronted with the loss or destruction of crucial pieces, while nothing in the unconscious is ever destroyed. Yet, it is precisely this divergence and the guarantee that psychical truth is there, somewhere, that leads Freud at times to collapse the opposition between construction and historical truth and thereby to bypass the subject's own discourse. It all depends on the conviction of the patient—his or her belief in the knowledge of the analyst: "Quite often we do not succeed in bringing the patient to recollect what has been repressed. Instead of that, if the analysis is carried out correctly, we produce in him an assured conviction of the truth of the construction which achieves the same therapeutic result as a recaptured memory."[36] There is a relation of transference at work here whereby the fictional and provisional status of the construction is elided.

Instead, the construction comes to match perfectly, in a one-to-one correspondence, the historical truth. At these moments, Freud forgets his own insight linking the construction of analysis to the delirium of the patient. As Roustang points out,

> Construction (which is always a part of the theory) is in an unstable position and can readily turn into madness if one takes it too seriously, if one forgets that, like an hysteric, it suffers from memories, that is, it cannot be separated from the particular discourse of a particular analyst. . . . Historical truth exists no more than do the origins of revolutions or of the Indo-European languages. What exist are delusions founded upon the supposition of its existence . . . truth has always had a strength which comes from the fact that it has none, that is, that it draws all its force from its nonexistence and that this nonexistence is precisely what provokes, through a horror of the void, the feverish and indefinite production of cultural substitutes.[37]

But if construction is acknowledged to be a fiction, a particularly potent myth or delirium which is open to rewriting, it is more easily aligned with the work of memory as transcription.

In analysis, transference provides the mirror image of the psychoanalyst's adherence to the historical truth of his own constructions. The patient, mimicking this presumption, believes that the analyst is the subject supposed to know. Feminist film theory can easily maintain such a transferential relation to psychoanalytic authority if it takes its constructions—its apparatuses—too seriously. It is at this point that they become totalizing, allowing of no resistance which is not foreseen, assimilated. What is productive for feminist film theory would then be that which stops—astonishes—the machine of analysis with its own incomprehensible particularity. In psychoanalysis, by Freud's admission, there are (at least) two unanalyzable phenomena. One would be psychosis in its refusal of a language directed toward the other. The second would be a certain type of woman whom Freud, in the course of a discussion concerning how the analyst can tame and exploit the transference-love of the female patient, describes in the following way:

> There is, it is true, one class of women with whom this attempt to preserve the erotic transference for the purposes of analytic work without satisfying it will not succeed. These are women of elemental passionateness who tolerate no surrogates. They are children of nature who refuse to accept the psychical in place of the material, who, in the poet's words, are accessible only to "the logic of soup, with dumplings for arguments." With such people one has the choice between returning their love or else bringing down upon oneself the

full enmity of a woman scorned. In neither case can one safeguard the interests of the treatment. One has to withdraw, unsuccessful; and all one can do is to turn the problem over in one's mind of how it is that a capacity for neurosis is joined with such an intractable need for love.[38]

Freud's failure here is not due entirely to the excess of female sexuality exhibited by this woman but to her literal-mindedness. She will accept no surrogates, no substitutes—no rhetorical blockades to her desire. The sheer force of her presence cannot be fended off through recourse to the trope. She cannot be abstracted; she is not "Everybody's Lady." Still, Freud tries. Symptomatic of his failure to make her love sublime is his recourse to the poet's words, subjecting her to the "logic of soup, with dumplings for arguments." She may be literal minded but he is not—he can find her trope.

It is this process of troping which feminist theory must resist. "Everybody's Lady" is no one. The refusal of the apparatus as fully adequate to its object is a refusal of its totalizing force and the concept of Woman which it produces. The task must be not that of remembering women, remembering real women, immediately accessible—but of producing remembering women. Women with memories and hence histories. The abstracting work of *La Signora di tutti* is the annihilation of the woman's memory through its appropriation and naturalization. Gaby remembers—the bulk of the narrative is in the form of her flashback—but it is a forced memory induced by the administration of anaesthesia, a blockage of consciousness. The poster, fixing her image as star, is produced at the cost of a subjective history, for her public cinematic life excludes her private melodrama. Similarly, in *Prix de Beauté*, the successful cinematic abstraction of the woman is simultaneous with her death. In both states, she becomes the desirable image.

There is a sense in which Sally Potter's explicitly feminist film, *The Gold Diggers* (1984), is a work of remembering or retranscription of *La Signora di tutti*, *Prix de Beauté*, and a host of other films in their embodiment of the cinematic Woman. In the course of its sustained meditation on the relations between the circulation of women and the circulation of money in a patriarchal and capitalist society, *The Gold Diggers* also produces a discourse about film history, the history of a representation of Woman. Julie Christie (and the use of Julie Christie, of course, triggers certain cinematic memories of the spectator) is that cinematic image and one of her distinctive attributes is amnesia—a total amnesia, for she lacks memory altogether. Ironically, Collette Lafonte, a black woman, is situated as the representative spectator in the film—spectator of a cinema which, in its abstraction of an ideal of white femininity, has traditionally excluded black audiences, so much so that their viewing can only be surreptitious, a form of guerrilla spectatorship. But it is Lafonte who performs the analysis of this abstraction.[39] When Lafonte interrogates her about her past, Christie can only reply, "I remember very little. I've been kept in the dark." *The Gold Diggers* is a resolutely literal reading of the woman as image, of the only discourse she can produce. In the beginning of the film, Christie's voice-over proclaims, "I'm born in a beam of light. I move continuously yet I'm still. I'm larger than life, but yet do not breathe. Only in darkness am I visible. You can see me but never touch me. I can speak to you but never hear you. You know me intimately and I know you not at all. We are strangers and yet you take me inside of you. What am I?" Christie's only memory is a cinematic one of various images and scenarios—"I was first seen tied to tracks and hanging from cliffs," she tells Lafonte. To the extent that the cinema is represented here as the space of an enclosure, a prison, *The Gold Diggers* explicitly reveals the impact of apparatus theory on feminist reasoning about the cinema. The apparatus obliterates memory and confines its figures. Like *La Signora di tutti*, and *Prix de Beauté*, *The Gold Diggers* traces the apparatus' production of the woman. With one difference of course: Christie is saved from the cinematic scene, saved from the confines of the apparatus by another woman, a woman who has been systematically excluded from that apparatus—Lafonte—riding in on a white charger. The film uses the cinema's own iconography to dislodge it— resistance is also a cinematic scene—this time retranscribed, remembered. *The Gold Diggers* is symptomatic of the influence of apparatus theory and of the consequent need to violently tear the woman from the screen.

From *La Signora di tutti* to *The Gold Diggers* what is returned to the woman is her memory through construction. The process of abstraction of Woman is undone through a laborious construction of a memory and hence a history. *The Gold Diggers'* analysis of the circulation of women and money as defined by a certain social symbolics is supplemented by the elaboration of a subjective history. The scenarios of the wooden cabin in a snowy landscape all concern this effort to recapture or construct a memory—and ultimately it is recaptured through representation, in the theater, where the woman, constituted through division, simultaneously plays the role of herself and is the spectator of her own drama. What is crucial here is the elaboration of a new process of seeing and remembering. The final words of Collette Lafonte's character in the film are, "I know that even as I look and even as I see I am changing what is there." Feminism must refuse empiricism. But at the same time it must avoid the enclosure of rigid theoretical constructions misrecognized as historical truth (in other words, the problem of apparatus theory). In *The Gold Diggers*, the compulsion to repeat is resisted through an active process of remembering. The compulsion to repeat, based on forgetting, is a loss of temporal differentiation, the collapse of the past onto the present. The term "history" can figure most prominently in feminist theory not as an appeal to the "real" of women's lives, but as precisely this refusal of the compulsion to repeat in its own theoretical formulations the abstraction of the woman.

II. Femmes Fatales

CHAPTER FIVE

Gilda: *Epistemology as Striptease*

I. NO DICE

In the first shot of *Gilda* (1946),[1] a slow tilt upward by the camera to face a frontal assault by a pair of dice thrown by Johnny/Glenn Ford is accompanied by the voice-over: "To me a dollar was a dollar in any language" (figures 5.1 and 5.2). This shot constitutes an introduction to a major character as well as the articulation of a central thematic of the film— the conflation of economics, risk, and desire represented by gambling. Later in the film it is paralleled by the shot which introduces Gilda herself. Only this time the movement is Gilda's. A shot in which Ballen/George Macready asks his new wife, "Are you decent?," is immediately followed by an empty frame whose function is simply the establishment and holding of a space. Gilda/Rita Hayworth, tossing her hair back with an almost violent gesture, rises into the frame and answers, "Me?" (later adding, after a reverse shot of Johnny and as she pulls her dress strap over her shoulder, "Sure, I'm decent"). In this case, the movement upward to fill the frame with a content is displaced from the camera to Gilda (figures 5.3 and 5.4).

The two shots sustain two different kinds of relations with each other which are, ultimately, paradigmatic for the cinematic institution itself. There is a sense in which the first shot is constituted retrospectively, according to the Freudian/Lacanian loic of *après coup,* as the negation of the second. This negation or exclusion of the feminine (concentrated in an extreme/excessive form in the figure of Gilda in this film[2]) is effected by Ballen's articulation, a condition of Johnny's employment, of the cliché "Gambling and women don't mix," preceded by "I must be sure that there is no woman anywhere." Within a capitalist patriarchy, gambling and women do not mix because both demand full concentration (they "use up" energy), both are risky, and both entail high stakes. The gambler's desire for money and his desire for a woman are incompatible precisely because the money and the woman are substitutable objects within essentially the same system and logic of exchange. Later, when Ballen breaks his own

Figure 5.1

Figure 5.2

Figure 5.3

Figure 5.4

rule by marrying Gilda, his only defense against Johnny's accusation is, "My wife does not come under the category of women." This denial repeats in explicit form the implicit strategy of the classical Hollywood narrative which has historically stated and re-stated the non-identity of the woman, her non-existence as subject within a phallocentric discourse. Ballen's articulation of this negation of the woman, his situation of Gilda outside of sexual taxonomies, can be explicit only because its absurdity is so easily "recognizable" by the spectator and his stand-in, Johnny, whose cynical reply to Ballen is "I could have been mistaken." For Johnny, as for the spectator, the obvious nature of sexual difference, the immediate recognizability of Gilda as woman, constitutes the fundamental ground of meaning itself. The illusory nature of that otherness, its delimitation as lack (the woman as castrated), as precisely non-male, remains unspoken.

While this first type of relation between the two shots (gambling as the negation of the woman) is mediated by the content of the image, the second type of relation concerns its production. Something takes place between the two shots, between the representation of the man and the representation of the woman, which transforms the relation between the signifier and desire. The movement upward by the camera (acting here as a metonymy for the cinematic apparatus itself) to reveal the throw of the dice is internalized—displaced to a movement within or into the frame on the part of the woman. Both movements have the same function, that of introducing a major character, or, of filling both frame and narrative with a content. The visual pleasure associated with the non-diegetic signifier in its moment of revelation bleeds over into the diegesis in the second shot and attaches itself to the figure of the woman. The spectacle constituted by the cinema imperceptibly becomes the spectacle of the woman by means of a certain sliding of signification. This relation, too, is paradigmatic for the cinematic institution and its representation of women. As Laura Mulvey points out in her highly influential article, "Visual Pleasure and Narrative Cinema":

> Going far beyond highlighting a woman's to-be-looked-at-ness, cinema builds the way she is to be looked at into the spectacle itself. Playing on the tension between film as controlling the dimension of time (editing, narrative) and film as controlling the dimension of space (changes in distance, editing), cinematic codes create a gaze, a world, and an object, thereby producing an illusion cut to the measure of desire.[3]

In the structures of seeing which the cinema develops in order to position its spectator, to ensure its own readability, an image of woman is fixed and held—held for the pleasure and reassurance of the male spectator. This holding process allies the woman with spectacle and in Mulvey's argument, the transfixing or immobilizing aspects of spectacle work against the forward pull of the narrative. Narrative's containment of the image of the woman is generally mediated by the male character who demystifies, possesses, or sadistically punishes the woman. Incorporating these medidated relations between the spectator and the female image within the temporal unfolding of narrative attenuates the more threatening aspects of the spectacular (woman as signifier of the possibility of castration). The affective value of Gilda's introduction is correlated with her localization as spectacle; her movement into the frame then is, paradoxically, the "moving" representation of stasis.

The story of the film is initiated by another movement, the throw of the dice, which cuts the frame in a different way, inviting/prescribing the spectator's attention. It is not accidental that this gesture which continually casts away and retrieves is reminiscent of a peculiarly "adult" version of the *fort/da* game described by Freud.[4] In attempting to explain the pleasure involved in the compulsion to repeat a traumatic experience, Freud seized upon a game played by his grandson. The little boy came to terms with the comings and goings of his mother by means of a game which consisted simply of throwing away a cotton-reel attached to a string and then pulling it in. While playing this game the child emitted sounds which Freud interpreted as *fort* (there it goes) and *da* (here it is). The psychical significance of the game is related to the fact that it represents the child's mastery through symbolization of the loss of that first object of desire—the mother. The game itself usurps the place of the woman ("Gambling and women don't mix"). It is the orchestration of signifiers, the emergence of meaning from the differential play of terms, which elicits pleasure. The woman is left behind outside of the realm of signification, its support. Gambling takes on an exemplary status in *Gilda* because its compulsive and repetitive gestures—its thrill in effect—echo in microcosm those of the cinema itself. For the cinema, like the *fort/da* game, constitutes itself as a continually renewed search for a lost plenitude.

Nevertheless, Johnny Farrell is always in control whem gambling. IIis dice are loaded.

II. "DID YOU LOSE SOMETHING, MR. FARRELL?," OR APPEARANCES CAN BE DECEIVING

During the 1940s a group of American gangster/thriller films were produced which were noticeably darker—both literally and in terms of the pessimism of their themes—than the earlier Hollywood product. The French labeled them films noirs. *Gilda* is clearly a member of this group. The films relied heavily on high-contrast lighting and the use of shadows and often employed a disillusioned voice-over which recounted the past systematically, giving the bulk of the film the form of a flashback . As Christine Gledhill points out, in film noir "certain highly formalized inflections of plot, character and visual style dominated at the expense of narrative coherence and comprehensible solution of crime, the usual goal of the thriller/detective film."[5] Film noir, instead, constitutes itself as a detour, a bending of the hermeneutic code from the questions connected with a crime to the difficulty posed by the woman as enigma (or crime). The fact that the femme fatale in film noir is characterized as unknowable (and this is the lure of her attraction) has frequently been noted. This unknowability is consistent with a broader cultural/social positioning of woman as having a privileged link with the pre-Oedipal or pre-symbolic. Female sexuality is spread out over the body, signified by all of its parts. And it is the very non-localizability of this sexuality which defines her as a proper "other" to the man whose sex is *in place,* a reassurance of mastery and control. Woman thus becomes the other side of knowledge as it is conceived within a phallocentric logic. She is an epistemological trouble.

In the classical Hollywood cinema, there are two types of films within which the contradictions involved in the patriarchal representation of woman become most acute—melodrama and film noir.[6] Of the two, it is film noir which establishes a disturbance of vision as a premise of the film's signifying system. The lighting style implies a distortion of an originally clear and readable image and the consequent crisis of vision. Since the epistemological cornerstone of the classical text is the dictum, "the image does not lie," film noir tends to flirt with the limits of this system, the guarantee of its readability oscillating between an image which often conceals a great deal and a voice-over which is not always entirely credible. Nevertheless, the message is quite clear—unrestrained female sexuality constitutes a danger. Not only to the male but to the system of signification itself. Woman is "the ruin of representation."[7]

What is particularly interesting about film noir for a feminist analysis is the way in which the issue of knowledge and its possibility or impossibility is articulated with questions concerning femininity and visibility. The woman confounds the relation between the visible and the knowable at the same time that she is made into an object for the gaze. *Gilda* is exemplary in this respect. There are two parallel scenes in the film in which Ballen invites Johnny to "drink a toast to the three of us." In the first, the third member of the triangle is Ballen's "other little friend"—the cane which at the flick of a switch turns into a knife. In the second scene, Gilda takes the place of the cane-knife. Johnny makes explicit the parallel between the two occasions when he refers to the other "friend." Gilda interrogates Ballen as to the gender of this friend (". . . a him or a her?") and Johnny answers, "A her . . . because it looks like one thing and right in front of your eyes it becomes another thing." The instability of the female sex is linked to the untrustworthiness of the image, to a conflict between "looking" and "being."

Nevertheless, Johnny's impotence, his sexual inadequacy, is associated with his exclusion from a primal scene, his inability to place himself so that he can see. After Johnny finds out that Ballen has married Gilda, he leaves the house angrily, walking through the jail-like bars of the outer door into an extreme close-up, his face lit from the side. The dramatic thrust of that movement into close-up is supplemented by the voice-over: "It was all I could do not to run back and hit her. I wanted to go back and see them together with me not watching. I wanted to know." Johnny's desire is to see without being seen, in effect, to duplicate not only the position of the child in the primal scene but that of the spectator in the cinema as well. Furthermore, knowledge is equated with this position.

Johnny's exclusion from the scene, therefore, is signaled as a type of castration/blinding (similar to that which Oedipus undergoes and which Freud comments on in his analysis of "The Sandman"[8]). When Gilda's apparent infidelity to Ballen in bringing home another man is interrupted by Johnny in his attempt to protect her image for Ballen, she is wearing a sequined coat which catches and reflects the light in a thousand different directions—almost blinding in its intensity. In contrast to Johnny, Ballen, in whom power, mastery, knowledge (together with possession of Gilda) are concentrated, has a type of perceptual omniscience which is indicated by the deployment of space in his casino. The citadel which is his office has both eyes and ears: mechanical venetian blinds which can be raised or lowered at will cover windows looking out in all directions over the floor of the casino, and a sound system makes accessible, at the flick of a switch, the sounds emanating from the various numbered territories of the floor. In spatial terms Ballen is given *the* point of view.

And it is also a point of view which Johnny attempts to appropriate even before his usurpation of Ballen's various other positions: head of an international cartel, husband of Gilda. But Johnny cannot maintain the same relation to that powerful position as Ballen. When Johnny occupies the citadel/office he is consistently placed under attack. The assaults are of both a visual and aural nature and emanate from an excessive and explosive display of female sexuality. In two instances, Johnny is disturbed (first while sleeping, second in a discussion with the detective) by the sound of Gilda's voice singing "Put the Blame on Mame," a song which attributes various types of natural and other disasters to female sexuality. The sound of her voice on both occasions prompts Johnny to pursue the image, opening the venetian blinds which cover the "eyes" of the citadel. Gilda's first rendition of the song tends to undercut its association of women with violence. Close-ups of her in soft focus, backlit, alternate with medium-shots of both Gilda and Uncle Pio, the representative in the film of the "common man" and down-to-earth or folk wisdom, absorbed in her singing. The second instance, however, consists of a more elaborate and public performance—the famous striptease in which Gilda removes only a glove and a diamond necklace. Johnny intervenes before the "act" is consummated. The props and stereotypes of the striptease are all there but its product—the completely nude body—is not (figures 5.5 and 5.6). Structurally, this modified striptease occupies the position of the climax in the narrative; everything that follows is a part of the denouement. It also marks

Figure 5.5

Figure 5.6

a textual return to the shot introducing Gilda at the beginning of the film, in which the question of whether she is clothed or not, the body covered, is articulated as a question informed by a code of moral behavior ("Are you decent?").

Striptease provides the perfect iconography for film noir, economically embodying the complex dialectic of concealing and revealing which structures it at all levels—particularly those of lighting and plot. The fascination of a Gilda is the fascination of the glimpse rather than the ambivalent satisfaction of the full, sustained look. For the head-on look is simultaneously pleasurable and threatening, the threat emanating from the construction which forces a reading of the female body as the site of negativity, of lack and hence, of the possibility of castration. And fetishism, with which striptease is inevitably linked, is precisely the avoidance of that full look, a prolonged hesitation at the outskirts, the margins of desire. Striptease presupposes, on the part of the spectator, an immersion in the very process of peeling away accretions of layers. In a sense the endpoint, the completely nude body, which structures the way in which the woman is looked at, is necessarily an anticlimax. *Gilda* knows this; the film institutes a continual flirtation with perception: the gaucho costume Gilda wears reveals a narrow strip of leg; one shoulder is bared as she sings "Love Me Forever"; a scene begins with the camera pulling back from a close-up of a leg raised in the middle of the frame as a stocking is eased on. Lighting patterns reiterate this fragmentation of the body, particularly in the scene in which Gilda is told by Ballen in reference to her relation to Johnny, that "Hate can be a very exciting emotion." She is lying on a bed in the second plane of the image while Ballen, in the foreground sitting on the bed, is lit almost as a silhouette. As he talks, Gilda rolls into and out of the light and Ballen, immobile, acts as a kind of pivot (figures 5.7–5.10). The scene clearly establishes Ballen as the "bad object," as emotionally perverse. But the lighting and framing belie this, lending to Ballen at least the attribute of stability against which Gilda is measured. He is predictable and does not deceive the eye.

As Roland Barthes points out, the function of the striptease is to naturalize the nakedness of the woman, and in this way to neutralize its threat.

There will therefore be in striptease a whole series of coverings placed upon the body of the woman in proportion as she pretends to strip it bare. Exoticism is the first of these barriers, for it is always of a petrified kind which transports the body into the world of legend or romance: a Chinese woman equipped with an opium pipe (the indispensable symbol of "Sininess"), an undulating vamp with a gigantic cigarette-holder, a Venetian decor complete with gondola, a dress with panniers and a singer of serenades: all aim at establishing the woman *right from the start* as an object in disguise. The end of the striptease is then no longer to drag into the light a hidden depth, but to signify, through the shedding of an incongruous and artificial clothing, nakedness as a *natural* vesture of woman, which amounts in the end to regaining a perfectly chaste state of the flesh.[9]

Figure 5.7

Figure 5.8

Figure 5.9

Figure 5.10

Gilda is certainly established "right from the start as an object in disguise." Like many noir heroines, her only power is derived from her ability to manipulate her own image.[10] Gilda literally confirms Johnny's comparison of her to Ballen's cane-knife by continually and duplicitously producing an image of herself as loose, as promiscuous, for Johnny's benefit. Her performances are all dependent upon Johnny's potential look, and the "striptease" rendition of "Put the Blame on Mame" is the ultimate and most convincing of these performances. The detective (whose relation to knowledge will be discussed later) tells Johnny, "She didn't do any of those things. It was just an act. And I'll give you credit—you were a great audience." There is a sense in which the narrative itself takes the form of a striptease, peeling away the layers of Gilda's disguises in order to reveal the "good" woman underneath, the one who will "go home" with Johnny. Barthes's description of striptease is most clearly appropriate for an analysis of the narrative trajectory in *Gilda*: the process/progress of the plot is to demonstrate that not nakedness but "goodness" is the natural vesture of the woman. Evil on the part of the woman is only a discardable garment—her threatening aspects can be detached, peeled away like layers from a core which is basically "good." This is the logic which supports the representation of the "good-bad" girl: feminine evil is not a fundamental condition but an accessory, an accident. It is the logic of "if only": if only she had not fallen into the company of gangsters, if only she didn't work in a saloon. But basically, she's not a bad sort after all. Appearances can be deceiving.

Nevertheless, in *Gilda* the logic slips—the appearance is too strong and the ending lacks credibility. The end of the film undermines everything that has gone before, the elaborate and prolonged construction of a threatening, explosive image of female sexuality and the devastating effect of that image upon Johnny. Gilda performs too well; and even though it may be "just an act," she becomes inseparable from that act. The ending does not "work" precisely because the image of volatile sexuality attached to Gilda is too convincing (the American soldiers who named a Bikini bomb after Gilda completely ignored the final scene of the film). Gilda is not amenable to domestication, to being turned "inside out" in order to expose an inner goodness. For the camera proves that she is all surface. The incoherency of the narrative, the dissatisfying quality of its closure, are demonstrations of the power that the cinematic institution invests in the look.

The drama of looking which is exploited by the striptease is supported at another level as well—that of dialogue. The mechanism of the striptease—the dialectic of concealing and revealing—is projected onto language. Sexuality exists in the interstices, gaps, and *double entendres* of dialogue. This signifying strategy, too, is characteristic of film noir. In *Double Indemnity* (1944), for instance, Fred MacMurray as an insurance salesman tells Barbara Stanwyck, standing at the top of the stairs in a bath towel, that she is not "fully covered" by her present insurance policy. In *Gilda*, the narcissistic aggressivity which defines all of the relations between Johnny and Gilda manifests itself in their language. When Johnny tells Gilda, "I take care of everything that belongs to the boss," she responds, "What's his is yours?" When Johnny says that he will lie to Ballen (about Gilda's promiscuity) and tell him that she "went to the movies," Gilda's comeback is "Do you want to know if I had a good time?" As Johnny and Gilda dance at the masquerade ball, she very slyly remarks, "You're out of practice . . . dancing, I mean. I could help you get in practice . . . dancing, I mean." At this moment, Johnny's very clear understanding of the unspoken meaning purportedly negated by the term "dancing" is signaled by the fact that he violently pushes Gilda away and leaves the scene. This extremely heavy reliance upon *double entendre* in film noir in general and *Gilda* in particular is of special interest. For the *double entendre* is simultaneously the social display or exposure and the *binding* of the polyvalency of language. Restricting signification at the same time that it allows for a certain "play" of meaning, the *double entendre* attempts to sexualize polysemy. An "innocent" meaning and a full, "loaded" meaning coincide. Upon disrobing, all language points to the same thing; pleasure is repetition out of phase with itself.

By walking away from Gilda's *double entendre,* Johnny insures that it is read correctly. In effect, he stabilizes meaning for the spectator. But meaning in the film can only be stabilized *through* Johnny not *by* him—for he is impotent both with respect to meaning and with respect to knowledge. It is the figure who represents the law in the film—the detective—who ultimately anchors interpretation. After walking away from Gilda, Johnny receives a note from her telling him to pick her up at the Hotel Centennario later that night. Johnny's wordless response is to crumple the note, to replace interpretative discourse with violence. At this moment, the detective assumes the hermeneutic labor of the text, providing an answer with his question, "Lose something, Mr. Farrell?"

III. SEX AND VIOLENCE

But it is too simple to locate all authority and textual power in the figure of the detective; for the text is schizophrenic. In a rewriting of the classic Oedipal trajectory, the Law is split in the oscillations between two Fathers— Ballen and the detective. As mentioned earlier, in spatial terms Ballen is given *the* point of view, a type of perceptual and paternal omniscience. His control extends to the realm of economics as well; he is the head of an international cartel with a monopoly on tungsten. Most crucially, however, Ballen is situated structurally by the text as the third term with respect to the imaginary dyad constituted by Johnny and Gilda. This intervention by Ballen as third term is evident from the first meeting between the two, but it is a gesture repeated (even in his absence, by means of an image) throughout the film. When Gilda and Johnny first meet within the diegesis, the film punctuates their confrontation with a rhetorical flourish. As Johnny hears Gilda's rendition of "Put the Blame on Mame" (accompanying the radio) and the signs of recognition appear on his face, the camera tracks in very quickly to a close-up, isolating him emphatically from Ballen. Gilda's introduction, her movement into an empty frame, marks the beginning of a sustained shot/reverse shot sequence. Ballen is present here only as voice-off, on the margins of desire.

Recent theorization of the cinema has placed it ineluctably on the side of the imaginary, in Lacanian terms.[11] The spectator sitting in a darkened auditorium repeats the scenario of the infant before the mirror, corroborating his[12] identity through an alienating image. Because the imaginary order is frequently defined in terms of the plenitude of the image, the cinema would seem to provide the perfect theater for its operations. Yet, as Jacqueline Rose has demonstrated, this description neglects the fact that aggressivity is a necessary corollary of the imaginary.[13] The mirror image is not the only imaginary other assumed by the child; the imaginary has a social dimension as well. The child situates himself in a social setting through a comparison with other children which becomes an equation—if one child is hit, the other one cries, aggression defining the terms of these relations. As Anika Lemaire points out, the imaginary order dictates "the constitutional aggressivity of the human being who must always win his place at the expense of the other, and either impose himself on the other or be annihilated himself."[14]

Within the filmic text, this aspect of the imaginary relation emerges in the structure of the shot/reverse shot, which is constituted by isolating the two characters (in this case, Johnny and Gilda)—each being defined as the exclusion of the other (figures 5.11–13). But the shot/reverse shot also operates by putting into place a type of mirror structure by means of which Gilda serves to reflect Johnny. The production of her image confirms his own. The mise-en-scène establishes the condition that Johnny meet Gilda as his image, his other. And since the pleasure attached to the cinematic apparatus in the first shot of the film is here appropriated by the figure of Gilda in her movement into the empty frame, she is also, in effect, Johnny's screen, his cinema. The imaginary aspect of the relation between the spectator and the film is mimicked within the diegesis. The mirror behind Gilda seems to confirm this (figure 5.11). It is not only the shot/reverse shot which formalizes the mirror linkage between Gilda and Johnny. They mirror each other in their relations with Ballen as well. Both define themselves to Ballen as having "no past, all future." Johnny, alone with Gilda for the first time, explains his affiliation with Ballen by saying, "I was down and out. He picked me up." And Gilda's response to this is, "Well, isn't that a coincidence . . . ." The narcissistic aggressivity which characterizes their relationship is further evidence that the metaphor of the mirror is appropriate here. Given the passivity and complacency attached to the position of the spectator by the classical cinema, it is apparent that the aggressivity proper to the imaginary relation must be displaced, incorporated within the diegesis. In the case of *Gilda,* that aggressivity is situated in the sadomasochistic alliance between Johnny and Gilda. Nevertheless, the leakage or excess of that aggressivity is siphoned off onto the figure of Ballen, whose disembodied voice-off acts to suture the two shots at the same time that it attains the authority of an Other outside of the image. Towards the end of the scene, Ballen recontextualizes that authority by walking into the frame between Gilda and Johnny, traversing the space which separates them (figure 5.14). Introducing a cut or division, Ballen assumes his function as symbolic father, a function encapsulated in the phallic cane-knife, the mark of difference which breaks or deflects imaginary energies.

Ballen's status as third term to the imaginary dyad of Johnny and Gilda is restated again and again by the film. When Johnny and Gilda kiss in the shadows of her bedroom, Ballen's off-screen presence is signaled by the sound of a slamming door, interrupting their kiss. After Johnny and Gilda are married, Gilda puts her arms around Johnny to thank him for the new house and furnishings but the embrace is once more broken by the off-screen "presence" of Ballen. The look of horror on Gilda's face indicates to the spectator, who is not yet privy to the object of Gilda's look, what the following shot confirms—the supposedly dead Ballen is present through his portrait hanging on the wall. Gilda's reaction is to tell Johnny "that's not even decent," the word she chooses echoing the earlier scene in which "decent" is applied to Gilda herself and indicates a state in which the body is covered. Gilda's attempt to appropriate the word is immediately canceled, negated by Johnny's repetition/interrogation, "Decent?," as though the word's conflation of morality and concealment of the body could apply only to the female. The final instance in which Ballen intervenes as third term parallels this scene quite closely, but reverses its positions. Johnny and Gilda, finally reconciled through the insights of the detective, are about to embrace once more when a glance/object cut between Johnny moving toward Gilda and a shot of the venetian blinds of Ballen's office closing again indicates Ballen's presence at the scene.

The voice-off, the sound of a door slamming, the portrait, the venetian blinds closing—all evince a lack in representation. Sound without image or image without sound; in any event, the representation is flattened, two-dimensional—in short, it is lacking. But isn't this precisely the function of the Father in psychoanalytic theory—to pose the possibility of lack through prohibition—to act as an incarnation of the *Nom (Non) du Père?* This is the threatening and containing aspect of paternity. In the case of Ballen, the two-dimensionality of the classical villain in melodrama is literally inscribed in an extraordinary scene which acts as a condensation of all the lacks in representation previously described. Johnny takes Gilda home to Ballen at five in the morning and Gilda explains her absence by telling a story about going swimming. After Gilda leaves the scene, the lighting scheme isolates Ballen as a very large black silhouette on the right of the

Figure 5.11

Figure 5.12

Figure 5.13

frame while Johnny, fully lit, stands in the left background, passively listening as the black figure who dominates the frame discusses Johnny's skill in swimming (figure 5.15). At the precise moment of Ballen's question, "Did you teach her to swim, Johnny?," the camera tracks very swiftly toward Ballen, turning slightly to accentuate the flatness of his silhouette now on the extreme right-hand edge of the frame. Johnny's rather violent reply is, "I taught her everything she knows . . . ." After Johnny leaves the house, the camera remains on Ballen for several moments as he slowly draws on his cigarette (figure 5.16). In the representation of Ballen in this scene there is no suggestion whatsoever of depth. The absoluteness of Ballen's two-dimensionality supports the uncanniness of the resultant disengagement of voice from body. The trauma of the uncanny attached to the image of the "bad father" is derived from the representation of prohibition as a voice without the fullness of a body to anchor it.

Ballen is deprived of corporeal reality in relation to Johnny and Gilda because his structural position is that of the zero-degree of textuality, of

Figure 5.14

placeholder in the narrative. His mini-scenario of intrigue—the international cartel, the tungsten monopoly, the confrontations with the two Germans—all of this is subject to condensation as the MacGuffin of the plot. The textual interest is largely sustained by the sadomasochistic relation between Johnny and Gilda, while Ballen's intrigue partakes of the machinery of narrative rather than its substance. This representation of Ballen as absent presence, or the literal translation of lack is also a demand for a counterbalance, a compensatory figure who would be endowed not only with the potency of the father but with the fullness of positionality with respect to the law. In *Gilda,* this need is answered by the character of the detective. Narrational authority, knowledge as it pertains to the text's unfolding, will always outweigh individual spatially and temporally bound articulations of authority. Thus, the question of the text is deflected—what is at stake is no longer the guilt or the innocence of the woman (since she is, invariably, the conflation of the two) but the choice between two fathers.

The trajectory of the narrative, then, is the tracing of Johnny's movement from false father to true father, from the wrong side of the Law (the imaginary and pre-Oedipality—the realm of women) to the right side (the symbolic, to which the man has unproblematic access). Overdetermining its own configurations, the text also presents this trajectory as a movement from homosexuality (Johnny's relation to Ballen in the early part of the film: the return of the key as a matter of "tact" after Ballen's marriage to Gilda) to

Figure 5.15   **Figure 5.16**

heterosexuality. Identification with the false father on the part of Johnny is bound to the terms of the imaginary because it is situated as the repetition of an image. Johnny's posturings, his attempts to assume Ballen's position are all tinged by the absurd and lack credibility until he is able to mime imagistically the sadomasochism of their master/slave relation. Compare, for instance, a shot toward the beginning of the film which confirms Johnny's recognition of Ballen's position to a shot toward the end of the film which inscribes the absolute nature of Gilda's subjection to Johnny. When Johnny attempts to make money by cheating at Ballen's casino, he is taken to the office and eventually slugged by one of Ballen's henchmen. The next shot frames Johnny, kneeling on the floor, between the massive legs of the henchman (figure 5.17). The subsequent cut to a shot of Ballen in the distant plane of the image corroborates Johnny's submission. Later in the film, Johnny will mime this perfect pose of mastery in relation to Gilda. When Gilda returns to Buenos Aires with the lawyer she trusts, only to be told by Johnny that there is no such thing as an annulment in Argentina, she falls to his feet, simultaneously crying and beating him with her fists (figure 5.18). This scene—of kneeling in subservience to a power which stands erect—constitutes *the* pose of mastery and subjection, dominance and submission. A microcosm of the representation of sexual difference within a patriarchal society, it has the clarity and precision of an image which is *too* explicit, the end result of a striptease which must be perpetually deferred. Johnny's desire to repeat this image is mimetic, registered entirely within the order of the imaginary. The imaginary relation is broken only by the reinsertion within the diegesis of the phallic mark, the cane-knife. As the instrument of death in the final scene, the cane-knife erases the memory, the effectivity of the first scene of dominance and submission described above and prepares the way for the domestication of the second.

Figure 5.17   **Figure 5.18**

The "Let's go home" at the end of the film becomes another version of the detective's earlier remark to Johnny, "I have the law on my side. It's a very comfortable feeling—something you ought to try."

IV. THE MEN'S ROOM OR THE PHALLUS AS EPISTEMOLOGICAL TOOL

Fascism haunts the text. In other words, the MacGuffin is not really a MacGuffin—the zero point is not empty but a shadow signaling the presence of a socio-historical scenario supporting the more fully elaborated scenario explicitly claimed by the text. *Gilda* situates itself temporally by invoking history only obliquely, as an afterthought. After Johnny is hired by Ballen to work in the casino, his voice-over commentary announces, "By the way, about that time the war had ended . . . ." This cynical remark introduces a scene of revelry which anticipates the later carnival scene in which one of the Germans is killed by Ballen. The fascism which haunts the margins of the narrative proper, which never seems to gain a secure foothold, a sure image, is displaced and reincorporated within the diegesis in two ways. First, its energies are sexualized by their containment in the sadomasochistic relations of both homosexuality (Ballen-Johnny) and aberrant heterosexuality (Johnny-Gilda). Thus, the condemnation of homosexuality and a heterosexuality not properly constrained within the bounds of the "normal" marriage gains force by its sleight-of-hand merger with an anti-fascist critique. It is within Ballen's sphere of influence that these "perverse" forms of behavior are allowed free play. And Ballen is contaminated by his association with fascism. Second, bourgeois ideology's ambivalence about the extremism of paternal authority attributed to fascist ideology demands a splitting and a separation of the functions assigned to fatherhood—hence, the emergence and balancing of two fathers (Ballen and the detective). Ballen assumes the weight of the connotations attached to fascism (he kills outside of the due process of legality, his primary desire is to control the world), thus leaving to the detective the space of neutrality, the law which because it is unquestionable makes one feel "comfortable." In a metonymic movement, this neutrality attaches itself not only to the detective as representative of a law associated with the police or the democratic state but also to the detective as the voice of narrative legality.

One might easily ask of this text—where, in effect, does knowledge reside? In the classical Hollywood text, knowledge is generally supported by the image, which ultimately acts as a guarantee of the reality-effect of the film. Individual characters may lie, but the image does not.[15] In a sense this is true of *Gilda,* but it is an attribute of the image which is revealed as self-contradictory—the cinema is lost and only partially regained. The last scene of the film, which unveils Gilda's essential "goodness" with the gesture of the striptease and finally presents Gilda as decent (a condition signaled by her clothing—a suit which adequately, in a business-like manner, covers the body) ultimately lacks credibility. The pleasure of the image, the spectacle, the cinema is given over to the woman who, reciprocally, contaminates them with her deception and her instability. *Gilda* is a dramatic elaboration of the way in which the visual representation of the woman carries with it the potential to provoke a crisis in the codification and coherency of ideological systems, and thus demands a redoubling of efforts towards containment. In *Gilda,* the work of containment is constituted by a proliferation of points of view, a multiplication of the means whereby the spectator is given access to knowledge.

In addition to the image, there are three sources of knowledge available to the spectator: the voice-over commentary of Johnny and the diegetically anchored commentaries of Uncle Pio and the detective. Each is defective in some respect. Johnny's voice-over, like most voice-overs in film noir, effects a confusion of temporalities. His commentary is formulated in the past tense, but the voice must deny the knowledge contained in the "present" of the enunciation—it must speak "as if" Gilda were really what she appeared to be. In other words, the voice-over is complicit with the deception characterizing Gilda's appropriation of the image—"it looks like one thing. . . ." Yet, this complicity is only retrospectively apparent to the spectator. But even in terms of the time of its own unfolding, the voice-over is clearly the locus of an activity of misrecognition, of self-deception. This is most explicit in the scene in which Johnny takes Gilda home after the masquerade ball. When she points out to him that nobody is home and then climbs the stairs to her bedroom, Johnny turns away angrily and goes to the bar to get a drink. The voice-over which immediately precedes his ascent to Gilda's bedroom and the resulting kiss is an extremely blatant instance of self-deception: "I thought about Ballen back in the casino fighting for his life. I had to get rid of her for him." Similarly, the voice-over justifies Johnny's later imprisonment and punishing of Gilda with reference to Ballen: "She wasn't faithful to him while he was alive; she would be faithful to him now that he was dead."

The impotence or inadequacy of the voice-over as conduit of knowledge is added to the instability and deception of the image. The consequent demand for another grounding of knowledge is answered by the insertion of figures within the diegesis who have a special relation to truth. Uncle Pio, significantly the character who ultimately kills the "bad father" with his own weapon, is the film's embodiment of both common sense and popular folk wisdom. He tells Gilda, for instance, that her personal frustration is evident from the fact that she smokes too much. He fulfills, however, a primarily phatic function. His continual comments concerning how interesting it will be to watch events unfold (particularly with respect to the relationship between Johnny and Gilda) act as a reconfirmation of the validity of the spectator's engagement by the film. The detective, who finds the atmosphere of the casino after Gilda's arrival "positively fascinating," also performs a phatic function in the narrative. However, the extent of his narrational authority is much greater than that of either Uncle Pio or Johnny. He is there at every turn in the narrative to indicate its direction. His first appearance is in the men's room where he tells Johnny, who is looking in the mirror and attempting to wipe a spot off his face, "The spot is not on your nose, yet." Later, he articulates an "old saying" which is particularly and almost uncannily appropriate. As Gilda wins at gambling, he tells her, "The superstitious have an old saying—lucky at cards, unlucky at love." The spectator's knowledge that Gilda is, in fact, superstitious is derived from Johnny's voice-over, an extra-diegetic signifier to which the detective should have no access. After Gilda leaves the gambling table the detective follows her, the camera following him. But as he sees the little man who is later ruined by Ballen he hesitates and decides to follow the little man rather than Gilda. Thus, he quite literally directs the camera's and the spectator's attention. At the masquerade party, he knows that "there's going to be trouble," and he is ultimately the one who tells Johnny that he is "breaking up in little pieces." Finally, and most importantly, he confirms Gilda's innocence by telling Johnny that it was all "an act." His discourse functions as a guarantee, in effect, of the validity of the narrative's entire trajectory, of the striptease whereby Gilda, disrobed by the epistemological power of cinematic narrative, is revealed in her essential "goodness." The threat offered by the woman is canceled. The spectator's position with respect to this passage of the "couple" into the symbolic is sanctioned by the detective's statement, "I'm a sucker for a good love story."

But the statement is too weak; it does not, cannot have the desired effect. The detective is a marginal figure within the body of the film and his guarantees and absolutions at the end have all the credibility of the *deus ex machina*. In a sense, the project that *Gilda* takes on is far too ambitious, and can only result in a text which unsuccessfully attempts to contain a myriad of contradictions. Because the woman confounds the relation between the visible and the knowable, the image is undermined, and the detective must bear the burden of narrational authority, buttressed only by a frequently deluded voice-over and a washroom attendant. Yet, the very fact that the detective is diegetic ultimately makes a hierarchy of discourses impossible. The detective resides at the same level of narrative realization as Ballen, the "bad father" who is contaminated by fascism (or, in a sense, surpasses it as absolute evil—cheating the Nazis, Ballen becomes a type of meta-fascist). The text can ultimately make no distinction between the two forms of authority.

What *Gilda* effectively demonstrates, in its contortions and contradictions, is the difficulty posed by the woman as a threat to epistemological systems—particularly those of cinematic narrative. Nevertheless, the text gathers together its forces. In a scene toward the beginning of the narrative which acts as a type of preparation for the introduction of Gilda, a mustering of strengths in the face of a threat, the tokens of narrational authority gather in the men's room. This congregation includes Johnny, the detective, and Uncle Pio. The only significant male character who is absent from this gathering is Ballen. This particular congregation is repeated at the end of the film, but this time Gilda is included and Ballen's representation of lack, of absence is made literal through his death. What the film effectively does is to expand the confines of the men's room. In the ultimate gesture of recuperation, these are the characters—Johnny, the detective, Uncle Pio— who surround Gilda with their benevolence, who accept her into the fold— of meaning, of knowledge, of sense.

CHAPTER SIX

The Abstraction of a Lady:
La Signora di tutti

The films of Max Ophuls consistently manifest an obsession with what the cinema—as a machine—is capable of doing. The extended, elegant tracking shots, which are his trademark, test the limits of the technology, and his play with image and mise-en-scène testifies to a desire to investigate fully the material basis of the medium. Nevertheless, many of Ophuls's statements belie an ambivalence toward the technology of the cinema and a certain anxiety about its relation to representation: "Technology has reached a stage in our profession where it is a threat to our heart"; or "This industrialization—which I have to keep reminding myself in my profession is the guarantee, the material side of its existence—it does leave so much out of account."[1] For Ophuls, one of the dangers of technology is the annihilation of difference, of uniqueness; as he puts it, "drama cannot be mass produced."[2] The processes of mechanical reproduction act both as the ground and condition of his signifying practice *and* as a limit against which he continually strains. In this respect, Ophuls participates in the widespread ambivalence about technology that is characteristic of much aesthetic activity in the first half of the twentieth century.[3]

A second, and quite prominent, aspect of Ophuls's work is his fascination with the figure of the woman and the vicissitudes of her romantic life. Ophuls, like George Cukor, is known as a "woman's director," undoubtedly because his films manifest a predilection for stories about passionate women and doomed love affairs played out in a bourgeois setting. Claude Beylie refers to Ophuls as "assuredly one of the most subtle portraitists of the woman that the cinema has ever given us."[4] The obsession with the cinema as a technology, a technique, merges in a curious way with the desire to represent and re-represent the woman in an early and seldom discussed film by Ophuls, the 1934 *La Signora di tutti*.[5] *La Signora*, the only film made by Ophuls in Italy, was commissioned by newspaper owner and aspiring film producer Emilio Rizzoli, who wanted to adapt the heavily melodramatic novel by Salvator Gotta (serialized in one of Rizzoli's newspapers) for the screen. The title of Gotta's book is linked to an episode narrated within it in which a woman walking by incites a man to think simultaneously of joy and death, causing him to name her "everyone's woman."[6] An associate of Rizzoli's, Ettore Margadonna, had seen and admired *Liebelei* (1932) and invited Ophuls, then in exile in Paris, to Italy to direct the film.[7] This invitation was consistent with the Cines studio policy of encouraging international talent to work in Italy and with the corresponding notion of the "art film." *La Signora di tutti* was a box office success and was awarded a prize as "best technical film" at the Venice Biennial. However, its critical reception was more problematic—film critics responding to it as, in Elaine Mancini's words, a "dangerous sign of decadence in the Italian cinema."[8] Accusations against the emptiness of technique abound in Ophuls criticism, but the attacks concerning an overemphasis upon technological or formal feats at the expense of "substance" or "ethics" seem to be particularly strong in relation to *La Signora*. This is somewhat ironic insofar as the film itself produces a discourse on the cinema as a technology—specifically, a technology of temporality.

La Signora traces the life of a brilliant yet tragic star of the cinema, Gaby Doriot, played by Isa Miranda. In the beginning of the film Gaby attempts to commit suicide and the anaesthetic she is given on the operating table induces a flashback memory which forms the body of the narrative. As a young girl Gaby is expelled from school when the music teacher falls in love with her and flees abroad, leaving his family. Subjected to the strict regulation of her father, a retired colonel, she is confined to her own home. However, Roberto Nanni, son of a wealthy businessman, invites Gaby and her sister Anna to a graduation party, dances with Gaby, and begins to fall in love with her. This encounter is interrupted by Roberto's invalid mother (Alma), fearful of Gaby's reputation. But Alma herself is attracted to Gaby and asks her to visit and later to stay with her as a kind of companion. After Roberto leaves on a trip to Rome, Leonardo—his father—returns and initiates a passionate romance with Gaby. One night, while Gaby and Leonardo meet secretly in the garden, Alma calls to Gaby. When she discovers Gaby's absence, she frantically searches through the halls of the large house in her wheelchair, ultimately falling down the steep staircase and killing herself. Leonardo and Gaby undertake an apparently endless journey throughout Europe, ignoring the pleas of Leonardo's business associates to return. When they do, Gaby is haunted by the empty house and her own guilt feelings, and Leonardo is on the verge of bankruptcy. Gaby leaves Leonardo (admonishing him to stay with his dead wife), and he is subsequently convicted of embezzlement and sent to prison. Gaby eventually becomes a major star of the cinema. When Leonardo, worn down and disoriented, is released from prison, he wanders around the foyer of the theater showing Gaby's new film (*La Signora di tutti*), staring longingly at her images. Improperly dressed for a premiere, he is expelled from the theater, and run over by a passing car. To avoid the ensuing scandal, Gaby's managers call in Roberto to exonerate her. Gaby discovers that it is Roberto she has cared for all along, but it is too late—Roberto has married her sister Anna. She commits suicide, leaving a note detailing the loneliness that has persisted despite her stardom. The film returns to the present, the ether mask is raised, and the doctors confirm her death. The printing presses producing the posters for her latest film are stopped.

The narrative of *La Signora di tutti* circulates around an absence which seems to reassert the inaccessibility of its central figure. The film within a film, also entitled *La Signora di tutti*, is never seen. The blind spot of the film's imaging of the woman, it is advertised, discussed, and attended but never given to the gaze of the film's own spectator. What does it mean to structure a filmic narrative around a film which is only mentioned, never viewed? The actual subject matter of Ophuls's film—as announced by its title (which ambiguously names both the unseen film and the woman)—is curiously marginalized, transformed into a kind of narrative afterthought— unless we are to assume that the film we are seeing is, indeed, Gaby Doriot's final film, evoking a vertiginous mise-en-abyme effect barely envisaged in *La Ronde* (1950). In this case, we would be seeing a film which accurately reflects, in a one-to-one correspondence, Gaby's own life, unlike the book Leonardo gazes at longingly late in the film (a book which produces an elaborate fiction of the star). But I prefer, initially at least, to think of the absent film instead as a pretext for Ophuls's obsession with the intricate and involved relations between the woman, the image, infidelity, exchange, and spectacle, most fully realized, perhaps, in *Lola Montès* (1955, spectacle) and *Madame de . . .* (1953, exchange). What informs Ophuls's work in general is a certain economy of the signifier upheld by sexual difference. But it is insofar as it is haunted by nothingness, by a void, that this economy becomes most interesting.

Absence is hence the basis of the process of abstraction which is so crucial to *La Signora di tutti*'s signifying work. Not only is the film within a film curiously absent, but its title specifies an unnamed woman as the generalized possession of "everybody" (in a similar way, another Ophuls film, *Letter from an Unknown Woman*, marks the anonymity of the woman in its title). Furthermore, this process of abstracting the woman and trans- forming her into a signifier of generalized desire is supplemented by the production of a discourse about mechanical reproduction and its techniques of abstraction. A privileged figure in the film is that of the machine spewing forth identical images of the woman—poster images which are later demonstrated to be absolutely inadequate to the "truth" of the protagonist, the details of her family melodrama. At first glance, film would appear to be a medium which is not particularly predisposed to abstraction, given its concreteness—cinematic concreteness measured by the image's indexicality, its potential to actualize, to make "present." The camera "remembers" everything it has seen without hierarchization, much like Funes in Borges's tale, "Funes the Memorious." Funes's hyperperception and flawless memory disallowed abstract thought, for, according to Borges, "to think is to forget differences, generalize, make abstractions. In the teeming world of Funes there were only details, almost immediate in their presence."[9] Film mechanically records, accumulating details, hypothetically allowing the spectator's gaze to wander at will through the image. Yet mechanical reproduction, through its pure repetition, its leveling of differences, contributes to abstraction, a movement away from the differentiating detail. And in *La Signora di tutti* there is a constant tension between the pull of abstraction (manifested in the film's insistence upon situating its protagonist as the signifier of a generalized desire) and the overly replete, inevitably *detailed* nature of the diegesis.

The technology which *La Signora* invokes so prominently in its framing sequences is closely allied with both the figure of the woman and a certain conceptualization of temporality. The woman is explicitly represented as a construction, as the sum total of a disembodied voice and an image (the two sensory registers of the cinema). Furthermore, it is precisely a technological construct which is at issue here; the mechanization of her voice and image is stressed. The woman becomes the exemplary work of art in the age of mechanical reproduction. The first indication of her presence within the diegesis is in the form of a recorded voice emerging from a spinning record, revolving in close-up. Here, as represented by her voice, she becomes the object of a financial transaction, a contractual dispute—signified metonymically by the hands gesturing over the record (figure 6.1). The spectator's first glimpse of Gaby is in the image of her poster, rolling repeatedly off a printing press. Later in the film, her death is represented as the bent or warped image produced as a result of the abrupt shutting down of the printing press (figure 6.2). From the combination of a disembodied voice and a mechanical image emerges the figure of a generalized Woman— "Everybody's Lady." Here, the woman is indeed the product of the apparatus.

But the woman is also *like* the cinematic apparatus insofar as she constitutes a lure for the male subject—more dangerous even than the cinema

Figure 6.1

Figure 6.2

since she frequently leads him to his doom. Yet, without knowledge of her effect, she has no access to subjectivity. The narrative of *La Signora di tutti* is grounded in Gaby's lack of agency. She is the pure object of the desires of men, subject of nothing. As her father points out early in the film, "The girl is dangerous and she doesn't realize it." She unwittingly or unknowingly causes death or disaster. This is accomplished without the category of deception precisely because all subjectivity is lacking. As the unconscious cause of desire, Gaby's operation is that of the detached image or the detached voice, both of which become the fetish objects of the film. Gaby is the Signora di tutti—everybody's lady. Possessed by all men and therefore by none in particular, she becomes the axiom of femininity.

Hence, the woman's abstraction in this film is a function of her alliance with a technology of images and sounds which simultaneously singles her out and annihilates her difference in a process of commodification. Gaby's final words—a response to the claim of her inaccessible lover that he will see her soon, when her current film comes to Italy—are "On film, on film, on film . . . ," musingly trailing off into nothing. They indicate the tautological nature of her relation to the medium. The film opens with an optical effect, a gradually widening circular iris, which mimics the mechanical circular movement of the record reproducing Gaby's voice. Similarly, the thumping sound of the machine printing her poster is taken up by the extradiegetic soundtrack in the next scene so that a music designed to evoke the mechanical is laid over a long tracking movement through the studio tracing the search for the absent woman. In this way, the filmic discourse's own status as a technology is linked to the rigorous repetitiveness of mechanical reproduction which, in its turn, is linked to the desirable image/sound of the woman.

Furthermore, the technology of the cinema is compatible with a particular view of temporality consistent with the age of mechanical reproduction. Mechanical reproduction, in its photographic, filmic, and phonographic manifestations, suggests a rigid, controllable, and absolutely repeatable ordering of temporality. There is a certain predictability of the machine. Technology presupposes a resolutely linear and teleological view of history which is bound up with this idea of time. From this perspective there is and can be *no dead time.* Taylorism would be, perhaps, the most extreme manifestation of the impact of the machine upon time as it is subjectively experienced. When Ophuls points to the fact that industrialization "leaves so much out of account," he is referring, at least in part, to *laziness:* "There's a great miracle. The miracle of laziness. There's no room for it any more, and it's such a beautiful miracle."[10] Laziness is empty time, non-productive time, the type of time which must be minimalized in a classical narrative structure. Technology appears to us in the guise of an inevitability—in its pace, predictability, and organization of time. In *La Signora di tutti* this inevitability is subjected to a slippage—from the machine to the woman—insofar as the woman comes to represent a repetitively fatal historical force.

The central character of *La Signora*, Gaby Doriot (born Gabriella Murge) has a familiar textual presence. All of Gaby's sexual relations are contaminated by death, but her fatal attraction is not really that of the femme fatale of film noir, that abstraction of the woman posited as simultaneously most fascinating and most lethal to the male. While the femme fatale of film noir is consciously manipulative or conniving, Gaby is apparently devoid of intention or motivation; she floats from experience to experience without awareness. The woodenness of Isa Miranda's acting, the clumsiness or awkwardness of her gestures, underscore her lack of deliberation or intentionality. Gaby's status as zero-degree or placeholder in relation to emotionality or personal psychology is thrown into relief by the mother's hysteria and paranoia (her anxious reactions to the thought of being left alone). Gaby simply *is* and it is her sheer existence which proves to be problematic. Late in the film, Leonardo is overwhelmed by her image, surrounded by these images and her fake "life story." Transfixed by her name in lights and her flashing image, he wanders in a disoriented state out into the street and is run over by a car: her image is murderous. As prefigured in the opening sequences of the film, it is indeed her image which seems to wreak the most havoc. In this context, the two instances in the film in which Gaby gazes (almost longingly) into the mirror—before the Nanni ball when she wonders whether anyone will dance with her (figure 6.3) and when she dresses in Roberto's mother's evening gown before the opera (figure 6.4)— are extremely significant. Both immediately precede the initiation of an erotic relation, first with the son, then the father. In a preparatory moment, displaying a kind of narcissistic self-sufficiency, the woman is taken in by her own image. It is almost as though her own desire for her image were deflected, dispersed outwards to infect the men in the film.

This figure of the woman as inadvertent cause, as sexuality without consciousness, is reminiscent of the tradition of the *diva* in the silent Italian cinema. Lyda Borelli, in *Ma l'amore mio non muore* (*Love Everlasting* [1913]), is usually referred to as the first *diva* of the cinema. The *diva* is a woman of exceptional beauty who incites catastrophe—not by means of any conscious scheming but through her sheer presence. She is also a figure of the silent cinema who is defined by her exaggerated gestures and incessant miming. According to Vinicio Marinucci, Borelli in the 1913 film was "the triumph of the *femmes fatales* with their languorous poses, their rapacious glances and their jerky movements, stifled by anguish and the imminence of catastrophe, like flowers strewn over the living and the dead."[11] Other nationally known female stars who assumed the role of *diva* include: Francesca Bertini, Leda Gys, Maria Jacobini, Diomira Jacobini, and Pina Menichelli. Georges Sadoul, speaking of the *diva*, refers to "exaggerated movements of the hips and arms, with the head thrown back, her hair

Figure 6.3

Figure 6.4

suddenly spilling down her back, contortions, rolling eyes. . . ."[12] The rise of the *diva* also introduced the development of the star system ("*divismo*") in Italy. The *diva*'s popularity ensured her generous contracts and the women were associated with extravagant spending and high living. With the star system, of course, there arose also the phenomenon of the fan. The neologism "borellismo" was coined to describe the excessive lengths to which Lyda Borelli's fans went to imitate her. As Vernon Jarratt points out, "Girls just leaving school, young married women, shop girls, shorthand typists—they walked like her, did their hair like her, dressed as near to her style as their purses allowed, and whenever they found themselves within reach of a divan they reclined on it with the best imitation they could muster of her peculiarly languid grace."[13] Few male stars achieved the stature or the ability to dominate the set attributed to the *diva*. The preferred narratives of the films, however, cast the *diva* in roles which undermined the off-screen aura of domination and manipulation. In Pierre Leprohon's account:

> Nino Frank shrewdly contrasts the *femme fatale* with the vamp invented in the Nordic countries, more deliberately devastating, the woman who lives off her victims' misfortunes, a kind of vampire. The fate of the Italian *femme fatale* is often as dreadful as that of her lovers, and this makes her even more appealing. She takes the form of a force against which one is powerless, since she herself is dominated by something stronger than herself. This may well be the reason for the name given to her in awe, which also defines her: *diva*, or goddess. The man whom she touches and condemns becomes the victim of a kind of holocaust; he is sacrificed to a mysterious superior power. There is something almost religious in the audiences' worship of the *dive*.[14]

The overwhelming sense of a fatal force, of a holocaust, an inevitability, suggests that what we are dealing with here is in fact a certain conceptualization of history, of temporal determination blocked and frozen in a perpetual war of the sexes. It is a history which is, of course, displaced, reworked, privatized, and sexualized—condensed onto the figure of the woman, the cause without consciousness, provoker of events. In histories of the Italian cinema, writers frequently note that the tradition of the *diva* and the melodramatic mode it entailed was competitive with, and gradually marked a change of direction from, the fascination with costume dramas and historical epics such as *The Last Days of Pompeii* (1908), *Garibaldi* (1907), and the well-known *Cabiria* (1914). Leprohon claims, "Reconstructed history gave way to passion—to psychology even."[15] Events of import were now constrained within the closed and claustrophobic sphere of a privatized space, their sole determinant the inexplicable but inevitable sexuality of the woman.

History, from this point of view, is pure repetition. This is why Gaby's "affair" with the music teacher at the girls' school is required in order to specify her relation with Leonardo as the inevitable, cyclical return of a scenario she is doomed to repeat. Even the words which she tries not to hear are the same—"I can't live without you." Gaby is a *diva* insofar as she is oblivious of her own destructive effects.[16] She differs from the *diva*, however, in the impassivity of her body, the absence of the exaggerated gestures of the heroine of silent film. That excess resides instead in the hyperbolic strategies of the Ophulsian style—in camera movement, mise-en-scène, and music, which take up in their repetitive *straining*, the thematic of the fatal inevitability of history. As in melodrama in general, affect is very much a function of the form and temporal structure of the narrative.

The melodramatic moment of irreversibility, the point in the narrative which Roberto will later refer to nostalgically as the moment at which things *might have gone differently*, is the scene in the garden at the Nanni ball when Roberto's declaration of love is interrupted by the message from his mother. The son's inability to articulate his love is also represented as a result of the father's intervention in the scene where the two cars meet in the road outside Gaby's house. Gaby's precarious position is then a function of a certain excess or perversion of the familial order. When father and son struggle over the same woman, the figure of the mother is quite definitively evoked. But here, the actual mother herself is also fascinated by and drawn to Gaby. In contrast, Gaby's own family is weakened by the overpresence of a bullying and demanding father (who is a retired colonel and exercises a military discipline over Gaby) and the marked absence of the mother. That absence is palpable in the very beginning of the film when Gaby tells the headmaster that her mother is dead and she has no one to confide in, and is repeatedly referred to in different instances of the narrative: Gaby murmurs "Mama" immediately before the ether cone descends and she loses consciousness; her father's lecture after the incident with the music teacher contains the phrase, "If only her mother were alive"; Gaby tells Alma that she knows her mother through a photograph taken when she was twenty; and finally, Gaby's manager ironically reinvokes that absence by producing a fiction of the mother, riding with Gaby in Paris. The lack of a mother, as an impairment of the family structure, leaves room for the excessive and transgressive (though largely unconscious) sexuality attributed to Gaby. Yet Gaby manages to find a form of mother-substitute in Alma. Above and beyond the Oedipal rivalry between father and son, the text invests much of its energy in delineating the place (or perhaps non-place) or the difficulty of the maternal.

For while the film situates Alma and Gaby in an affectionate quasi-mother-daughter relationship, it also produces a signifying framework within which the two women are juxtaposed as competitive and radically incompatible figures, one taking or resuming her place at the expense of the other. In the first part of the film, Gaby dons the mother's evening gown for the opera and becomes, on the stairway, a spectacle for the gaze of the father. This same stairway is later the site of the mother's grotesque death. When Gabriella returns with Leonardo to the house after their seemingly endless railway journey across Europe, a shadowy bar literally crosses out or negates the portrait of the mother over the fireplace. And the return of the same portrait to Roberto at the auction prepares the way for Gaby's death. In this way, *La Signora di tutti* emphatically demarcates and opposes the roles of mother and lover and their respective sexualities. The mother's sexual stability (or even asexuality given the fact that she is presented as an anxious invalid) is contrasted with Gaby's sexual mobility, her inability to remain *in place*. This sexual precariousness of the woman, her inevitable infidelity whether in or out of marriage, is a frequent topic of Ophuls's work (most prominently in *Lola Montès* and *Madame de*). It is also, as Tony Tanner points out, the obsession of the nineteenth-century novel in the form of a continual return to adultery—adultery understood in "its larger sense of an improper conjunction, or the bringing together of things that law decrees should remain apart."[17] For Stephen Heath, this concentration of the novel on adultery implies a differential diagnosis of the roles of mother and wife (or by extension, lover).

> Adultery, in fact, is "category-confusion," the slide from identity to indifference, a total indistinction of place. What guarantees identity is the woman who is then equally the weak point in its system: if she gives, everything gives; moving from *her* right place, the adulterous woman leaves *no* place intact . . . "*Pater semper incertus est*," while the mother is "*certissima*," recalled Freud . . . As mother the woman is sure, as wife always potentially unsure; she is mirrored by the unsureness of the man as father and the compensatory sureness of his juridical instatement as husband-father, *pater familias*. It is there, in the difficulty of the images of that mirroring reflection, that the society of the novel casts its stories—adultery in the novel, everywhere.[18]

While Gaby is not literally in this sense an adulteress, she does transgress the law of marriage, of the family. And *La Signora di tutti* does appear, at least at one level, to polarize mother and daughter/lover through the opposition between sexual certainty and uncertainty.

Yet it is crucial to examine more closely the status of Gaby's transgression for, again, it is devoid of intention or motivation. The "crossing over of a border" which would constitute her transgression is inadvertent, almost accidental or coincidental. Her anguish at the death of Alma is much keener than that of Leonardo. Ophuls's privileged topic in his European films— the adultery or infidelity of the woman—does not presuppose that the female protagonist is characterized as villainous. Rather, her sexual deviation from a norm is usually quite clearly socially imposed. A rigorous and unrelenting social order governs her options (in *La Signora* this order is incarnated in the figure of Gaby's father). Hence the spectator is persuaded not to castigate the woman but to sympathize with her, even to mourn her death all the while acknowledging its inevitability. The solicited investment of affect aligns the spectator to some degree *with* the woman. In the case of the novel, as Tanner points out, "it is just such a tension between law and sympathy that holds the great bourgeois novel together, and a severe imbalance in either direction must destroy the form."[19] One can cry at the injustice of her life and its vicissitudes and simultaneously bow to their necessity. The obligatory balance between law and sympathy emphasizes even more strongly the inexorability of her fate (and of those surrounding her), the obsessiveness of its quasi-historical force.

When sexuality bears the burden of history, space is constricted and time deprived of linearity. The displacement from the realm of the public onto that of the private, where oedipalization becomes excessive and all conflicts and contradictions are sexualized, bears witness to the suffocating closeness of the familial. That closeness is mirrored in the mise-en-scène of *La Signora di tutti*. As in many melodramas, much of the narratively crucial material is organized around the space of a dominating, semi-spiral staircase. In a long crane shot, Roberto observes the unfortunate and melancholy Gaby, seated on the sidelines at the dance, and descends to waltz with her. Gaby meets Leonardo on that same staircase, Alma dies on it, and Gaby hallucinates the opera music there. Events are anchored to a space whose function is to articulate the public and private realms within the home. In an earlier scene in Gaby's home, the constraints of space, its lack of potential, are even more perceptible in a scene which stresses the horizontal rather than the vertical dimension of the image. As Gaby's father lectures her sister and aunt behind closed doors on the subject of her incorrigibility, Gaby begins to clear the table. She opens the doors of the dining room and moves back along the hallway, past a dog in the middle plane to the lit door of the kitchen, activating the deep space of the image (figure 6.5). But far from invoking the subjective freedom that Bazin associates with the spectator's reading of depth of field, this image, invaded by the harsh and unrelenting voice of the father, suggests its own absolute limitations, a termination of options. Like the bars of the staircase, space repeats itself; it does not open out.

This concentration on sexuality as it is played out within a closed private space and the consequent dehistoricizing tendency of Ophuls films are

Figure 6.5

analyzed by Virginia Wright Wexman in relation to *Letter from an Unknown Woman* (1948). She refers to Ophuls's

> repression of history, so eloquently alluded to by the film's fin-de-siécle Viennese setting, that creates the atmosphere of tragic inevitability that hangs over the narrative. Beyond human control, the temporal systems that govern the characters' lives remain fixed and unyielding, impervious to manipulation or negotiation. . . . For Ophuls's style combines lyrical movements of incandescent emotion with endlessly repetitive patterns that only signify within the private space of memory, never as part of a larger historical reality.[20]

But there are critical differences between the two films as well. While Lisa in *Letter* submits to a fate which is external and unrelenting, Gaby *is* that fate. She is also a star, the framing narrative of the film insistently aligning her more closely with the technology of the cinema. The star is in some sense the conflation of the realms of the public and private—she is given a constructed private life for public consumption ("The glamorous impersonates the ordinary," as Laura Mulvey points out).[21] According to Geoffrey Nowell-Smith, the two themes of *La Signora di tutti*, one concerning her personal love life, the other her life as a successful film star with an idealized image, are combined in an unusual and disconcerting way: "In show-biz movies, the heroine is usually good by nature but becomes corrupted by artifice and the falsity of her image. But Gabriella is not, in an unambiguous way, naturally good, and if she is to be counted as corrupt it is not the movies that have made her so."[22] If the relation between the two themes is not one of cause-effect, if the cinema does not corrupt Gaby, what is the relation? Why juxtapose an artificial and somewhat mechanical cinematic existence to the heavy melodrama of personal life enclosed within the central portion of the film?

Perhaps the relation is, instead, one of analogy. The woman does not have to be corrupted by the cinema because in her essence—in the abstract—she *is* the corruption of the image, her hypnotic effect on the male comparable to that of the cinema. By withholding the film within a film, *La Signora di tutti*, from the spectator's gaze, Ophuls allows the spectator to imagine that the two films *may* be the same, that ultimately, there is no difference between the image which circulates and is exchanged (the cinematic image) and the image as determinant cause (the woman as fatal force). Ophuls himself has recourse to revealing language in his description of the way in which the cinema lured him away from the theater: "The camera, this new means of expression which I had at my disposal for the first time, distracted me irresistibly from speech, a little like a young mistress distracts a married man from his wife."[23] In a curious abstraction which would wed the seductive woman to the pictorial, Ophuls links infidelity and the image. The cinematic image, in its power and ubiquity, is like the fatal *diva*. In the beginning of the film the technology surrounding the cinema is also associated with the driving obsessive force of the *diva*: the producer's voice, mechanically chanting "Continue, continue, continue" is laid over the image of the presses systematically producing posters of Gaby. Later, this strategy of disembodying a voice and ritualizing it as a chant is evoked with the term *Vergogna* (shame). The similarity of the two moments suggests that the shame of the woman is here mechanized—mechanically reproduced— even spectacularized through melodrama. Yet the rigidity of the image— its death-like pose and its association with death (the warped poster)—is contested by a work which reveals the precariousness of that image, its susceptibility to decomposition and hence the difficulty of smoothly maintaining the commodification of desire. This interrogation of the image takes place on several different levels: in the use of the dissolve, the sustained recourse to camera movement, the deployment of sound in relation to space, and the structuring of the narration.

More than other Ophuls films, *La Signora di tutti* makes use of overlapping images, so that the integrity of the image as a unit often seems to be threatened. When Gaby and Leonardo attend the opera, an image of the orchestra is superimposed over the couple watching from the balcony, forming a kind of filmic palimpsest. However, in this case, the strategy allows the camera to fixate on Gaby, neglecting the reverse shot of her point of view, and to reveal that Leonardo, far from watching the opera, is directing his look at Gaby. But more commonly and consistently, the dissolve is the preferred mode of transition from scene to scene, and even from shot to shot within a scene. The dissolve is one of the few cinematic devices which have been subjected to a kind of grammatical codification. Through habitual use, the dissolve has come to designate either a temporal or a spatial change (or both), thus its frequent appearance as a transition between two scenes. Within a scene, it is specifically related to time when it introduces a memory; to space, when it moves us from the outside of a building or house to a room inside. The dissolve receives a psychological codification when a close-up dissolves in order to reveal the thoughts, memories, or dreams of a character.

La Signora di tutti, however, *overuses* the dissolve to the extent that its status as a more or less willful disintegration of the image becomes manifest. There are dissolves not only between scenes but within scenes as well, often reducing the legibility of temporal and spatial coordinates.[24] In the operating room, a shot of the ether cone descending dissolves to Gaby watching in fear. The opening shots of Gaby's memory of the young women singing in the music class are joined by long, slow dissolves. An image of Gaby's family eating dissolves to a menacing close-up of the father. There are numerous other instances where the film departs from the traditional use of the dissolve, but the most disorienting, perhaps, is in the scene of the initial meeting between Alma and Gaby. The first shot of this scene is already a dissolve between Gaby listening to Roberto's conveyed invitation to visit his mother and Alma sitting in her wheelchair. The camera tracks back slowly from Alma and the image dissolves to a similar slow track backwards from Gaby standing at the fireplace. This image, in its turn, dissolves to a two shot of the characters. Since the dialogue is continuous, the dissolves clearly are not being used in the usual way to signal an elision of time. Rather, the dissolves demonstrate an affinity between the mother and Gaby, revealing that there is a sense in which the two female figures are *in the same place*, despite the narrative's other and massive attempts to polarize them spatially that I discussed earlier. The traditional heavy grammatical codification associated with the dissolve is indicative of the precariousness of its signifying position. When used to signify a temporal or spatial elision, the dissolve signals that there is a time or a space which the image does not cover—that the narrative is effectively based on a *loss of time*. When used *within* a scene, these connotations do not fully disappear. Rather, the dissolves suggest that there is a lack which inhabits even the normally spatially and temporally homogeneous unit of the scene. The dissolve potentially bears witness to the image's mimetic and historical inadequacy. The image fails to hold its boundaries stable.

That instability of the image is also a function of Ophuls's frequently noted hyperbolic use of camera movement. The camera generally stays with the characters, often in a somewhat convoluted or elaborate manner, as though operating a constant, paranoid refusal of or anxiety about off-screen space. The camera must, at all costs, keep the character *in sight*. For instance, in the beginning of the film an intricate and sustained camera movement follows a man through the film studio in his search for Gaby. Later, when her agent visits her apartment, the camera's ubiquity is demonstrated by its seeming ability to pass through walls in order to align itself with the agent's movements. A similar capacity is illustrated when Gaby dances with Roberto at the ball. The shot, in a constant production and annihilation of space, takes on something of the fatalistic force attributed to the woman. Yet in its frantic attempt to negate the haunting absence of off-screen space, to promote the sense of total presence—a gaze which is fully adequate to its object—in its sheer desperation, excessive camera movement constantly points to that absence as a taunting gap. Like the dissolve, camera movement in this film has a perilous relation to the absence which haunts the frame at its borders.

The deployment of sound in relation to space also participates in this interrogation of the image and its limits. Sound is consistently associated with a kind of violence evocative of the effects of Gaby's inadvertently destructive sexuality. But sound is also consistently elsewhere—displaced in relation to the image, calling attention to that space to which the camera must be blind. The non-coincidence of sound and image, of voice and body, is marked. The schoolmaster's repetition of "*Vergogna*" appears both over a forbidding image of Gaby's father and later as an accompaniment to the ticking clock as Gaby sits and waits for Roberto's return from his mother's room. The father's voice of reproval after the scandal is a disembodied, despatialized voice lecturing as she traverses a long, empty hall. The opera music returns to haunt Gaby after the death of the mother, emerging from the fireplace, on the stairs. Even the disembodied voice of Gaby singing "*La Signora di tutti*" at the beginning of the film is subjected to the violence signaled initially by gesturing hands and off-screen voices. Gaby's only emotionally forceful action is the destruction of the radio, the silencing of the opera music after the mother's death.[25]

In this context, it is significant that the mother is presented as, above all, an auditor, and hence the recipient of the text's greatest degree of violence. In one of the film's many narrational acts, Leonardo and Gaby jointly recount the plot of the opera as Alma listens, not understanding that at a second level they are recounting, or even enacting, something of their own story (the young officer and the older emperor coveting the same woman, one of the rivals going mad in prison—as Gaby points out, "When a man does that for a woman, isn't it magnificent?").[26] Representation here is always "off," somewhat decentered. At the opera, the spectator's access is primarily to the image of Gaby and Leonardo—the representation takes place off-screen. While narrating the opera's plot to Alma, Leonardo and Gaby move behind a large curtain which blocks them from Alma's view so that the image of Leonardo's attempt to kiss Gaby is withheld from her. The only sign of the mother's continued presence is her voice-off, "Is that the end?" She overhears a love scene but mistakenly understands it as a representation.

Alma is also a strangely displaced auditor of the love scene between Gaby and Leonardo in the garden. Listening to the radio rendition of the same opera music and noting Gaby's absence, she becomes anxiety-ridden. The musical representation here seems to drive her to her death, to violently exclude her from the text.[27] But the music is also the most "proper" or appropriate accompaniment to the love scene (Leonardo, in the garden, tells Gaby, "Listen. That is our music"). The crosscutting between Gaby and Leonardo's tryst and the frantic search of the mother for Gaby, represented in glimpses of her shadow falling across an empty bed, her cane hitting a window, and the wheel of her wheelchair traveling across the hallway, seems to intensify the hysteria of the other woman, the woman left outside—unsuccessful spectator and distant auditor of a love scene which necessitates her exclusion. In a rather convoluted reorganization of the primal scene, it is strangely appropriate that the mother cannot look back, cannot see what is going on between father and daughter. And what she overhears is ultimately fatal. When Gaby destroys the radio, it is an acknowledgment that what has killed the mother, what has undermined the relation between the two women in the text, is the myth of romantic love.

The scene of the mother's death is a critical turning point in the narrative structure and the intensity of the affect associated with it is unusual—in a way it is the most thoroughly melodramatic moment of the film. The tragedy is exacerbated by the erotic implications of the scene which precedes her death on the stairway—a scene in which Gaby climbs into bed with Alma and the older woman strokes and caresses her. The *diva* or femme fatale is generally the cause of the *man's* destruction or downfall so that Nanni's bankruptcy and degeneration are actually more legible aspects of the traditional scenario. The formal organization of the scene of Alma's death seems to suggest that the real tragedy is in the separation of the two women. Alma overhears, sees nothing, and dies. Later, Gaby also overhears in the sense of hearing *too much*—hearing what is not there (the opera music emanating from the fireplace, the stairway). Off-screen sound is generally used in narrative film to guarantee the existence of off-screen space—to deny that the frame is a limit and to affirm the unity and homogeneity of the depicted space. Here the close affiliation between sound and anxiety, death, and hallucinatory effects indicates the ever-present potential of diegetic instability and narrative incoherence.

Yet, this constant threat of incoherence is manifested much more explicitly at the level of the structuring of narration in *La Signora di tutti*. Gaby's story is organized as a long flashback, induced by the anaesthesia, and further reinforced by the idea of memory's return in the moments before death. As the memory of her life, it is chronologically ordered and quite legible in its depiction of events. But the source of the narration proves to be more problematic. The narrative is continually starting again—from another place. In the scene in which Roberto waits outside to meet Gaby and is confronted by the driver of another car, a voice-over explains, "The other car stopped. I heard a man talking to him, but I couldn't make out what was said." The source of the voice-over and its context are not made clear until the following scene when the camera moves downwards from a view of the mountains to Gaby and Alma talking on a patio. Yet the extent of the material preceding this scene which can be attributed to Gaby's narrative to the mother remains uncertain. Later this technique is repeated, much more ambiguously, when Gaby leaves Leonardo, their broken communication signaled by phones left off the hook. Gaby's voice-over accompanies the images of the two phones, "I did not have the strength to hang up . . ." The next scene reveals that this is the final section of Gaby's life story as presented to her manager. But we are only given the endpoint of the narrative; there is no starting point, and it is conceivable that the entire flashback up until that moment is a narrative addressed to the manager. The limits and origins of the act of narration are destabilized, continually shifting. It is as if Gaby's life were presented as a series of originless narratives defined only by the terms of their address. To complicate matters further, Gaby's flashback memory also contains a flashback attributed to Roberto (his memory of the auction and his meeting with Gaby's sister, Anna). As representations and narratives proliferate in the film (the posters, the opera and its various incarnations, the portrait of the mother, Gaby's suicide letter, her stories), the act of narration itself appears to vacillate, to lose its place, to undermine its own spatial and temporal coordinates. Ironically, it is the film within a film, *La Signora di tutti*, which retains its power despite, or perhaps because, of its absence. Its power is the power to name, to categorize Gaby most precisely outside the constraints of a potentially disruptable and insecure diegesis. For the film within a film is known to the spectator only as a title, an abstraction, without any concrete spatial or temporal coordinates—without, in effect, a diegesis.

La Signora di tutti puts into play an abstraction of a lady, "Everybody's Lady", the *diva* as the fatal inexorability of history misunderstood as uncontrollable sexuality. But its narrative falters. With the various movements of modernism in the early twentieth century, narration becomes more precarious, language loses its stability, its ability to construct a coherent spatio-temporal realm—the illusion of the real—or its ability to convey an experience adequately, as Walter Benjamin points out. Benjamin connects the loss of the art of storytelling with the catastrophic contradiction between bodily experience and mechanical warfare, where even hostility and aggression are made anonymous through technology.[28] The body's increasing insignificance and the consequent decrease in the communicability of experience are further emphasized through industrialization and the mechanization of labor. For Benjamin, storytelling is an exemplary instance of craftsmanship; the "traces of the storyteller cling to the story the way the handprints of the potter cling to the clay vessel."[29] The art of the storyteller is hence the art of the craftsman coordinating hand, soul, and eye, a phenomenon lost with the advent of mechanical reproduction which no longer permits the slow accumulation of layers of retellings specific to the oral tradition. What is lost is, above all, a certain relation to temporality. The sheer duration attached to the storytelling process is countered by a new attitude toward work which insists upon the compression of time. According to Benjamin, that sense of duration is necessary not only in the production of the story but in its reception as well. For the listener is predisposed to remember and repeat the tale only when "the rhythm of work has seized him,"[30] a rhythm most closely associated with the crafts of weaving and spinning which induce a certain boredom, and hence receptivity.[31] Benjamin stresses the critical nature of the new orientation toward time by quoting Valéry, ". . . the time is past in which time did not matter. Modern man no longer works at what cannot be abbreviated."[32]

For Benjamin, then, narrative, in being "removed from the realm of living speech" through mechanical reproduction (first through printing in the dissemination of the novel—later, it might be added, through photographic reproduction as the basis of film), loses its specific relation to temporality. Modernism would be one response to such a destabilization of narrative. In the avant-garde of the 1920s and in much modernist work, narrative space and time begin to lose their contours and narrative as history is riddled with gaps. But narrative is clearly restabilized, the threat countered (certainly in the cinema), and the figure of the *diva* demonstrates that this is partially accomplished through a projection onto the woman of a certain view of history—a view of history which compensates for the growing unreliability of narrative as a process. The incapacity, inadequacy, or lack of narrative is covered over by the displacement onto the woman of historical determination (and hence, in this context, narrative determination) conceived as inexorable fate. If narrative now lacks the power of the solitary storyteller, the embeddedness in an oral tradition which also once lent to it the weight of its authority, it refinds its mechanism in an internal representation of determination (if not authority)—in the image of the woman as cause without consciousness. The *diva*, in the very predictability of the doom she incarnates, in the mechanicity of her effects, embodies a view of history and temporality which is consonant with the era of mechanical reproduction. For all her allure, her aura, her eroticism, the *diva* is a machine, a narrative machine. Ophuls perhaps perceives this in his recourse to a framing device in which the image of the woman is a function of the machine (the shots in which posters roll off the assembly line). The ostensible desire here may very well be to demonstrate the contrast between the commodified image of the star and the "real" woman of the personal melodrama, but the result is the opposite insofar as the woman—as *diva*—is shown to have an affinity with the machine.

The crisis of narrative and that of history are linked—to the extent that both are constituted by orderings of events in time. For Benjamin, the historiographical form of the chronicle epitomizes the narrative tendency because the explainability of events is always located *elsewhere*—for the chronicle, in a divine or natural order which is always already understood; for the story, in the listener's activity of reception. In French and German, the same word denotes both "story" and "history" (*histoire, Geschichte*). And narrative's failure, its loss of credibility receives a response at the level of a buttressing or reconceptualization of history. Historical determination and temporality are now subject to a thinking inflected by a technological restructuring of space and time. Technology involves the harnessing of time; time is now managed, organized, directed, compressed, confirming the fears of Valéry, Benjamin, and Ophuls concerning the historical loss of duration and its subjective corollaries—boredom and laziness. Technological time is, above all, sensed as irreversible and linear. It becomes difficult to conceive of technological evolution as anything but progress toward a total state of control over nature. Technology does not move backwards. Its effects are predictable and unyielding.

History, then, in the early years of the twentieth century, is conceptualized in alignment with the mechanical, predetermined movements of an inexorable technology, epitomized perhaps in the cinema and its unrelenting temporality. The time of film viewing is irreversible, determined by the movements of the machine and, unlike the temporality of reading, it does not allow for lingering or contemplation. The technique of film editing, montage, is dependent upon that compression of time cited by Valéry and Benjamin as symptomatic of the modern era. But even the cinematic shot, in its temporal unfolding, suggests a notion of fatalistic determination, the certainty of its own demise. In an analysis of the long-take in Murnau, which in a way aims at a phenomenological description of the essence of the cinema, Alexandre Astruc describes this temporality in revealing terms. Murnau's image is

> the meeting place for a certain number of lines of force . . . brought to this point of extreme tension so that henceforth only their destruction can be conceived and supported. With Murnau, each image demands annihilation by another image. Every sequence announces its own end.
>
> And this is, I think, the key to all of Murnau's work—this fatality hidden behind the most harmless elements of the frame; this diffuse presence of an irremediable something that will gnaw at and corrupt each image the way it wells up behind each of Kafka's sentences. . . . The story of the sequence is the accomplishment of that promise of death. Its temporal unravelling is no other than the definitive realization in time of an original plastic fatality in which everything that must play itself out in these few seconds will be given once and for all.[33]

Cinematic temporality is a temporality which is linear, irreversible, and demanding. One cannot look away for a moment. The image insistently advances, continually producing, annihilating, and reproducing its own time and space.

The relation between the cinema and the woman, as it is delineated in *La Signora di tutti*, shares in this understanding of temporality in terms of fatalistic determination. Mechanical reproduction seems only to solidify and ensure Gaby's inherently dangerous power of seduction. But the film is also clearly uneasy about this alliance between the cinema and the woman, evidencing an anxiety about technology's hold over representation. Ophuls is always at some level the heir of Romanticism, a filmmaker of nostalgia (setting many of his films in turn of the century Vienna, before the age of mechanical reproduction), who through the sheer force of his style attempts to resuscitate the aura of art, despite the limits of cinema as a machine. Undoubtedly, his predilection for including an opera in his films is a way of counterbalancing his dependency upon mechanical reproduction. Opera activates the same signifying materials as the cinema—voice, music,

Figure 6.6

mise-en-scène, sound effects—but its major difference from filmic signification lies in its *presence*, its independence from technical reproducibility. In *La Signora*, as in other Ophuls films, the opera is staged in a space off-screen; it is never shown directly. Nevertheless, the opera is literally *enacted* by the filmic characters when Leonardo and Gaby narrate its story for Alma. The film within a film, on the other hand, remains entirely divorced from diegetic incarnation; the film's absence is more extreme. Nevertheless, any attempts to maintain a strict opposition between the sign unadulterated by technology (the opera) and mechanical reproduction ultimately fail. For the opera is infiltrated by the technological and tainted by death when its music, reproduced on the radio, instigates Alma's fatal fall. In the same vein, the machine which prints the warped poster signifying Gaby's death is similar, in its operation and appearance, to a film projector or a camera, continually producing still images which only provide the illusion of movement and are contaminated by death (figure 6.6). Starkly reminiscent of the filmic movement of frames—twenty-four frames per second—the posters are generated and fall more and more slowly until one is frozen. When the woman dies, the cinema dies and history/the story has achieved its teleological goal.

The cinematic image, the woman, and a view of history as inexorable fate thus interact in an intricate way to produce the figure of the *diva* and her descendants. *La Signora di tutti* puts that abstraction into play, makes it the structural center of the narrative, but does not necessarily agree to all its terms. For the frame of the film and its inner story do not fit together comfortably. In Ophuls's text, we are made aware of the uneasy conjunction between a narrative whose spatial and temporal coordinates are beginning to lose their equilibrium and the machinery of the cinema which produces the death-like pose of the spectacle. The complicity of the cinema in an abstraction of woman which complements its abstraction of temporality and historicity is revealed in the process. *La Signora di tutti*, through its concentration on absence—the absence of the film of its title, the absence which always threatens to invade the borders of the image—displays that mechanism of abstraction and exposes the basis of its power as a hollowed-out image.

CHAPTER SEVEN

The Erotic Barter:
Pandora's Box

At Lulu's trial for the murder of Dr. Schön in G.W. Pabst's *Pandora's Box* (*Die Büchse der Pandora*, 1929),[1] the ostensible question seems at first to be the usual legal one of guilt versus innocence.[2] Yet the arguments produced by both the prosecutor and the defense lawyer displace the ordinary terms of legalistic discourse—evidence, motivation, alibi, eyewitness, etc.—and instead, have recourse to a language which evokes the register of fiction, drama, myth. Immediately after the scene of Schön's death, there is an abrupt cut to Lulu's lawyer who proclaims, "Honored Court: in a rapid series of pictures I have shown you a fearful destiny."[3] The phrase, "a rapid series of pictures" invokes, of course, the cinematic mechanism and, in a self-reflexive gesture, refers back to the film's own narration of events. That narration, in turn, is highly inconclusive insofar as the decisive moment is presented as a blockage of vision—Schön's broad back nearly covers the field of the frame and the only indication that a shot has been fired is the puff of smoke rising between Lulu and Schön. The prosecutor's recourse to "evidence" is even more problematic—the sole support of his argument for Lulu's guilt is a reference to the Greek myth of "Pandora's Box" and the disaster unleashed by the woman in this tale. It is symbolic evidence which proclaims her guilt. The trial indeed becomes a travesty after a false fire alarm, and in the ensuing pandemonium Lulu escapes the court's jurisdiction altogether as she is surrounded by her friends, mostly representatives of the lumpenproletariat, and whisked out of the courtroom. The dilemma is whether, in *Pandora's Box*, the question of Lulu's guilt or innocence is ever really posed in a way which makes it legally resolvable.

This strategy is consonant with the tendency of Weimar society in general to test continually the limits of sexuality in relation to legal (or moral) jurisdiction. The cultural artifacts of the Weimar Republic evince a fascination with sexual transgression and the violation of traditional taboos through the exploration of pornography, prostitution, androgyny, homosexuality.

Modernity to the Berlin of the mid-1920s entails a sexual expressivity outside the constraints of law or convention. Sexual secrecy—aligned with the bourgeois repression confronted by the newly popular psychoanalysis— is annihilated in an excessive exhibitionism. Accounts of Berlin, such as the following by Stefan Zweig, were common.

> Berlin transformed itself into the Babel of the world. . . . Germans brought to perversion all their vehemence and love of system. Made-up boys with artificial waistlines promenaded along the Kurfüstendamm . . . Even the Rome of Suetonius had not known orgies like the Berlin transvestite balls, where hundreds of men in women's clothes and women in men's clothes danced under the benevolent eyes of the police. Amid the general collapse of values, a kind of insanity took hold of precisely those middle-class circles which had hitherto been unshakeable in their order. Young ladies proudly boasted that they were perverted; to be suspected of virginity at sixteen would have been considered a disgrace in every school in Berlin.[4]

And Louise Brooks, describing the city in which she worked on the film, refers to "girls in boots advertising flagellation," a nightclub which displayed "an enticing line of homosexuals dressed as women," another with "a choice of feminine or collar and tie lesbians," and the "collective lust" which "roared unashamed at the theatre."[5]

In Weimar Germany, exposure of the flesh became tantamount to a confrontation with the facts, with the real. The period cultivated a modern sophistication wherein not to be deceived meant to know that everything is deception—a knowledge which seemingly compensated for the losses effected by modernization. Weimar's strategic immoralism was an aspect of its pervasive sexual cynicism, a rejection of the romantic idealism and corresponding repression of an earlier era. Such a cynicism does not attempt to unmask or unveil the true sexuality but rather to demonstrate that sexuality resides in the mask, the game, the deceptiveness of vision associated with the crossing of the boundaries of sexual identity. It perceives the structure of sexuality as an economic one but, further, perceives that economic status as an intractable reality. Cynicism involves an acute self-consciousness, reflectiveness, and a matter-of-factness about the necessary existence of evil. Peter Sloterdijk argues that Weimar culture is the "essential 'founding period' of this cynical structure in its culturally dominating dimension"[6]—a cynical structure which is still with us today (in a more exhausted form) and which provides us with the optics by means of which we can better understand Weimar Germany. Sexual cynicism "washes old sexual-romantic jetsam ashore."

If one puts erotic idealism to one side, firmer contours in personal transactions become visible. The erotic barter comes more clearly to light; the animal, capricious side of sexual energy makes itself felt; the projective components of being in love and the resignative components of fidelity cannot be over-looked in the long run. And like everywhere else where ideals collapse, cynicism, which lives out its disappointment by pushing over what is already falling, is not far behind.[7]

Collapsing ideals haunt a cynicism which, according to Sloterdijk, is not only sexual but political, medical, religious, military, and epistemological. Sloterdijk links Weimar cynicism to the widely discussed notion of a crisis in male identity provoked by the defeat of World War I. The cynicism attached to modernity is thus approached by its analysts as the symptom of a difficulty in male subjectivity, a lack in subjectivity which is then compensated for by a knowing wink which understands the emptiness of ideals and the obtuseness of the real.

What is the place of the female subject in such a configuration? Can she share in the cynicism whose function is to bandage a wounded male identity? Or does she act, instead, as the symbol of all the losses and catastrophes afflicting modern consciousness? The intersection of cynicism, feminism, and modernity is complex and problematic but requires analysis. For is not cynicism a necessary moment in the development of feminist theory? Insofar as cynicism involves an active suspicion of romantic ideals and the sexual identities they dictate and an interrogation of the mores and mor-alisms of a patriarchal order, it would seem to ally itself with the feminist enterprise. Yet cynicism, if it could be described as a form of reflective consciousness or knowledge, is a knowledge which nevertheless accepts or resigns itself to the status quo. Hence, cynicism as an operational strategy for feminist theory has its limits. And, historically, within the limitations of a modern cynical consciousness, the image of the woman has played a crucial—and not always a positive—role. Nowhere, perhaps, is this more evident than in Pabst's cinematic construction of the figure of Lulu in *Pandora's Box*.

Insofar as *Pandora's Box* puts into play the signifiers of sexual transgres-sion—incest, androgyny, lesbianism, prostitution—it partakes of the perva-sive sexual cynicism of the Weimar period. The film erects no counter-values to replace those which have been lost and its closure, in this respect, is uncertain, evoking a curious hollowness or emptiness. It is not surprising that, in the climate of sexual permissiveness and openness characterizing Weimar, Pabst would have recourse to Wedekind as a source. *Pandora's Box* is an adaptation of two plays by Frank Wedekind which constitute the

Lulu cycle—*Der Erdgeist* (*Earth-spirit*, 1895) and *Die Büchse der Pandora* (*Pandora's Box*, 1904). Influenced by Nietzsche, opposed to the women's emancipation movement because it sought to annihilate the specificity of female sexuality (which he linked to a primitive animal nature), Wedekind fought against bourgeois repression in his works and was continually pursued by censorship and accusations of pornography. He was strongly influenced by the slightly illegitimate or marginal forms of French theater: the little theater revues, Grand Guignol horror shows, popular pantomimes, and perhaps, most importantly, given his later impact upon Brecht, the circus.[8] *Erdgeist* opens with a prologue in which an animal tamer with a revolver in one hand and a riding whip in the other introduces the "snake," Lulu, to the audience. Louise Brooks claims that Pabst cast himself as the animal tamer in this "tragedy of monsters" and used the revolver to "shoot straight into the heart of the audience."[9]

For many critics, the film could not possibly measure up to the literary work. In an era when the cinema was constantly compared, often disdainfully, to the more legitimate forms of theater and the novel, *Pandora's Box*—a silent film—was viewed as an inadequate attempt to approximate a literary work with intricate and provocative language. Cognizant of the different material demands and possibilities of the two media, the film's most influential critics, Harry Alan Potamkin and Siegfried Kracauer, disagreed with this criticism but produced others. Kracauer praises Pabst for what he sees as a realist tendency in his other films (specifically *The Love of Jeanne Ney* [1927] and sections of *The Joyless Street* [1925]): "Pabst arranges real-life material with veracity as his sole object. His is the spirit of a photographer."[10] Yet, although *Pandora's Box* deals with the relation between "social disintegration and sexual excesses," Kracauer finds it to be too abstract due to the nature of the play upon which it is based: "It was a texture of arguments; its characters, instead of living on their own, served to illustrate principles."[11]

Similarly, Potamkin faults Wedekind's play as a "network of negotiations and not the experience of people" and claims that the film has an ethereal or immaterial quality, manifesting an obsession with surfaces (Pabst is "an anatomist of surfaces").

In Pabst's *Pandora* (after Wedekind) the camera-caress of surfaces, agile enough as *lichtspiel*, was a nonchalance that offended, rather than realized, the theme.[12]

It is "too diligent, too tasteful, too beautiful" because its diligence, taste and beauty are errant, refer to *no concrete edifice*.[13]

Potamkin continually attacks the film for Pabst's overconcern with "delicacy" and "finesse" and associates it with "the polishing of surfaces, the feints, the detachment, the rarified atmosphere of the ineffable."[14] The language and tone of these critiques parallel in intriguing ways a more general tendency to label and hence dismiss derogatorily the Weimar social scene itself as "decadent" or "degenerate"—an era which exhausted itself through an obsession with the nonessential.

It is striking that neither Kracauer nor Potamkin stress the single point of fascination for many later critics of the film, the figure of Lulu. One might suspect that the two socially minded critics view the centering of a highly sexualized female figure as incompatible with a sustained analysis of social conditions. But they do not say so directly. Rather, any diatribe against Lulu is displaced by a condemnation of Pabst's fetishism of cinematographic technique, his penchant for "*Lichtspiel*," his obsession with surfaces and atmosphere, his "delicacy" and "finesse." The puzzle for Potamkin and Kracauer is how a director such as Pabst, so skilled in the realism inspired by the *Neue Sachlichkeit*, could become fascinated and *held* by the lure of the image (an "image" which increasingly connotes feminine style versus substance). *Pandora's Box*, tinged with expressionism in sets and lighting, constituted for these critics a capitulation to the demands of the image versus the referent, the decorative versus the substantial. To claim that Pabst has the spirit of a photographer in his more socially conscious films, as Kracauer did, is to stabilize or domesticate the image by insisting upon its indexical relation to the real. In much of *Pandora's Box*, the image (and the woman who dominates it) are derealized. But they are also stabilized and contained in a way which is more consistent with modernism and its cynical consciousness than with social realism.

At first glance, the "modernity" of *Pandora's Box* would seem to be more a function of its attitude toward sexuality than of its textual strategies. The narrative is classical, legible, and linear, and the editing of the film shares many of the strategies of the traditional Hollywood cinema, particularly in its establishment of continuity. Constant cutting on movement tends to decrease the visibility of cuts, create a homogeneous space, and develop a linearity of action. The shot/reverse shot construction is also used, linking the characters by establishing a common space for them during dialogue. Characters are related to the space in which they move through the mise-en-scène—the fog of London, the chaos of scenery and movement in the backstage scene, the expressionist shadows and daunting sculpture emerging from the wall in Schön's death scene, an attention to details such as the placement of a stuffed crocodile just behind and above Rodrigo's head as he threatens Lulu on the ship or the ceramic donkey with which

Schön fiddles as he attempts to tell Lulu of his engagement to another woman.

An unusually large number of the cuts which are not cuts on movement or characters entering or leaving a frame are glance/glance cuts (or a cut which moves significantly from glance/object to glance/glance). Although the glance/object cut in the Hollywood system insures a kind of continuity, Pabst emphasizes it so heavily and combines it with such extreme close-ups that, instead of corroborating the homogeneous space created by the cuts on action, it tends to fragment that space. Lotte Eisner describes the impact of the close-up in *Pandora's Box*: "It is the close-ups which determine the character of the film; the flamboyant or phosphorescent atmosphere and the luminous mists of London remain throughout merely a kind of accompaniment to these close-ups, heightening their significance."[15] The close-ups, which would conventionally denote or specify metonymically something within a larger field of significance, tend to absorb and contain the semantic energy of the text. Furthermore, the close-ups often function as ruptures in the text, both spatially (the characters become literally disembodied) and temporally (the close-up arrests the gaze of the spectator, temporarily halts the flow of the action). Perhaps the best example of this occurs in the scene in which Lulu, after being rejected by Schön, visits Alwa and Geschwitz in Schön's home. After Alwa abruptly catches Lulu as she swings back and forth from a curtain rod, Lulu says, "Alwa is my best friend—he's the only one who wants nothing from me." There is a cut-away to Geschwitz, observing this with jealousy and anxiety, and subsequently an extreme close-up of Alwa and Lulu (figure 7.1). They are two profiles at the edges of the screen and there is a black background between them. Alwa's face is highlighted, Lulu's outlined by a thin pencil of light; the black background removes them from any recognizable space. The highly erotic nature of the image is a function of its despatialization, its lack of anchoring in any context which might weight it with a diegetic purpose. Although shared here with Alwa, for the most part this type of shot is allotted to Lulu alone as the focus of the constant demands and desires of the other characters.

Pandora's Box is structured by an optics of eroticism based on a network of gazes which signal the momentous events of the scenario and an acting mode which relies heavily on the expressivity of the eyes as a readable text. Its narrative very self-consciously strings together scenes which are staged for an internal audience. Climaxes and turning points—Schön's discovery of Lulu at the theater, his son's and fiancée's surprise encounter with Schön and Lulu in each other's arms, and Schön's death—are all represented as *sights* whose significance is underlined by the shock, awe, or terror legible

Figure 7.1

on the faces of the beholders (figures 7.2–8; 7.9–12; 7.13). The horror as well as the eroticism of seeing are inscribed within the mise-en-scène. Through their structuration as a *sight*, the woman, illicit sexuality, and death display an affinity and the woman is guaranteed her position as the very figure of catastrophe.

While the lines of force and spaces between characters are constructed largely through an emphasis on the gaze, the eyes are also the crucial indicators of emotions and reactions, the highly legible texts of desire, hatred, fear, and fascination. Lulu's eyes are generally flirtatious in an indiscriminate manner—everyone, including Jack the Ripper, is the potential recipient of a look which acknowledges no boundaries of class or position. In the economics of sexuality which govern the text, she *gives* her look freely. Schön possesses the castrating look of the Father, a look allied with the monocle which forces him to squint maliciously. A monocle is also worn by the State Prosecutor as he associates Lulu with Pandora and relates the myth. Halted by her gaze and smile, he is forced to stop and clean the monocle before he can continue. The prosecutor represents the Law; however unconvincing, based as it is on a mythological problematic, his speech results in a conviction. Alwa is the terrified observer: his eyes are wide open when his father tells him to watch out for Lulu. They are wide open again when Lulu performs the sacrilegious action of throwing her mourning cap at the relief in the room where Schön was killed. As the representative of lesbianism in the film and, according to Wedekind, the true "tragic central figure of the play,"[16] Geschwitz is given eyes which are associated with jealousy (when she asks Alwa, "How's Lulu?," her eyes become slitty through the smoke). Most intriguingly, perhaps, Jack the Ripper has a psychotic gaze. In the notice warning the women of London about him, he is described as having "small unsteady eyes." In his scene with Lulu, as long as the directness of the gaze is sustained (during the eye-line matches between Jack and Lulu), he is docile, almost infantile. His gaze becomes less and less steady as Lulu leans on his shoulder and closes her eyes. In her one moment of repose in the film, she becomes the victim of male psychosis. The eye is not only the organ of desire, but that of performance and deception as well.

Within this network of close relations and dependencies sustained primarily by the directionality and semantic qualities of the gaze, disjunction and rupture play a crucial role. Through certain deviations in the editing, Pabst suggests the existence of a non-wholistic space beside a seemingly organic one. In a shot/reverse shot construction, Schön tells Alwa to "watch out for that girl." In the first shot, Schön is on the left, Alwa on the right. The cut to the reverse shot (Alwa reacting) breaks the 180 degree rule and Alwa suddenly appears on the left, Schön on the right. This cut—transgressive from the point of view of cinematic technique—marks an exchange of places: the son replaces his father as Lulu's lover. But it does so at the expense of a clear orientation in space and produces a rupture of diegetic stability. Similarly, in the opening scene of the film, in which Lulu is introduced in her encounter with the meter man (introduced as well in her capacity as the object of desire and fascination), there is a break in continuity in relation to the directionality of the gaze. Such deviations from the traditional rules might be dismissed as mere "mistakes." However, Pabst's knowledge of and desire to conform to the rules of continuity editing is evidenced by a conversation he had with Kenneth Macpherson about the film made just previous to *Pandora's Box*, *The Love of Jeanne Ney*.

He [Pabst] told me there where two thousand cuts in the entire film. When I saw it one was not conscious of any. When I said this he explained his method. "Every cut is made on some movement. At the end of one cut somebody is moving, at the beginning of the adjoining one the movement is continued. The eye is thus so occupied in following these movements that it misses the cuts. Of course," he added, "this was very difficult to do."[17]

In *Pandora's Box*, a film which on the whole bows to the necessity of smooth continuity and the construction of a legible, homogeneous space, isolated moments are singled out and lent a quasi-extradiegetic quality through deviations in glance/glance relations.

Perhaps the most striking example of this occurs during the backstage scene at the theater, when Schön and Lulu confront one another. Schön, standing next to his fiancée, the daughter of the Minister of the Interior,[18] first catches a glimpse of Lulu as she adjusts her costume before her performance (figures 7.2 and 7.3). In the next series of shots, which constitute a crucial turning point in the narrative, the two are linked by glance/glance editing (figures 7.4–8). Although the clear implication is that they are looking at one another, they are both looking in the same direction—towards the left of the screen, momentarily effecting a spatial disruption. Their glances never "meet," suggesting that his vision of and desire for her are unreal, slipping past any actual intersubjective relation to the realm of the ethereal and the fantastic. Desire belongs to an irrational space. While Schön's stern and distrustful look is embedded in a context—chaotic stage preparations form the background of his close-up and his fiancée's face appears on the right of the frame—the close-up of Lulu is in soft focus, separating her from her surroundings in a scene which otherwise establishes depth of field and the manipulation of different planes as a strategy. Lulu's face is softly lit, her only context her own somewhat diaphanous headdress; she is pure image. Earlier in the film, in the first scene, there is a similar soft-focus shot of Lulu—again, just before she seduces Schön against his will. In her most desirous (and disruptive) state, Lulu is *outside of* the mise-en-scène. There is a somewhat fantastic hallucinatory quality attached to her image.

The aspiration of her representation toward the timeless and the spaceless realm of the idea rather than the fact is suggested by an excess of representations of Lulu within the narrative; she is self-consciously *pictured* for the audience within the film and the spectator outside. There is the huge painting of Lulu dressed in a Pierrot costume in the first scene, her various mirror images, the court photographer's photo of Lulu which allows Casti-Piani to recognize her and to blackmail Alwa on the train, the photographs of Lulu posing which Casti-Piani uses in his bargaining with the Arab, and the costume sketch by Geschwitz (which becomes a representation of Lulu for Dr. Schön and his son and suggests that possession of Lulu is not so much the object of desire as the ability to look at her). Framed in two senses, her image circulates and is exchanged as a form of currency.

Lulu is clearly, although always in motion, the fixed textual center—the focal point around which all the other characters circulate. Their dominant reactions to her are those of an awe-filled desire and a desire to exploit, foregrounding the economic substratum of seduction. While Geschwitz,

Figure 7.2

Figure 7.3

Figure 7.4

Figure 7.5

Figure 7.6

Figure 7.7

Figure 7.8

Schön, and Alwa seem to be under her spell, Schigolch, Rodrigo, and Casti-Piani perceive her largely in economic terms. Lulu herself is oblivious to class distinctions, displaying her smile and her charms freely to members of the lumpenproletariat (Schigolch and Rodrigo), the petty-bourgeoisie as well as Kracauer's *Angestellten* (the meter man of the opening scene),[19] and the upper class/aristocracy (Schön, Alwa, Geschwitz). She is able to travel comfortably through all social spaces and, not recognizing or acknowledging these distinctions herself, is situated in a realm somewhere beyond or outside of social hierarchy.

That realm would appear to be one of sheer being; Lulu, through her very existence, is conceptualized as an eroticized ontological problem. Because she is consistently despatialized through her relegation to some extradiegetic territory, one is led to wonder how and why—if not where— she exists. In Wedekind's play, Lulu is at least given a veneer of intellectuality; she thinks, she schemes and plots, she even dictates Schön's discourse for him in the scene in which she gives him the words for a letter in which he breaks all relations with his fiancée. What strikes one about Lulu in Pabst's film is that she is totally devoid of thought, a blank surface. Thomas Elsaesser refers to the emptiness of her smile.[20] There is no suggestion of a depth—only depths which are projected onto her by the various male characters, in an apparent confirmation of Potamkin's diatribe against Pabst's overconcern with surface. This is a process of projection which also exceeds the limits of the film text. Subsequent critical discourse surrounding *Pandora's Box* exhibits a compulsive fascination with the figure of Lulu or with the American actress who played her, Louise Brooks—so much so that the film often seems to be more accurately described as a star vehicle rather than as the work of an auteur. The following are some typical critical responses to the film which fasten on an analysis of Lulu's traits as key to the text.

> From that eroticism which reunites sensuality and love, tenderness and cruelty, Louise Brooks forms the first cinematographic expression (Charles Jameux).

> The success of Pabst lies first and foremost in the nuanced art with which he sumptuously deploys the ensemble of magical qualities of Louise Brooks: firm flesh and satin skin, the looks and smiles and bewitching sweetness of a being consecrated to the exaltation of the instant, to the plenitude of pleasure (Raymond Borde, Freddy Buache, Francis Courtade).

> In this "realist" drama, the "metaphysical meaning" is only suggested through the simultaneously guileless and demonic character of a girl whose eroticism is in the image of the sinister seductions of the night (Jean Mitry).

Many times Pabst films Lulu's features on a slant. Her face is so voluptuously animal that it seems almost deprived of individuality. In the scene with Jack the Ripper, this face, a smooth mirror-like disc slanting across the screen, is so shaded out and toned down that the camera seems to be looking down at some lunar landscape. (Is this still a human being—a woman—at all? Is it not rather the flower of some poisonous plant?) (Lotte Eisner).

Those who have seen her can never forget her. She is the modern actress par excellence because, like the statues of antiquity, she is outside of time . . . She is the intelligence of the cinematographic process, she is the most perfect incarnation of photogénie. . . . (Henri Langlois)[21]

The above quotes, whether consciously or unconsciously, acknowledge the fact that Lulu acts as a narrative mechanism, the provoker of events. All that happens in the film happens through or around her, although she can in no sense be described as a traditional protagonist.

The fatality, the morbid sexuality associated with Lulu, together with the fact that what she generally provokes are catastrophes, would seem to suggest that she occupies the position of the classic femme fatale. Elsaesser, however, disagrees strongly with this characterization insofar as it assumes a knowledge and an intentionality in relation to evil which Lulu lacks. He points, quite accurately, to "the principal ambiguity that preoccupied critics of Lulu, both in the plays and the film—whether she is a victim or an agent, whether she has a passive or an active role in the events of which she is the centre."[22] It is a question which, according to Elsaesser, follows directly from the sexual ambiguity ascribed to Lulu, her androgyny. Her lithe—almost boyish—body is often emphasized by the camera, her association with the lesbian Geschwitz seems to call into question sexual identity, and her exchange of clothing with the sailor on the ship also suggests a certain bisexuality. I would agree that there *is* a play with sexual roles in the film but, ultimately, it is a very limited play. It is important to note that the concepts of androgyny and bisexuality are more freely and easily associated with the *female* figure, indicating, once again, that the woman is ultimately perceived as inherently more bisexual than the man (in the film we do not see the sailor in Lulu's clothing) and, indeed, that this is a part of her allure. Furthermore, in her interaction with Geschwitz, Lulu's femininity is maintained and the signifier of Geschwitz's lesbianism is her masculinization. Geschwitz consistently occupies the margins of a masculine scenario structured around Lulu. The androgyny attributed to Lulu is a fundamental aspect of her mutability, her free-spiritedness, the transgression of conventional boundaries—all of which constitute her eroticism, her desirability.

Nevertheless, the question whether Lulu is agent or victim, subject or object, guilty or innocent remains, and is crucial to one's reading of the film. Elsaesser ultimately argues that Lulu is neither passive nor active, that she collapses all of these oppositions and produces an entirely different dynamics. The urgency of the binary opposition in the critical discourse surrounding *Pandora's Box* has to do with the ability to ascertain guilt: "Agency is a crucial question because in our society moral evaluation of guilt or innocence, evil or virtue attaches itself to intentionality and agency."[23] For Elsaesser, then, the film's modernist signifying problematic, by illustrating the bankruptcy of these oppositions, produces a discourse beyond guilt. In this respect, the backstage scene at the theater revue is crucial.

> Pabst here recasts and reformulates the central "moral" issue of the play: is Lulu active or passive, evil or innocent? The answer that the film gives is that she is neither, that it is a false dichotomy. Instead, it becomes a matter of presence or absence, of spectacle, of image and *mise-en-scène*: Lulu puts on a show of her own disappearance—and reappearance. The spectacle of her person, about which she controls nothing but the cadence and discontinuity of presence, is what gives rise to desire and fascination.[24]

Elsaesser spells out all the consequences of Langlois's intuition that Louise Brooks is "the intelligence of the cinematographic process" and is certainly astute in his depiction of Lulu's status as, first and foremost, image, representation, spectacle. Yet, the issue of guilt does not disappear. For the amazing thing about feminine culpability is that guilt does not necessarily attach itself to the woman through intentionality or motivation. Her sheer existence, particularly in its spectacular capacity, is often the cause of disaster or catastrophe. And *Pandora's Box* is a catastrophile's film. Lulu's guilt is a guilt which is not legalistic (particularly if this is viewed as a function of individual agency) but imagistic. She exemplifies the power accorded to images which aligns them with a malignant femininity—most symptomatically when the images are not firmly anchored diegetically or referentially (recall Potamkin's "camera caress of surfaces"). Hence, Lulu's trial is a battle over images—with that of Pandora, *the* figure of feminine catastrophe, ultimately winning. This is also why Lulu, escaping the court's justice, must die at the hands of Jack the Ripper in the end, throwing the film back (from the register of the fascinating, spectacular image) to the realm of a sordid realism, where the image is, at last, finally contained. Within the film as a whole, femininity constitutes a danger which must be systematically eradicated. The fiancée of Schön disappears early in the narrative, Geschwitz is eliminated before the final scenes in London, and Lulu is finally murdered by a sexual maniac. The film takes some pains to accomplish the total negation of the feminine. Only Alwa, the son, is left at the end of the film, in his solitary misery, the narrative retrospectively becoming *his* tragedy.

Alwa's survival is dictated by the fact that, although he might seem to be a relatively marginal character, he is in fairly subtle ways a point of origin of the discourse—so that its demise is dependent upon his lonely figure in silhouette, leaving the scene of the crime. In Wedekind's plays, Alwa is explicitly situated as the author-figure, constantly commenting on the potential literary interest of Lulu's life, its suitability for drama, and referring in *Pandora's Box* to "my play *Earth-Spirit*."[25] Although the film specifies that he is a writer, it only indirectly and implicitly links him to its own enunciation. Alwa is the producer of the musical revue and this scene, in its concentration on voyeurism, exhibitionism, spectacle, and image is most suggestive of the function of the cinematic apparatus. There is also a strong emphasis on Alwa's status as silent witness or observer of the climactic moments of the narrative: standing with his father's fiancée, he surprises Schön and Lulu in their backstage embrace (this is his "primal scene"—see figures 7.9–12); with Lulu, he looks down at his father dying off-screen (figure 7.13). Less literally, the narrative presents itself as a slightly revised Oedipal fantasy which would be that of a *son*. The theatricality of this Oedipal drama is revealed by the placement of the "primal scene" backstage during Alwa's revue. And, in a deviation from the standard Oedipal plot, the son is not guilty of the murder of the father; instead, that guilt is displaced onto the mother (Lulu, in her extremely limited maternal aspect). Immediately before the shooting, Alwa lays his head on her lap in a shot which invokes the memory of the Pietà (figure 7.14). The father enters the frame holding the gun at his side and completes the triad (figure 7.15). In a wish-fulfilling fantasy of true Oedipal yearning, the mother eliminates the father and opens the way for the consummation of the son's desire. Geschwitz, who according to Wedekind is "burdened" with "the terrible destiny of abnormality,"[26] is significantly locked outside the door of this familial scene. And, ultimately, it is the mother who is punished—through the arbitrary justice of a Jack the Ripper. It is always someone else who murders for Alwa: in the first instance, Lulu, in the second, Jack the Ripper, as Alwa's double and exemplification of his violent underside.[27]

For Kracauer, the gesture by means of which the German male in the Weimar cinema rests his head upon the lap of a woman constitutes *the* filmic trope of a crisis in masculinity. It is a gesture which signifies immaturity, a desire to return to the maternal womb, resignation, capitulation, and

Figure 7.9

Figure 7.10

Figure 7.11

Figure 7.12

inferiority.[28] In Kracauer's analysis, subordination to or dependency upon a woman is collapsed onto social disintegration. From this point of view, Alwa would exemplify the conflict-ridden male psyche of Weimar Germany. Alwa's two addictions in the film are Lulu and gambling, linking a peculiarly modern conceptualization of free sexuality with the idea of unrestrained speculation at the economic level; in both cases the returns can be either extremely pleasurable or unpleasurable. But both addictions also manifest a desire to escape history, to move into the realm of the infinitely repeatable idea or gesture. Desire for Lulu is desire for a femininity which is outside of time (hence the critic's description of her as "a being consecrated to the exaltation of the instant" and the association of Lulu with momentary pleasures—she has no memory). Her temporality is that of the moment—the glance, the smile that signifies no lasting commitment. It is also a femininity which is despatialized, a hallucinatory image characterized by diegetic resistances. Its modernity, then, in a somewhat paradoxical manner, is constituted by its ahistoricity. Similarly, gambling, as Walter Benjamin has pointed out, is comparable to modern factory work on the

Figure 7.13

Figure 7.14

Figure 7.15

assembly line insofar as its constantly repeated gestures bear no necessary connection with each other, insure no continuity through time. Each operation at the machine is like a *coup* in a game of chance because it is entirely separated from and unrelated to the preceding operation (being its exact double).[29] According to Benjamin, betting is "a device for giving events the character of a shock, detaching them from the context of experience."[30] With its valorization of chance, gambling disallows the cause-effect determinations which support historical understanding. When Alwa, influenced by Schigolch, attempts to cheat, and hence to introduce a directionality and a continuity into the game, reducing the element of chance, the entire fragilely ordered (or disordered) social system of the gambling ship (which Elsaesser specifies as "the fictional metaphor for the economic chaos of the Weimar Republic")[31] is disrupted.

As significant as the figure of Alwa is as a kind of discursive control, his position and his point of view are not, ultimately, those of the film. Alwa's vision is constrained by the fact that he is one, diegetically bound character—and a particularly naive, deluded, and innocent one at that. The filmic discourse promotes a broader view of sexuality, seduction, speculation, and spectacle. While Alwa may be represented in the film as an author-producer, it is not his musical revue we are given to see but the backstage machinations which support it, in the spirit of a cynical exposure of the substructure of spectacle. In terms of both style and representational structure this scene has something of a modernist impulse—in the desire to unveil the mechanisms of image production, to initiate a process of textual self-reflection. In its emphasis on elaborate costuming and careful choreography, the backstage sequence dwells on the theme of exhibitionism. Throughout most of this scene there is an activation of different planes in the image and the frame is always full. Whereas in the rest of the film the look of the spectator is more classically *directed* (through the use of close-ups and cuts on movement), the theater scene effects a confusion of that look. Off-screen space continually invades the frame (the characters—the director or actors—are thrown into the frame at several points). The audience of the revue is never shown; the only spectators are the other actors or backstage visitors. When Lulu creates a "spectacle" by refusing to go onstage and arguing with Schön, other actors gather around to watch. (In one shot, they gradually fill the first plane while Schön and Lulu fight in the background.) The exhibitionism of the revue is self-contained—the voyeurs are the exhibitionists and vice versa, producing a kind of ocular claustrophobia. The narrative proper can only be continued after the reconstruction of the opposition between voyeur and exhibitionist in the "primal scene," where son and fiancée become voyeurs of parental exhibitionism.

The backstage machinations all work toward the production of a spectacle of sexuality which we observe only marginally, from the sidelines. The one we do see, seemingly more "real" in terms of the film's narrative, is only another performance. Although the strategy of the scene is aimed at cynically unveiling the mechanics of the show, nothing is revealed. Behind the wings at the theater is played out a movie scene, a drama which, in its turn, stages a primal scene, producing a mise-en-abyme structure of performance. According to Sloterdijk, "Without a theory of bluff, of show, seduction, and deception, modern structures of consciousness cannot be explained at all properly."[32] The modernist impulse here is that of a sexual cynicism which conceptualizes sexuality as the seduction of an image without depth; the freely mobile, referentless image is the cause of desire. From this perspective, seeing would operate in the register of seduction rather than that of perception.[33] At the same time, and because the voyeurs are the exhibitionists, everyone is "in the know"—seduction is simultaneous with mistrust.[34]

Nevertheless, even this type of sexuality would be viewed by the cynic as too utopian, too idealistic. Sexual desire for the modern consciousness is never an entity in itself (recall the erotic barter) but the by-product of the moral ideals which will never fully and finally collapse and whose taboos engender its excitement and terror. At the core of this free-flowing, chaotic backstage scene, where spectacle and sexual mobility are paramount, lie the fixity and heaviness of the classical primal scene, the consequence of the split between ethical behavior and sexuality which begets the repression characteristic of the class represented by Schön. Schön belongs to a premodern order where sexuality, riddled by contradictions, is nevertheless contained by the polarization of morality and secret desire. The cynic's "fact" which the film confronts is that sexual desire always only relies upon the moral boundaries which dictate its very existence as well as its inevitable demise. This is what constitutes its melancholy attraction. Within this view, morality is in the realm of sexuality what referentiality is in the realm of linguistics—difficult to demonstrate or rationalize, but impossible to abandon completely. Still, when one believes in it (morality, referentiality) too fully, the economy of the system (of sexuality, of signification) is destroyed. Lulu's allure is a function of the illicit, unbounded nature of her sexuality, but the attempt to legalize that sexuality through marriage is fatal, disastrous. Perhaps it is unnecessary to add that such a view leaves the hierarchy of sexual difference intact.

This dialectic of sexuality, the curious dependency of law and desire, subject and object, projection and introjection, is registered in the structure of Schön's death scene, in which a mirror plays a pivotal role.[35] Lulu, gazing admiringly at her own image in the mirror, begins to take off her wedding gown (figure 7.16). In a closer shot, she removes her necklace (figure 7.17) and as she bends down to set it aside, the ghostly image of Schön appears in the mirror (figure 7.18) to fill the space she leaves vacant (figure 7.19). When she rises again, Lulu is startled by the image of Schön, his gaze fixed upon her (figure 7.20). Schön's presence here as a virtual image lends to his figure an even greater terror. Because the mirror image, psychoanalytic mark of an illusory identity, is shared by both Lulu and Schön, it can be interpreted from a double perspective. The free and joyful sexuality represented by Lulu seems to call forth in response its weighty, cumbersome other, signaled by the presence of Schön and his problematic of sexual guilt. On the other hand, Schön's guilt requires Lulu's image. In Wedekind's play, Lulu's subjectivity is linked to the mirror in an entirely different way. In a conversation with Alwa about her appearance, Lulu says, "When I looked at myself in the mirror I wished I were a man . . . my own husband."[36] Similarly, in Alban Berg's opera, the following

Figure 7.16

Figure 7.17

Figure 7.18

Figure 7.19

Figure 7.20

statement is attributed to Lulu: "When I looked at myself in the mirror I wished I were a man—a man married to me."[37] In this definitive discourse of narcissism and lost subjectivity, the man's existence is summoned up to fill the desiring void of her own reflection. While Wedekind and Berg after him link desire, identification, and projection in their scenario of female subjectivity at the mirror, in Pabst this entire problematic is tinged with horror. When Schön looms up in the place of Lulu's lost image, the film suggests that she is there by virtue of the other—a projection of male desire. But, while her image is dependent upon him, the scene also indicates the dependency of a tormented male subjectivity upon a certain image of female sexuality. Here the film seems to recognize and even attempt to analyze the dialectic of subjectivity and objectivity which underpins sexual desire.

This recognition is lost at the end of *Pandora's Box* in a scene which provides a rewriting of the existential angst of the mirror scene. If Schön is the representative of sexuality bounded by morality and the conventional, Jack the Ripper, through the tabloid reporting of his crimes, is the very figure of perversion, of sexuality gone awry.[38] Both scenes are structured as an attempt to kill Lulu. Yet, in the scene of Lulu's death, struggle and conflict are not represented through the complex play of mirror images, as an exchange, however unequal, between the man and the woman; instead, they are internalized as the man's battle with himself. The emphasis here, particularly in the prolonged stairway sequence where Lulu's smile is crosscut with Jack's grip on his knife, is on the man's internal struggle. The gentleness of the scene, its lack of explicit violence, together with the tenderness of the previous encounter with a Salvation Army worker, tend to align spectatorial sympathy much more fully with Jack. Lulu's romanticized—even mystical—death takes on a kind of inevitability as the symptom of the modern male's split consciousness.[39] The significant exchange here is not between Lulu and the man as in the mirror scene, but between Alwa and Jack the Ripper as their glances meet outside the tenement in the fog of London. (Elsaesser claims that "a sign of recognition seems to pass between the men that sets Alwa free and allows him, too, to disappear into the fog, having found his sexual salvation from ambivalence.")[40] The silent pact between Jack and Alwa is formed over the corpse of Lulu. Male subjectivity cuts itself loose from the terror of otherness.

What is particularly striking about the ending is the sudden appearance of Jack the Ripper on the scene—a key character who seems to require no introduction due to his extratextual notoriety. Lulu escapes the justice of the court only to fall into the embrace of Jack the Ripper. Early in Wedekind's *Pandora's Box*, Lulu says, "Every few nights I used to dream that I'd fallen into the hands of a sex-maniac,"[41] so that the end, in a very classical manner, seems to reply to the beginning, fulfilling Lulu's dream. But in Pabst's film there is no preparation whatsoever for the appearance of Jack the Ripper. In a way, it is appropriate that, when the justice of the court fails, Lulu should be subjected to a purely contingent punishment. Accident, chance, coincidence—the contingency of her death shares the logic of the *coup* in gambling rather than that of the law and its court. The throw of the dice which characterizes the modernist impulse to dehistoricize becomes coincident with the exclusion of women from the scene. Lulu's luck has run out.

In Elsaesser's analysis, Pabst in *Pandora's Box* presented a nuanced image of the ambiguities of sexuality and, in his framing, mise-en-scène, and editing, demonstrated a recognition of the "modernist promise" of the cinema. Yet, according to Elsaesser, Pabst could not prevent the film industry's later "betrayal" of this modernist promise—its subordination of the image to the logic of fetishism and commodification.[42] There are admittedly significant differences between the Weimar cinema of the twenties and the classical Hollywood cinema. Nevertheless, modernity and modernism do not necessarily promise anything to the woman; or, if they do, that promise is always already broken. *Pandora's Box*, fairly classical in much of its design, does not, in its modernist moments, escape the power-knowledge relations of the problematic of sexual difference. Lulu occupies the derealized image, the image released from referential constraints—an image that only magnifies an exploitative desire and calls forth the modern anxieties of male consciousness. A cynical modernity resigns itself to this erotic barter as the "real" of sexuality.

III. The Body of the Avant-Garde

CHAPTER EIGHT

Woman's Stake:
Filming the Female Body

We know that, for want of a stake, representation is not worth anything.

—Michèle Montrelay

To those who still ask, "What do women want?," the cinema seems to provide no answer. For the cinema, in its alignment with the fantasies of the voyeur, has historically articulated its stories through a conflation of its central axis of seeing/being seen with the opposition male/female. So much so that in a classical instance such as *Humoresque* (1946), when Joan Crawford almost violently attempts to appropriate the gaze for herself, she must be represented as myopic (the moments of her transformation from spectacle to spectator thus captured and constrained through their visualization as the act of putting on glasses) and eventually eliminated from the text, her death equated with that of a point of view. Cinematic images of women have been so consistently oppressive and repressive that the very idea of a feminist filmmaking practice seems an impossibility. The simple gesture of directing a camera toward a woman has become equivalent to a terrorist act.

This state of affairs—the result of a history which inscribes women as subordinate—is not simply to be overturned by a contemporary practice that is more aware, more self-conscious. The impasse confronting feminist filmmakers today is linked to the force of a certain theoretical discourse which denies the neutrality of the cinematic apparatus itself. A machine for the production of images and sounds, the cinema generates and guarantees pleasure by a corroboration of the spectator's identity. Because that identity is bound up with that of the voyeur and the fetishist, because it requires for its support the attributes of the "non-castrated," the potential for illusory mastery of the signifier, it is not accessible to the female spectator, who, in buying her ticket, must deny her sex. There are no images either *for* her or *of* her. There is a sense in which Peter Gidal, in attempting to articulate the relationship between his own filmmaking practice and feminist concerns, draws the most logical conclusion from this tendency in theory:

> In terms of the feminist struggle specifically, I have had a vehement refusal over the last decade, with one or two minor aberrations, to allow images of women into my films at all, since I do not see how those images can be separated from the dominant meanings. The ultra-left aspect of this may be nihilistic as well, which may be a critique of my position because it does not see much hope for representations for women, but I do not see how, to take the main example I gave round about 1969 before any knowledge on my part of, say, semiotics, there is any possibility of using the image of a naked woman—at that time I did not have it clarified to the point of any image of a woman—other than in an absolutely sexist and politically repressive patriarchal way in this conjuncture.[1]

This is the extreme formulation of a project which can define itself only in terms of negativity. If the female body is not necessarily always excluded within this problematic, it must always be placed within quotation marks. For it is precisely the massive reading, writing, filming of the female body which constructs and maintains a hierarchy along the lines of a sexual difference assumed as natural. The ideological complicity of the concept of the natural dictates the impossibility of a nostalgic return to an unwritten body.

Thus, contemporary filmmaking addresses itself to the activity of uncoding, de-coding, deconstructing the given images. It is a project of defamiliarization whose aim is not necessarily that of seeing the female body differently, but of exposing the habitual meanings/values attached to femininity as cultural constructions. Sally Potter's *Thriller* (1979), for instance, is a rereading of the woman's role in opera, specifically in Puccini's *La Bohème,* in terms of its ideological function. Mimi's death, depicted in the opera as tragedy, is rewritten as a murder, the film itself invoking the conventions of the suspense thriller. In Babette Mangolte's *The Camera: Je/La Caméra: Eye* (1977), what is at stake are the relations of power sustained within the camera-subject nexus. The discomfort of the subjects posing for the camera, together with the authority of the off-screen voice giving instructions ("Smile," "Don't smile," "Look to the left," etc.), challenge the photographic image's claim to naturalism and spontaneity. And, most interestingly, the subjects, whether male or female, inevitably appear to assume a mask of "femininity" in order to become photographable (filmable)—as though femininity were synonymous with the *pose*.[2] This may explain the feminist film's frequent obsession with the pose as position—the importance accorded to dance positions in *Thriller,* or those assumed by the hysteric in Terrel Seltzer's *The Story of Anna O.* (1979)— which we see as the arrangements of the body in the interests of aesthetics and science. In their rigidity (the recurrent use of the tableau in these films) or excessive repetition (the multiple, seemingly unending caresses of the woman's breasts in Mangolte's *What Maisie Knew* [1974]), positions and gestures are isolated, deprived of the syntagmatic rationalization which, in the more classical text, conduces to their naturalization. These strategies of demystification are attempts to strip the body of its readings. The inadequacy of this formulation of the problem is obvious, however, in that the gesture of stripping in relation to a female body is already the property of patriarchy. More importantly, perhaps, the question to be addressed is this: what is left after the stripping, the uncoding, the deconstruction? For an uncoded body is clearly an impossibility.

Attempts to answer this question by invoking the positivity or specificity of a definition have been severely criticized on the grounds that the particular definition claims a "nature" proper to the woman and is hence complicit with those discourses which set woman outside the social order. Since the patriarchy has always already said everything (everything and nothing) about woman, efforts to give those phrases a different intonation, to mumble, to stutter, to slur them, to articulate them differently, must be doomed to failure. Laura Mulvey and Peter Wollen's *Riddles of the Sphinx* (1977), for instance, has been repeatedly criticized for its invocation of the sphinx as the figure of a femininity repressed by the Oedipal mythos. Femininity is something which has been forgotten or repressed, left outside the gates of the city; hence, what is called for is a radical act of remembering. The radicality of that act, however, has been subject to debate. As Stephen Heath points out,

> The line in the figure of the sphinx-woman between the posing of a question and the idea that women are the question is very thin: female sexuality is dark and unexplorable; women, as Freud put it, are that half of the audience which is the enigma, the great enigma. This is the problem and the difficulty—the area of debate and criticism—of Mulvey and Wollen's film *Riddles of the Sphinx* where the sphinx is produced as a point of resistance that seems nevertheless to repeat, in its very terms, the relations of women made within patriarchy, their representation in the conjunction of such elements as motherhood as mystery, the unconscious, a voice that speaks far off from the past through dream or forgotten language. The film is as though poised on the edge of a politics of the unconscious, of the imagination of a politics of the

unconscious ("what would the politics of the unconscious be like?"), with a simultaneous falling short, that politics and imagination not yet there, coming back with old definitions, the given images.[3]

What is forgotten in the critical judgment, but retrieved in Heath's claim that "the force remains in the risk"—the risk, that is, of recapitulating the terms of patriarchy—is the fact that the sphinx is also, and crucially, subject to a kind of filmic disintegration. In the section entitled "Stones," the refilming of found footage of the Egyptian sphinx problematizes any notion of perceptual immediacy in refinding an "innocent" image of femininity. In fact, as the camera appears to get closer to its object, the graininess of the film is marked, thus indicating the limit of the material basis of its representation.

Most of this essay will be a lengthy digression, a prolegomenon to a much needed investigation of the material specificity of film in relation to the female body and its syntax. Given the power of a certain form of feminist theory which has successfully blocked attempts to provide a conceptualization of this body, the digression is, nevertheless, crucial.

The resistance to filmic and theoretical descriptions of femininity is linked to the strength of the feminist critique of essentialism—of ideas concerning an essential femininity, or of the "real" woman not yet disfigured by patriarchal social relations. The force of this critique lies in its exposure of the inevitable alliance between "feminine essence" and the natural, the given, or precisely what is outside the range of political action and thus not amenable to change. This unchangeable "order of things" in relation to sexual difference is an exact formulation of patriarchy's strongest rationalization of itself. And since the essence of femininity is most frequently attached to the natural body as an immediate indicator of sexual difference, it is this body which must be refused. The body is always a function of discourse.

Feminist theory which grounds itself in anti-essentialism frequently turns to psychoanalysis for its description of sexuality because psychoanalysis assumes a necessary gap between the body and the psyche, so that sexuality is not reducible to the physical. Sexuality is constructed within social and symbolic relations; it is most *un*natural and achieved only after an arduous struggle. One is not born with a sexual identity (hence the significance of the concept of bisexuality in psychoanalysis). The terms of this argument demand that charges of phallocentrism be met with statements that the phallus is not equal to the penis, castration is bloodless, and the father is, in any case, dead and only symbolic.

Nevertheless, the gap between body and psyche is not absolute; an image or symbolization of the body (which is not necessarily the body of biological science) is fundamental to the construction of the psychoanalytical discourse. Brief references to two different aspects of psychoanalytic theory will suffice to illustrate my point. Jean Laplanche explains the emergence of sexuality by means of the concept of propping or *anaclisis*. The drive, which is always sexual, leans or props itself upon the non-sexual or presexual instinct of self-preservation. His major example is the relation of the oral drive to the instinct of hunger whose object is the milk obtained from the mother's breast. The object of the oral drive (prompted by the sucking which activates the lips as an erotogenic zone) is necessarily displaced in relation to the first object of the instinct. The fantasmatic breast (henceforth the object of the oral drive) is a metonymic derivation, a symbol, of the milk: "The object to be rediscovered is not the lost object, but its substitute by displacement; the lost object is the object of self-preservation, of hunger, and the object one seeks to refind is an object displaced in relation to that first object."[4] Sexuality can only take form in a dissociation of subjectivity from the bodily function, but the concept of a bodily function is necessary in the explanation as, precisely, a support. We will see later how Laplanche denaturalizes this body (which is simply a distribution of erotogenic zones) while retaining it as a cipher. Still, the body is there, as a prop.

The second aspect of psychoanalysis which suggests the necessity of a certain conceptualization of the body is perhaps more pertinent, and certainly more notorious, in relation to a discussion of feminism: the place of the phallus in Lacanian theory. Lacan and feminist theorists who subscribe to his formulations persistently claim that the phallus is not the penis; the phallus is a signifier (the signifier of lack). It does not *belong* to the male. The phallus is only important insofar as it can be put in circulation as a signifier. Both sexes define themselves in relation to this "third term." What is ultimately stressed here is the absolute necessity of positing only one libido (which Freud labels masculine) in relation to only one term, the phallus. Initially, both sexes, in desiring to conform to the desire of the other (the mother), define themselves in relation to the phallus in the mode of "being." Sexual difference, then, is inaugurated at the moment of the Oedipal complex when the girl continues to "be" the phallus while the boy situates himself in the mode of "having." Positing two terms, in relation to two fully defined sexualities, as Jones and Horney do, binds the concept of sexuality more immediately, more directly, to the body as it expresses itself at birth. For Jones and Horney, there is an essential femininity which is linked to an expression of the vagina. And for Horney at least, there is a sense in which the little girl experiences an empirical, not a psychic, inferiority.[5]

But does the phallus really have nothing to do with the penis, no commerce with it at all? The ease of the description by means of which the boy situates himself in the mode of "having" one would seem to indicate that this is not the case. And Lacan's justification for the privilege accorded to the phallus as signifier appears to guarantee its derivation from a certain representation of the bodily organ:

> The phallus is the privileged signifier of that mark in which the role of the logos is joined with the advent of desire. It can be said that this signifier is chosen because it is the most tangible element in the real of sexual copulation, and also the most symbolic in the literal (typographical) sense of the term, since it is equivalent there to the (logical) copula. It might also be said that, by virtue of its turgidity, it is the image of the vital flow as it is transmitted in generation.[6]

There is a sense in which all attempts to deny the relation between the phallus and the penis are feints, veils, illusions. The phallus, as signifier, may no longer *be* the penis, but any effort to conceptualize its function is inseparable from an imaging of the body. The difficulty in conceptualizing the relation between the phallus and the penis is evident in Parveen Adams's explanation of the different psychic trajectories of the girl and the boy.

> Sexuality can only be considered at the level of the symbolic processes. This lack is undifferentiated for both sexes and has nothing to do with the absence of a penis, a physical lack.
> Nonetheless, the anatomical difference between the sexes does permit a differentiation within the symbolic process. . . . The phallus represents lack for both boys and girls. But the boy in having a penis has that which lends itself to the phallic symbol. The girl does not have a penis. What she lacks is not a penis as such, but the means to represent lack.[7]

The sexual differentiation is permitted but not demanded by the body and it is the exact force or import of this "permitting" which requires an explanation. For it is clear that what is being suggested is that the boy's body provides an access to the processes of representation while the girl's body does not. From this perspective, a certain slippage can then take place by means of which the female body becomes an absolute tabula rasa of sorts: anything and everything can be written on it. Or more accurately, perhaps, the male body comes fully equipped with a binary opposition—penis/no penis, presence/absence, phonemic opposition—while the female body is constituted as "noise,"[8] an undifferentiated presence which always threatens to disrupt representation.

This analysis of the bodily image in psychoanalysis becomes crucial for feminism with the recognition that sexuality is inextricable from discourse, from language. The conjunction of semiotics and psychoanalysis (as exemplified in the work of Lacan and others) has been successful in demonstrating the necessity of a break in an initial plenitude as a fundamental condition for signification. The concept of lack is not arbitrary. The fact that the little girl in the above description has no means to represent lack results in her different relation to language and representation. The work of Michèle Montrelay is most explicit on this issue: ". . . for want of a stake, representation is not worth anything."[9] The initial relation to the mother, the determinant of the desire of both sexes, is too full, too immediate, too present. This undifferentiated plenitude must be fissured through the introduction of lack before representation can be assured, since representation entails the absence of the desired object. "Hence the repression that ensures that one does not think, nor see, nor take the desired object, even and above all if it is within reach: this object must remain lost."[10] The tragedy of Oedipus lies in his refinding of the object. And as Montrelay points out, it is the sphinx as the figure of femininity which heralds this "ruin of representation."

In order for representation to be possible then, a stake is essential. Something must be threatened if the paternal prohibition against incest is to take effect, forcing the gap between desire and its object. This theory results in a rather surprising interpretation of the woman's psychic oppression: her different relation to language stems from the fact that she has nothing to lose, nothing at stake. Prohibition, the law of limitation, cannot touch the little girl. For the little boy, on the other hand, there is most definitely something to lose. "He experiments, not only with chance but also with the law and with his sexual organ: his body itself takes on the value of stake."[11]

Furthermore, in repeating, doubling the maternal body with her own, the woman recovers the first stake of representation and thus undermines the possibility of losing the object of desire since she has, instead, become it.

From now on, anxiety, tied to the presence of this body, can only be insistent, continuous. This body, so close, which she has to occupy, is an object in excess which must be "lost," that is to say, repressed, in order to be symbolised. Hence the symptoms which so often simulate this loss: "there is no longer anything, only the hole, emptiness . . ." Such is the *leitmotif* of all feminine cure, which it would be a mistake to see as the expression of an alleged "castration." On the contrary, it is a defence produced in order to parry the avatars, the deficiencies, of symbolic castration.[12]

There are other types of defense as well, based on the woman's imaginary simulation of lack. Montrelay points to the anorexic, for instance, who diminishes her own body, dissolving the flesh and reducing the body to a cipher.[13] Or the woman can operate a performance of femininity, a masquerade, by means of an accumulation of accessories—jewelry, hats, feathers, etc.—all designed to mask the absence of a lack.[14] These defenses, however, are based on the woman's imaginary simulation of lack and exclude the possibility of an encounter with the symbolic. She can only mime representation.

Montrelay's work is problematic in several respects. In situating the woman's relation to her own body as narcissistic, erotic, and maternal, Montrelay insists that it is the "real of her own body" which "imposes itself," prior to any act of construction.[15] Furthermore, she does, eventually, outline a scenario within which the woman has access to symbolic lack, but it is defined in terms of a heterosexual act of intercourse in which the penis, even though it is described as "scarcely anything," produces the "purest and most elementary form of signifying articulation."[16] Nevertheless, Montrelay's work points to the crucial dilemma confronting an anti-essentialist feminist theory which utilizes psychoanalysis. That is, while psychoanalysis does theorize the relative autonomy of psychic processes, the gap between body and psyche, it also requires the body as a prop, a support for its description of sexuality as a discursive function. Too often anti-essentialism is characterized by a paranoia in relation to all discussions of the female body (since ideas about a "natural" female body or the female body and "nature" are the linchpins of patriarchal ideology). This results in a position which simply repeats that of classical Freudian psychoanalysis in its focus upon the little boy's psychic development at the expense of that of the little girl. What is repressed here is the fact that psychoanalysis can conceptualize the sexuality of both the boy and the girl *only* by positing gender-specific bodies.

Even more crucially, as Montrelay's work demonstrates, the use of the concepts of the phallus and castration within a semiotically oriented psychoanalysis logically implies that the woman must have a different relation to language from that of the man. And from a semiotic perspective, her relation to language must be deficient since her body does not "permit" access to what, for the semiotician, is the motor-force of language—the representation of lack. Hence, the greatest masquerade of all is that of the woman speaking (or writing, or filming), appropriating discourse. To take up a discourse for the woman (if not, indeed, by her), that is, the discourse of feminism itself, would thus seem to entail an absolute contradiction. How can she speak?

Yet, we know that women speak, even though it may not be clear exactly how this takes place. And unless we want to accept a formulation by means of which woman can only mimic man's relation to language, that is, assume a position defined by the penis-phallus as the supreme arbiter of lack, we must try to reconsider the relation between the female body and language, never forgetting that it is a relation between two terms and not two essences. Does woman have a stake in representation or, more appropriately, can we assign one to her? Anatomy is destiny only if the concept of destiny is recognized for what it really is: a concept proper to fiction.

The necessity of assigning to woman a specific stake informs the work of theorists such as Luce Irigaray and Julia Kristeva, and both have been criticized from an anti-essentialist perspective. Beverley Brown and Parveen Adams, for example, distinguish between two orders of argument about the female body which are attributed, respectively, to Irigaray and Kristeva:

> We can demand then: what is this place, this body, from which women speak so mutely?
>   Two orders of reply to this question can be distinguished. In the first there is an attempt to find a real and natural body which is pre-social in a literal sense. The second, more sophisticated reply, says that the issue at stake is not the actual location of a real body, but that the positing of such a body seems to be a condition of the discursive in general.[17]

Although the second order of argument is described as "more sophisticated," Brown and Adams ultimately find that both are deficient. I want briefly to address this criticism although it really requires an extended discussion impossible within the limits of this essay. The criticisms of Irigaray are based primarily on her essay, "That Sex Which Is Not One,"[18] in which she attempts to conceptualize the female body in relation to language/discourse, but independently of the penis/lack dichotomy. Irigaray valorizes certain features of the female body—the two lips (of the labia) which caress each other and define woman's auto-eroticism as a relation to duality, the multiplicity of sexualized zones spread across the body. Furthermore, Irigaray uses this representation of the body to specify a feminine language which is plural, polyvalent, and irreducible to a masculine language based on restrictive notions of unity and identity. Brown and Adams claim that "her argument turns upon the possibility of discovering that which is already there—it is a case of 'making visible' the previously 'invisible' of feminine sexuality."[19] While there are undoubtedly problems with the rather direct relation Irigaray often posits between the body and language, her attempt to provide the woman with an autonomous symbolic representation is not to be easily dismissed. Irigaray herself criticizes the logic which gives privilege to the gaze, thereby questioning the gesture of "making visible" a previously hidden female sexuality. Her work is a radical rewriting of psychoanalysis which, while foregrounding the process of mimesis by which language represents the body, simultaneously constructs a distinction between a mimesis which is "productive" and one which is merely "reproductive" or "imitative"—a process of "adequation" and of "specularization."[20] An immediate dismissal of her work in the interests of an overwary anti-essentialism involves a premature rejection of "the force that remains in the risk."

The criticism addressed to Kristeva, on the other hand, is directed toward her stress on pre-Oedipal sexuality, allying it with a femininity whose repression is the very condition of Western discourse.[21] For Kristeva, the woman's negative relation to the symbolic determines her bond with a polymorphous, prelogical discourse which corresponds to the autonomous and polymorphous sexuality of the pre-Oedipal moment. Brown and Adams formulate their criticism in these terms: "Setting up this apolitical autonomy of polymorphous sexuality is, in effect, the positing of sexuality as an impossible origin, a state of nature, as simply the eternal presence of sexuality at all."[22] However, pre-Oedipal sexuality is not synonymous with "nature"; it already assumes an organized distribution of erotogenic zones over the body and forms of relations to objects which are variable (whether human or non-human). Both male and female pass through, live pre-Oedipality. Hence, pre-Oedipality can only be equated with femininity retrospectively, *après coup,* after the event of the Oedipal complex, of the threat of castration, and the subsequent negative entry into the symbolic attributed to the woman. Insofar as Kristeva's description of pre-Oedipality is dependent upon notions of the drive, it involves a displacement of sexuality in relation to the body. As Laplanche points out, the drive is a metonymic derivation from the instinct which is itself attached to an erotogenic zone, a zone of *exchange.*

The drive properly speaking, in the only sense faithful to Freud's discovery, *is* sexuality. Now sexuality, in its entirety, in the human infant, lies in *a movement which deflects the instinct, metaphorizes its aim, displaces and internalizes its object, and concentrates its source on what is ultimately a minimal zone, the erotogenic zone* . . . . This zone of exchange is also a zone for care, namely the particular and attentive care provided by the mother. These zones, then, attract the first erotogenic maneuvers from the adult. An even more significant factor, if we introduce the subjectivity of the first "partner": these zones *focalize parental fantasies* and above all *maternal fantasies,* so that we may say, in what is barely a metaphor, that they are the points through which is *introduced into the child that alien internal entity* which is, properly speaking, the *sexual excitation.*[23]

The force of this scenario lies in its denaturalization of the sexualized body. The conceptualization of the erotogenic zone as a zone of exchange demonstrates that the investment of the body with sexuality is always already social. Since it is ultimately *maternal* fantasies which are at issue here, it is apparent that, without an anchoring in the social, psychoanalysis can simply reiterate, reperform in its theorization, the vicious circle of patriarchy.

The rather long digression which structures this essay is motivated by the extreme difficulty of moving beyond the impasse generated by the opposition between essentialism and anti-essentialism. In the context of feminist film theory, both positions are formulated through a repression of the crucial and complex relation between the body and psychic processes, that is, processes of signification. From the point of view of essentialist theory, the goal of a feminist film practice must be the production of images which provide a pure reflection of the real woman, thus returning the real female body to the woman as her rightful property. And this body is accessible to a transparent cinematic discourse. The position is grounded in a misrecognition of signification as outside of, uninformed by, the psychic. On the other hand, the logical extension of anti-essentialist theory, particularly as it is evidenced in Gidal's description of his filmmaking practice, results in the absolute exclusion of the female body, the refusal of any attempt to figure or represent that body. Both the proposal of a pure access to a natural female body and the rejection of attempts to conceptualize the female body based on their contamination by ideas of "nature" are inhibiting and misleading. Both positions deny the necessity of posing a complex relation between the body and psychic/signifying processes, of using the body, in effect, as a "prop." For Kristeva is right—the positing of a body *is* a condition of discursive practices. It is crucial that feminism move beyond the opposition between essentialism and anti-essentialism. This move will entail the necessary risk taken by theories which attempt to define or construct a feminine specificity (not essence), theories which work to provide the woman with an autonomous symbolic representation.

What this means in terms of the theorization of a feminist filmmaking practice can only be sketched here. But it is clear from the preceding exploration of the theoretical elaboration of the female body that the stake does not simply concern an isolated image of the body. The attempt to "lean" on the body in order to formulate the woman's different relation to speech, to language, clarifies the fact that what is at stake is, rather, the syntax which constitutes the female body as a term. The most interesting and productive recent films dealing with the feminist problematic are precisely those which elaborate a new syntax, thus "speaking" the female body differently, even haltingly or inarticulately from the perspective of a classical syntax. For instance, the circular camera movements which carve out the space of the mise-en-scène in *Riddles of the Sphinx* are in a sense more critical to a discussion of the film than the status of the figure of the sphinx as feminine. The film effects a continual displacement of the gaze which "catches" the woman's body only accidentally, momentarily, refusing to hold or fix her in the frame. The camera consistently transforms its own framing to elide the possibility of a fetishism of the female body. Chantal Akerman's *Jeanne Dielman, 23 Quai du Commerce—1080 Bruxelles* (1975) constructs its syntax by linking together scenes which, in the classical text, would be concealed, in effect negated, by temporal ellipses. The specificity of the film lies in the painful duration of that time "in-between" events, that time which is exactly proper to the woman (in particular, the housewife) within a patriarchal society. The obsessive routine of Jeanne Dielman's daily life, as both housewife and prostitute, is radically broken only by an instance of orgasm (corresponding quite literally to the "climax" of the narrative) which is immediately followed by her murder of the man. Hence, the narrative structure is a parodic "mime" that distorts, undoes the structure of the classical narrative through an insistence upon its repressions.

The analysis of the elaboration of a special syntax for a different articulation of the female body can also elucidate the significance of the recourse, in at least two of these films, to the classical codification of suspense. Both *Jeanne Dielman* and Sally Potter's *Thriller* construct a suspense without expectation. *Jeanne Dielman,* although it momentarily "cites" the mechanism of the narrative climax, articulates an absolute refusal of the phatic function of suspense, its engagement with and constraint of the spectator as consumer, devourer of discourse. *Thriller,* on the other hand, "quotes" the strategies of the suspense film (as well as individual films of this genre—for example, *Psycho* [1960]) in order to undermine radically the way in which the woman is "spoken" by another genre altogether, that of operatic tragedy. This engagement with the codification of suspense is an encounter with the genre which Roland Barthes defines as the most intense embodiment of the "generalized distortion" which "gives the language of narrative its special character":

"Suspense" is clearly only a privileged—or "exacerbated"—form of distortion: on the one hand, by keeping a sequence open (through emphatic procedures of delay and renewal), it reinforces the contact with the reader (the listener), has a manifestly phatic function; while on the other, it offers the threat of an uncompleted sequence, of an open paradigm (if, as we believe, every sequence has two poles), that is to say, of a logical disturbance, it being this disturbance which is consumed with anxiety and pleasure (all the more so because it is always made right in the end). "Suspense," therefore, is a game with structure, designed to endanger and glorify it, constituting a veritable "thrilling" of intelligibility: by representing order (and no longer series) in its fragility, "suspense" accomplishes the very idea of language. . . .[24]

It is precisely this "idea of language" which is threatened by both *Jeanne Dielman* and *Thriller* in their attempts to construct another syntax which would, perhaps, collapse the fragile order, revealing the ending too soon.

While I have barely approached the question of an exact formulation of the representation of the female body attached to the syntactical constructions of these films, it is apparent that this syntax is an area of intense concern, of reworking, rearticulating the specular imaging of woman, for whom, in the context of a current filmmaking, the formulation of a stake is already in process.

CHAPTER NINE

The Retreat of Signs and the Failure of Words: *Leslie Thornton's* Adynata

The images in Leslie Thornton's 1983 film, *Adynata*, are *lush* and one consistently gets the sense of an overwhelming surplus of the significer: a rippling piece of bright red silk which fills the frame; jewelry, ornamentation, and clothing designed to connote the Otherness of the "Oriental"; exotic flowers and grasses in lavish botanical gardens; a close-up of bright blue, undulating waves of water; silk slippers against wicker edged by peacock feathers and deep green leaves of tropical plants. The colors are extremely vivid and work to amplify what at first glance appears to be an unruly fetishism of the exotic object. There is *too much* for the eye—the film seemingly capitulates to the seductive force of visual pleasure. But this richness of the image is somewhat deceptive. It is itself already a second-order signifier of an exoticism associated with the discourse of Orientalism which is both quoted and criticized by the film. And, for Thornton, the discourse of Orientalism is precisely a discourse of excess, of hyperbole, of the absurd. In *Adynata* she investigates the mise-en-scène of Orientalism—the conglomeration of sounds and images which connote the Orient for a Western viewer/auditor.

Here, Thornton's work converges with the theoretical explorations of such figures as Edward Said (*Orientalism*), Roland Barthes (*Empire of Signs*), and Julia Kristeva (*About Chinese Women*). The film's organizing image is a formal portrait of a Chinese Mandarin and his wife taken in 1861, its fascination a function of both its age and its evocation of the faraway, the inaccessible. The portrait seems to authorize a sustained meditation on the iconography and the morphology of Orientalism. The obsessive and seductive "That has been" which Barthes associates with the photograph is translated into the inescapable "Here it is" of the cinematic image when Thornton herself assumes the position, pose, and dress of first the Mandarin's wife and then the Mandarin. The cinematic image *mimes* the photographic image and *acts out* the perverted analogical gesture of Orientalism whereby the Orient comes to mirror the underside of the Western subject's own desire. Putting herself in the picture, Thornton embodies identificatory procedures by means of which the lure of representation is revealed to reside in its relation to the subject rather than to the referent. Orientalism functions both to insure the coherent, cohesive identity of the Western subject and to sustain desire in representation. *Adynata* delineates the various ways in which desire converges on the Other.

In the film, the excesses of Orientalism are even more visible/audible in the soundtrack than in the image. Rare ethnographic recordings of Chinese opera from the 1920s are combined with the "Hartz Mountain Canary Orchestra," recurrent "pings" associated with an Oriental musical instrument, old 78 RPM love songs and blues, TV-style background music which connotes "Pacific island-ness" and the suspense associated with police dramas, microphone hum (the "noise" of the apparatus), "nature" sounds including crickets, birds, thunderstorms, and dialogue from a Korean soap opera. The relation of sound to image is often contentious rather than supplementary, producing ruptures and disjunctive moments which force the discourse of Orientalism to stutter and falter. When rock and roll music accompanies a television image of an Oriental wedding dance, the absurdity of the Western desire to grasp (in the sense of both holding or fixing and understanding) the Orient through representation is foregrounded. In an age of satellite communications, television technology brings the exotic and the "faraway" closer, but it cannot reduce the inevitable distance from the referent entailed in all representation. The words of the rock song are, "I am a TV savage." In its insistence upon problematizing the relation of sound to image, *Adynata* finds its greatest affinity with Barthes's approach in *Empire of Signs*. In a short prologue to the series of essays which constitute the book, Barthes explains the alignment or misalignment of text with photographs, paintings, and drawings:

> The text does not "gloss" the images, which do not "illustrate" the text. For me, each has been no more than the onset of a kind of visual uncertainty, analogous perhaps to that *loss of meaning* Zen calls a *satori*. Text and image, interlacing, seek to ensure the circulation and exchange of these signifiers: body, face, writing; and in them to read the retreat of signs.[1]

For Thornton as well, the cinematic sign is dismantled through the mismatch, the asynchronism of sound and image.

But in many crucial respects, Thornton's project differs markedly from that of Barthes. If the sign "retreats" in *Adynata*, it does not get very far. Barthes, on the other hand, would like "to 'entertain' the idea of an unheard-of symbolic system, one altogether detached from our own."[2] Barthes's writing about his trip to Japan is evidence of an impossible desire for *absolute* and irreducible otherness—with no point of contact with the West. One gets the sense that he finds the Western episteme constraining, if not suffocating, in its insistence upon the ideological hold and closure of meaning. Barthes's search is therefore for an "outside"—and the Japanese "text" seems to offer him a material order of signifiers which never coagulate in the production of a signified. What he looks for is, in effect, something pre-Symbolic. Barthes travels to Japan in some sense to experience the originary. In contrast, there is nothing originary in *Adynata*; everything articulated about the Orient has already been respoken. The film delineates a representation of the Orient which flaunts its own inadequacy, its status as cliché. As Jonathan Rosenbaum points out, spectatorial engagement with such a discourse reveals "all sorts of ideological positions and forms of ignorance about the Orient" demonstrating that "one's misconceptions and uncertainties about what one sees and hears are not a distraction from the film's focus but part of its subject. . . ."[3] Orientalism is hence a kind of continuous misreading which does not, however, presuppose a "correct" or "accurate" reading. Rather, the discourse of Orientalism is a perpetual deviation without a norm. Its desire to escape or avoid signification is exemplified by Barthes's attraction to languages (particularly tonal ones) which he does not understand: "The murmuring mass of an unknown language constitutes a delicious protection, envelops the foreigner . . . in an auditory film which halts at his ears all the alienations of the mother tongue. . . ."[4] In one section of *Adynata*, some pinkish found footage, which is reminiscent of a faded technicolor 1950s science fiction film about either creatures from outer space or irradiated monsters on earth, depicts a man with a headset listening intently and looking somewhat perplexed. The soundtrack which is rather violently appended to this image is dialogue in an Oriental language, apparently taken from the soundtrack of either a film or TV show. The man thus appears to be perplexed (in a strange evocation of the Kuleshov effect) by his inability to decipher the dialogue. Such a juxtaposition seems to produce a direct (and mocking) commentary on Barthes's dream of an unknown language and his celebration of its opacity to the Western auditor. For Thornton, opacity is opacity—it has no deeper implications.

This thwarting of the invocatory drive is paralleled by a scene which aligns Orientalism with scopophilia or a desire to see which is similarly blocked. A figure in an ornate red robe (echoing Thornton's "reproduction" earlier, of the subjects of the photograph) is glimpsed at the edge of the frame, at a point just prior to its movement out of frame, in a "walking" point-of-view shot through a sculptured Oriental garden. The image is fogged and the point of view always fails to "catch up" with its object, to achieve a secure and stable relation with it. Any fixing of the object is quite literally its death, and it is clear that the film's project entails an investigation of the murderous tendencies of representation. Toward the end of *Adynata*, there is a long section which is constituted by a distorted refilming of the final scene of Truffaut's *Shoot the Piano Player* (1960). The images are almost illegible—a shaky camera traces the movements of pencil-thin dark figures, themselves out-of-focus, against a blurry and snowy background. The most recognizable image in this context is that of the dead woman's face toward the end of the scene, accompanied by the familiar gesture of closing the eyes of the dead. The original subtitle of *Adynata* was "Murder Is Not A Story"—death is more compatible with the still image (e.g. the photograph of the Mandarin and his wife and, later, the stiff poses of the entire family) than with the narrative procedures of Truffaut's film. Here, photography becomes a form of murder (in line with both Bazin's and Barthes's theories of the relation between photography and death), particularly when it concerns the representation of the woman. In a description of the formal portrait of the Mandarin and his wife, Thornton points out that ". . . while the man appears wholesome and animated, the woman seems quite lifeless by comparison, her features made up in the stylized manner of a 'china doll.' "[5]

Hence, one of the most prominent aims of *Adynata* is comparable to that of Sally Potter's *Thriller* (1979)—to investigate the determinants of the woman's murder in/through representation. Part of that endeavor involves the examination of the "deathly" discomfort of the pose. In front of an expanse of silver cloth which fills the frame, two hands join, clasp, fidget, and rejoin, unable to find and maintain a comfortable position. Their maneuvers are accompanied by a strained and off-key humming. The thick white make-up, ornate headwear, beads and jewelry which constitute the costume of German filmmaker Karen Luner (who also masquerades as the Mandarin's wife) clearly inhibit movement (figures 9.1–2). The fact that she is seated in front of a movie light establishes her position as, precisely, a pose (figure 9.3). In a walking point-of-view shot of the ground, "bound" feet in Oriental slippers shuffle in and out of the frame. In its Western representation, the Oriental body displays a perpetual awkwardness and lack of fluidity. It is constrained, constricted, regulated—the bound foot is its most telling image. Eroticism is the rigidly ornate. The pose—"being" for the camera—forcefully orchestrates and arranges the body just as the

Figure 9.1

botanical garden organizes and controls the vicissitudes of nature for the
purposes of aestheticization.

It is not surprising that the "otherness" of Orientalism would be aligned
by Thornton with the culturally determined otherness of femininity. Both
partake of the exotic, both function to stabilize the identity of the Western
male subject.[6] The mechanism of the construction of beauty or eroticism
coincides with that by means of which otherness becomes desirable as a
deviant reflection of the same. There is a kind of morpho-logic at work
here through which shapes or forms achieve value (become obsessional)
through the mere fact of their repetition, recall, re-echoing of other shapes
or forms. One scene in *Adynata* involves a speeded-up perusal of a book
on the "art" of foot-binding in which the body is deformed in order to
produce a shape reminiscent of the perfection and delicacy of a flower petal.
And the next shot is exactly that of a languid, exquisitely shaped flower
which picks up and repeats the outline of the bound foot. The perfect
woman is a copy of nature but nature, in *Adynata*, is largely constituted by
the hyper-order of "man"-made botanical gardens. As Barthes points out,
"beauty cannot assert itself save in the form of a citation . . . left on its

Figure 9.2

Figure 9.3

own, deprived of any anterior code, beauty would be mute."[7] At points, the discursive moves of *Adynata* play out all the permutations of a sustained meditation on the function of analogy as the sometimes concealed mechanism of representation. This can be seen not only in the reiteration of comparisons between the bound and fetishized foot and flowers but also in the constant return to a process of "miming" the figures in the photograph as well as in the construction of a metonymic chain which traces a recurrent form in various objects—slippers, hands, petals (figures 9.4, 9.5). Interspersed between shots of hands wearing slippers posing in front of a wicker chair and shots of bare hands assuming the shape of those slippers as they slide into frame over lush green grass are images of a naked female torso pinned beneath a male arm. Citations of "beauty," of perfect form, circumscribe the representation of the female body.

This kind of "morpho-logic" is even more explicit in an excerpt from Thornton's *Peggy and Fred in Hell* (1985). A close-up of vibrating vocal cords is accompanied by Handel's opera, "Rinaldo" (a *bricolage* of earlier operatic pieces), superimposed over pop-Latin music by Yma Sumac from Peru (alias Amy Camus from Brooklyn), known for the range of her voice (seven octaves). The black and white image of quivering vocal cords is from a (1950s?) science film and, taken out of context, it is almost unrecognizable. The vocal cords' resemblance to female genitalia is inescapable and one gets the strange sense that we are witness to the body producing speech—a singing vulva. It is difficult to avoid a reference here to the work of Luce Irigaray, particularly her two essays, "When Our Lips Speak Together" and "This Sex Which Is Not One."[8] Irigaray's project is the extended development of a morpho-logic whereby a psychical sexuality mimics a bodily sexuality and in which the phallus is no longer the supreme arbiter of sexual difference. In Thornton's film, documentary is investigated as a site for the "scientific" dissection and analysis of the voice in its minutest bodily movements. Fragments of intertitles relating pitch to the rapidity of movement underline the fact that this is a discourse which strives to be scientific.

Yet, it is a "science" which constantly returns us to questions of sexual difference, the cultural construction of femininity and masculinity. In her film work, Thornton has consistently been interested in elaborating the way in which sexual difference is a matter of sound as well as image. In an early film, *Jennifer, Where Are You?* (1981), a man's voice, incessantly repeating the film's title in various tones and inflections, with connotations of appeal, command, and anger, accompanies an image of a little girl playing with lipstick and matches. His voice is all the more terrorizing insofar as he remains unseen.[9] She is all image; he is all voice. In the excerpt from *Peggy and Fred in Hell*, an image of the lower half of a television set is presented along with a voice which is reminiscent of "educational" voices associated with "learning by rote." The voice tells us: "Listen to the two voices which follow and decide which is the higher in pitch." The sentence produced by the two voices whose pitch we are to decide is: "The pitch most people

Figure 9.4

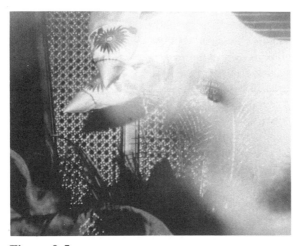

Figure 9.5

prefer for the female voice is about A flat below middle C." Later, the multiple choice test activates a male voice which informs us, "The pitch most people prefer for the male voice is around low C." The second, "preferable" male voice is recognizable as the overly familiar "neutral" voice-over of the documentary—the voice which inhabits that space outside the image, a space of reserve, authority, transcendental Otherness, in short—knowledge. In Thornton's work one often gets the sense that the most oppressive site of patriarchal authority is the soundtrack rather than the image. In *Adynata*, "maleness" on the soundtrack is evidenced not in a voice but as heavy measured footsteps which contrast with the image of simultaneous deformation and delicacy associated with the bound female foot.

Thornton's obsession with found footage usually linked with the documentary or "science film" is partially prompted by the fact that the genre of the scientific film purports to be most neutral—or perhaps more accurately, *neuter*—with respect to its inscription of subjectivity. It is nature which appears to speak to us when *Adynata* presents time-lapse photography of emerging seedlings, shots of swaying underwater flowers blooming or pinkish shots of the earth taken from space. Other images taken from the science film or documentary include a slow track in to a spinning globe at the beginning of the film and a shot of a NASA technician monitoring communications during an early John Glenn space flight (which, interestingly, I initially misrecognized as a shot taken from a 1950s science fiction film—see above), as well as the entire section on pitch in *Peggy and Fred*. Recontextualizing this found footage, however, effects a defamiliarization of the scientific discourse and its claim to provide an objective norm for cinematic language. I am again reminded of Irigaray's work on the concealed "subject of science" and her parodies of the allegedly "voice-less" examination question: "The female child develops, according to a certain number of observations, at a more rapid pace than the male child. In particular, she talks at an earlier stage and her social skills are more advanced. Yes? No? Verifiable? Falsifiable? Are those fundamental skills employed by her to become a more desirable object for others? Hence her regression? True? False? Support your answer."[10] Similarly, Thornton's mimicking, through reinscription, of scientific genres works toward the revelation that these are, indeed, science *fictions*. The scientific film strives to connote, ironically, pure denotation and is evidence of the strength of the desire for a neutral linguistic norm, an evacuation of all subjectivity. Thornton's films remind us that all discourse—from Orientalism to the science film—involves desire.

In the dystopia of *Peggy and Fred in Hell*, the subjects are overwhelmed by a kind of technological clutter and a mise-en-scène of dysfunctional objects, out of place. In one fairly sustained shot of a TV set, wires fall from the ceiling and eventually fill the space in front of the television. Before the eyes of the spectator, the cinematic image is disemboweled, its technological substrate exposed. The only interiority, however, is a technological one. In both *Peggy and Fred* and *Adynata*, the misalignment of sound and image and the forced juxtaposition of images or objects totally alien to one another indicate the failure of any reasonable syntax. Indeed, "Adynata" is a rhetorical term meaning "A stringing together of impossibilities; sometimes a confession that words fail us." Note that "we" do the confessing but it is words that fail. And there is ultimately little to confess since the words are not "us." The topology of Thornton's filmmaking evinces a concern with surface rather than interiority—meaning spreads, it does not deepen. Words fail us, not because they are inadequate for the expression of a full interiority, but because meaning leaks out, cannot be contained by a logic of morphemes; it contaminates the gaps and absences language depends upon for the very differentiating power of their emptiness. On the soundtrack of the early *X-Tracts* (1975), Thornton *cuts* language differently, producing alternative minimal units and hence different differences. One is tempted to compare her endeavor to Kristeva's emphasis upon *echolalia* or Barthes's "grain of the voice" (both pointing toward the otherness which inhabits language). These are theories of asignification or, perhaps more accurately, the signification which escapes the constraints of socio-symbolic ordering. Yet, Thornton's choice of sounds and images often has less to do with any otherness in relation to the symbolic than with an over- or hyper-codification (e.g. Truffaut's film refilmed and combined with the soundtracks of a Betty Boop cartoon, *The Bride of Frankenstein* [1935], and a TV cop show). Readability is diminished through a surplus of codification. The "marriage" of sound and image is often an unlikely juxtaposition of two heavily regulated discourses and it is clear that what is at stake is not a dream of getting beyond codification. In *Peggy and Fred*, language speaks *through* the two children who chant limericks, folk songs, and a version of Michael Jackson's "Billie Jean." What is involved here is not Barthes's dream of an unknown language but the nightmare of a language which is overly familiar. Thornton seeks to explore its interstices.

CHAPTER TEN

"When the direction of the force acting on the body is changed": The Moving Image

I

There is a scene in *Letter from an Unknown Woman* (1948) which is frequently singled out as a metacinematic moment.[1] Lisa and Stefan, in the course of their extremely short-lived time together, visit a carnival attraction which involves sitting together in a simulated train compartment as a series of painted scenes depicting nationally specific landscapes is rolled by outside an artificial window. At one point in the scene, the forward progression of the landscapes is halted and Stefan is forced to emerge from the compartment and buy more tickets so that he and Lisa, as he tells the ticket-seller, can "revisit the scenes of our youth." His emergence from the compartment draws attention to the old man who rides a bicycle in order to provide the power for the image-producing machine. The metacinematic nature of this moment lies in the revelation of an apparatus which simulates not only a train but the cinema as well, in its simple provision of an image which *moves*. The railway passenger, like the cinema spectator, is subjected to a succession of images mediated by a frame. Similarly, the cinema, in opening onto another space—a new or "other" place—, takes the spectator somewhere he/she has never been before (or, obeying the compulsion to repeat, back to revisit familiar scenes). Whatever its particular fiction, the film produces a pleasure akin to that of the travelogue.[2]

Perhaps this explains the persistent fascination of the classical cinema with trains and railroad stations, its narrative fixation upon moments of arrival and departure. Lisa's twice-suffered loss of the object of desire (Stefan, her son) is encapsulated both times as the departure of a train (there are similar moments in *Since You Went Away* [1944] and *Now Voyager* [1942], the flickering effect of light and shadow reflected from the departing train onto the woman's face as a reinscription of the alternation of presence and absence which supports cinematic signification). Just as the half-opened door seems to condense onto a single figure the semantic value of narrative's hermeneutic codification (provoking the question, "What is behind the door?"), the train embodies its proairetic codification, its sequencing as a movement from here to there, its assumption of a causal connection, the "coupling" of discrete actions and events, the ultimate termination, terminus, terminal as closure. The invention of the railroad train in the early nineteenth century, as Wolfgang Schivelbusch demonstrates in an extensive study, effects a reorganization of the modern perception of space and time—a reorganization which is, peculiarly, entirely compatible with that required by filmic narrative, for it activates the spatial and temporal ellipsis, the annihilation of the space and the time "in-between" events. Schivelbusch himself finds more than an analogy here:

> . . . on one hand, the railroad opens up new spaces that were not as easily accessible before; on the other, it does so by destroying space, namely, the space between points. That in-between space, or travel space, which it was possible to "savor" while using the slow, work-intensive eotechnical form of transport, disappears on the railroads. The railroad knows only points of departure and destination. . . . In the filmic perception—i.e., the perception of *montage*, the juxtaposition of the most disparate images into one unit—the new reality of annihilated in-between spaces finds its clearest expression: the film brings things closer to the viewer as well as closer together.[3]

Schivelbusch invokes the work of Benjamin to support his claim that just as the film, the art of reproduction *par excellence,* destroys the "aura" of individual objects, the train annihilates the "aura" of the spatial/geographical location, its isolation and hence its individuality.[4]

Thus, the train is not simply a faster means of transportation. It is a crucial element in a chain of new technologies and machines (including photography, the cinema, and television as well as the automobile and the airplane) which profoundly affect perception. It heralds no less than a technological restructuring of the relation between the traveler/spectator, vision, and space. Vision becomes, as Schivelbusch points out, "panoramic." The velocity of the train dissolves the foreground, the preindustrial basis of the relation between traveler and landscape. Because the traveler had previously seen himself/herself as a part of the foreground, joined to the landscape, the speed of the train radically *dis*places that traveler, allotting to him/her a kind of non-space of anonymity. The traveler is "removed from that 'total space' which combines proximity and distance" and is separated from the space of perception by an "almost immaterial barrier," in the same way that glass architecture transforms the viewer into a non-inhabitant of the space which he/she can nevertheless see.[5] Such a process positions the traveler more properly as a spectator: "Panoramic perception, in contrast to traditional perception, no longer belongs to the same space as the perceived objects: the traveler sees the objects, landscapes, etc. *through* the apparatus which moves him through the world."[6]

The train, and the cinema as well, thus contribute to the detachment or dissociation of the subject from the space of perception—what might be termed a despatialization of subjectivity effected by modern technology. Because the train and "panoramic perception" appear to destabilize and fundamentally alter the terms of understanding of subjectivity and perception, effecting a crucial realignment of subject and image, the train becomes a figure of fascination not only for the cinematic but also for the philosophical and scientific imaginations. The classical cinema, through a regularization of vision and the subject's relation to the screen, reasserts and institutionalizes the despatialization of subjectivity. Yet, there are other discourses as well which take up the obsession and attempt either to theorize or rewrite the relation between the subject, vision, and space: psychoanalysis, in its insistence upon the alienating effects of identification with an image; that segment of experimental psychology which concerns itself with "visual spatialization"; and a contemporary avant-garde cinema which sets itself up in opposition to the regularizing effects of the classical cinema. These discourses represent, in part, the effects at the level of theory, the reverberations as it were, of a technological restructuring of subjectivity and perception. The purpose of this essay is to trace, in these three discourses, the repercussions of an obsession with the subject's positionality in relation to an image.

II

Three disparate but related train scenarios:

1) A black and white shot of a train platform. The only mediation between spectator/camera and the content of the image appears to be the film frame. The shot is held while on the soundtrack a voice reads one of Freud's analyses from *The Interpretation of Dreams*. After a few seconds the existence of a windowpane separating the camera lens from the object and the fact that the camera is situated in a train car are revealed by the movement of the train out of the station, a movement which temporarily destabilizes the spectatorial position on the scene. A camera set up on the

platform on the other side of the window presents a mirror image of the camera on the train. The dream analyzed on the soundtrack is attributed to a patient whose father had died six years earlier and its absurdity aligned with the representation of the father as alive. In the dream, the derailing of a train causes the father's head to be "compressed from side to side." This compression, as Freud's unraveling of the dream thoughts demonstrates, could be traced to a judgment about the mimetic value of a bust commissioned from a sculptor who had never seen the father. The trajectory of the analysis leads Freud to speculate about the relation between representation and represented object with respect to both the bust and photography. He concludes: "The absurdity of this dream was thus no more than the result of a piece of carelessness in verbal expression which failed to distinguish the bust and the photograph from the actual person. We might any of us say (looking at a picture): 'There's something wrong with Father, don't you think?' " It is at this point in the film that the train begins its movement. (This first scenario is a partial description of the last shot of Joanna Kiernan's film *Dream-Work* [1980].)[7]

2) The psychoanalyst sits in a train compartment. When the train is subjected to a particularly violent movement, the door of the adjoining washing-cabinet swings open and a man whose appearance the psychoanalyst dislikes seems ready to enter the compartment by mistake. Jumping up, the psychoanalyst recognizes that the ugly man is his own image reflected in a mirror and he experiences this momentary deception as uncanny. (This is from a footnote to Freud's essay, "The 'Uncanny.' ")[8]

3) The physicist and the philosopher of science, Ernst Mach,[9] also cited by Freud in the same footnote of "The 'Uncanny' " as a disliker of his own image, glances out the window of the train as his car travels around a curve and notices that the scenery appears to tilt over. Fascinated by this illusory phenomenon, he attempts to duplicate it in the laboratory by having himself driven around a circular track in an enclosed cardboard box. As the box is accelerated it appears to Mach to tilt over more and more. The circular movement results in a modification of the direction of the felt gravitational force acting on the body and therefore affects the subject's perception of what is upright. Mach concludes, as a result of the experiments conducted on himself, that orientation toward the upright is based primarily upon bodily or postural experiences and not upon a relation to the visual field. Seventy-five years later, in 1950, H. A. Witkin, an American experimental psychologist, writes a scientific article entitled "Perception of the Upright When the Direction of the Force Acting on the Body is Changed"—an article which cites this perceptual experience of Mach as a kind of Ur-narrative authorizing Witkin's own series of experiments. Witkin constructs

a rotating room apparatus, very similar to that of Mach—a kind of train without windows, in his attempt to ascertain the relative contributions of postural/bodily experiences and dependence on the visual field to the determination of what is upright. Witkin's results demonstrate that Mach, generalizing from only his own experience, fixated on an extreme point of what is in fact a very broad spectrum of individual differences in the relative extent of dependency on the body or vision as a standard for locating the upright. Statistics prove, according to Witkin, that on the whole, dependency upon the visual field is more significant despite degrees of individual difference.[10] He will later organize these differences in particularly interesting ways.

Aside from the fact that all three scenarios take place on a train, they each exhibit a fascination with appearances which are deceiving, mobilizing the trompe l'oeil as a structuring device. The relations between the first two scenarios are, perhaps, the most explicit. The first scenario contains the barest articulation—the minimal number of elements: a frame, an image, movement, a threshold (the pane of glass), the voice expounding the principles of mimesis and its bottom line—a carelessness in wording. Furthermore, the absent author represented by the reading voice-over— Freud—is both character in and author of the second scenario. The third scenario delineates the fictional origin of a discourse which strives to be both author-less and character-less—a scientific discourse. The undoubtedly overly ambitious goal of this essay is to examine certain connections between these three types of discourse: a contemporary independent avant-garde cinema insofar as it appeals to psychoanalysis as a pretext for its signifying activities in an attempt to restructure the relation between spectator and image; psychoanalysis itself insofar as it is dependent upon the registers of narrativity and visual imagery; and experimental psychology in its attempt to articulate the "scientific" laws connecting vision, space, and the body.

Freud relegates the determination of the uncanny effect of his particular trompe l'oeil (apprehending a mirror image as real) to that other scene— the unconscious. In the subsequent theorization of a split subjectivity which Lacan so ardently pursues—in which Freud's dislike of his own image during his rather late experience of the mirror phase can be easily linked to the aggressivity characteristic of the imaginary register—the trompe l'oeil is a structuring element of subjectivity. The distinctions between fiction and the real, internal and external, subject and object are established in relation to an image of the self which is, ultimately, alienating. Within the discourse of psychoanalysis, the trompe l'oeil is internal to the construction of subjectivity. In the discourses of science and the cinema, on the other hand, the trompe l'oeil can only be defined as external, accidental in relation to subjectivity. The trompe l'oeil is constituted as a threat which must be contained. For Jean-Louis Comolli, this scenario describes a prehistory and a history of the alliance between the cinema and a scientific discourse on perception.

Comolli argues that the cinema can be understood as a compensation at the level of ideology for the scientific obsession with evidence that the eye can be fooled, that it no longer offers a guarantee of epistemological security. Photography provides the major challenge to the supremacy of the human eye, mechanizing and hence displacing/replacing the power attributed to the eye. At the same time that photography strengthens confidence in perspective and analogy (the eye's "principles of representation"), it also promotes "a crisis of confidence in the organ of vision which till then had reigned over all representation as its official standard scientifically." The renewal and intensification in the late nineteenth century of an obsession with optical illusions and the instruments which exploit them is a symptom of this crisis of confidence. And, according to Comolli's account,

> the doubt on the scientific level in some sense provoked a compensating and cushioning reaction on the level of ideology, so that the inscription of the doubt and deficiency was systematically compensated for by the inscription of the normality and centrality of the eye. It is in this sense that we can agree with Marcelin Pleynet that the code of the *perspectiva artificialis* has acted as a repressive system.[11]

Because the trompe l'oeil constituted a threat, it was necessary to break down the adherence to the visual field and to systematically organize relations to that field in ways which required a machinery, a technology. The cinema (and, in fact, all systems for the reproduction of images, photography and television included) introduces a separation between vision and the individual subject through mechanization and the easy collusion of science and technique. It allows for the possibility of thinking vision through structures which exceed but nevertheless corroborate individual subjectivity. Vision, which had formerly quite clearly "belonged" to the individual subject, is expropriated by the machine. Mainstream cinema, in both its very form and its privileging of narrative, contributed to what Comolli describes as the historical and ideological necessity of a "perspective and analogous representation of the world (the photographic image can't be argued with, it shows the real in its truth). . . ."[12] As a machine for stabilizing the relation to the visual field, the cinema is an institutionalized control of the trompe l'oeil. Sporadic critiques of the cinema or television as socially harmful are the leakages, the excesses which escape that controlled modulation of the "trick."

But why is the trompe l'oeil threatening? Or, more accurately perhaps, why does it operate simultaneously as fascination and threat? From the psychoanalytic point of view, the trompe l'oeil exhibits without mediation or modification the splitting of the subject, the subject's lack of presence to itself, by foregrounding the image's potential to mislead. The eye, as a metonymy of the "I" of subjectivity is "taken in." The first image which "fools" the human subject is its own, the mirror reflecting an unfamiliarly unified and coherent body—a more secure image in which the subject would prefer to reside, the first glimpse of subjectivity thus constituting itself on the basis of an alienating identification which is not acknowledged as such. Yet, in the trompe l'oeil in art, the eye is "taken in" or deceived only momentarily, the entire aesthetic effect being dependent upon the eventual recognition that the painting is, in fact, a painting. While "*trompe l'oeil,* i.e., 'that which deceives the eye,' strives relentlessly to achieve perfect duplication of reality to the point of *de*lusion," it must also be clear that "from the nature of things, the delusion or 'trickery' cannot endure very long, so that the ultimate result will indeed be precisely 'to impress . . . with a demonstration of technical virtuosity.' "[13] While the deception of the eye is in process, however, the trompe l'oeil elicits the desire to touch, to transgress the barrier between spectator and image (as one art critic points out, its objects are "teasingly tangible"[14]). The eventual revelation of its status as deception or pretense is jolting because it demonstrates that the eye/"I" does not possess an unshakeable position of knowledge.

There is a sense, then, in which the trompe l'oeil effects a hyperbolization of the positioning of the spectator in illusionistic or realistic artistic practices. Realism in representation always requires the spectator to adopt the stance of the fetishist, weighing simultaneously the belief that the represented matter conveys the truth of the real and the knowledge that the representation is only a representation. The trompe l'oeil, on the other hand, operates a separation in time of the two components of fetishism, belief and knowledge, so that the contradiction between the two is more apparent. This delaying of "knowledge" as a secondary temporal effect is demonstrated by one of the "rules" of the trompe l'oeil aesthetic which demands that the frame contain but in no instance cut off the elements of the painting: ". . . the composition of a *trompe l'oeil* should exist strictly within the limits of the frame—that is to say that there should not be any cutting off by the frame of any of the objects as can happen in a still-life. For instance a shelf of objects which may be exquisitely painted will not deceive the eye if the ends are cut off abruptly by the frame."[15] Acknowledgment of the frame must clearly succeed the moment when the eye is "taken in." The ultimate recognition of the frame in trompe l'oeil thus produces a shock or a jolt which is uncharacteristic of realism or illusionism.[16] It is for this reason that Lacan produces the neologism *dompte-regard,* as a parallel to trompe l'oeil: ". . . there is in painting a certain *dompte-regard,* a taming of the gaze, that is to say, that he who looks is always led by the painting to lay down his gaze. . . ."[17] Realist painting involves a process of taming or reassuring while the trompe l'oeil on the one hand fascinates or thrills and on the other threatens.

The threat of the trompe l'oeil lies in the fact that it is constituted as the undoing of a psychical defense. For fetishism, in psychoanalytic theory, binding together knowledge and belief, acts as a defense against a castration which signifies to the subject his own structuring lack, a fundamental splitting of subjectivity. Similarly, fetishism in the cinema holds at bay this trauma of lack or absence, producing a coherent subject-spectator. In the tromple l'oeil, however, fetishism as a defense is broken down into its elements and analyzed, forcing a gap between knowledge and belief, indicating the re-emergence of lack and unveiling the subject's unity as fundamentally contradictory. This is why the cinema operates as an institutionalized control of the effects of trompe l'oeil.

Yet the apparent neutrality and undifferentiation—in relation to sexual politics—of this description is misleading. For the splitting of subjectivity in psychoanalysis is given meaning (or holds meaning in the balance) not through sight in general but by means of a quite specific sight—that of the female body as representation of castration. For the masculine subject, the most threatening sight of all, the woman, is the trompe l'oeil *par excellence.*[18] The absence she represents can only be a trick against which the masculine subject must constantly be on guard. The use of the concept of fetishism in film theory (whether applied to technique, special effects, or the impression of the real) acquiesces to a view of the cinema itself as a defense against femininity—quite apart from any relay of looks within the diegesis and quite apart from specific representations of the female body. For the psychical threat which the cinema as an institution allays is inextricably bound up with the construction of sexual difference.

III

Is the avant-garde cinema any different with respect to this aspect of phallocentric mechanisms? For independent films are not, of course, independent of the technological base of the cinema. Classical cinema diminishes and controls the threat of the trompe l'oeil by making the image central to its reality, by constituting itself on a large scale as a trick of the eye with a deeper, more profound truth which justifies the trick. And because it is the eye which is threatened and not the ear, sound is subordinated to image. Outside its positioning within a specific economic circuit of distribution and exhibition, a film presents itself to us as avant-garde in the measure to which the image is seen as inadequate to the real (in terms of any notion of immediacy) or displaced from its classical function as narrative support. As an investigation of the repressed of the dominant cinema, the avant-garde film explores the extent of the image's deception. In all but the most lyrical of avant-gardes the task is to interrogate the integrity of the image rather than to preserve it. Far from feeling threatened by the trompe l'oeil, the independent avant-garde film explores its multiple ramifications.

Nevertheless, there is a sense in which a contemporary independent cinema and its theorization resuscitate, in a different way, a fear which is historically linked with the trompe l'oeil. The fear elicits defensive signifying strategies which are, however, the underside of those of the classical narrative text. There is a certain metonymic slippage here between vision, the image, the eye, and the "I" of subjectivity. In the terms of Comolli's argument, the cinema as an institution is a response to the fact that human vision is threatened by its mechanization. Because vision is an extremely important register of the credibility of the subject's knowledge, because it has acted as a guarantee of the subject's centeredness and unity, a strict codification of imagistic systems of signification was necessary. Much of the work of the contemporary independent cinema is, however, predicated upon a slippage—a movement from the idea that vision is threatened from without to the notion that vision is in itself threatening. It is the image itself which is a lure and a trap. The threat of the image is located in what is specified as its automatic attribute of immediacy—a closeness to the real which can only be illusory. In other words, a fear of the trompe l'oeil, of the image which may deceive, which is undependable, is transformed into a fear of the image which is somehow inherently, even naturally deceptive. An ontology of the image slips in and the deception of the image is naturalized. Of course, this idea is not new. Plato and other philosophers have warned against the deceptiveness of perception and the illusory nature of painting—as a mere appearance of an appearance, copy of a copy. Yet, this tendency in the conceptualization of vision and imagery is undergoing a strong resuscitation at the moment, and it is a revival which clearly hopes to differentiate between itself and idealism.

Such a localization of the image as danger and threat is given substantial support by psychoanalytical theory, particularly in its conceptualization of the imaginary register, a register frequently conflated with that of the image. One can, for instance, cite Lacan's claim that, "In this matter of the visible, everything is a trap . . . ."[19] Lacan's use of such terms as "trap," "capture," and "lure" in his discussion of visual imagery situates the question of the subject's relation to an image as the problem of defining the borderline between two realities—that of the animal and that of the human. Roland Barthes, forgetting momentarily that Lacan specifies the relation to the mirror as a boundary between the chimpanzee and the "little man," invokes a "zoological horizon" in his discussion of the imaginary: "The image-system (*l'imaginaire*), total assumption of the image, exists in animals (though the symbolic does not), since they head straight for the trap, whether sexual or hostile, which is set for them."[20] Yet, in the case of the mimetic image, the question of the extent to which human beings and animals are "lured" and whether or not they are "fooled" in quite the same way becomes much more complex, as Lacan attempts to demonstrate by invoking the story of Zeuxis and Parrhasios (discussed earlier in Chapter Three). Challenged by his rival, Parrhasios, Zeuxis drew a painting of grapes which attracted birds who attempted to peck at them. But when Zeuxis demanded that Parrhasios draw aside the veil which covered his painting, he was shocked to find that the veil itself was painted. Lacan uses the story to establish a distinction between the "natural function of the lure" and that of trompe l'oeil: ". . . if one wishes to deceive a man, what one presents to him is the painting of a veil, that is to say, something that incites him to ask what is behind it."[21] Absence not presence informs the human involvement with the image and Parrhasios's painting invokes the fundamental dimension of lack and desire.

Nevertheless, despite Lacan's construction of an opposition between the lure and the trompe l'oeil, contemporary filmmakers and theorists of the avant-garde have been quick to isolate the function of the image as that of the lure, describing it as entrapping, fascinating, captivating. From this perspective, the work of an alternative cinema must be a work against these properties of the image. Far from a promotion of "heading straight for the trap," the contemporary avant-garde could be described as a proliferation of means of avoiding the snare of the image. The image which threatens to capture and immobilize the spectator must constantly be held at bay, for there is always the danger that the spectator may lose himself/herself in that image.

This is, of course, a bit of an overstatement of the problem and is ultimately more true of the theorization of the independent cinema than of the independent cinema itself, which cannot help but resort to the image in the construction of its discourse. Nevertheless, the theory and the fear which it embodies do have their effects. Constance Penley, in arguing against the minimalist structural cinema of Peter Gidal and Malcolm Le-Grice, presents a precise and very articulate statement of a widespread understanding linked with the theorization of the cinematic signifier as imaginary and hence associated with the realm of the lure. Penley's formulation casts serious doubt on Vertov's notion of a "politics of perception."

> In terms of a political filmmaking practice, a practice whose emphasis is on transformation rather than transgression, is there any way to eliminate the imaginary relation between spectator and screen? . . . There is perhaps only one way to complicate this particular (imaginary) relation: language can offer us an oblique route through the image; it can "unstick" us a little from the screen as Barthes would say. The films of Godard have systematically taken into account this work of language on image, as have those of Straub and Huillet and Laura Mulvey and Peter Wollen. Images have very little analytical power in themselves; their power of fascination and identification is too strong. This is why there must always be a commentary *on* the image simultaneously with the commentary *of* and *with* them.[22]

This suspicion of the image is not carried over to the technico-sensory unity of sound—although it too can partake of the imaginary. Nor does the approach question the way in which language is inhabited by the imaginary. Rather than promoting the regulation of a deceptive image by language, it might be better to attempt an understanding of how many of these films concern themselves with what Peter Wollen refers to as the "interface between image and word."[23]

Yet, in many ways it is apparent that the independent cinema has taken this demand to "unstick" the spectator from the screen quite seriously. It has done so primarily through a recourse to other already highly formalized and regulated discourses—in particular, psychoanalysis. In Surrealism, psychoanalysis was used to provide a logic, a syntax (even though this takes form as an anti-logic, or anti-syntax). In contemporary independent cinema, psychoanalysis is mobilized as a text—a text which is necessary to mediate the spectator's relation to a dangerous image, a "sticky" image. While it is quite hazardous and ultimately inaccurate to generalize about *an* independent cinema as a homogeneous entity (a "unity" which in fact conceals a diversity of filmmaking practices), there is nevertheless a marked tendency in many contemporary independent films to resort to psychoanalysis as a mediating language. Examples—which vary greatly in the extent and type of references to psychoanalysis—include: *Dream-Work, Sigmund Freud's Dora* (1980), *Raw Nerves: A Lacanian Thriller* (1980), *Journeys from Berlin/1971* (1980), *Riddles of the Sphinx* (1977), and *The Story of Anna O.* (1979). *Journeys from Berlin/1971* radically circumscribes the limits of psychoanalysis in its discourse, inscribing the transformation by means of which the dialogical becomes the monological in a sustained relation to the camera/spectator which redefines the psychoanalytic session. Films like *Dora* and *The Story of Anna O.*, on the other hand, are structurally dependent upon the form of the case history—whether or not they embody a critique of the psychoanalytic writing of the woman. The project of *Raw Nerves* consists of extracting narrativity from the Lacanian drama and subjecting it to a textual play. While psychoanalysis is often mobilized specifically in conjunction with an analysis of sexual difference (*Dora, Riddles of the Sphinx*), this is not always the case.

This sustained activation of intertextuality, the strategy of multiplying discourses, operates as a defense against the homogeneity of realism and its presumption of an innocent, transparent image. It is a strategy which is not foreign to psychoanalysis itself. Freud mediates an inevitably problematic contact with the unconscious through a sporadic but consistent appeal to literature as a privileged site of its access. This is not, however, because the unconscious is composed of images but because its principles are linguistic through and through.

In some independent avant-garde films the use of psychoanalysis to mediate a relation to the image is quite literal in that the division of labor between image and sound corresponds to the extreme reduction whereby the image is designated imaginary lure and language becomes the sole realm of the symbolic. Think of the extent to which the "voice of Freud" figures in films like *Dream-Work* and *Dora* for instance. Nevertheless, the recourse to psychoanalysis is clearly an overdetermined configuration. While part of the film-work involves the importation of the seemingly heterogeneous discourse of psychoanalysis, there is also a claim that this discourse *is* only *seemingly* heterogeneous to that of the cinema—witness the constantly cited coincidence of the births of psychoanalysis and the cinema as well as the demonstrations of a convergence of psychical mechanisms in the function of spectatorship. The contemporary fascination of psychoanalysis is also indissolubly linked with its status as a kind of image-repertoire, a treasury of images and scenarios—even narratives—which can be invoked at will, redistributed and rearranged and whose very process of citation seems to insure a buffer against any potential ideological complicity. The imaginary is reinserted at another level—psychoanalysis becomes cinema's new imaginary. It allows this cinema to qualify images and narrative while still exploiting their structure.

IV

Whether it is the eye which is described as deceptive (as manifested in the fear of trompe l'oeil against which the classical cinema defends itself) or the image (as a lure which the avant-garde cinema either critiques or mediates)—the idea is the same: to regulate and secure access to the visual field. But the cinema is also clearly not the only institution which has a stake in the organization of modes of seeing. Upon the birth of the cinema, science did not cease its investigation of the effects and determinations of trompe l'oeil. But while the cinema effected a synthesis of vision and of movement, science was interested in their breakdown and analysis (as, for instance, in the work of Marey and Muybridge). Marey claimed that "animated photographs," i.e. the cinema, could "remove none of the illusions" of our eyes: "The real value of a scientific method is the way that it compensates for the inadequacy of our senses and corrects their errors."[24] The third scenario presented at the outset of this paper outlines one tendency in this extended project to "compensate for" and "correct" the errors of our senses. The narrative of Ernst Mach, a narrative of pure observation—the chance glance of a man out the window of a train which appears to confirm the neutrality and indifference of science, its impartiality—motivates and authorizes a series of investigations by an experimental psychologist, Witkin. Witkin's project is the mapping and thus constraining of the inadequacy of vision—its susceptibility to the trompe l'oeil.

Experimental psychology, because it assumes a unity of consciousness as an attribute of the subject, is a discourse which for most theorists is diametrically opposed to psychoanalysis. From the point of view of psychoanalysis, experimental psychology is complicit with the defensive, unifying function of the ego—a function which constantly seeks to conceal from the subject its own fundamental splitting, the fact of the unconscious. Another problem with the purportedly "scientific" investigations of experimental psychology is that the subject is treated as pure object. The dialogical relation of psychoanalysis is reduced to the monological and effects of anticipation on the part of the subject—the engagement of another subjectivity, in short—can never be taken fully into account. There is always a remainder, a margin, in a discourse which assumes a certain fullness. While psychoanalysis is not without its own dreams of scientificity, it has the decided advantage of situating the desire of the analyst as a crucial element in the process of theorizing.[25] Nevertheless, and despite such marked differences between the two types of discourse, it is also interesting, and far less frequent an enterprise, to note their convergences. For both discourses, in their attempts to map the relations between vision, space, and subjectivity, reinscribe a certain understanding of the sexual differentiation of processes of looking. In this sense, both can be read symptomatically as privileged theoretical rationalizations of a broader cultural positioning of the feminine and the masculine. Witkin's project, with its quite divergent assumptions about subjectivity and what constitutes a science, converges with psychoanalysis on this issue.

Witkin developed and popularized a number of tests and experiments which came to be classified under the general rubric of "spatial visualization." The experiment inspired by Mach's story, because it involved mimicking the effect of a train ride, necessitated a fairly complex technological apparatus whereby the subject was situated in a closed car which was rotated along a circular track at two different speeds. During this process, the subject was asked to adjust a rod in the car to the true vertical and horizontal. Because the rod was covered with luminous paint, it was possible for the experimenter to remove the visual field (provided by the corners of the car, outlined with white tape and two framed pictures hung on the front wall of the car) simply by turning off the lights. In a second series of experiments, the subject was asked to adjust either the chair or the box itself to the true upright position. This apparatus allowed Witkin to dissociate what he posited as the two determinants of perception of the upright: 1) visual space (which is "filled with proper verticals and horizontals" which "provide a basis for judging the direction of the upright"[26]) 2) the gravitational pull on the body. When the subject is rotated by the apparatus the effective force on the body is changed—it is calculated as the resultant of the lateral centrifugal force and the downward gravitational force. Earlier experiments effected a change in the visual field simply by tilting the only visual frame available to the subject for the determination of the vertical and the horizontal. Witkin found, unlike Mach who tested only himself, that his subjects depended much more heavily on the visual field in the determination of the upright than on bodily sensations.

But he "found" much more. Granted an overall significantly greater dependency on the visual field, there was a very wide range of individual differences in relative dependency on that field. Witkin found a satisfactory means of organizing these differences by aligning them with the "most indisputable" difference of all—sexual difference. It is not until the second article ("Further Studies of Perception of the Upright When the Direction of the Force Acting on the Body Is Changed") that the decision is made to correlate individual differences with sexual differences—apparently insuring retrospectively the sexual neutrality of the very categories of description, the separation of perception into its two components—visual space and the body. Witkin concluded that "women rely less on bodily experiences, or adhere more strongly to the standard offered by the visual field, in determining the upright."[27] Interestingly, this formulation allows women to be more accurate than men in the train-simulation experiments which effect a change in the force acting on the body. But Witkin and others multiplied the number and kinds of experiments which claimed a kinship in their testing of what were called visual-spatial skills: the rod and frame test where the frame is tilted, imbedded figure tests, experiments on bodily steadiness in the face of an unstable visual field, and tests of the relative dependency on visual and auditory phenomena. In almost all of these areas, the purportedly demonstrable overadherence of women to the visual field puts them at a disadvantage in relation to any norm of accuracy. Men's relatively greater dependence upon the body as a standard puts them at a disadvantage only in very limited and highly regulated situations—in trains which travel in circles. The image is indeed a lure in this context. Women, like animals, seem to head straight for the trap, whether sexual or hostile, which is set for them.

In an article entitled "Sex Differences in Perception," Witkin attempted to synthesize and interpret his findings in terms which are particularly revealing. While most subjects "go along with" the visual field, women "go along" with it further than men. In a test in which the subject was required to straighten his/her body when the room was tilted, women tilted themselves farther in the direction of the field than did men; they manifested a tendency to align their bodies with the visual field. Witkin concludes: "Thus, women, in their perception of body position also, tended to be more strongly influenced by the surrounding field and to give less credit to bodily sensations than men."[28] In the rod and frame tests "women tended to adjust the rod in accordance with the position of the frame to a greater extent than did men, and they proved less able to involve the body in making their adjustments."[29] Glued to their surroundings, unable even to take their own bodies into account, women are at the mercy of an unstable visual field. What this demonstrates, for Witkin, is that women are unable to make distinctions, to differentiate, and ultimately, to be as analytical in their perception as men. This is why women cannot read maps.

As one feminist biologist points out, "When all else fails, spatial visualization is the one arena cited again and again as a clearcut example of how the members of each sex think differently."[30] Spatial visualization is an extremely malleable concept; it can and does authorize a variety of repressive operations without appearing to be overtly sexist. It is flexible enough to be linked not only with general intelligence and analytical ability (or the lack thereof) but with conformity and passivity as well.[31] Michèle Le Doeuff describes the claim to authority made by a scientific discourse, "Here, an author speaks in the name of facts; his discourse, which thus boasts an extrinsic criterion of legitimacy (as indeed religious discourse had done), can thereby occult its own discursive operation, and so proceed to dogmatise as it chooses."[32] She delineates the chiasma which is proper to the "spatial imagination": sexual difference does not reside in the genitals but everywhere else—in the brain, the senses, the nervous system, etc. A contemporary scientific discourse finds that the inevitable psychosexual brain differences are manifested in the area of *spatial* aptitude because

> "spatial aptitudes" are a vague enough datum ("seeing in three dimensions") to be said to operate everywhere. An inequality of this order can have an indefinitely wide domain of application, in everyday life (driving a car, reading a map) as much as in work (the whole of mechanical industry; scientific education too; the professions of architecture, engineering, art). And as space means the right-hand hemisphere and the right-hand hemisphere means creation, if your daughter doesn't compose music you can blame space for that as well . . . . A mere hump or lobe, or some single convolution of the cerebral cortex would not have been enough. It was not sufficient to invoke some "narrowly specialized" handicap; it had to be some general dimension of existence. Hence, a whole hemisphere . . . . The practical consequences are easily arrived at: if small girls are less gifted at mastering spatial relationships, one would be wise to keep them at home.[33]

Agoraphobia is only the most extreme instance of such a construction of the feminine just as anorexia is symptomatic of a cultural denegation of the female body—its wished for disappearance. More pertinently for this study, the woman's purported lack of skills in the area of visual spatialization—her overadherence to the visual field—would seem to indicate that she is more susceptible to the trompe l'oeil. Far from being a better spectator of the cinema, adhering more closely to the image she is more likely to be "taken in" by it.

The discourse of experimental psychology is, on this point, fully compatible with that of psychoanalysis. For experimental psychology relegates women once again, and in its own fashion, to the realm of the imaginary. The terms of Witkin's experiment presuppose a division in the subject's relation to perception which is articulated with sexual difference only apparently "after the fact." The paradigm which informs the structuration of the experiment opposes the body to visual space, distance (from the image) to closeness, and an internal frame of reference to an external frame of reference (the actual terms used by the experimenters are "field independent" and "field dependent"). The woman "goes along with" the visual field—if the image sways, she sways. Her deficiency is pinpointed as an inability to differentiate—space is all enveloping and the limits of her own subjectivity are not acknowledged. In short, she is incapable of dealing with difference, the analytical category *par excellence*. In the terms of another discourse, she has a negative entry into the Symbolic—is denied access to the distancing effects of Symbolic operations. Experimental psychology gives to the male a more rational, more discursive control of the image, the ability to balance knowledge and belief (in vision) which is characteristic of fetishism. In the experiments conducted by Witkin, the man, unlike the woman, uses his own body (and its felt gravitational pull) as a standard of judgment; it is fully representable within discursive operations. The male body "has that which lends itself to the phallic symbol";[34] the female body, an undifferentiated presence, denies her access to the processes of representation. Gravity and the phallus are in collusion. Two theories which maintain entirely antithetical understandings of subjectivity cooperate in the assignment of a place to the woman—a standard relation to vision, the body, and space.

From this perspective, it is quite problematic to refuse or invalidate Vertov's "politics of perception" based on psychoanalytic ideas concerning the lure of the image, its insufficiency. For, a politics of perception is already in process whether we acknowledge it or not. Visual space is continually being outlined, territorialized, divided along sexual lines. Women have not only the specific space which is their allotment (the home, the kitchen) but a *relation* to space which is assigned to them. And it is this relation which is ultimately more oppressive—because it covers, controls, secures, oversees in advance all possibilities. What is elided in the strategy of fastening upon the image as lure, as non-analytical in itself, is the sexual specificity of such a description. The image *is* a lure to the extent that it draws one closer, but fetishism allows the male spectator to maintain a distance. Classical cinema controls the possibility of trompe l'oeil by institutionalizing it and simultaneously invoking fetishistic mechanisms. To protect the spectator (whether through critique or mediation) against the "deceptive" image is to redouble fetishistic mechanisms, not to escape them. In the hopes of increasing knowledge at the expense of a regressive belief (the two being apparently locked together in a restrictive economy), this theory can only further the cause of a knowledge which is phallocentric. The figurative matrix generated by the alliance of closeness with belief and distance with knowledge involves the transformation of an epistemology into spatial terms. If it is true that one has to start from where women are or, more accurately, from the place to which they have been assigned—instead of immediately assuming an elsewhere—this strategy can only leave them behind.

It might, perhaps, be more useful to encourage work on the possible modes of transformation of the relation to space in film. As Stephen Heath points out, in the narrative film space is organized, ruled, and regulated by the notion of "place." "Space becomes place" and the "point of that conversion" is the frame, its limits and certainty legalized by an academy ratio: "What is crucial is the conversion of seen into scene, the holding of signifier on signified: the frame, composed, centered, narrated, is the point of that conversion."[35] The frame is thus the crucial site for a narrative work on space. It is difficult to imagine, however, a relation to space which would be independent of the coherency and stability of the notion of place—its narrativizing effects: "every picture tells a story." In an article entitled "Place Names," Julia Kristeva attempts to delineate the attributes of that threshold which marks the transformation of space (the field of laughter as a non-differentiated semiosis invoking a participation of the body) into place (named and hence rationalized, symbolized through the mediation of the Father):

> Chronologically and logically long before the mirror stage (where the Same sees itself altered through the well-known opening that constitutes it as representation, sign, and death), the semiotic disposition makes its start as riant spaciousness . . . . We note that beginning with the "first point of psychic organization," light-giving marker or mother's face, which produced laughter along with the first vocalizations, the future speaker is led to separate such points into *objects* (transitional at first, then simply objects) and add to them *no longer laughter but phonation*—archetype of the morpheme, condensation of the sentence. As if *the laughter that makes up space had become, with the help of maturation and repression, a "place name."*[36]

While the image is implicated in the recognition/misrecognition of self, visual space is also framed (transformed into a series of "this's" and "that's") and contributes to the very possibility of recognition, nameability. The use of "this" and "that" in language precedes the recourse to "I" and "me." It is as though it were absolutely crucial to outline a space which the "I"—not yet formulated—could subsequently inhabit. Positionality—not necessarily the visual image in itself—is the coagulant of identity.

Work on the transformation of identities—sexual identities included—

will thus necessarily involve a reworking of the relations between space and place. A redefinition of narrative, forcing it to conform to another logic, will affirm the ambiguity of its central signifying dictum—"to take place." The phrase "to take place" points toward a dialectic of passivity and activity—connoting both "that which happens" and the seizure of a position.

The pleasure generated by the final shot of Joanna Kiernan's film, a pleasure in some ways peripheral to the project of the film as a whole—its leakage or excess—lies in its articulation of movement, process, and the stasis of recognition. It is the movement of the train/camera which makes the image fully recognizable, locatable, readable. The pleasure in non-recognition, in the subject's displacement, is by definition momentary, temporary. It is only retrospectively, from a position of stability (paradoxically moving), which itself may be upset at any moment, that the pleasure is possible. And this is accomplished through a disphasure of the two frames—the frame of the film, the frame of the train window. From inside the train, where women finally have the advantage, the train figures differently. It is no longer the privileged trope of the classical narrative, embodiment of a masculine imperative to dominate space, fetishizing moments of arrival and departure in the service of a proiaretic chain linking car to car and cause to effect. Taking one from here to there no longer rationalizes narrative—is no longer the elision of an absent space and time. (A film like *Jeanne Dielman, 23 Quai du Commerce, 1080 Bruxelles* [1975] is explicit on this point: the elided moments of traditional narrative are constitutive of the woman's story.) The narrative train of Freud, Mach, and of Witkin—the site of philosophical, psychological, and psychoanalytic speculation about perception, the self, and sexual difference—becomes, contradictorily, the site of both trompe l'oeil and its recognition/affirmation—a mimesis which is no longer threatening.

IV. At The Edges of Psychoanalysis

CHAPTER ELEVEN

Dark Continents: Epistemologies of Racial and Sexual Difference in Psychoanalysis and the Cinema

I. THE DARK CONTINENT AS TROPE

Freud's use of the term "dark continent" to signify female sexuality is a recurrent theme in feminist theory. The phrase transforms female sexuality into an unexplored territory, an enigmatic, unknowable place concealed from the theoretical gaze and hence the epistemological power of the psychoanalyst. Femininity confounds knowledge while male sexuality is its stable guarantee. Yet, the more pertinent question may not be "What is the dark continent?," but "Where is it?" The fact that Freud himself borrowed the phrase from Victorian colonialist texts in which it was used to designate Africa is often forgotten. As Patrick Brantlinger points out, "Africa grew 'dark' as Victorian explorers, missionaries, and scientists flooded it with light, because the light was refracted through an imperialist ideology that urged the abolition of 'savage customs' in the name of civilization."[1] The term is the historical trace of Freud's link to the nineteenth century colonialist imagination. In its textual travels from the colonialist image of Africa to Freud's description of female sexuality as enigma to feminist theorists' critique of psychoanalysis (particularly in Luce Irigaray's *Speculum of the Other Woman*), the phrase has been largely stripped of its historicity. Something of Freud's link to this colonialist imagination has been lost as well. For although Freud did not recapitulate "an imperialist ideology that urged the abolition of 'savage customs' in the name of civilization," the binary opposition between the savage and the civilized in their relation to sexuality was a formative element of his thinking, one often dismissed in Lacanian influenced accounts as a "pre-Freudian" aspect of the Freudian text.

In a footnote to her essay on metaphor and metonymy in *Reading Lacan*,

Jane Gallop seems less concerned with the dark continent's geographical location than with its textual location.

> "Dark continent" is a term Freud used for female sexuality, a term frequently quoted in French psychoanalytic works ("continent noir"). I have not yet succeeded in locating this term in Freud's text, but that may be my blind spot.[2]

The lack of knowledge of the source of the term is not Gallop's personal "blind spot" but the blind spot of many; for the text in which it is located (or at least the only one that I have found) is quite marginal in the Freudian corpus. The dark continent trope cannot be found in any of the more obvious places one might look—it is not in "Femininity" or "Female Sexuality" nor in *Three Essays on the Theory of Sexuality*. Instead, it is tucked away almost unnoticeably in "The Question of Lay Analysis," a general treatise on psychoanalysis inspired by the quite technical problem of whether or not psychoanalysis should be practiced only by medical doctors. In the course of his discussion of the psychoanalytic theory of infantile sexuality, Freud explains that the female sexual organ plays no role in this sexuality since the child has not yet discovered it.

> Stress falls entirely on the male organ, all the child's interest is directed towards the question of whether it is present or not. We know less about the sexual life of little girls than of boys. But we need not feel ashamed of this distinction; after all, the sexual life of adult women is a "dark continent" [this term is in English in the original] for psychology. But we have learnt that girls feel deeply their lack of a sexual organ that is equal in value to the male one; they regard themselves on that account as inferior, and this "envy for the penis" is the origin of a whole number of characteristic feminine reactions.[3]

The dark continent trope is hence invoked in the context of a return to the motifs of castration, lack, and envy. The argument here is that the psychoanalyst's diminished knowledge about the sexuality of little girls is justifiable or at least understandable because he knows little or nothing about adult female sexuality as well. A metonymic chain is constructed which links infantile sexuality, female sexuality, and racial otherness. For the adjective "dark" in dark continent signifies not only unknowability but blackness in its racial connotations. Africa is "dark" because its inhabitants are "dark."

And, indeed, in the paragraph immediately preceding the one invoking the dark continent trope, Freud defends the psychoanalytic account of "the early sexuality of children" by comparing this product of psychoanalytic theory to the imagination of "primitive man." He goes on to claim that

> in the mental life of children to-day we can still detect the same archaic factors which were once dominant generally in the primaeval days of human civilization. In his mental development the child would be repeating the history of his race [*Stammesgeschichte*] in an abbreviated form, just as embryology long since recognized was the case with somatic development.[4]

This is an elaboration of Freud's well-known claim that ontogeny recapitulates phylogeny. In the English translation, "race" might seem to be more accurately replaced by "species" since Freud insists, here as well as elsewhere, on mapping the difference between the primitive and the civilized onto a temporal or historical axis rather than a spatial one. The "primitive" is the remote in time, it is the "childhood" of modern man (as the term *Stamm*—stem, trunk—suggests). Yet, Freud's dependence upon anthropological sources suggests that the notion of primitiveness is understood not only diachronically but synchronically as well—as marking the differences between races within the species. Elsewhere in this text Freud delineates how civilization is born at the expense of sexuality (whose "free rein" is henceforth associated with the "primitive" races, some of whom are undoubtedly located on the "dark continent").

> Among races [*Völkern*] at a low level of civilization, and among the lower strata of civilized races [*Kulturvölker*], the sexuality of children seems to be given free rein. This probably provides a powerful protection against the subsequent development of neuroses in the individual. But does it not at the same time involve an extraordinary loss of the aptitude for cultural achievements?[5]

These "lower" races, with their free sexuality and lack of neuroses, would be, in a sense, unpsychoanalyzable and would hence constitute the limits of psychoanalytic knowledge. The force of the category of race in the constitution of Otherness within psychoanalysis should not be underestimated. When Freud needs a trope for the unknowability of female sexuality, the dark continent is close at hand. Psychoanalysis can, from this point of view, be seen as a quite elaborate form of ethnography—as a writing of the ethnicity of the white Western psyche. Repression becomes the prerequisite for the construction of a white culture which stipulates that female sexuality act as the trace within of what has been excluded.

What is at issue in the essay, "The Question of Lay Analysis," is also in a broader sense the question of psychoanalytic knowledge and who can lay claim to its possession. It is a response to a quite specific and local debate about Austrian laws which would prohibit the practice of psychoanalysis to anyone without a medical degree ("layman" in this instance means "non-doctor"). Freud wrote "The Question of Lay Analysis" in defense of Theodor Reik who was charged by a patient with breaking an old Austrian law against "quackery" because he did not have a medical degree. The essay is subtitled "Conversations With An Impartial Person" and is structured as a dialogue. The "impartial person," whom Freud characteristically constructs, is by no means impartial, demonstrating the usual resistances to psychoanalytic theory in order to provide Freud with a forum for the exhibition of his rhetorical powers. The essay, a curious mixture of the broadly pedagogical and the narrowly polemical, poses the problem of knowledge in two ways: 1) as the question of what, properly speaking, constitutes the specificity of psychoanalytical knowledge 2) as the question of who has the right to speak as a psychoanalyst   who has access to this knowledge, in other words, as the issue of the legalization of a position of discourse. It is not coincidental that the trope of the dark continent— merging, as it does, two unknowabilities, racial difference and sexual difference—should appear within such a context. For Otherness, whether sexual or racial, is usually articulated as a problem of the limits of knowledge and hence of visibility, recognition, differentiation. In Freud's text, women (and it should be stressed that these are *white* European women) and "primitive" races function in a similar way and through opposition to buttress the knowledge of the psyche to which psychoanalysis lays claim— with the crucial difference that white women constitute an internal enigma (Hegel's "enemy within [the community's] own gates")[6] while "primitive" races constitute an external enigma.

The dark continent trope indicates the existence of an intricate historical articulation of the categories of racial difference and sexual difference.[7] In it, there is an extraordinary condensation of motifs linking the white woman and the colonialist's notion of "blackness." Just as Africa was considered to be the continent without a history, European femininity represented a pure presence and timelessness (whose psychical history was held, by Freud, to be largely inaccessible). The trope, however, reduces and oversimplifies the extremely complex relations between racial and sexual difference articulated by the colonialist enterprise. For that enterprise required as a crucially significant element the presence of the black woman (who is relegated to non-existence by the trope). The colonialist discourses of photography, poetry, and the essay frequently equated the African woman and the African continent—the conquest of the former signified the successful appropriation of the latter. Within the context of a collection of photographs taken in Africa between 1840 and 1918, and with specific reference to a photograph entitled "Girl of Beggiuk tribe," Nicolas Monti writes,

> In a very peculiar way eroticism became a medium for establishing contact, for penetrating the secrets of nature, the reality and the "otherness" of the continent. The seduction and conquest of the African woman became a metaphor for the conquest of Africa itself. A powerful erotic symbolism linked a woman's femininity so strongly to the attraction of the land that they became one single idea, and to both were attributed the same irresistible, deadly charm.[8]

Indeed, the photographic terms of the visibility of the dark continent dictated the incessant visualization of native eroticism.[9] Within a photographic discourse which brought the dark continent home to Europeans, the exotic and the erotic were welded together, situating the African woman as the signifier of an excessive, incommensurable sexuality. These images were later invoked to blame black women for the victimization inflicted upon them by white males.

As Sander L. Gilman has demonstrated, the female Hottentot became, for Europeans, the exemplary representative of this hyperbolic sexuality. Medical dissections and treatises established her sexuality as a form of pathology associated with "enlarged buttocks" and "distended labia." Gilman also describes the nineteenth century's cultural investment in constituting a close affinity between the female Hottentot and the white prostitute who is, similarly, the object of a certain medical pathology. The prostitute's physical anomalies as delineated by "scientific" investigation as well as aesthetic representation are often strikingly comparable to those of the Hottentot, so much so that "the perception of the prostitute in the late nineteenth century . . . merged with the perception of the black."[10] In Manet's portrait, *Nana*, certain physical features such as enlarged buttocks and "Darwin's ear" indicate that "even Nana's seeming beauty is but a sign of the black hidden within. All her external stigmata point to the pathology within the sexualized female."[11] And in Zola's novel, Nana dies of smallpox and in death "begins to revert to the blackness of the earth, to assume the horrible grotesque countenance perceived as belonging to the world of the black, the world of the 'primitive,' the world of disease."[12] Yet, this special kinship between the white woman and the black woman is a quite limited one. The white woman, in her unknowability and sexual excessiveness, does indeed have a close representational affiliation with blackness. On the other hand, the "civilized" white woman, exemplar of culture, racial purity, and refinement, is situated as the polar opposite of the Hottentot. Nevertheless, what the representational affinity seems to indicate is a strong fear that white women are always on the verge of "slipping back" into a blackness comparable to prostitution. The white woman would be the weak point in the system, the signifier of the always too tenuous hold of civilization.

Whether in the colonialist discourse of photography, the medical discourse delineated by Gilman, or the aesthetic languages of the nineteenth century, the hyperbolic sexualization of blackness is presented within a visual framework; it is a function of "seeing" as an epistemological guarantee—Nana's "blackness" emerges to the surface so that it can be seen and hence verified. It is not surprising, therefore, that the cinema as an institution would embrace the colonialist project and reinscribe its terms within its uniquely optical narrative logic. The privileged genre for this inscription is the travel narrative or adventure film of the 1930s, within which Merian C. Cooper's 1933 *King Kong* would be an exemplary instance. The eroticism of *King Kong* is a result of its titillating conjunction of blonde white femininity and the immense sexual power suggested by King Kong—undoubtedly linked to fears of black masculinity and its alleged uncontainability. Here, in the Hollywood cinema, as in Freud's trope of the dark continent, the term which undergoes erasure, becomes invisible, is the black woman. The representational violence inscribed within Hollywood's colonialist project would be most predictable within the adventure/horror genre of the 1930s. But it is particularly interesting to note the presence of such violence within the genre most closely associated with the white woman—the maternal melodrama. In Josef von Sternberg's 1932 *Blonde Venus*, Marlene Dietrich does cross over the line separating respectable femininity from prostitution (whiteness from blackness in the nineteenth century imagination). Yet, within the maternal melodrama, the figure of the prostitute is not the target of an unambiguous censure but of a sympathy manifested in the textual organization of pathos. Revised sexual mores connected with the emergence of the "New Woman" in the 1920s required a more flexible understanding of white female sexuality which weakened the polarization between the respectable Victorian lady and the prostitute. Marlene Dietrich is, in fact, recuperated by the nuclear family at the end of the film. Yet, the near collapse of the moral opposition between types of white femininity also threatened to collapse certain racial distinctions as well. Nana's "blackness within" is predicated upon her role as a prostitute (the nineteenth century locus of excessive female sexuality). If the white woman's excessive sexuality cannot be contained within that subclass, the status of the upper-class white woman as guarantee of racial purity is seriously threatened.

There is a scene in *Blonde Venus* which seems to constitute a violent response to such a dilemma by reversing the process associated with Manet's and Zola's Nana. When Marlene Dietrich emerges from the ape costume in the "Hot Voodoo" number, blackness is transformed from Nana's essence within into a disguise which can be easily shed.[13] When Dietrich slowly removes the huge gorilla paws to reveal slender white hands and when she pulls off the gorilla head to exchange it for an intensely blonde wig adorned with sequined arrows, she trades one icon for another. It is as though white femininity were forcefully disengaged from blackness once and for all in the process of commodification of the image of white female sexuality.[14] Such a commodification is already announced by the neon sign flashing "Blonde Venus" which introduces the sequence and slowly dissolves into an image of Dietrich preparing for her act in front of the mirror. Blackness functions here not so much as a term of comparison (as with the Hottentot and the prostitute), but as an erotic accessory to whiteness. The black woman (represented by the chorus primarily composed of white women in black face with huge black wigs and shields and spears) becomes the white woman's mise-en-scène. Black masculinity is so fully exhausted representationally by the gorilla costume that the black bartender can only be presented in relation to a stuttering fear produced for comic effect—he tells a white female customer, "If that animal was real, I wouldn't b-b-b-b-be here." But perhaps the white woman poses a greater threat than the animal. The dark continent is inscribed here as a topos with its own value as spectacle, as *stage*.

The representational topography which situates the black woman in relation to the white woman is one which activates the registers of foreground and background, presence and absence. There is a certain mutuality in their cultural construction which is strongly inscribed in a number of discourses: psychoanalysis, the cinema, feminist theory. The purpose of this essay is to trace some of these interconnections against the larger background of the historical articulation of racial and sexual ideologies since the late nineteenth century. Why have racial differences been insistently infused with sexual desires and prohibitions? Is psychoanalysis simply complicit in this operation or is it potentially useful in its analysis? Here, I single out the work of Freud and Frantz Fanon as instances of a psychoanalytic engagement with these questions. The pivotal position of the white woman in a racist economy—a position which often relegates the black woman to a realm outside of femininity—is *enacted* in psychoanalysis in Freud's appeal to the dark continent metaphor as well as in Fanon's analysis of rape and its relation to female subjectivity. It is also enacted in the cinema, in films as diverse as D. W. Griffith's *Birth of a Nation* (1915) and Douglas Sirk's *Imitation of Life* (1959), both analyzed in some detail here. But Fanon also provides a psychoanalysis of the surface and of visibility which is potentially useful in the analysis of the cinema's racial politics. For *Birth of a Nation*, instrumental in the historical development of the classical system of narrative, directly confronts the issue of visibility and its relation to racial politics by transforming the visible aspects of racial identity—blackness and whiteness—into signs whose theatricality is marked. Sirk's *Imitation of Life*, produced at the apex of Hollywood's power, also deals with problems of visibility, racial identity, knowledge, and recognition by articulating black passing and white acting in a complex dialectical relation. The former film provides a culturally and historically specific inscription of the relations between black men and white women; the latter film, a regulated discourse on the relations between black women and white women. Both of the films raise crucial questions about the white woman's position in the articulation of racial and sexual difference and the consequences of that position for the representational status of the black woman. They also demonstrate something of the strength of the historical reverberations of the dark continent metaphor—its representational stakes.

II. PSYCHOANALYSIS AND RACE:
THE CASE OF FANON

Feminist neglect of or disregard for *where* the dark continent is located is symptomatic of a problem recently brought to the foreground in critical discourse. A psychoanalytically informed feminist theory is accused of hierarchizing sexual difference over racial difference and of being ill-equipped to deal with issues of racial oppression.[15] The allegation is not simply that psychoanalytic feminist theory has *neglected* the analysis of racial difference but that there is an active tension between them. If certain races (associated with the "primitive") are constituted as outside or beyond the territory of the psychoanalytic endeavor—insofar as they lack repression or neurosis (perhaps even the unconscious)—the solution cannot be simply to take this system which posits their exclusion and apply it to them. The trope of the dark continent, through its territorialization of the trope of knowledge, indicates a difficulty here which is both theoretical and histori-cal, to the extent that Freud's project is linked to the colonial imagination and its structuring binarism. Psychoanalysis, unshaken in its premises, cannot be *applied* to issues of racial difference but must be radically destabilized by them.

The work of Frantz Fanon (particularly *Black Skin, White Masks*) consti-tutes one of the few attempts to activate psychoanalysis in the examination and indictment of the relation between colonizer and colonized—a relation subtended by racism.[16] For Fanon, a psychoanalytical understanding of racism hinges on a close analysis of the realm of sexuality. This is particularly true of black-white relations since blacks are persistently attributed with a hypersexuality. Why is it sexuality which forms a major arena for the articulation of racism?[17] From a psychoanalytic point of view, sexuality is the realm where fear and desire find their most intimate connection, where notions of otherness and the exotic/erotic are often conflated. Whether heterosexual or homosexual, sexuality is generally thought to be indissociable from the effects of polarization and differentiation, often linking them to structures of power and domination. Fanon's Sartrean influenced *Black Skin, White Masks* organizes its investigation of colonialism and racism to a large extent through a tracing of the various permutations in the relations between black men and white women, black women and white men, and white men and black men (the excluded relation is that between white women and black women—a relation to which I will return later).

Fanon's methodology—as eclectic and unstable as it is—consistently undermines the very category of race and hence cancels the question which might appear to be its premise: Is psychoanalysis applicable to blacks? According to Fanon, the black becomes psychoanalyzable only when he/she comes in contact with whites/colonizers. It is the conjuncture between the two which produces neurotic effects and the disorienting vision of a double narcissism. For Fanon, the psyche is always already articulated with the social and the object of his analysis is not the individual but the social network of gazes, desires, fears, and transgressions born of the colonialist/imperialist enterprise. Furthermore, Fanon is intensely aware of the extent to which psychoanalysis operates at "the level of the 'failures,' "[18] the extent to which it is dependent upon categories of loss, lack, and alienation rather than the promise of an ontological fullness. His study is framed by two rather extreme statements: 1) The first, in the introduction (and repeated in the conclusion), has been the object of a great deal of perplexity and speculation—"However painful it may be for me to accept this conclusion, I am obliged to state it: For the black man there is only one destiny. And it is white" (10). 2) The second, which has received much less commentary, appears in the conclusion—"There is no white world, there is no white ethic, any more than there is a white intelligence" (229). The second could be read as a form of reply to the first, a reply which de-essentializes both blackness and whiteness (and hence race as a category). In the course of his analysis, racial identity becomes radically differential. Fanon's extremely critical relation in *Masks* to the negritude movement—its philosophy and poetry extolling "blackness"—and his persistent remarks about the inadequacy of ontology underline the destabilization of racial categories which is a fundamental aspect of his project.[19] Race relations are ensconced within the imaginary.

To the extent, however, that there *are* material and economic effects of racism, race does exist as a category of both political and psychical significance. But its meaning would be socially variable rather than biologically essential. Fanon himself acknowledges the primacy of the economic factor in the "inferiority complex" attributed to the black (11). Yet, because Fanon situates his psychoanalysis at the borders, where cultures meet, he must confine his analysis to those blacks whose extended contact with white culture qualify them as an educated elite—the *évolués*. Historically, psychoanalysis has always targeted the upper or upper-middle classes to the extent that, for Freud, neurosis is intimately associated with the degree of intensity of culture or "civilization" (recall how Freud compares the free sexuality of "races at a low level of civilization" with that of the "lower strata of civilized races"). Fanon's analysis hinges on the experience of the black man from Martinique who travels to France to study—with a persistent focus, in his text, upon the moments of departure, arrival, and return.[20] And early in *Masks*, Fanon claims that in his psychoanalysis, "The 'jungle savage' is not what I have in mind" (12). The exclusion of the "jungle savage" from the terms of Fanon's analysis is reminiscent of Freud's relegation of the "primitive" to the realm of the unpsychoanalyzable. In fact, Fanon gives assent to the homostatic system which requires Freud's structuring binarism of the primitive and the civilized. Racism is the result of the surplus sexual guilt of the white man which is generated in the process of building culture. According to Jock McCulloch,

> Fanon's account of the psychodynamics of negrophobia in both white men and white women presupposes a certain psychic dependence of the European upon the black. Through the mechanism of projection, the imago of the "genital nigger" absorbs that fund of sexual guilt which is the inevitable product of cultural development. . . . It is in this territory that Fanon absorbs the fundamental tenets of the Freudian theory of personality as a homostatic system which has culture as its product.[21]

The black man's desire to be white, much discussed by Fanon, would be the result of his identification with this conceptualization of culture and hence his automatic alienation—the black becomes his own phobic object. Fanon's acceptance of Freud's homostatic system is symptomatic of a rather conservative veneration of European culture which leads him, in *Masks*, to treat that culture as a normative standard. This is at least partially what makes it impossible for him to embrace negritude's valorization of a black cultural history, an African heritage which could ground the idea of an alternative and autonomous intellectual realm. [22] For Fanon, the confrontation and interaction of cultures is a crucial historical fact. And with it, the advent of neurosis.

The neuroses which Fanon studies circulate around the question of identity. Black desire, delineated here only in its collision with whiteness, is specified as the desire for a different ontology, the desire to be white. But, "every ontology is made unattainable in a colonized and civilized society" (109). Fanon argues that the black family, unlike the white family, is not isomorphic with the nation and the transition from one to the other by the black subject is always accompanied by trauma. The black's confrontation with whiteness is automatically pathological and most frequently takes the form of a certain mimicry. This mimicry is characteristic of both sexes and Fanon devotes a separate chapter to each, making his analysis circulate around a literary text in each instance. In the chapter entitled "The Woman of Color and the White Man," the primary text is the autobiographical *Je suis Martiniquaise* by Margotte Capécia (although there are also references to a short story, "Nini," by Abdoulaye Sadji). Fanon is relentless in his critique of Capécia's overwhelming desire to marry a white man—"She asks nothing, demands nothing, except a bit of whiteness in her life" (42). The expressed desire on the part of the black woman is to lighten and hence "save" the race; Fanon reads this as a form of pathology to which he applies the label "affective erethism." The constant slippage of pronouns here— from "she" to the generic "he" indicating the black man in general—signals the extent to which Fanon sees the black woman's desire as representative of a black pathology which he despises. There is no talk of cure—referring to Capécia, Fanon states, "May she add no more to the mass of her imbecilities. Depart in peace, mudslinging storyteller . . ." (53).

In contrast, the chapter entitled "The Man of Color and the White Woman," is a much more sympathetic account of the allegedly autobiographical novel, *Un homme pareil aux autres*, by René Maran, in which the protagonist, Jean Veneuse, experiences strong inner conflict over his desire for a white woman. Surprisingly, Fanon adamantly claims that Jean's neurosis is not color-specific, it is not representative of anything outside itself: "Jean Veneuse is a neurotic, and his color is only an attempt to explain his psychic structure. If this objective difference had not existed, he would have manufactured it out of nothing. . . . I contend that Jean Veneuse represents not an example of black-white relations, but a certain mode of behavior in a neurotic who by coincidence is black" (78–79). To the extent that *Un homme pareil aux autres* presents itself as an account of race relations, it is a "sham." Why the abrupt shift from one chapter to the next? How can one explain the vacillation of Fanon when confronted with the relations between race, psychopathology, the individual, and the social? One is tempted to see the vacillation as the effect of a certain conceptualization of sexual difference. The woman of color, Mayotte Capécia, no matter how white the color of her skin, becomes the exemplary representative of a blackness delineated as the inevitably impotent desire to be other. Jean Veneuse, on the other hand, does actually achieve otherness through his intense intellectual endeavors—he is only accidentally, "coincidentally" black. Given the fact that his pathological behavior is unrelentingly *individual*, according to Fanon, and whiteness confers upon the subject the "right" of individuality, Jean Veneuse has indeed attained a form of whiteness in Fanon's schema. The white mask is most perceptible as a mask in the case of the woman of color who seems more at home in the realm of mimicry.

The other side of the "psychoexistential complex" Fanon associates with the colonial relation is also considered in his analysis of "negrophobia" on the part of both white men and white women. Fanon is very much aware of the sexual logic subtending the relations between white men, black men, and white women. The phobia associated with blackness is a phobia of sexual anxiety and fear revolving around the imago of the "genital nigger" or the oversexed black male who is envisaged as having an enormous penis. From this point of view, what is at stake is the white male's simultaneous fear and desire in relation to a sexual potency he believes he can never achieve. Invoking a Freudian economics once again, Fanon situates this dynamic as a by-product of cultural development.

> Every intellectual gain requires a loss in sexual potential. The civilized white man retains an irrational longing for unusual eras of sexual license, of orgiastic scenes, of unpunished rapes, of unrepressed incest. . . . Projecting his own desires onto the Negro, the white man behaves "as if" the Negro really had them. (165)

Although this schema would seem to be grounded by and focused upon the white male's compensatory behavior and his consequent delegation of his own fear to the white woman, it is in fact the white woman who becomes the pathological linchpin of Fanon's analysis, who is the primary site of a psychic trauma linked to racial difference. Almost all of the individual cases Fanon cites in this chapter ("The Negro and Psychopathology") are white women: from "the girl who confides to me that to go to bed with a Negro would be terrifying to her"(151) described in the opening to the rather inscrutable case of the woman with a classic case of hysteria whose somatic symptoms (agitation, motor instability, tics, and spasms) are linked to a fantasy of primitive blacks, tom-toms, and hallucinatory circles. Fanon is fascinated by a prostitute's fascination with the story of a white woman who slept with a black man and went mad ("what she [the prostitute] wanted was the destruction, the dissolution, of her being on a sexual level" [171]). In the concrete and phenomenologically detailed terms of his description, psychical excess is on the side of the white woman within a scenario largely orchestrated by white male subjectivity—so much so that it is white female subjectivity which becomes the greatest textual stake.

The only case of negrophobia in which Fanon brings the apparatus of psychoanalysis to bear in all the complexity of its detail is a case which concerns not an individual but white female subjectivity in general. In a textual echo of Freud's "A Child is Being Beaten" essay, Fanon proposes an explanation of the fantasy, "A Negro is raping me." He has previously established his notion that the white woman's fear of the black man acts as a denial of her true desire—which is that of being raped ("Just as there are faces that ask to be slapped, can one not speak of women who ask to be raped?" [156]). Accepting the work of Helene Deutsch and Marie Bonaparte as the logical extension of Freud's theory of female sexuality, Fanon finds that the fantasy of being raped by a Negro constitutes the assimilation by the woman of a cultural treasurehouse of images concerning blackness and their incorporation within what is a basic structure of femininity. This structure is characterized by the necessity of managing a surplus aggression associated with her clitoral (i.e. masculine) phase which must be repressed: "when a woman lives the fantasy of rape by a Negro, it is in some way the fulfillment of a private dream, of an inner wish. Accomplishing the phenomenon of turning against self, it is the woman who rapes herself" (179). Hence, the white woman's pivotal role within a racist psychical economy is a function of what Fanon describes as a form of perverse narcissism/masochism—the core fantasy is not "A Negro is raping me" but "I am raping myself."

This analysis clearly rests on a serious confusion between rape and sex with which feminists of any color might take issue. Nevertheless, there is another structural difficulty with Fanon's reading which is more pertinent here and concerns its structuring absences. The overpresence of the white woman is coincident with the almost complete disappearance of the black woman from the analytic schema. At the end of his exegesis, Fanon states, "Those who grant our conclusions on the psychosexuality of the white woman may ask what we have to say about the woman of color. I know nothing about her" (179–80). Fanon is very much aware of the history which subtends his cultural and psychical scenario—a history which links lynching, castration, and the white man's alleged need to protect white womanhood from violation by oversexed black males (particularly in the United States).[23] In this historical context, the white woman's fantasies about black men and sexuality would be bound up with the white male's sexual fears in the face of a perceived threat to his racial superiority and power. But more importantly, Fanon's analysis situates rape only as the white woman's fantasy and neglects its status as the historical relation between the white male and the black female both in the colonial context and in that of slavery.[24] Rape undergoes a displacement—from the white man's prerogative as master/colonizer to the white woman's fears/desires in relation to the black male. This confers upon race relations an extremely intense psychical charge which compensates a white psychical economy for the loss of the physical constraints of slavery or colonialism. In the historical schema of rape, lynching, and castration, which reveals a complex articulation of power and sexuality in relation to both white women and black men, the black woman disappears as an actor because she can only be an embarrassment to any lingering ideals of white male morality or white female compassion. Unfortunately, in his attempt to produce a psychoanalysis of the historical problematic, Fanon repeats the gesture which results in the black woman's erasure. He foregrounds white female sexuality.

It could be argued (and has been) that contemporary white feminism also repeats this historical gesture (which is reminiscent of earlier white feminism's exclusion of the black woman). It is important to acknowledge this despite, or perhaps because of, my intention of exploring the historically and psychically pivotal position of white femininity in a racist economy which articulates racial and sexual differences. Fanon asks few (if any) questions about the white man's psycho-sexuality in his violent confrontation with the black woman—fewer still about how one might describe black female subjectivity in the face of such violence. In the historical scenario conjoining rape and lynching, the emotional charge attached to miscegenation, its representational intensity, are channeled onto the figure of the white woman, effectively erasing the black woman's historical role. It is clear that psychical reality and historical reality are not directly reflective of one another, although they are related. As a number of feminists have pointed out, lynchings were in fact very rarely related to a black man's rape of a white woman (or even to a consensual sexual relation between the two).[25] Nevertheless, lynching—as the spectacular form of a disciplinary machine—*signified* first and foremost fears about sexuality, race, and power. Its representational valence exceeded, and was meant to exceed, any contingently defined individual cases.

III. VISION, THE BODY, AND
THE CINEMA

Fanon, although he focuses upon black *male* subjectivity in this respect, produces an extremely insightful analysis of the representational power of racism and of its intersection with the psychical. And because this analysis circulates around questions of vision, visibility, and representability, there is a sense in which it is strongly applicable to black women, who are the objects of a double surveillance linked to race and gender. Yet Fanon, like Sartre, transforms the problematic of racial vision into an affair between men. In "Black Orpheus," his introduction to an anthology of poetry by blacks espousing negritude,[26] Sartre discusses the seeing/being seen nexus from the white man's point of view.

> Here, in this anthology, are black men standing, black men who examine us; and I want you to feel, as I, the sensation of being seen. For the white man has enjoyed for three thousand years the privilege of seeing without being seen. It was a seeing pure and uncomplicated; the light of his eyes drew all things from their primeval darkness. The whiteness of his skin was a further aspect of vision, a light condensed. The white man, white because he was man, white like the day, white as truth is white, white like virtue, lighted like a torch of creation; he unfolded the essence, secret and white, of existence. Today, these black men have fixed their gaze upon us and our own gaze is thrown back in our eyes . . .[27]

The transgressiveness of the notion of the black man "looking back," actively appropriating the gaze, is underlined by its resistance to the biblical myth used to rationalize slavery and colonization, the story of Ham who after "looking upon his father's nakedness" was cursed with descendants who would be both dark skinned and slaves.[28] In Sartre's account, "the sensation of being seen" is alien to the white man—his own privileged vision makes him effectively invisible. Fanon's emphasis in his analysis of the black psyche is on a form of constant visibility—a disabling overvisibility—which is a function of skin color.

Skin becomes the locus of an alienation more acute to the extent that it is inescapable—*at first sight*, racial identity is ineluctably established and the Manichaean polarity of black/white with all its metaphysical implications is activated. As the site of various barriers as well as transactions between inside and outside, skin is a primary signifier of psychical intensity. In his psychoanalysis of surface (which often confounds the concept of the unconscious),[29] Fanon foregrounds the corporeal prison of acute visibility inhabited by the black. Homi Bhabha, in an analysis of Fanon, maintains that

> the fetish of colonial discourse—what Fanon calls the epidermal schema—is not, like the sexual fetish, a secret. Skin, as the key signifier of cultural and racial difference in the stereotype, is the most visible of fetishes, recognized as common knowledge in a range of cultural, political, historical discourses, and plays a public part in the racial drama that is enacted every day in colonial societies.[30]

At one point Fanon begins to write of the "internalization" of inferiority on the part of the black, but reconsiders and decides that the term "epidermalization" is more appropriate. Wherever the black goes, his or her identity is immediately given as a function of the most visible organ—the skin. Fanon persistently returns to the imperative call—"Look, a Negro!"—uttered by a little white boy in a state of fascination and terror. The call is a somewhat perverse version of the Althusserian process of interpellation or hailing. Although it addresses and at the same time refuses to address the black directly (the second person pronoun is not used), the exclamation fixes the black person, producing a subjectivity which is fully aligned with a process of reification. As Fanon puts it, "I am overdetermined from without. I am the slave not of the 'idea' that others have of me but of my own appearance" (116).

Whiteness hence relegates blackness to a certain corporeal schema or, more accurately, to corporeality itself. The black *is* the body, *is* the biological. Fanon explains in detail how the black is subject to a hyper-awareness of the body which attends his/her overvisibility. The specificity of the black male's situation becomes apparent in its comparison with that of the Jew. Strongly influenced by Sartre's *Anti-Semite and Jew*, Fanon compares the punishment usually meted out to the Jew (murder or sterilization) to that associated with the black (castration).

> The penis, the symbol of manhood, is annihilated, which is to say that it is denied. The difference between the two attitudes is apparent. The Jew is attacked in his religious identity, in his history, in his race, in his relations with his ancestors and with his paternity; when one sterilizes a Jew, one cuts off the source; every time a Jew is persecuted, it is the whole race that is persecuted in his person. But it is in his corporeality that the Negro is attacked. It is as a concrete personality that he is lynched. It is as an actual being that he is a threat. The Jewish menace is replaced by the fear of the sexual potency of the Negro. (163–4)[31]

The collapsing together of the concrete, the corporeal, and sexuality indicates that the fate of the black is that of a body locked into its own non-generalizability. Such a contingently defined threat would need to be countered repeatedly in a constantly renewed racism.

Yet, it is clearly the black *male* body which is at issue here and which poses the greatest threat to white male subjectivity. Fanon invokes Lacan's theory of the mirror stage in order to illuminate the articulation of image, identity, body and racial otherness. Although Fanon begins the discussion by pointing out that the black man is the "real Other" for the white man and is perceived entirely on the level of the body image as "the not-self," "the unidentifiable, the unassimilable" (161), his analysis transforms itself into a discussion of the black's identification of himself as white (e.g., young Antilleans claiming in school compositions that they like vacations because they give them "rosy cheeks" [162]). But earlier, he hints at a more extensive interpretation of the mirror stage in its interracial dimension. Referring to the "influence exerted on the body by the appearance of another body," Fanon claims, "the Negro, because of his body, impedes the closing of the postural schema of the white man" (160). In Lacanian psychoanalysis, the significance of the mirror phase lies in its provision of an illusory yet strong identity based on a body image. The image of a completely whole and unified body which props up the ego also provides the basis of the psychical terror associated with castration anxiety. To the extent that the black "impedes the closing of the postural schema of the white man," to the extent that he poses the possibility of *another* body, his position would appear analogous to that of the woman in psychoanalysis, who embodies the threat of castration. Yet, the woman's threat is configured as a physical lack or absence while the black male's threat is posited as that of an *overpresence*, a monstrous penis. This overpresence is not unrelated to the hypervisibility associated with skin color (the penis being, in the Freudian account, not only the most visible of sexual organs but also metaphorically linked with the eye).[32] The *obviousness* of racial difference appears as the symptom of this surface politics of the psyche. This drama of the white male ego, which undoubtedly plays itself out differently in different historical epochs according to their varying distributions of bodies, can contribute to an explanation of the intense sexualization of racism in the colonialist and post-colonialist period.

The symbolic network which welds visibility, skin color, identity, image, and ego to castration anxiety gives a clue to the reasons for the disappearance of the black woman in Fanon's account, to the limitations of his knowledge about her. For within this schema, she is figuratively invisible, penis-less. This is true for Fanon even in the context of his discussion of the cinema, where one might anticipate the conjunction of spectacle and female sexuality. Fanon is concerned not so much with the spectacle on the screen as with the spectacle in the audience, the deeply troubling aspect of cross-over identification. The black spectator has no access to the "seeing pure and uncomplicated" of Sartre's white man. Identificatory procedures are instead testimony to the effectivity of the cultural imperialism of Hollywood. In another context, Kwame Nkrumah has delineated what Brantlinger calls the "special impact of the American mass media on the African situation."[33]

> The cinema stories of fabulous Hollywood are loaded. One has only to listen to the cheers of an African audience as Hollywood's heroes slaughter red Indians or Asiatics to understand the effectiveness of this weapon. For, in the developing continents, where the colonialist heritage has left a vast majority still illiterate, even the smallest child gets the message. . . . Here, truly, is the ideological under-belly of those political murders which so often use local people as their instruments.[34]

Fanon is also deeply concerned with the phenomenon of black identification with whites in their exploitative relation to the Other—particularly when the black is forced to realize that he *is* the Other. His privileged example is the reception of *Tarzan*, which takes on a different affective valence in different viewing contexts.

> Attend showings of a Tarzan film in the Antilles and in Europe. In the Antilles, the young Negro identifies himself *de facto* with Tarzan against the Negroes. This is much more difficult for him in a European theater, for the rest of the audience, which is white, automatically identifies him with the savages on the screen. It is a conclusive experience. (152–3n)

Fanon's "white mask" would be most fully in place in the cinema theater up until the moment of unmasking accomplished by the gaze of others. Fanon is extremely sensitive to the psychical impact of the representational field of race relations—children's stories, comic books, films. But because the oppressiveness of black cultural identity is so intimately connected to the anguish and anxiety of the visible, of the epidermal schema, the cinema would potentially be a prime site for the corroboration of such an identity. Its corroboration, however, takes place not on the screen (or not only on the screen) but in the theater itself.

> I cannot go to a film without seeing myself. I wait for me. The people in the theater are watching me, examining me, waiting for me. A Negro groom is going to appear. My heart makes my head swim. (140)

The space of the theater becomes a space of identificatory anxiety, a space where the gaze is disengaged from its "proper" object, the screen, and redirected, effecting a confusion of the concept of spectacle.

IV. BLACKNESS AND WHITENESS AS SIGNS: *BIRTH OF A NATION*

The cinema which Fanon addresses in *Black Skin, White Masks* is the white cinema of mainstream Hollywood[35] with its extensive problematic history of representing racial difference. The filmic tradition in which Fanon's exclusion is inscribed both in the film and in the theater, the space of its screening, represents blacks primarily in marginal, stereotyped roles with no pretensions of depth. Nevertheless, the Hollywood cinema as travelogue, as historical spectacle, as melodrama acknowledges in numerous ways, consciously or unconsciously, the force of Fanon's analysis of racism's sexual fears and desires as they circulate around issues of knowledge and its possibility or impossibility, masks, pretense, and masquerade. From this point of view, it is highly significant that *Birth of a Nation* (Griffith, 1915), often cited as the moment of coagulation of the classical system of narrative, is also a discourse on disguise as the operative mode of race relations.

Although the historical framework for the development of Fanon's psychoanalysis of race relations is that of colonialism, his analysis is not totally unrelated to the representational field of a Hollywood cinema more immediately influenced by the American context of slavery, abolition, and Civil War. For the master/slave relation and that of the colonizer/colonized share a certain tropic repertoire, particularly with respect to the construction of sexualities and the psychical configurations accruing to each. In fact, *Birth of a Nation* can be read as an inscription of the schema Fanon deals with linking rape, lynching, and castration—an inscription traversing the genres of melodrama and historical spectacle. In the cinema, melodrama is a particularly crucial site for the elaboration of sexual questions and dilemmas. Indeed, melodrama has been consistently defined as the cinematic mode in which social anxieties or conflicts are represented as sexual anxieties or conflicts. From this point of view, it would seem to be a particularly appropriate arena for the observation of the intersection of race and gender. Griffith's projection of the melodramatic mode onto that of historical spectacle intensifies the articulation of sexual and racial anxieties.[36]

In a film which constantly announces its own historicity, Griffith seeks to proclaim and maintain the purity of family, race, and nation. The historical drama of the Civil War and its aftermath intersects with a family melodrama tracing the relations between a Southern family, the Camerons, and the Northern Stonemans. Successful romantic engagements between members of the two families signify the reunification of North and South and hence of the nation. As in Fanon's analysis, it is the white family which is the microcosm of the nation—the black family is non-existent. Whatever their ideological differences, what ultimately binds together the Camerons and the Stonemans is the perceived/constructed threat posed by black men to white womanhood.

In *Birth of a Nation* the white woman is the stake of a virulent racism. The blacks, once freed from slavery, exhibit a massive sexual appetite for white women (euphemistically presented as the desire to "marry" them), and this is represented as their principle threat and the rationalization of the birth of the Ku Klux Klan. Sexual danger is signaled by the black appropriation of the voyeuristic gaze—Gus, for instance, consistently lurks in the background hoping to catch a glimpse of the Cameron little sister, while Silas Lynch's sidelong looks at Elsie betray his lustful intentions. Michael Rogin argues that in *Birth of a Nation*, the sexually active woman in Griffith's earlier films (usually played by Blanche Sweet) disappears in favor of the presexual Lillian Gish. The sexuality previously associated with the notion of the New Woman becomes the excessive sexuality of the black male: "Griffith displaces sexuality from white men to women to blacks in order, by the subjugation and dismemberment of blacks, to reempower white men."[37] The white woman would hence act as the textual pivot for the elaboration of a discourse on blackness as economic, political, and, most importantly, sexual threat.

What is perhaps most striking about *Birth of a Nation* is the second order form of signification it invokes in relation to its ordering of whiteness and blackness. It is as though it were crucial to dissociate racial difference from the epidermal schema described by Fanon and to transform it into a floating signifier of itself. Hence, blacks are allowed to represent blacks only in their most marginal roles, as elements of a crowd or background. The black figures with the most important roles are actually acted by whites in blackface. In a kind of textual echo effect, whiteness is not a characteristic of the skin but is hyperbolized and ritualized as the white robes of the Ku Klux Klan which function to conceal identities. Blackface and white robes both potentially destabilize the fetishized reality effect of the classical Hollywood cinema (and, in particular, of the historical genre which *Birth* strives to epitomize). They act as a denial of the body and any claims it might have to signification. As Rogin points out, "Dressed in blackface (or watching others so dressed) whites played with blackness as part of their self-fashioning. Griffith took an interest in clothes as a young man, he later wrote, because he could not change his body. Griffith discovered in *Birth* that changing clothes allowed him to leave the body behind."[38] A denial of the body in a discourse on racial difference is also an economic and symbolic denial of the power of blackness as it was conceived within a white epistemological framework (as *the* mark of the biological). Knowledge, as authorized by the body, is destabilized in the interests of ideological containment.

Hence, *Birth of a Nation* effects a curious ordering of the relations between visibility, knowledge, and power. Skin—which would seem to be the most stable guarantor of racial difference and the ground of its instant recognizability—is transformed from immediacy to sign. Blackness is a costume which is worn or removed at will by whites, while whiteness in its symbolic dimension (the white robes of the Ku Klux Klan) is also a form of masquerade which conceals an identity. This disengagement of knowledge about racial identity from skin color is consistent with the fact that the legal criterion for racial identity in the United States has historically been linked to blood rather than skin. The polarization of white and black insures that there are no gradations in racial identity—one drop of "black blood" effectively makes one black.[39] Genealogy, a potentially *invisible* history, ultimately determines racial identity. The mulatto, as the sign of a historical miscegenation and a potential disabling of the polarization between black and white, is a particularly dangerous figure who requires extensive textual containment. In *Birth of a Nation*, mulattoes are the actively evil representatives of a free black population: Lydia Brown, Stoneman's housekeeper, malevolently seduces him into political support for her race while Silas Lynch, at first a mere tool of Stoneman, ambitiously assumes the prerogatives of a white man in desiring Stoneman's daughter.

The fact that blood is the historical determinant of racial identity and allows of no mixture or gradation is dramatically underlined by the scene of a strange ritual following the death of the Cameron little sister and the murder of Gus by the Ku Klux Klan. The ritual focuses on the purity of the little sister's blood and on how "the red stain of the life of a Southern woman" became "a priceless sacrifice on the altar of an outraged civilization." The white woman's blood is a testimony to the purity of whiteness itself. The genealogy which insures that purity is distinct from the question of skin color is not immediately accessible to vision but seems to call forth, instead, the symbolic ritual. Yet, Griffith was dealing with a medium (the cinema) in which it was becoming increasingly evident that the realm of the visible was the ultimate epistemological guarantee. Blackface could only be a hangover from vaudeville or the stage where the operation of the symbolic was not as intimately endangered by the emerging codes of photographic realism. And in other respects Griffith constructs *Birth of a Nation* as an obsessive appeal to historical authenticity. Merging vision and knowledge, his "historical facsimiles" constitute a staging of the historical scene (e.g. Lee's surrender to Grant at the Appomattox Court House, the assassination of Lincoln at Ford's Theater) in its most exact details (usually as they are conveyed in historical paintings or photographs). There is a constant tension in the film between the codes of melodrama and those of historical spectacle, between an appeal to the symbol and an appeal to the real. This struggle is resolved, or at least mediated, by the representation of the white woman.

If the realm of white men and black men and women is the realm of masquerade (blackface and white robes), there is on the other hand a certain naturalization of the white woman's representation of whiteness. She is simply there, undisguised, *naturally* symbolic of all that the white men struggle to safeguard—white purity, white culture, whiteness itself (in contrast, Lydia Brown, a mulatta and the major representative of the black woman in the film, is defined in terms of excessively melodramatic gestures). There is a small photograph of Elsie Stoneman which circulates in the film as the sign of desire, of racial purity, and of national unity. The photograph is first introduced in a pastoral scene in which the Cameron and Stoneman youths walk through a cotton field where a black man and woman are happily picking cotton, an anticipatory sign of nostalgia for a way of life soon to be lost. Ben Cameron snatches the portrait away from the Stoneman brother who reveals it, clearly enamored with her image. There are a number of points to be made about this scene. First, presaging what was to become a major mechanism of the cinematic institution, desire is sparked by an image. Visibility and desire are mediated by photographic codes of lighting and portraiture which naturalize, realize, and construct "beauty." On the other hand, the fact that the white woman is represented by a photographic portrait which is displaced, circulates, and gains value within a certain political economy of desire, gives to that portrait a symbolic status. Here, Griffith successfully merges the symbolic and the iconic, melodrama and historical spectacle, the theatrical and the photographic. The portrait has both something of the melodramatic and of the historical authenticity associated with Griffith's "historical facsimiles." And this drama of cinematic representation in its emergence is played out against the backgrounding of the figure of the black, whose smiling labor in the fields infuses the mise-en-scène with another kind of "historical authenticity." Blacks will habitually be confined in the Hollywood cinema to providing an environment, a space, "local color," a background for the unfolding of white dramas. In *Birth of a Nation*, it is white womanhood which becomes the stake of this representational politics.

The complex power network linking the roles of the white man, the white woman, and the black man in *Birth* ought to make clear the impossibility of any valid parallel between the position of the white woman and that of blacks. Nevertheless, it is particularly tempting, in light of the theories of visual politics informing analysis of the cinema, to see certain similarities between the two. When Fanon claims that the black represents to the white the body, the biological, or corporeality in all its specificity, when he speaks of the hypersexualization of the black or of a kind of paranoia of the visible attending an identity chained to appearance, it is difficult not to recognize these categories as playing an important role within feminist analysis (particularly feminist film theory) where they have been applied to the situation of the woman and her representation/self-representation. Both the woman and the black would be, in a sense, overvisible.

But this temptation must be resisted precisely because of what it relegates to the realm of the invisible. It is dangerous and very misleading to claim that the position of white women is analogous to that of blacks simply because both take on the role of Other in relation to the white man. As Hazel Carby has argued, parallelism may seem at first sight to be justified: categories of race and gender are both socially constructed; racism and sexism both ground their notions of common sense in the "natural" and the "biological," etc. But, ultimately, "The experience of black women does not enter the parameters of parallelism. The fact that black women are subject to the *simultaneous* oppression of patriarchy, class and 'race' is the prime reason for not employing parallels that render their position and experience not only marginal but also invisible."[40] As has been frequently pointed out, the category of women is usually used to refer to white women, while the category of blacks often really means "black men." What is lost in the process is the situation of the black woman. Her position becomes quite peculiar and oppressively unique: in terms of oppression, she is both black and a woman; in terms of theory, she is neither. In effect, she occupies a position which is difficult to think within current paradigms. This may be linked to the fact that, as Bell Hooks (Gloria Watkins) points out, the black woman has no institutionalized other. The institutionalized other of the white man is constituted by black men and women and white women; the white woman has blacks as her institutionalized other; the black man can situate black women in that position. But there is no other of the black woman. Her identity cannot be oppositional in the traditional way. This is perhaps what leads Fanon to maintain, "I know nothing about her."

Given this unique position of the black woman, it is crucial to examine the intersection of sexual difference and racial difference not only as it concerns the relations of black men and white women (in melodramas like *Birth of a Nation*), but insofar as it inflects the represented relations between white women and black women as well (the relation which Fanon neglects). As has been frequently pointed out, the differences which have been forgotten in feminist criticism's emphasis upon sexuality as the major locus of its analysis, are differences of class and race. As Bell Hooks has claimed, white feminist theory has attempted to deracinate itself by systematically misrecognizing the limits and specificity of its own categorization of "women."

> The force that allows white feminist authors to make no reference to racial identity in their books about "women" that are in actuality about white women is the same one that would compel any author writing exclusively on black women to refer explicitly to their racial identity. That force is racism. In a racially imperialist nation such as ours, it is the dominant race that reserves for itself the luxury of dismissing racial identity while the oppressed race is made daily aware of their racial identity. It is the dominant race that can make it seem that their experience is representative.[41]

White theorists have historically monopolized the operation of abstraction, displacing the characteristics of discreteness, particularity, and concreteness onto racial others. The differences that are forgotten in order to produce "thought" are often racial differences. From this point of view, whiteness does not constitute a racial or ethnic identity but is posited as the norm against which all deviations are measured.

V. ONE BODY TOO MUCH: *IMITATION OF LIFE*

Black women are not absent from the realm of Hollywood cinema, but their representations are highly circumscribed and limited even within the few films Hollywood produced with all-black casts (e.g. musicals such as *Stormy Weather* [1943] and *Cabin in the Sky* [1943]). In analyzing the represented relations between white women and black women within the Hollywood cinema, it is particularly interesting to isolate and examine the genre which has received intense scrutiny in feminist film criticism—the "woman's film" (or, more accurately, the "white woman's film"). The "women's problems" which these films purportedly address are problems which can be specified as white, heterosexual, middle class. When black women are present, they are the ground rather than the figure; often they are made to merge with the diegesis. They inhabit the textual sidelines, primarily as servants. Black servants haunt the diegeses of films like *The Great Lie* (1941), *Since You Went Away* (1944), and *The Reckless Moment* (1949).

Within this context of white constructions of black femininity, Douglas Sirk's 1959 version of *Imitation of Life*, made at a time which was already beginning to witness the demise of the "woman's film" as a viable commodity, offers a particularly rich site for the examination of the relation Fanon excludes from his psychoanalytic study—that between the white woman and the black woman. Here, the correlations between visibility, knowledge, power, and masquerade are the very focus of the narrative. Sirk's version is the third—it was preceded by Fannie Hurst's original 1933 novel *Imitation of Life* and John Stahl's 1934 film adaptation.[42] All three versions make the theme of "passing" a central element of their narratives. Passing had been a popular theme of both African-American and white novelists from the mid-nineteenth century on. However, it received particularly intensive treatment in the 1920s, during the Harlem Renaissance,[43] in novels such as Walter White's *Flight* (1926), Jessie Fauset's *Plum Bun* (1928), and Nella Larsen's *Passing* (1929). Like many whites, Fannie Hurst was fascinated with the cultural life of Harlem and with an exoticism and primitivism she associated with blacks. Participating in the system of white patronage of black artists, Hurst hired Zora Neale Hurston first as her secretary and later, when it became clear that Hurston's typing and shorthand skills were minimal, as her chauffeur and companion. One advantage of this relationship to Hurst was clearly the opportunity to absorb black culture. As one historian of the Harlem Renaissance claims, "Hurst . . . gained a crash course in black life and culture from the mercurial Hurston, who became the inspiration for and the model for her later best-selling novel of black life, *Imitation of Life*."[44] Although it is highly inaccurate to claim that Hurst's *Imitation* is a "novel of black life" and it is not clear which of the characters Hurston would act as a model for, Hurst's relation with Hurston demonstrates a desire to immerse herself in a black culture which is then appropriated in the theme of passing within *Imitation*.

While the theme of passing is not equivalent to the convention of the tragic mulatta (the mulatta may or may not choose to pass), the two are intimately connected since passing always suggests the historical dimension of miscegenation. The tragic mulatta is "tragic" because she is usually delineated as caught between two cultures and her dilemma is seen as irresolvable in any satisfactory way. Her skin color allows her economic and cultural opportunities which would otherwise be denied to her, but grasping these opportunities means denying her own cultural heritage and familial connections. Hence, she is described as the victim of "double consciousness,"[45] as "caught betwixt and between,"[46] or, as Claudia Tate claims in an essay on Nella Larsen's novel, as "a character who 'passes' and reveals pangs of anguish resulting from forsaking his or her Black identity."[47] The figure of the tragic mulatta also provides the occasion for an examination of relations between the races, of cultural/social mobility and its possibility or impossibility. Hazel Carby understands the mulatta figure as a "literary convention for an exploration and expression of what was increasingly socially proscribed"—as a literary denial of "an increasing and more absolute distance between black and white as institutionalized in the Jim Crow laws."[48] The mulatta, in moving back and forth between the black and the white worlds, could express their relation.

The mulatta is also the figure of an epistemological quandary. In an early scene of Nella Larsen's *Passing*, both Irene Redfield, the protagonist/ narrator, and Clare Kendry, her girlfriend from a distant childhood, are passing in an upper-class restaurant. Irene, misrecognizing Clare as white, gradually becomes increasingly paranoid that Clare, who has been staring at her intensely, has somehow discovered her racial identity, afraid that she will be able to read her body as a text, to decipher its origin ("Absurd! Impossible! White people were so stupid about such things for all that they usually asserted that they were able to tell; and by the most ridiculous means, finger-nails, palms of hands, slopes of ears, teeth, and other equally silly rot"[49]). Passing lends to issues of race a certain narratability insofar as it raises hermeneutic problems of knowledge, identity, and concealment. Recurrent motifs in the passing novel circulate around the trauma of recognition: either through an accidental meeting with someone from one's past, a betrayal by one's own body of racial identity (e.g. the blue half-moons of fingernails attributed to blacks by white folklore), or the possibility of a "throwback," i.e., having a child with more blatantly black characteristics. The mulatta always signifies a potential confusion of racial categories and the epistemological impotency of vision. The fact that these are dramas of recognition and misrecognition and, as one critic points out, scenes of revelation are crucial to the genre,[50] indicates an affinity with the structure of melodrama. Indeed, a number of black feminist literary critics have criticized the use of conventions of passing and the tragic mulatta as "melodramatic."[51] But melodrama has been an extraordinarily significant genre historically both in literature and in the cinema with an ideological impact on questions of class and sexual antagonism. From this point of view, the alignment of the maternal melodrama with the convention of the tragic mulatta in both the screen versions of *Imitation of Life* would be particularly potent. For the maternal melodrama is perhaps *the* cinematic subgenre most fully associated with narratives of recognition and misrecognition, consequent upon the fateful separation of mother and child. In each case, the impulse is to embed a story of race relations within a genre directed primarily at white women—the maternal melodrama. In Stahl's 1934 version, the motif of passing is simply an appendage to the white woman's narrative; in Sirk's film, the two are deeply interconnected and racial hierarchies subjected to both an explicit and an implicit critique.

Given the passing narrative's juxtaposition of issues of knowledge, identity, and visual verifiability, it is somewhat surprising that it is not utilized more extensively in the Hollywood cinema. However in the cinema it produces a dilemma which is absent in its literary incarnation, for film requires an actual embodiment of the figure of the tragic mulatta—and hence a choice of the racial identity (defined genealogically) of the actress who represents the figure. In Stahl's *Imitation*, the mulatta daughter is played by a mulatta (Fredi Washington as Peola), but in Sirk's version as well as in *Lost Boundaries* (1949), *Pinky* (1949), and the 1929, 1936, and 1951 versions of *Show Boat*, the tragic mulatta/o was represented by a white actress or actor. This tendency has been interpreted as a symptom of the films' primary address to a white audience, allowing the white spectator to identify with and feel pain for a character who is, after all, reassuringly white.[52] But it also tends to demonstrate inadvertently the quiescent discordance between ideologies of racial identity (defined by blood) and cinematic ideologies of the real (as defined by the visible). The practice of typecasting has often served historically to organize the deployment of bodies in film and to confirm a certain imprint of the real. In this case, who could better represent a black attempting to "look white," or a black who is "white enough" to pass than a white herself? The success of typecasting hinges upon assumptions based on visual certainty or the immediate unthought knowledge one gains from looking. The mulatta, whose looks and ontology do not coincide, poses a threat to the epistemological basis of typecasting (as well as to the very idea of racial categorization). A curious distanciation attends the knowledge that one is watching a white pretending to be a black pretending to be a white. There is one body too much.

Sirk's version of *Imitation of Life* takes this intricate relation between pretense, ontology, and the visible real as the core of its discourse. Hurst's novel and Stahl's first adaptation capitalized upon the fascination blacks held for whites during the Harlem Renaissance. In addition, Stahl's film emerged in the mid-1930s, the apex of popularity of the Hollywood maternal melodrama. Sirk's remake was one of the last ambitious maternal melodramas and it was made at a historical moment far removed from the Harlem Renaissance, on the brink of the Civil Rights movement of the

1960s. Like all remakes separated by decades from their originals, Sirk's *Imitation* effected a historical dislocation of generic conventions in their relation to social problems. Nevertheless, what the two versions of *Imitation* have in common is a focus on some variant of the New (white) Woman whose changing relation to work/career is frequently made economically feasible by the labor of the black woman. Generically, in terms of the confrontation of conventions of the maternal melodrama with those of the novel of passing, and historically, in terms of its delineation of an economic hierarchy of types of labor, *Imitation of Life* forces the articulation of a relation between the white woman and the black woman.

Sirk's version takes more seriously than Stahl's the implications of the concept of "imitation" presented in the title. Parallels are consistently drawn between the black mother (Annie) and the white mother (Lora) in their relations with their daughters (Sarah Jane and Susie)—parallels which tend to corroborate Annie's aptness for the maternal and Lora's alienation from that role due to her career. This is fully in line with the generic imperative of the maternal melodrama which tends to pit the concept of the "good mother" against the concept of the "bad mother." But there is another parallel which crosses racial lines and yokes both Sarah Jane and Lora to the notion of "pretending" and hence imitation. Sarah Jane's passing is presented as a radical disjunction between being and appearing, a counterfeit claim to something she is not. In this sense, Sarah Jane is associated with a discourse on acting, pretending, artificiality which is also linked to Lora and her desire for a successful acting career. Sarah Jane's refusal of her racial identity is paralleled by Lora's refusal of her maternal identity, a corollary of her insistence on a career which not accidentally involves pretense. The two are bound together in structures of recognition and misrecognition from the very beginning of the film. In the first scene on the beach, Lora immediately assumes that Sarah Jane is a white woman's daughter and that Annie has the job of taking care of her. There is a certain metonymic slippage whereby Lora's misrecognition is immediately taken up by Sarah Jane, who, in the very next scene, refuses the black doll Susie offers her. This initial misrecognition is not "righted" until the end of the film when Sarah Jane accepts her own racial identity by recognizing her position as Annie's daughter. In a sense, misrecognition is shared: for the bulk of the film, Sarah Jane does not understand she is a daughter while Lora does not understand she is a mother. By insistently comparing the black daughter to the white mother the film suggests that racial confusion leads to familial confusion—and ultimately to the breakdown of the white family.

The racial specificity of Lora's "acting" lies in its association with extreme artificiality. Her success is equated with an increasingly artificial, plastic lifestyle. The house is modern and overdecorated, Susie's bedroom is blindingly pink, Lora's costumes become hyperbolically expensive and tasteless. Susie and Lora become vacuous characters, with no attempt made to rescue them from the two-dimensionality they come to represent. And, significantly, as a consequence of Lora's successful career, the background of her modernist house is increasingly populated by mute black servants, an echo of the echo provided by Annie and Sarah Jane. These servants are insistently *there*, waiting on table, passing silently through the background. The pretense associated with Lora's acting career gradually infiltrates and contaminates her entire lifestyle.

On the other hand, when Sarah Jane *acts*, she paradoxically acts the real. At one point in the film, Sarah Jane is asked to serve Lora who is meeting with her agent and an Italian director in the living room. Sarah Jane carries the tray of food on her head and announces, "I fixed you all a mess of crawdads." When Lora asks her where she learned this, Sarah Jane replies, "I learned it from my mammy and she learned it from her massuh befo' she belonged to you." This is the film's most blatant presentation of the intersection of racial relations and property relations and the history of slavery that subtends them. In acting in front of Lora, the actress, Sarah Jane acts her constructed self, the truth or the real in its historical dimension. She assumes the expectations about blackness which are imposed upon her. She becomes the representation of blackness which is implicitly contrasted with her passing. The representational convolutions involved in this scene are mind-boggling. The spectator is faced with a white (Susan Kohner the actress) pretending to be a black pretending to be a white pretending to be a black (as incarnated in all the exaggerated attributes of Southern blackness). Ontology is out of reach. However, the threat to the stability of racial identities is contained by the placement of Lora Meredith as the white female spectator of this scene, the one who extracts its meaning. Characteristically, she misreads it, telling Sarah Jane, who has retreated to the kitchen and claims as her defense that Lora and her mother are "so anxious about my being colored," "You weren't being colored," as though there were a proper colored identity which Sarah Jane simply misunderstands. "Being" acts as an ideological anchor for the potential semiotic slippage of pretense.

Sarah Jane's desires, nevertheless, tell us something about conceptualizations of white femininity and their interaction with conceptualizations about black femininity. What Sarah Jane demonstrates is the historical alienation of black women from ideas of womanhood or femininity elaborated within white culture. There is a sense in which when the black woman aspires to "whiteness" she becomes most representable within a Hollywood problematic which is so heavily dependent upon structures of voyeurism and fetishism. For Sarah Jane, to be a white woman means to become a sexual commodity, to perform for the male gaze in seedy nightclubs and scanty costumes which situate her identity first and foremost in relation to the body.[53] Her desire to be white, to pass, is not represented as the attempt to be a cashier in a store (as in the first version of *Imitation*) or any of the more "acceptable" feminine roles. What the film stipulates as reprehensible about passing, i.e. about refusing one's racial identity as a black, is linked to fears of excessive white female sexuality which are particularly characteristic of the 1950s. What is "wrong" with passing is articulated with what is "wrong" with excessive female sexuality—both refuse the stability and security of place, of social position. The character within the Sirkian corpus who seems most comparable with Sarah Jane is Marylee (Dorothy Malone) in *Written on the Wind* (1956) who, although she is white, as an undisputed nymphomaniac is the very embodiment of excessive female sexuality. A scene in *Imitation* in which Sarah Jane dances in her bedroom over records scattered across the floor (one of which is *Porgy and Bess*) is reminiscent of the scene in *Written on the Wind* in which Marylee dances while her father dies of a heart attack on the stairs outside her bedroom. It could be said that Sarah Jane also dances while her mother dies, although here the connection is implicit. In this way, racial issues seem to be entirely assimilated to the problematic of white female sexuality. The alienation of the black woman whose skin color fixes her racial identity and disallows passing is manifested by Annie's predicament. Each of the nightclub scenes in which Sarah Jane performs is presented from the point of view of Annie as spectator and in each, not only is she excluded from the stage of this sexuality (her character is deliberately asexual), she is not even allowed to look. A white male either orders or escorts her away from the scene.

The narrative of *Imitation of Life* thus seems to be very much concerned with producing and allaying anxieties about identity, position, social categorization. In novels of passing, the tragedy of passing is often linked to the consequent loss of cultural identity as an African-American. *Imitation of Life*, in the spirit of 1950s melodrama, translates this tragedy into a loss of familial identity, specifically, a distortion of the mother-daughter relation. In effect, this gesture depoliticizes passing as a narrative device by yoking it to a familial ideology produced by a white society. And ultimately, Sirk's *Imitation* seems to privilege the notion of stable identity— the white mother finally recognizing her position as mother, the black daughter returning to assume simultaneously her daughterhood and her blackness. Any racial and familial confusions have been resolved at the level of plot, and all identities are consolidated simultaneously. If this were the final word on the film's significance, it would not be of particular interest in its delineation of the relations between racial difference and sexual difference or between white women and black women. However, the critical power of much melodrama has always resided to a large extent not in its plot structure so much as in its mise-en-scène. By destabilizing the relation of decor to character, of background to foreground, and enacting their potential reversibility, Sirk marshalls the power of melodrama to make visible the tensions of race and gender.

In the subgenre of the "woman's film," to which *Imitation* belongs, blacks are insistently *there*, never central, but an important component of the discourse, of its reality-effect. In *The Great Lie*, for instance, blacks supply the music, the "local color" as it were, which provides the background for Bette Davis's romantic relationship with George Brent. Because they are so resolutely placed in the background, blacks become effectively elements of the decor, grounding and verifying the textual universe and hence the construction of white femininity. And in melodrama, the relation between character and decor is a highly charged one, which is often unstable and potentially reversible. There is a process of reification in relation to the representation of blackness which can collide with the tendency of melodrama to invest emotion in decor, objects, the clutter of "things" which becomes so oppressive for the white woman in the middle-class setting. Thomas Elsaesser describes the prototypical setting of melodrama as the middle-class home, "filled with objects" which are often heavy with symbolic significance. This obsession with objects

> brings out the characteristic attempt of the bourgeois household to make time stand still, immobilise life and fix forever domestic property relations as the model of social life and a bulwark against the more disturbing sides in human nature. The theme has a particular poignancy in the many films about the victimisation and enforced passivity of women—women waiting at home, standing by the window, caught in a world of objects into which they are expected to invest their feelings.[54]

Certainly, the black servants who inhabit the dieges of these films are never entirely reducible to objects, but they are reified as elements of the mise-en-scène. In melodrama, mise-en-scène is charged with a significance indissociable from a discourse on property relations. Frequently this involves the resuscitation of the "poor little rich girl" theme, in which what the white woman owns threatens to overwhelm her. Hence, the hierarchical relation of character to decor in melodrama is always potentially reversible. Such an inversion is never, however, fully possible in the relation of white women to their black servants, since power relations there generally remain intact. Furthermore, it would be less than accurate to suggest that white women are emotionally invested in their female black servants in the same way in which they overinvest in objects. Rather, the black servants often function as a kind of textual echo of the white female protagonists, or at least, an echo of what they have allegedly lost as the price of their middle-classness. The intuitive knowledge or maternal power credited to the black woman acts as a measure of the distance between the white bourgeoise woman and the nature or intuition she *ought* to personify. In these narratives, the black woman has no independent function. Which is to say, she is not awarded the status of a *character*.

This is why Sirk's 1959 version of *Imitation of Life* (as opposed to Stahl's 1934 version) is such a significant reworking of the genre. In general, the pathos of melodrama is the pathos of the white woman (or, sometimes, the feminized white male). Sirk's *Imitation of Life* revises this scenario through a gradual displacement of emotive and narrative value from the white characters to the black characters. The film becomes Annie's story. The final scene of Sirk's film chronicles the elaborate, excessive spectacle of Annie's funeral and the return of her daughter, Sarah Jane. Stahl's 1934 version, on the other hand, does not end with the funeral but appends an additional scene which delineates the postponement of heterosexual desire for the sake of an emotional bonding between white mother and daughter. Delilah (Stahl's version of Annie) is definitively relegated to the background in a shot of the neon sign of her beaming face advertising the pancake mix. In contrast, Sirk's version inscribes and offers a commentary upon the instability and potential reversibility of the melodramatic relation of decor to character, figure to ground.

In sharp contrast to the funeral scene and its lush extravagance of objects and colors, the beach scene in the beginning of the film, which introduces the scenario of the lost child, is characterized by a certain drabness and anonymity—presented in a series of long shots. But from this point on, the film mobilizes the familiar claustrophobia of melodrama, the crowded spaces in which objects threaten to overwhelm the characters with a significance which is not symbolic but tactile. This semiotic role of objects is not reserved for the white characters. In one of the earliest and most "melodramatic" instances of Sarah Jane's denial of her mother, Annie's discovery that Sarah Jane is passing at school, the placement of objects and colors calls attention to the depth of the image as sign, to the gap between foreground and background. As Annie climbs the steps to the school, a large red fire hydrant dominates the left front section of the frame, its color made more startling by the wet snow falling heavily. When Sarah Jane, traumatized by the sudden revelation of her racial identity, runs outside and is stopped by her mother, an imposing Christmas tree sign in bright red forms the backdrop as Annie gives Sarah Jane her red rubbers and helps her with her coat. And this entire drama of identity and recognition/misrecognition takes place against the background of a whiteness whose overwhelming presence is made tangible by the thick white snow. Without the extreme polarization and hierarchization of whiteness in relation to blackness, passing would have no affective valence.[55] Later in the film, after a scene in Harry's Bar in which Annie is again rejected by Sarah Jane, there is a scene which opens with Lora's return to her spacious, overdecorated house. A large vase of red roses occupies the left portion of the frame, infusing the scene with some of the pathos attached to Annie's situation. And, as in many scenes of the film, a dark figure glides up the stairs in the far background, signaling the presence of the black servants whose labor has made Lora's lifestyle possible. In this way, the mise-enscène and the signifying force of the objects within it are mobilized in relation to a drama of recognition linked fundamentally to racial difference.

This becomes most clear in the final scene of the film. The hierarchization of plot and subplot has been transgressed and the usual relations of dominance and subordination between them disturbed. The trajectory of the narrative insures that the affective operations of the film are organized primarily in relation to the black characters. Most significantly, melodrama's major mechanism for the production of pathos—a recognition which occurs too late, on the point of death—is associated with Sarah Jane's return to her mother's funeral. Sarah Jane, who earlier told her mother, "If by chance we should ever pass in the street, please don't recognize me," is confronted with the understanding that such a meeting is now impossible, that it is "too late." Spectatorial tears in such melodramas are not shed directly for the sake of the characters but as the recognition of a lost ideal of fullness and harmony. It is the sheer fact of loss or absence which is mourned. But it is not unimportant that this loss is articulated in relation to a specifically racial dilemma. In the context of discursive mechanisms which usually function to insure her *invisibility*, the film makes visible the plight of the black woman (which is, precisely, a problem of nonrecognition). For white feminists, it is a reminder of the extent to which abstraction in the representation of women is always haunted by loss.

The ending is also definable as the classical Sirkian happy/unhappy ending, where the fragility of the happiness of the characters is subtly undermined or put into question. Although Sarah Jane has returned and apparently accepted her racial and familial roles, Lora seems ready to fulfill her role as mother, Susie has given up the possibility of having Steve, and

Steve seems assured of a calm, stable relation with Lora, the tensions of earlier sections of the film outweigh the tenuous security. Furthermore, the ending is put under the mark of masquerade. An early shot of the funeral, whose point of view seems to taint the scene with the "imitation" of the title, is taken from behind the storefront window of a costume shop. Fassbinder reads the pathos of the relation between Annie and Sarah Jane somewhat differently, but his explanation of the terms produced by the film is telling.

> It is the mother [Annie] who is brutal, wanting to possess her child because she loves her. And Sarah Jane defends herself against her mother's terrorism, against the terrorism of the world. The cruelty is that we can understand them both, both are right and no one will be able to help them. Unless we change the world. At this point all of us in the cinema cried. Because changing the world is so difficult.[56]

Fassbinder is referring specifically to the scene in which Annie visits Sarah Jane backstage, in the Las Vegas nightclub (the scene in which Annie, in her one moment of masquerade in the film, *pretends* to be Sarah Jane's mammy when confronted with her white co-worker), but his remarks are applicable to the ending as well. They are also reminiscent of Fanon's exhortation, when faced with the black's acceptance of a white value system and consequent desire to be white: "We shall see that another solution is possible. It implies a restructuring of the world" (82).

The imbrication of the black motif of passing with the conventions of the white woman's maternal melodrama shatters the complacency of that genre (and its feminist critics) about the identity of Woman. The film demonstrates that it is not possible to read the white woman's dilemma as the incarnation of a "woman's problem" which excludes consideration of the black woman's situation. The two are interlocked both economically and representationally. However, the tendency to pit racism against sexism is not absent in feminist criticism of the film. Christine Gledhill, for instance, argues that the much-applauded Sirkian irony is aimed entirely at a critique of racial relations and hence neglects the problematic role of the woman.

> John Stahl's version [of *Imitation of Life*] (1934), however myopic it may be on the issue of race, is thoroughly a woman's film, suppressing the male role to the margins in the interests of an all female household. Sirk's remake turns the story into a problem of the absent husband and father and obtains his critique of white values at the cost of turning poor, struggling Lana Turner into a "bad mother"—a judgmental temptation few Sirkian commentators have

been able to resist, despite the possibility within the logic of the "Sirkian system" for ironically exposing ideologies of motherhood. Ironic value in this context has an implicitly misogynist edge.[57]

Once again, the figure who mysteriously disappears from this analysis is the black woman. If the earlier *Imitation of Life* is myopic about race relations but is nevertheless "thoroughly a woman's film," black women lose their status as women. Similarly, the misogyny Gledhill associates with Sirk's version is clearly directed against white women. The fact that Gledhill feels it is necessary to choose between a critique of racism and feminism is, at least in part, the symptomatic effect of a system which situates the white woman in a strategic representational locus in the discourse on the "racial problem."

Lana Turner as Lora is by no means marginalized in the film. But she is gradually drained of any psychological significance and, together with her daughter, Susie, becomes something of a cipher, a placeholder. Barbara Christian claims that "Each black woman image was created to keep a particular image about white women intact."[58] She is referring primarily to the hypersexualization of the black woman, her association with an unrestrained promiscuity which left the white woman free to occupy the pedestal of sexual purity. But this Victorian schema, so vital to the Southern plantation economy, is complicated by the changing mores concerning female sexuality in the twentieth century. This is why Marlene Dietrich in *Blonde Venus* had to emerge and disengage herself so forcefully from blackness. Notions of racial purity could no longer be adequately supported by ideas about sexual purity. The white woman, from being the intensely charged vehicle of a violent racism in the late nineteenth, early twentieth centuries, becomes a placeholder, seemingly deprived of meaning in the racial schema. The intense artificiality associated with Lora constitutes an acknowledgment of this semantic loss. Nevertheless, the figure of Lora retains one meaning—perhaps the most important— in relation to this schema. She exemplifies whiteness. In her blondeness, her lifelessness, her positioning as "mistress," her artificiality, her solipsism (she tells Annie at one point that she didn't realize Annie had her own friends), she exemplifies whiteness in the film. Her daughter Susie echoes this construction. Perhaps the only "racially neutral" character is Steve Archer, Lora's patient, hardworking, upright lover. In the final scene, inside the car at the funeral, Sarah Jane lays her head on Lora's shoulder, Lora grasps Susie's hand, and all three are locked into the paternalistic approving gaze of Archer. With the return of the white male, the family regains its tenuous composure and the authority of his gaze lends meaning to the scene. Such a position of authority is usually, and certainly in this case, presented as race-less, or *beyond* racial identity. The white male delegates the representation of racial identity, insofar as race can only be apprehended as specificity, embodiment, limitation, to the white woman. Her association with an overembodiment and hence lack of access to the abstraction of the generic "he" facilitates her positioning as the incarnation of white racial identity. As in *Birth of a Nation*, whiteness becomes most visible, takes form, in relation to the figure of the white woman. Fanon has understood this value system very well in claiming that the black who marries a white woman as part of his desire to be white marries "white culture, white beauty, white whiteness" (63). The white woman's "white whiteness" allows the white male access to the universal, the transcendent.

Yet, this interpretation is complicated by a number of factors. There is a fundamental contradiction in the representational schema. What allows the white woman to represent whiteness, her association with the body and contingency, collides with the substance of that representation: whiteness as the general, the abstract, the universal. For as Richard Dyer has pointed out, whiteness is characterized by its very lack of specificity, its invisibility, so that it should not be accessible to representation at all.

> In the realm of categories, black is always marked as a colour (as the term "coloured" egregiously acknowledges), and is always particularising; whereas white is not anything really, not an identity, not a particularising quality, because it is everything—white is no colour because it is all colours.[59]

What allows whiteness to be represented (unlike the case with blackness) is a certain conceptualization of sexual difference.

The contradiction which is internal to the white woman's representation of "white whiteness" is, however, somewhat ameliorated by her mobile position in this respect. When a white patriarchal culture requires a symbol of racial purity to organize and control its relations with blacks (usually black men but sometimes black women as well), the white woman represents whiteness itself, as racial identity and as *the* stake of a semiotics of power. But in her own relation to blacks (men and women), she has the "luxury of dismissing racial identity" to which Bell Hooks refers. She becomes the norm rather than a limited, racially defined being. Her appeals to universality are perhaps nowhere more apparent than in contemporary white feminism's claims to speak about "woman" or "women" in the abstract. But there is a significant history as well in which the white woman profited from her place in the protected shadow of the white male's assertion of racial power and mastery. As Hazel Carby points out, with respect to the nineteenth century, "White women who felt that caste was their protection aligned their interests with the patriarchal power that ultimately confined them."[60] They hence had and have now access to the power guaranteed by the universalization and abstraction associated with the exercise of whiteness rather than its representation. There is no sphere in which the black woman or black man could lay a similar claim to the authority buttressed by a denial of racial identity.

VI. IDENTITIES AND THEORIES

The trope of the dark continent is an early symptom of the white woman's fundamental and problematic role in the articulation of race and sexuality. The nature of the white woman's racial identity as it is socially constructed is simultaneously material, economic, and, as we have seen, subject to an intense work at the level of representation, mobilizing all the psychic reverberations attached to (white) female sexuality in order to safeguard a racial hierarchy. Hence, any analysis of race relations cannot afford to neglect textual analysis and psychoanalysis (with the understanding that both would be destabilized by the encounter with questions usually excluded from their paradigms). Fassbinder's and Fanon's injunctions to change or restructure the world have readily been understood as marking that which is beyond the limits of psychoanalysis—in effect, polarizing the world and the psyche. It is difficult, however, to imagine how such a restructuration could be accomplished without a restructuration of the psychical. Fanon's unenviable position as a black psychiatrist involves the activation of therapies which evolved within white culture to psychopathological conditions made possible by the colonialism and imperialism of that culture. His double bind is still ours.

To the extent that my analysis is about the white woman's pivotal role in a racist representational economy, it is at least partially a response to the demands of black feminists that white feminists examine their own racial identity, that they not assent to an understanding of race as a specialized topic of interest only to those upon whom the cultural burden of signifying Race is imposed. But analysis of the white woman's racial identity is made difficult by precisely this fact. When whiteness is defined in terms of a universal norm,[61] delineating its limits, its attributes, the specific features of its representation can be a hopeless task or, alternatively, can produce the paradoxes and contradictions detailed above. Undoubtedly, part of the difficulty is that I have examined its representation primarily within texts produced by a white culture. Whiteness can take on an entirely different semantic value in texts produced from within a black culture which feels no imperative to define it as non-specificity. This is, unfortunately, more difficult to demonstrate in the Hollywood cinema than in the American novel since African-American women have had greater (although still heavily circumscribed) access to the institution of literature than to the institution of cinema.[62] Nevertheless, whether the point of view is white or black, Fanon is ultimately right in insisting that race is radically differential. As Henry Louis Gates, Jr. points out, "Race as a meaningful criterion within the biological sciences, has long been recognized to be a fiction,"[63] and he goes even further to claim that "Race is the ultimate trope of difference because it is so very arbitrary in its application. The biological criteria used to determine 'difference' in sex simply do not hold when applied to 'race.' "[64] To some degree, this is what makes "passing" the narrative object of fascination. In any event, there is nothing essential about the racial identity of the white woman, nor is there anything in it to embrace or to invest with pride. There are often compelling political reasons for the black's espousal of blackness, but this is not the case for the white's relation to whiteness. To espouse a white racial identity at this particular historical moment is to align oneself with white supremacists. If race is an arbitrary signifier, as Gates suggests, whiteness and blackness are the most artificial of racial categories. For both whiteness and blackness cover and conceal a host of ethnicities, of cultural backgrounds whose differences are leveled by the very concepts of white and black. Whiteness and blackness are historically *real* categories only in their lengthy and problematic collision with each other in the context of systems of colonialism and slavery.

What I have attempted to do here is examine in some detail primarily white formulations of the intersection of race and sexuality. The obvious and necessary extension of such a project is to examine black constructions of race and sexuality (beyond those contained in Fanon's analysis of blacks who desire to be white and hence accept a white framework). But even within my limited purview, difficulties arise which may seem to have to do with my own racial identity as analyst. The difficulty of writing this essay has been for me a persistent and troubling sense of the limitations of my own knowledge. On a certain level, that feared lack of knowledge is linked to a deficient "mastery" of the field—the feeling that the more one reads the more one discovers how much one has not read. The field constituted by histories and theories of race relations, of colonialism and post-colonialism, of African-American Studies is an immense one. On the other hand, there is a lurking suspicion that this isn't really the problem, that the difficulty instead inheres in the not fully articulated or acknowledged belief that this limitation of knowledge is fundamentally the effect of an identity (whether social or essential is irrelevant) and its corresponding claims to a knowledge based on experience. What can a white woman know about racial difference or oppression when her social regime is constituted as the denial or evacuation of racial identity, when whiteness aspires to signify that it is color-less, absence, no race at all?

The dilemma seems initially to mimic one outlined by Jacques Derrida in an essay written at the onset of structuralism, "Structure, Sign, and Play in the Discourse of the Human Sciences."[65] Derrida specifies two possible reasons for the impossibility of totalization in the human sciences. The first is that the field is simply too large; infinitely expandable, it can never be grasped completely. This would be the empiricists' point of view. The second reason, favored by Derrida, would be that while the field is finite, manageable in its richness, it cannot be grasped in a totalizing analysis because it lacks a center which would ground the play of its elements. Unfortunately, Derrida's elaboration of the dilemma is not, in fact, analogous to the situation outlined above, in which the white feminist confronts issues of race. For her not quite consciously acknowledged sense that she has no "right" to speak about issues of race, that she does not know enough, is linked not to the recognition that there is no grounding, secure, stable center, but rather to her desire for, and perhaps unacknowledged belief in, such a place insofar as it would/could authorize her relation to feminism. For the parallel question—What can the white woman know of sexuality or sexual difference?—is perhaps just as relevant. Does her identity as a woman authorize a position in discourse with *automatic* claims to a form of knowledge? Does it make the act of writing any less formidable, any less uncertain? The institutional space which feminist theory opens for the white woman writer seems to posit this as a distinct possibility.[66]

So too do the seemingly endless debates about men writing on feminism, heterosexuals writing about homosexuality, whites writing about blacks, etc. For many, writing about something one is not constitutes a serious transgression of almost theological magnitude. But such a position threatens to collapse together experience, discourse, and ontology by transforming every type of writing into pure autobiography. The solution is not simply to place the word "white" before each use of woman in white feminist texts. The situation instead calls for a reexamination and reevaluation of the concept of experience in feminist theory. That concept seems to adhere persistently to the vicissitudes of the first person singular. What "I" know best is what "I" experience. The emphases of feminism must be shifted toward that which, precisely, exists at the limits of (or better, beyond) the regime of the "I." Gayatri Spivak has stated, "what I cannot imagine stands guard over everything that I must/can do, think, live, etcetera."[67] What I cannot imagine often has to do with other people's "experiences."

This is what constitutes the limits of the approach adopted in this essay in its attempt to delineate some of the implications of the white woman's status as image/symbol/agent in a racist representational economy. A major drawback is that the analysis, in its emphasis upon white racial identity, could readily be seen as a reinscription of the white woman's centrality and a repetition of the gesture consigning the black woman to invisibility. This is why it is crucial to go further, to investigate black representations of whiteness as well as black representations of blackness. The two representational regimes—black and white—are by no means entirely isolated from one another. Patrick Brantlinger ends his essay on the genealogy of the myth of the dark continent with a quote from Chinua Achebe about travel writing: "travellers with closed minds can tell us little except about themselves."[68] The pressing question here would seem to be—"Can travelers tell us about anything *other* than themselves?" I would hope that all feminisms could agree this is not only possible but necessary.

CHAPTER TWELVE

Sublimation and the
Psychoanalysis of the Aesthetic

In the course of his lectures on sublimation, Jean Laplanche poses a question about what he considers to be the "particularly irritating" concept of sublimation: "*Is there a nonsexual destiny of the sexual drive, but a destiny which would not be of the order of the symptom?*"[1] From the point of view of aesthetics, this is an especially tantalizing question since it seems to suggest the possibility of something other than a symptomatic reading of texts. In film theory, it could be said that the treatment of the film text as repressive or hysterical—and, therefore, precisely as symptomatic—has been the dominant mode of psychoanalytic criticism, with the inevitable implication of a pathologization of textual activity. But repression and sublimation, according to Freud, are two distinctly different vicissitudes of the drive. Both involve a displacement of sexual libido onto what is non-sexual, but in repression the sign or symptom is characterized as occupying the level of the socially trivial: compulsive habits or obsessions, tics, disturbances of vision, paralyses, etc. Sublimation, on the other hand, has as its product the highest manifestations of human culture, that which constitutes, most exactly, the sublime. Freud claims that in sublimation "a higher, eventually no longer sexual, goal is set up. . . . We probably owe the highest achievements of our culture to energy which has been liberated in this way."[2] Intellectual activity, art, scientific investigation, and the very process of thought itself have all been associated by Freud with sublimation. Hence, the concept has a decided advantage over that of repression in accounting for the social status of works of art, in acknowledging their weighty association with cultural value. Yet, Freud did not seem to be particularly interested in investigating the process of sublimation and he never gave it an adequate theorization. As Laplanche and Pontalis point out, "The lack of a coherent theory of sublimation remains one of the lacunae in psychoanalytic thought."[3]

Perhaps Freud was simply not intrigued by success. And sublimation is certainly successful, that is to say, a healthy way of dealing with sexual energy which does not risk the isolating effects of a repression which virtually insures the unwanted re-emergence of that energy in the symptom. In his one extended treatment of sublimation, *Leonardo da Vinci and a Memory of His Childhood*, Freud's fascination with the figure is sustained by Leonardo's failure, the incompletion of many of his projects together with the refusal to contemplate the difficulties of preserving his own work (as in the case of *The Last Supper*). In that sense, much of Leonardo's work would be more readily classified in relation to repression. There is a certain irreversibility associated with the process of sublimation which disallows a return from the intellectual or artistic endeavor—its transformation back into the libidinal energy from which it is derived. Within the Freudian schema, "desublimation" is either impossible or extremely difficult; it is as though the "raising," "lifting," or "elevating" effects associated with the etymological roots of sublimation could not be undone. Its product is deposited safely beyond the grasp of the psychoanalytic operation, beyond the regime of a perverse sexuality which constitutes its origin. To that extent, sublimation bespeaks both psychical health and a non-relation to the origin which makes it an absolutely unique concept within the Freudian problematic. Although they are originally intimately linked, the perverse and the sublime are ultimately and definitively dissociated.

This alignment of the opposition between sublimation and repression with that between the healthy and the pathological can, predictably enough, be mapped onto sexual difference. While women can have recourse to the process of repression—indeed, the hysteric is at the origin of the theorization of repression and the symptom, Freud frequently and consistently pointed out that women are less capable of sublimation than men. In other words, access to the pathological is insured to women while access to health is less certain. Luce Irigaray argues that "woman has the task of maintaining the 'object' end of the subject-object polarity of sexual difference; she will therefore be unable to perform the 'substitution of objects' that occurs in the process of sublimation."[4] If the woman cannot aspire to sublimation, perhaps she can represent its product, just as she acts as the support of so many tropological systems in our culture. But, according to Irigaray, she can represent it only badly, mired as she is in the hysterical symptom: "Enigmatic 'somatizations,' hysterical 'dreams' in which we are supposed to see 'the caricature of a work of art,' as Freud puts it in *Totem and Taboo*. Woman's special form of neurosis would be to 'mimic' a work of art, to be *a bad (copy of a) work of art*."[5] She goes on to specify woman's neurosis as a "counterfeit," a "parody," or a "forgery" of an artistic process. In this sense, women would, while not exactly lying or deceiving, *incarnate* in their illness inauthenticity, the disappearance of the Benjaminian aura, the faulty reproduction of an original.

Successful art, then, would be the outcome of a specifically masculine process, sublimation, which is, nevertheless, marginalized in the theoretical literature of psychoanalysis. Sublimation is the fourth vicissitude of the instinct specified by Freud in "Instincts and Their Vicissitudes," but it literally drops out of the discussion while repression, the third vicissitude, gets its own essay later. Perhaps this is why there are seldom appeals to the concept of sublimation in discussions of the contributions psychoanalysis can make to aesthetics. Less fully developed than other relevant concepts—identification, the symptom, fantasy, the uncanny—it falls by the wayside. The implicit question informing the work of the psychoanalytic critic is "Where does sexuality reside in a text?," or "What is the link between sexuality and textuality?" Feminist theory has seemed to require that sexuality be attached to the attribute of identity, hence linking it primarily to the function of character. Unfortunately, this nearly always entails the dangerous assumption that the major attribute of character is mimetic, that the character is somehow directly comparable to the patient on the couch, that the character in fact *has* a psyche that can be analyzed, a psyche which is, moreover, accessible to the analyst. Such an assumption subtends some of the most sophisticated feminist film theory as well as the maligned genre of psychobiography (of which *Leonardo* is an example) and Freud's crudest attempts at aesthetic analysis. What the approach neglects is the fundamental fact that character is first and foremost a textual mark, a trace, or more accurately, a bundle of such marks onto which the reader or spectator projects a personality, a psychology.

The etymology of the term "character" would seem to confirm such a view. As John Frow points out in his extensive analysis of the ramifications of the concept of character, "Etymologically the lexeme derives from the Greek *kharattein*, 'to make sharp, cut furrows in, engrave,' and it yields two primary 'literal' senses in English: that of mark or stamp, and more specifically that of a significant mark: for example, 'a graphic symbol. . . .' "[6] The Oxford English Dictionary distinguishes between this "literal" level of the term and the "figurative" meanings associated with the understanding of character as a moral and a fictional entity, as indicating a personality or an individuality. Frow claims that this opposition "suggests the possibility of thinking character (both fictional *and* moral) in terms of effects of readability produced by conventional systems of signification, rather than in terms of nonconventional structures of human nature (which in practice turn out to be the universalizing projection of a set of historical conventions: those of bourgeois individualism)."[7]

Ultimately, Frow argues that there are two one-sided and hence insufficient approaches to the analysis of character, which might be aligned with the figurative and literal meanings of the term as specified by the OED. One would treat the character as simply the "analogue of the person," the mimetic representation of a subject with all the attributes usually associated with subjectivity (individuality, morality, personality, drives, desires, sexuality, etc.)—this would be the approach of the crude psychoanalysis of character discussed earlier. Here the form or strategies, the very *work* of representation itself would be neglected. The second approach would reduce character completely to the status of textual mark, hence neglecting the necessary dependence of character upon "cultural schemata defining the nature of the self." This would be a formalism resting upon an absolute denial of the character's status as a quasi-subject, whose impact upon the reader/spectator raises questions about affect and identification. Consequently, Frow concludes, "the concept is both ontologically and methodologically ambivalent; and any attempt to resolve this ambivalence by thinking character either as merely the analogue of a person or as merely a textual function avoids coming to terms with the full complexity of the problem."[8] Frow cannot envisage a non-anthropomorphic literary or filmic narrative and associates the concept of character with *readability* and the affective engagement of reader or spectator with the text. Although it is not conducive to a simple psychoanalysis of symptoms, character is clearly an anchoring point in the reception of the text.

In reaction against the potential crudeness of the psychoanalysis of character and the concomitant notion of identification in film theory, several feminist critics have appealed to the concept of fantasy, in the process marginalizing the complex issue of character.[9] This tendency relies heavily on Jean Laplanche's analysis of fantasy—an analysis which accentuates the notions of space and setting rather than character. According to Laplanche, "fantasy . . . is not the object of desire, but its setting"[10]; in *The Language of Psychoanalysis*, the function of fantasy is specified as the "*mise-en-scène* of desire."[11] It is a certain arrangement of space and its rearrangement across time—rather than the characters who occupy that space—which is central to the concept of fantasy. Although Laplanche claims that the distinction between conscious and unconscious fantasy is far less relevant to Freud than the distinction between original and secondary fantasies, the concept is nevertheless resolutely associated with repression and the symptom. Hence, fantasy comes to be seen as the final product, the endpoint of analysis, "a latent content to be revealed behind the symptom. . . . the symptom has become the *stage-setting of fantasies* (thus a fantasy of prostitution, of street-walking, might be discovered beneath the symptom of agoraphobia)."[12] (The example of prostitution is revealing and I will return to it later.)

What is crucial to Laplanche's analysis is a desubjectivization of fantasy; in the structure of deepest fantasy, the idea of the subject disappears altogether. The subject can occupy the fantasy in a "desubjectivized form," in the syntax of the fantasy's sequence[13] and what the most intense fantasy ultimately effects is the loss of the very distinction between subject and object. Subjectivity is defined by its sheer amorphousness and fluidity. In feminist film criticism, this notion of fantasy is activated to demonstrate the mobility and fluidity of the spectator's relation to the text, particularly with respect to sexual identity. What is valued here is the psychical instability which thwarts the fixing of identity, and the constant slippage between various textual roles and positions. Fantasy theory's desire is to annihilate an identity which has been oppressive—but to annihilate it by fiat, simply declaring it non-operational at the level of an indisputable psychical reality of slippage, splitting, and failure. While there is no desire to eliminate the category of character altogether, it is sometimes reduced to the idea of position (spectators would identify with positions rather than characters) and is always unfixed, unanchored. I would suggest that character is a concept which cannot be so readily abandoned. Because character is *embodied* in the cinema (unlike in the novel where it is the effect of linguistic signals), it is an even more resistant, difficult, intransigent concept than it is in literature. In fact, the process of characterization proliferates; it exceeds the boundaries of the isolated text and attaches itself to the "real" actors and actresses whose personal lives become the object of intense scrutiny in fan magazines and the press.

Psychobiography (whether of the non-fictional or the fictional) and fantasy theory thus represent two extremes of the discourse on character. In the first, character is reified, fixed in a one-to-one correspondence with the person, the individual whose psychohistory is legible, analyzable. In the second, character is unmoored and dispersed while desire is unloosed to traverse without limit the space of the narrative. I want to shift attention to the process of sublimation not because it is the heroic psychoanalytic concept which will resolve all of these problems associated with the relation between psychoanalysis and aesthetics or because it is capable of moderating the excesses of psychobiography and fantasy theory. In any event, it is immediately apparent that this would be difficult since sublimation is designed to explicate the relation between the artist and the work and would resist theorization in terms of reception. But it is not as an interpretive method, a hermeneutic tool, or an appropriate psychoanalytic concept that I invoke it here. Instead, I want to investigate it as a recurrent problem, a trouble spot, an irritation as Laplanche would have it, in Freud's approach to questions of aesthetics. Ultimately it is a concept which does not work the way it is supposed to work. Nevertheless, it will eventually return us to the question of character, although not as a means of accounting for the concept in general but in relation to a specific—yet emblematic—case of female characterization. It is my contention that an examination of the problematic development of the concept of sublimation can elucidate the operation of a historically specific signifying process. It is therefore not a question of the *application* of something drawn from psychoanalysis to, for instance, a film text, but an investigation of the conjunction of certain historical and epistemological quandaries. What is the difficulty represented by sublimation? Why is it surrounded by so much eloquent silence and so confused an articulation in psychoanalysis?

The concept of sublimation may ultimately only testify to Freud's desire and inevitable failure to delimit an area outside of sexuality, to safeguard at least a small realm of uncontaminated cultural value. These cultural achievements arise *instead of* sexuality (perverse sexuality to be precise, since Freud claimed that it was the energy from polymorphous perversion which is channeled in sublimation). Hence the concept of sublimation depends on the rather fragile and tenuous opposition between cultural work and sexuality—and this despite the fact that Freud has taught us to be instantly suspicious of the notion of an inviolate or innocent cultural value. But it is important to be precise. Although Freud equates sublimation with desexualization, it is still the case that sublimation is subtended by sexuality: "the energy for the work of thought itself must be supplied from sublimated erotic sources."[14] But while the source or origin of sublimation is sexuality, sublimation is sublimation by virtue of a radical disjunction between the two, a gap which is unbridgeable—the displacement is irreversible. This is what marks the distinction between repression and sublimation—the symptom is interpretable, readable as the delegate of a repressed sexual conflict. Repression is in the final analysis reducible to sexuality. Sublimation, on the other hand, designates a realm of meanings which are not interpretable as sexual; they are excessive. Sublimation, in other words, marks the limit of psychoanalytic interpretation.

Laplanche attempts to understand sublimation as the reversal of the process of propping or *anaclisis*. While in *anaclisis* the sexual drive props itself upon the instinct of self-preservation (the oral drive upon hunger for instance), in sublimation, the non-sexual would prop itself upon, that is, emerge from, the sexual. However, the notion of a simple reversal of *anaclisis* is ultimately complicated by Laplanche's admission that in sublimation, the non-sexual would have to prop itself upon a sexuality which is in its turn propped upon the non-sexual—the Moebius strip logic of which seems to threaten the separation between the two sides. Furthermore, Laplanche finally finds it necessary to invoke the concept of repression in order to buttress that of sublimation, which often cannot stand on its own, and the return to sexuality is complete: "sometimes, indeed, sublimation does work in opposition to sexuality, but sometimes, on the contrary, the two complement each other, work together; which is along the lines of what I am attempting to suggest today, namely, that sublimation can be linked to a kind of neogenesis of sexuality."[15]

Sublimation, for Freud, was consistently associated with the drive to know, or epistemophilia. Yet, epistemophilia at times seems barely distinguishable from scopophilia, and the knowledge which is sought has to do with sexual secrets withheld from the child. The first theories constructed by the child circulate around the dilemmas of reproduction and sexual difference. Laplanche distinguishes between "intelligence," a faculty shared by animals, libidinally neutral and concerned with self-preservation, and "investigation," which seeks to uncover, to discover, to reveal, apparently for the sake of knowledge itself. But the very act of revealing that which was concealed, of delving beneath appearances, of a hide and seek game associated with vision, suggests that the urge to investigate (which was certainly characteristic of Leonardo da Vinci) is intimately bound up with sexuality. Investigation, for Laplanche, is "the search for something hidden, something necessarily capable of representation, beyond appearances. It is not surprising that the 'hidden' and 'representable' should be linked to the emergence of the sexual."[16] And because the sexual does not emerge in its totality, all at once, once and for all, but instead continually re-emerges, Laplanche links sublimation with the concept of a "neogenesis" of sexuality.

Laplanche's researches keep tripping against the difficult relation of the sexual and the non-sexual.[17] And it would seem that in each of Freud's readers, the concept of sublimation is brought back to sexuality. Theorists such as Jacques Lacan and Michèle Montrelay stress a definition of sublimation which makes it the point of articulation between language and sexuality. Lacan claims that sublimation is "an enigma, which, like all Freud's enigmas, was sustained as a wager to the end of his life without Freud deigning to offer any further explanation."[18] He attempts to explicate sublimation in relation to the concepts of drive and satisfaction, using his own speech act as a privileged example.

Well, in this article ["Instincts and Their Vicissitudes"], Freud tells us repeatedly that sublimation is also satisfaction of the drive, whereas it is *zielgehemmt*, inhibited as to its aim—it does not attain it. Sublimation is nonetheless satisfaction of the drive, without repression.

In other words—for the moment, I am not fucking, I am talking to you. Well! I can have exactly the same satisfaction as if I were fucking. That's what it means. Indeed, it raises the question of whether in fact I am not fucking at this moment. Between these two terms—drive and satisfaction—there is set up an extreme antinomy that reminds us that the use of the function of the drive has no other purpose than to put in question what is meant by satisfaction.[19]

Here it is the extreme displaceability of the drive with respect to object and aim which is at stake. For Freud it was the plasticity, the very malleability of sexuality which dictated its susceptibility to processes such as repression and sublimation.

In Lacan's account of the concept, sublimation is the result of a crisis concerning the object; it is motivated by the void which signals the relation between the real and the signifier—"In all forms of sublimation the void will be determinant."[20] Art is perhaps the pre-eminent form of sublimation and the most primordial artistic activity may very well be that of the potter who produces the vase which, for the archaeologist, is the irrefutable sign of a human presence. For Lacan, the vase creates the void in its very form and through this fact suggests the perspective of fullness—"if the vase can be full, it is insofar as, in its very essence, it is empty."[21] Given the fundamental lack or emptiness Lacan associates with the signifier, the vase deserves its archaeological prominence because it incarnates the signifying function. What is at stake in sublimation is the problem of dealing with this emptiness or void. Art is characterized by a certain mode of organization around the void; religion is constituted by all the means of avoiding the void (or, perhaps, as Lacan later amends it, "respecting" the void); and the discourse of science simply rejects the void in favor of a realistic discourse which is adequate to the object.

Sublimation in Lacan's account thus concerns the drama of signification as it plays itself out in the relation to the object. His fundamental definition of sublimation is a process which "elevates an object to the dignity of the Thing [*la Chose*]."[22] And Lacan later claims that *la Chose* has the character of an *au-dela du sacré*. From this point of view, the exemplary form or paradigm of sublimation would be courtly love, which is dependent upon the very inaccessibility of its object. Courtly love inscribes inaccessibility as the proper form of relation between man and woman. In courtly love, according to Lacan, "what the man demands, all that he can demand, is to be deprived of something of the real."[23] The various stipulations, the rules and regulations of the poetry of courtly love, the attribution of arbitrary demands to the lady involved—all act as interruptions, as mediations, as indirections.

It is quite striking that Lacan locates sublimation, which Freud associated with the sphere of the non-sexual, in a desexualized sexual relation between man and woman. Shot through with sexuality insofar as sexuality for Lacan is always infused with absence, courtly love would also represent the opposite of sexuality in what Lacan calls the "crude" sense. In any event, the difficulty of desexualizing sublimation is manifest in Lacan's discourse as well as in Freud's. In fact, for Lacan, sublimation exemplifies the work of the drive—it "reveals the proper nature of the drive (*Trieb*) insofar as it is not purely the instinct, but has a relation with *das Ding* as such, with *la Chose* as it is distinct from the object."[24] In this sense, sublimation is a privileged psychoanalytic concept insofar as it embodies the very slippage of the signifier which is fundamental to Lacan's linguistic approach.

In Montrelay's work, sublimation is even more explicitly bound up with the process of articulation. She claims that it is in fact a "misinterpretation" to define sublimation as the passage from the sexual to the non-sexual. For sublimation is the way in which the woman is able to reconstruct her sexuality in the realm of the symbolic (and hence escape the claustrophobia of incestuous pleasure). Sublimation, like the joke, is "an operation which consists in opening up new divisions and spaces in the material that it transforms."[25] In short, sublimation *is* articulation.

What is particularly intriguing about Montrelay's approach is that she undoes all the binary oppositions which uphold Freud's definition of sublimation—so much so that the supreme example of sublimation/articulation in her argument is an act of heterosexual intercourse: "the penis, its throbbing, its cadence and the movements of lovemaking could be said to produce the purest and most elementary form of signifying articulation. That of a series of blows which mark out the space of the body."[26] This would appear to be an extreme caricature of Freud's attempt to separate sublimation from sexuality. It is also somewhat scandalous from a feminist point of view since it situates woman's access to the symbolic in a heterosexual act of intercourse (whose definition is dependent upon the penis' metaphorical status as the pen which writes). Yet, Montrelay intends in this way to dephallicize the penis, to dissociate it from the "terrifying representations of the super-ego," to make it "an object of not-much-meaning."[27] It is in this evacuation of meaning from the process of sublimation that Montrelay's analysis reapproaches that of Freud. For sublimation, insofar as it is opposed by Freud to repression, ought to be uninterpretable, i.e. meaningless, within the realm of psychoanalysis, non-symptomatic. Montrelay's collapse of the opposition between the sexual and the non-sexual demonstrates the extreme instability of the concept of sublimation.

Laplanche, Lacan, and Montrelay share a certain nervousness with respect to a concept which emerges in Freud's discourse, which Freud in fact produces, but which remains somehow free-floating, without proper metapsychological grounding, lacking the rigorous systematicity usually associated with Freud's work. It is also a concept which at some level—and Montrelay's analysis seems to indicate this—does not make sense. Yet, despite its status as textual enigma or cipher, as empty of psychoanalytic content, all three theorists feel the urge to transform it into a concept which might almost be described as metapsychoanalytic, as a limit concept which defines the very essence of the psychoanalytic endeavor and the boundaries of its epistemic project. This is in keeping with the etymology of the term which evokes the notion of limits—a combination of the Latin *sub* (under, up to) and *limen* (threshold). It is also consistent with the philosophical definition of the sublime as that which marks "the unthinkable."[28] Nevertheless, the difficulties post-Freudian psychoanalysts experience with the term can be traced back to Freud's text. And I would like to suggest that there is a historical reason for the instability and uncertainty surrounding sublimation. Hence, a return to Freud's own elaboration of the concept is necessary.

It is in terms of the question of interpretation that Freud's most extensive treatment of sublimation, the study of Leonardo da Vinci, founders, particularly with respect to the issue of aesthetic sublimation.[29] As has been frequently pointed out, Freud attempts to distinguish sharply between Leonardo's artistic work and his scientific investigation, the latter increasingly overshadowing, making impossible, the former. But when confronting the pictorial work, Freud cannot refrain from interpreting it—and interpreting it in sexual terms. The products of Leonardo's sublimation—the portrait of the Mona Lisa, the painting *Madonna and Child with St. Anne*—are infused with sexuality. Freud interprets them as the symptomatic evidence of a family scenario which is colored by an ambivalent relation to the mother—a mother who, in the absence of the father, instills a premature eroticism in her own child hence "robbing" him of his masculinity. The intense effort to disjoin the product of sublimation from the symptom, to safeguard a realm of culture from sexuality, stalls, subverted by a desire to read. When Freud *interprets* Mona Lisa's smile it becomes a symptom and the concept of sublimation collapses.

What motivates an opposition which is so fragile, indeed, so anti-psychoanalytic to begin with? What are the terms which Freud is attempting so desperately to keep apart, insuring that one is not contaminated by the other? It would seem that this is psychoanalysis striving to think its own limits, to situate something beyond the grasp of its own methodology. In this way a topography is produced wherein cultural value would occupy its own space, irreducible to sexuality gone awry, and criticisms of Freud for pansexualism would be parried. Sexuality would *not* be everywhere; it could *not* explain everything. And ultimately, what it cannot explain is work. Sublimation does not name the aesthetic artifact, the mathematical equation, the bridge which is built but instead the process, the activity, the work which leads to this result. Freud consistently refers to the replacement of sexual instinctual forces by "professional activity." He is most inclined to describe sublimation in relation to *intellectual* work but, fundamentally, it can be adequate to any type of labor. In a footnote to *Civilization and Its Discontents*, he refers to

> the significance of work for the economics of the libido. No other technique for the conduct of life attaches the individual so firmly to reality as laying emphasis on work . . . The possibility it offers of displacing a large amount of libidinal components, whether narcissistic, aggressive or even erotic, on to professional work and on to the human relations connected with it lends it a value by no means second to what it enjoys as something indispensible to the preservation and justification of existence in society.[30]

Unfortunately, according to Freud, men do not value work very highly—"they do not strive after it as they do after other possibilities of satisfaction." In other words, Freud assumes the alienation of labor but dehistoricizes it by universalizing it (referring to the "natural human aversion to work").[31]

Sublimation is, furthermore, inscribed within an economy of energy, efficiency, and conservation which is not unrelated to theories of labor in the early period of industrialization. Sublimation is born from the energy provided by the perversions and Freud refers to the fact that in it "a not inconsiderable increase in psychical efficiency results from a disposition which in itself is perilous."[32] The plasticity of the sexual drive makes possible the displacements from the sexual to the non-sexual involved in sublimation but, in warning that this is not an infinitely repeatable process, Freud makes use of a machine metaphor: "To extend this process of displacement illimitably is, however, certainly no more possible than with the transmutation of heat into mechanical power in the case of machines. A certain degree of direct sexual satisfaction appears to be absolutely necessary for by far the greater number of natures. . . ."[33] Hence, sublimation at a metapsychological level is elaborated through the vocabulary of labor: energy, efficiency, machines, work.

In its simplest, most reduced terms, then, sublimation puts into play an opposition between sex and work. It is somewhat striking that a strategy for defining the epistemological limits of psychoanalysis would confront an opposition which is reminiscent of the grand opposition of twentieth century cultural theories between the intellectual frameworks of Freud and Marx: sex vs. work, subjectivity vs. class consciousness, psychoanalysis vs. political economy. The quandaries confronted in theorizing sublimation would be one index of the difficulty in maintaining such an opposition. Freud's own dilemma in delimiting the field of psychoanalysis is made evident in a humorous autobiographical detail related in his essay on the uncanny. Freud, lost in a provincial town in Italy, finds himself suddenly in the red light district, with "nothing but painted women" at the windows. He hurries away from the area along winding streets only to find himself back in the same place where "my presence was now beginning to excite attention."[34] He again attempts to evade the area but is no more successful and arrives a third time in the same square. For Freud, this story serves to illustrate the relation between the repetition compulsion and the uncanny. But clearly it could be used to "tell" much more. Freud is not like Laplanche's agoraphobic whose symptom conceals a fantasy of street-walking or prostitution. Indeed, he might be said to be a kind of master of space, of topographies. Freud's fear is not of space, but of never advancing—of always returning to the same place. And that place is a place of sexuality. There is other evidence of Freud's anxiety about the association of psychoanalysis with an all too predictable determinism whose explanations always lead back to sexuality. In case studies such as *Dora* and *Leonardo da Vinci*, Freud repeatedly strives to anticipate and defuse the incredulity of the reader when he is about to present an explanation in terms of sexuality, prefacing his statements with claims like, "Now, you will not believe me when I tell you. . . ."[35]

Yet, in the story from the essay on the uncanny, the mise-en-scène reveals not just a fear of always returning to sexuality as an explanation, but an anxiety about a quite specific form of sexuality—one which, far from inevitably being called upon in interpretation, is generally excluded from the realm of psychoanalysis. For the inhabitants of that area Freud tries to avoid are "painted women," prostitutes, and the prostitute is the very figure of the collapse of the opposition between sex and work—her labor is the selling of sexuality. Not only are women incapable of sublimation in Freudian theory, they potentially represent the confounding of the binary opposition which sustains cultural value—again, they function like a "bad copy of a work of art" in Irigaray's terms.[36] The economy which subtends psychoanalytic theory is strongly influenced by a nineteenth century version of thermodynamics in which the notion of the conservation of energy dictates the arrangements and displacements of a finite amount of libido. Sublimation is an exemplary consequence of this economy since it depends upon the notion that sexual energy is displaceable and modifiable and can be released, liberated for cultural work. This economy, however, is also used as a buttress against another kind of economy, one which involves prices, labor, and exchange value. What is at least partially at stake for Freud in the fragile concept of sublimation is keeping the two economies separate. The place Freud would like to avoid in his uncanny fantasy is the place where sexuality meets exchange value, for this is a merger which strains the interpretive powers of psychoanalysis.

Hence, the prostitute is not a particularly central character in Freud's narrative. In fact, she tends to be marginalized as a figure who threatens the always already tenuous opposition between sex and work, cultural value and perverse sexuality. The prostituted body, according to Christine Buci-Glucksmann, is "a disfiguration of the 'sublime body.'"[37] Freud consistently associates the prostitute with the polymorphously perverse. For instance, in his attempt to argue the claim that neurosis is the negative of perversion, that perversion can be displaced by neurosis in the same individual, he cites the proverb, "A young whore makes an old nun."[38] Prostitutes are thus, in their work, aligned with a psychically regressive movement: "Prostitutes exploit the same polymorphous, that is infantile, disposition for the purposes of their profession."[39] This regressiveness is in sharp contrast to the connotations of uplifting, raising, elevating associated with the concept of sublimation. On the other hand, prostitutes do not *embody* this perversion—they "exploit" it, performing work which could be perceived as the ruin of sublimation. The notion of exploitation itself indicates a missing dimension of the Freudian problematic.

Freud's relative neglect of the figure of the prostitute is atypical of his historical milieux. In the late nineteenth century, the prostitute constituted a social and representational problem of enormous proportions. In fact, her seemingly stronger presence in greater numbers—perhaps merely her greater visibility—indicated a veritable contagion of sexuality, disease, and wasted energy. The influence of Alexandre Parent-Duchâtelet, who moved effortlessly from a study of the sewers of Paris to a detailed statistical analysis of prostitution, urging that it be subject to heavy surveillance and extensive regulation, was still strong in the latter half of the century.[40] For Parent-Duchâtelet, prostitution was a statistical problem and a geographical problem—it could be controlled by the processes of counting, categorizing, regulating, and containing (often through spatial containment in the aptly named *maisons de tolerance*). There was a certain continuity between his work on the sewer system and that on prostitution because in each case it was a question of the ordering and management of expenditure, waste. And nineteenth century bourgeois ideology was characterized by anxieties about waste, excess, refuse, disease. According to Alain Corbin, the brothel and the unregistered prostitute's room were perceived as "places of waste, as theaters for a triple degradation—of the prostitute, the client, and money."[41] In this sense, the prostitute represented the antithesis of the bourgeois economy of thrift and moderation. Her degradation of money is a function of her affiliation with its potentially excessive and dangerous mobility in speculation, its disengagement from a reassuring use value. From this point of view, she also degraded the concept of work.

Given the fact that the prostitute was characterized in the nineteenth century as lazy, fond of idleness and pleasure, it might be difficult to argue that her activity was even perceived as a form of work. However, the images are contradictory. There was also recognition of the fact that prostitution was frequently a response to low wages, poverty, or unemployment and that it was sometimes a sideline among working-class women.[42] It continued to be regarded as the "oldest profession in the world." Also, one of the major functions of regulationism was, according to Corbin, to transform the prostitutes into good workers who "above all would not enjoy their work."[43] Most significantly, in the social imaginary, prostitutes were affiliated with the laboring classes who were regarded as "vicious classes" or "dangerous classes," and whose corrupting influence they shared. In the 1920s, an assembly-line type organization of prostitution leads Corbin to refer to it as "Taylorized prostitution."[44]

Although they were seen to constitute a serious threat, prostitutes were also the subject of an almost obsessive fascination in the second half of the nineteenth century, a fascination which lingered into the early years of the twentieth century. This fascination had little to do with the actual experience of the prostitute. Nevertheless, the prostitute's representational value transformed her into an exemplary character in literature, art, and the theater. In the work of Baudelaire, Flaubert, Zola, Manet, Degas, Wedekind, and somewhat later, Benjamin, a precise social imaginary is constructed around the figure of the prostitute. In the cinema, on the other hand, despite the fascination with the prostitute exhibited in a limited number of films— *Traffic in Souls* (Tucker, 1913), *Pandora's Box* (Pabst, 1929), *Blonde Venus* (von Sternberg, 1932), and *Diary of a Lost Girl* (Pabst, 1929) would be some examples—her representation is nowhere near as pervasive and insistent as in literature or art, even in the pre-censorship era. This may be linked to the fact that prostitution gradually loses its attraction as a privileged aesthetic trope after the 1920s, but it also has something to do with the social function of the cinema and its deployment of bodies, which mobilizes some of the connotations of prostitution conceived on a figurative level (I will return to this phenomenon later). In a discussion of the changing places and techniques of prostitution in the early twentieth century, Corbin points out that "the number of cinemas was expanding, but they did not lend themselves to soliciting."[45] The spectacle and exhibitionism associated with prostitution in its take-over of the streets were now on the screen, and the rearrangement of public space transformed the processes of commodification of the body.

In the literature and art of the late nineteenth century, however, the increased fascination with the figure of the prostitute, as the epitome of the female *flâneur*, was emblematic of the new woman's relation to urban space. The conjunction of the woman and the city suggests the potential of an intolerable and dangerous sexuality, a sexuality which is out of bounds precisely as a result of the woman's revised relation to space, her new ability to "wander" (and hence to "err"). This was perceived as a peculiarly modern phenomenon. The "painted woman" of Freud's anecdote became the very figure of a modernism associated with illusion, deception, artificiality. It was becoming more and more difficult to distinguish between the well-attired prostitute and the bourgeois lady since both were now found, unaccompanied, in the streets. The free and unanchored circulation of sexuality and money epitomized the modernity associated with the increased traffic of urban space. Benjamin referred to the prostitute as an aspect of the "allegory of the modern." Most significantly, the prostitute ostentatiously exhibited the commodification of the human body, the point where the body and exchange value coincided, where capitalism's ruse was exposed. It was in this sense that she represented what T.J. Clark refers to as "the danger or the price of modernity."[46] The prostitute is so resolutely linked with modernism because she demonstrates the new status of the body as exchangeable and profitable image.

Hence, the prostitute collapses not only the opposition between sex and work but that between the human being and the commodity as well. Sexuality is on the market, and while this has certainly been the case for centuries, it achieves a new significance at the end of the nineteenth and beginning of the twentieth centuries. For Benjamin, an expanding capitalism ensured the striking intimacy between prostitution and labor: "Prostitution can claim to count as 'work' at the moment work becomes prostitution," and "The closer work comes to prostitution, the more inviting it is to describe prostitution as work. . . ."[47] The status of labor power as commodity becomes manifest in the body of the prostitute. As Buci-Glucksmann points out in her investigation of Benjamin's theorization of prostitution in its relation to commodification,

> Such a "commodity" conveys a new correlation between sex and work—the prostitute claims "worth" as labor and has a price at the very moment "when work becomes prostitution." There is much more than a superficial historical analogy between the prostitute who obtains an increasingly well-accounted for, both profitable and exploitative, payment for her time and attentions, and a commercial economy where everything has its price. For if salaried labor and the general extension of commodities mark the "decline" of the qualitative, of use value, of distinctions for the benefit of a more generalized social submission to the universality of exchange—by the very abstraction of its universality—so prostitution expresses the end of the aura and the decline (*Verfall*) of love.[48]

This process could also be interpreted, in a similarly nostalgic vein, as further substantiating the notion that the prostitute represents the collapse of sublimation as a concept and hence the downfall of the "sublime"—the "end of the aura and the decline of love." The sublime, for Kant, was indissociable from an individual subjective experience. It could not be located in objects *per se* but was irrevocably attached to individual consciousness, and therefore buttressed one's consciousness of one's own individuality and uniqueness. According to Frances Ferguson, this ensures that the sublime is the locus of non-exchangeability.

> For the peculiar feature of the sublime is that it affirms individual identity at the expense of the notion of private ownership and the privileged access that seems to be accorded an owner and in that sense exposes not so much a drive into spirituality as a dissatisfaction with the limitations imposed by the notion of property. The trouble with property is that its essential nature is not determined by its owner; it would not be property unless it were exchangeable, unless it were alienable and survived the process of being removed from its original owner. The virtue of the sublime is that it cannot be exchanged, that each experience of sublimity is permanently bound not just to a subjective judgment but to its particular subjective judge.[49]

The body would seem to be the very support of that individual consciousness, of that particularity and uniqueness which characterizes the subjectivity which has access to the sublime. When the body becomes a form of property which is exchangeable, when subjectivity and sexuality themselves are perceived as being on the market, the concept of the sublime is seriously threatened.

What is at issue here is certainly the commodification of the human but the reverse is true as well—the prostitute comes to represent the humanization of the commodity (her characterization is, quite frequently, a sympathetic one—it is only through an accident of fate that she has become a prostitute; there is no moral fault).[50] Such a humanization of the commodity is, curiously enough, a way of selling the commodity form of culture itself. In the prostitute, sexuality and exchange value coincide most explicitly. But she is not an isolated case—to be confined within the walls of the bordello. One could plausibly argue that the prostitute in the late nineteenth and early twentieth centuries becomes a kind of meta-character—that is to say, she exemplifies or embodies what becomes *the* task of characterization in the twentieth century—particularly in the cinema—the humanization of the commodity. Perhaps this is why her literal representation in the cinema is unnecessary as such and the fascination with the figure of the prostitute declines in the twentieth century (in comparison with the obsessions of the nineteenth). The process of characterization now endows the commodity with speech, with emotions, with a moral psychology which strives to give the lie to both alienation and commodification.

From this point of view, a psychobiography of character would simply fuel the process, multiply its ramifications, not demystify it. It would be to assent fully to the humanization of the commodity at the level of theory. Furthermore, to psychoanalyze characters is to place Freud's work outside of time and history, to situate his concepts in relation to, if not a universal human nature, a universal, transcendent human psyche—in effect, to dehistoricize these concepts. In such an approach, the conventionality of character is at least momentarily forgotten. Sublimation seems to me to be a crucial concept not because it can deepen or extend our understanding of characters or the relations of authors to texts. Instead, its significance stems entirely from its collapse as a concept—its failure to delineate certain categories at a specific moment in time. The concepts of psychoanalysis cannot be applied haphazardly to the text (the notion of application always suggests a pasting on, an afterthought which doesn't *take*). It would be far more productive to trace and delineate the lapses in its logic which can elucidate another textual logic. By examining closely the vicissitudes of the development, the articulations of psychoanalysis' concepts, we can perceive the way in which they are traumatized by history.

What Freud experienced and attempted to deny was a certain historical assault on the sublime. Aesthetics and aesthetic activity held an important place for Freud, sometimes a quasi-sacred one. This inevitably motivated his constantly failing attempt to safeguard an area of culture from his own interpretive psychoanalytic techniques, in particular, symptomatic reading. But in the nineteenth and early twentieth centuries, notions of the aesthetic were severely destabilized—by the growth of urban spaces, the process of commodification, the lure of the counterfeit, the invasion of mass culture (including the cinema). Baudelaire not only made the prostitute a key figure in his poetry, he identified with her (writing of that "holy prostitution of the soul which gives itself wholly, poetry and charity, to the unexpected that appears, to the unknown that passes"[51]). Aesthetics as a category could be preserved by Freud by making it at some level immune to psychoanalytic understanding, unthreatened by a symptomatic reading which would transform the work into an expression of perverse sexuality. Freud's failure, and the failure of many who came after him, to maintain the distinction between the sexual and the non-sexual subtending the concept of sublimation is an indication of both the pressures of modernity and the extent to which Freud found it extremely difficult to accept certain limits for his own psychoanalytical enterprise.

Does this shatter the hopes that reside in sublimation as an alternative concept which allows a reading that would not be symptomatic?[52] Is critical language informed by psychoanalysis delegated the sole function of demonstrating the pathological nature of the text? I would suggest that psychoanalytic criticism does not necessarily have to think itself as exhausted by the operation of analyzing symptoms, although in any reading attuned to the vicissitudes of ideology this will continue to be an important aspect.[53] Yet, an alternative conceptualization of its role is not allowed by the concept of sublimation, but rather by its transformation in psychoanalytic discourse, indeed, by its misreading. While in Montrelay's analysis Freud's concept of sublimation collapses entirely, re-emerging in a different guise as articulation, what also emerges in the process is a different way of conceptualizing the function of psychoanalytic language (one which is not, ultimately, unindebted to Freud). The therapeutic function of psychoanalytic language is linked by Montrelay to its structuring effect. The analyst's word does not explain or interpret (symptoms), it structures, it articulates. Psychoanalytic discourse is not adequate to a truth concealed within the text of the patient's discourse. According to Montreley, "the analyst's discourse is not reflexive but different" and sublimation is "an operation which consists in opening up new divisions and spaces in the material that it transforms."[54] In a sense, then, the analyst's language is performative, producing effects in the patient's own discourse, in her cathexis of the word.

In the relation between the critic and the text, on the other hand, the transferential connection will always be missing, precisely because the text is a work which has outlines, boundaries, limits—a work which cannot speak back, cannot return the look of the analyst. But the relation between the critic and her reader is different. Critical language, and in particular a critical language informed by psychoanalysis, is always in some sense a performative language with its own peculiar effects. It mobilizes, it scandalizes, it articulates—it is itself generative of other texts. The symptom is too fundamental a category in psychoanalysis to disappear from this discourse. But at the same time that a psychoanalytically informed critical language must act *as if* it were adequate to an interpretation of the symptom, it must also acknowledge that it is itself a structuring discourse, which necessarily exceeds any meanings anticipated by the text. It exceeds them in view of its own reader and hence of its own historical context, inevitably blind to its own most telling symptoms. In psychoanalysis, the effectivity of the word lies in its ability to produce another word. If one concedes that the text (literary, artistic, filmic) generates the critical text, there is no reason to suppose that such a critical text should be the end of the line.

Notes

INTRODUCTION

1. Christine Buci-Glucksmann, *La raison baroque: de Baudelaire à Benjamin* (Paris: Éditions Galilée, 1984) 34. All translations of this text are mine.

2. Buci-Glucksmann 203–4.

3. Virginia M. Allen, *The Femme Fatale: Erotic Icon* (Troy, N.Y.: Whitston, 1983) 4.

4. Allen 2.

5. See, for instance, Jean-Louis Baudry, "The Apparatus," trans. Jean Andrews and Bertrand Augst, *Camera Obscura* 1 (Fall 1976): 104–26; Baudry, "Ideological Effects of the Basic Cinematographic Apparatus," trans. Alan Williams, *Film Quarterly* 28.2 (1974–75): 39–47; Stephen Heath, "Narrative Space," *Screen* 17.3 (1976): 19–75.

6. Walter Benjamin, "The Work of Art in the Age of Mechanical Reproduction," *Illuminations*, ed. Hannah Arendt, trans. Harry Zohn (New York: Schocken, 1969) 217–52.

7. For a more extensive discussion of this point, see Lesley Stern's contribution in Lesley Stern, Laleen Jayamanne, and Helen Grace, "Remembering Claire Johnston," *Framework* 35 (1988): 114–29; and Janet Bergstrom and Mary Ann Doane, "The Female Spectator: Contexts and Directions," *Camera Obscura* 20–21 (May–September 1989): 5–27.

8. The significance of this opposition varies, of course, according to the individual feminist film theorist and her specific intellectual background. See, for instance, Judith Mayne's contribution to the special issue, "The Spectatrix," *Camera Obscura* 20–21 (May–September 1989): 230–34. I would not want to imply that my experience is representative of that of feminist film theorists in general. This is crucially so, given the wide variety of fields (English, French, comparative literature, art history, as well as cinema studies) from which film scholars have emerged.

9. Claire Johnston, ed., *Notes on Women's Cinema* (London: Society for Education in Film and Television, 1973).

10. Christian Metz, "The Imaginary Signifier," *Screen*, 16.2 (1975): 14–76.

11. Michel de Certeau, *Heterologies: Discourse on the Other*, trans. Brian Massumi (Minneapolis: U of Minnesota P, 1986) 19.

12. Nancy K. Miller, *Subject to Change: Reading Feminist Writing* (New York: Columbia UP, 1988) 5.

13. For particularly sophisticated arguments to this effect, see Denise Riley, *"Am I That Name?" : Feminism and the Category of 'Women' in History* (Minneapolis: U of Minnesota P, 1988); and Elizabeth V. Spelman, *Inessential Woman: Problems of Exclusion in Feminist Thought* (Boston: Beacon, 1988).

14. Teresa de Lauretis, *Alice Doesn't: Feminism, Semiotics, Cinema* (Bloomington: Indiana UP, 1984) and *Technologies of Gender: Essays on Theory, Film, and Fiction* (Bloomington: Indiana UP, 1987); Jane Gaines, "White Privilege and Looking Relations: Race and Gender in Feminist Film Theory," *Cultural Critique* 4 (Fall 1986): 59–79. A revised version of this essay appeared in *Screen* 29.4 (1988): 12–27.

15. Isaac Julien and Kobena Mercer, "Introduction—De Margin and De Centre," *Screen* 29.4 (1988): 8.

16. In a recent paper, "Tracking the Vampire," delivered at the 1989 Modern Language Association Convention, Sue-Ellen Case singled out feminist film theory as being particularly guilty of a blind heterosexism. While it is clear that most of the work of feminist film theory has emphasized an interrogation of heterosexuality, it is not clear that this focus is synonymous with heterosexism. Even before Laura Mulvey's ground-breaking article on visual pleasure, feminists had fixed their glance on the Hollywood Cinema as the locus of an especially powerful and influential filmic organization of sexual difference. The Hollywood Cinema is a major enforcer of what Judith Butler has referred to as "the epistemic regime of presumptive heterosexuality" (*Gender Trouble: Feminism and the Subversion of Identity* [New York: Routledge, 1990] x). One need only register the compulsive heterosexual coupling which constitutes the closure of innumerable Hollywood films. In fact, the excessiveness of this tendency, the obsessive, even hysterical, inscription of heterosexuality as the narrative support of the Classical Hollywood text transforms this cinema into the source of an insistent camp reappropriation in gay and lesbian subcultures. For in the Hollywood cinema, heterosexuality is magnified, performed and reperformed. Feminist film criticism has hopefully gone some distance in defamiliarizing heterosexuality as a natural and normalized mode of being. As Freud points out, heterosexuality is itself "a problem that needs elucidating" (*Three Essays on the Theory of Sexuality*, trans. James Strachey [New York: Basic, 1962] 12). To believe otherwise is to fully accept the naturalization of heterosexuality. This is not to deny that an in-depth analysis of gay and lesbian representations in relation to the cinema is necessary. But Case's analysis neglects the substantial work that has been done in this area. This work includes that of Chris Straayer ("Sexual Subjects: Signification, Viewership, and Pleasure in Film and Video," diss., Northwestern University, 1989; *"Personal Best*: A Lesbian Feminist Audience Analysis," *Jump Cut* 29 [1985]: 40–44; "Sexuality and Video

Narrative," *Afterimage* 16.10 [1989]: 8–11), B. Ruby Rich ("From Repressive Tolerance to Erotic Liberation: *Maedchen in Uniform*," *Re-vision: Essays in Feminist Film Criticism*, ed. Mary Ann Doane, Patricia Mellencamp and Linda Williams [Frederick, MD: University Publications of America, 1984] 100–130), Teresa de Lauretis (*Alice Doesn't* and *Technologies of Gender*), and Judith Mayne ("Dorothy Arzner and Lesbian Looks," MLA Convention, Washington, D.C., 29 Dec. 1989, also published as Chapter Three, "Female Authorship Reconsidered" in *The Woman at the Keyhole: Feminism and Women's Cinema* [Bloomington: Indiana UP, 1990]).

17. See the special issue, "The Essential Difference: Another Look at Essentialism," *differences* 1.2 (1989).

18. Henry Louis Gates, Jr., "Editor's Introduction: Writing 'Race' and the Difference It Makes," *Critical Inquiry* 12.1 (1985): 4.

CHAPTER ONE

1. Sigmund Freud, "Femininity," *The Standard Edition of the Complete Psychological Works of Sigmund Freud*, vol. 22, ed. James Strachey (London: Hogarth and the Institute of Psychoanalysis, 1964) 113.

2. This is the translation given in a footnote in *The Standard Edition*, vol. 22, 113.

3. Heinrich Heine, *The North Sea*, trans. Vernon Watkins (New York: New Directions, 1951) 77.

4. In other words, the woman can never ask her own ontological question. The absurdity of such a situation within traditional discursive conventions can be demonstrated by substituting a "young woman" for the "young man" of Heine's poem.

5. As Oswald Ducrot and Tzvetan Todorov point out in *Encyclopedic Dictionary of the Sciences of Language*, trans. Catherine Porter (Baltimore and London: Johns Hopkins UP, 1979) 195, the potentially universal understandability of the hieroglyphic is highly theoretical and can only be thought as the unattainable ideal of an imagistic system: "It is important of course not to exaggerate either the resemblance of the image with the object—the design is stylized very rapidly—or the 'natural' and 'universal' character of the signs: Sumerian, Chinese, Egyptian and Hittite hieroglyphics for the same object have nothing in common."

6. Ducrot and Todorov 194. Emphasis mine.

7. See Noël Burch's film, *Correction Please, or How We Got Into Pictures*, Great Britain, 1979.

8. Laura Mulvey, "Visual Pleasure and Narrative Cinema," *Screen* 16.3 (Autumn 1975): 12–13. The essay is also reprinted in Mulvey, *Visual and Other Pleasures* (Bloomington: Indiana UP, 1989) 14–28 and in *Feminism and Film*

Theory, ed. Constance Penley (New York: Routledge; London: British Film Institute, 1988) 57–68.

9. Charles Affron, *Star Acting: Gish, Garbo, Davis* (New York: E.P. Dutton, 1977) 281–82.

10. This argument focuses on the image to the exclusion of any consideration of the soundtrack, primarily because it is the process of imaging which seems to constitute the major difficulty in theorizing female spectatorship. The image is also popularly understood as a metonymic signifier for the cinema as a whole and for good reason: historically, sound has been subordinate to the image within the dominant classical system. For more on the image/sound distinction in relation to sexual difference, see my article, "The Voice in the Cinema: The Articulation of Body and Space," *Yale French Studies* 60 (1980): 33–50.

11. Noël Burch, *Theory of Film Practice,* trans. Helen R. Lane (New York: Praeger, 1973) 35.

12. Christian Metz, "The Imaginary Signifier," *Screen* 16.2 (Summer 1975): 60. See Metz, *The Imaginary Signifier: Psychoanalysis and the Cinema,* trans. Celia Britton et. al. (Bloomington: Indiana UP, 1982). Excerpts from the essay are included in *Narrative, Apparatus, Ideology,* ed. Philip Rosen (New York: Columbia U P, 1986) 244–78.

13. Metz 61.

14. Luce Irigaray, *This Sex Which Is Not One,* trans. Catherine Porter with Carolyn Burke (Ithaca: Cornell UP, 1985) 31.

15. Luce Irigaray, "Women's Exile," *Ideology and Consciousness* 1 (May 1977): 74.

16. Hélène Cixous, "The Laugh of the Medusa," *New French Feminisms,* ed. Elaine Marks and Isabelle de Courtivron (Amherst: U of Massachusetts P, 1980) 257.

17. Sarah Kofman, "Ex: The Woman's Enigma," *Enclitic* 4.2 (Fall 1980): 20.

18. Michèle Montrelay, "Inquiry into Femininity," m/f 1 (1978): 91–92.

19. Freud, "Some Psychological Consequences of the Anatomical Distinction Between the Sexes," *Sexuality and the Psychology of Love,* ed. Philip Rieff (New York: Collier, 1963) 187–88.

20. Freud, "Femininity" 125.

21. Freud, "Some Psychological Consequences . . . " 187.

22. Molly Haskell, *From Reverence to Rape* (Baltimore: Penguin, 1974) 154.

23. Irigaray, "Women's Exile" 65.

24. Laura Mulvey, "Afterthoughts on 'Visual Pleasure 'and Narrative Cinema' inspired by *Duel in the Sun,*" *Framework* 6.15–17 (Summer 1981):13. The essay is also reprinted in Mulvey, *Visual and Other Pleasures,* 29–38 and in *Feminism and Film Theory* 69–79.

25. Joan Riviere, "Womanliness as a Masquerade," *Psychoanalysis and Female Sexuality,* ed. Hendrik M. Ruitenbeek (New Haven: College and UP, 1966) 213. The essay was originally published in *The International Journal of Psychoanalysis* 10 (1929). My analysis of the concept of masquerade differs markedly from that of Luce Irigaray. See *Ce sexe qui n'en est pas un* (Paris: Les Éditions de Minuit, 1977) 131–32 (*This Sex Which Is Not One,* 133–34). It also diverges to a great extent from the very important analysis of masquerade presented by Claire Johnston in "Femininity and the Masquerade: Anne of the Indies," *Jacques Tourneur* (London: British Film Institute, 1975) 36–44. I am indebted to her for the reference to Riviere's article.

26. Moustafa Safouan, "Is the Oedipus Complex Universal?," *m/f* 5–6 (1981): 84–85.

27. Montrelay 93.

28. Silvia Bovenschen, "Is There a Feminine Aesthetic?," *New German Critique* 10 (Winter 1977): 129.

29. Montrelay 93.

30. Linda Williams, "When the Woman Looks . . . ," in *Re-vision: Essays in Feminist Film Criticism,* ed. Mary Ann Doane, Patricia Mellencamp and Linda Williams (Frederick, MD: U Publications of America and the American Film Institute, 1984).

31. Johnston 40.

32. Freud, *Jokes and Their Relation to the Unconscious,* trans. James Strachey (New York: Norton, 1960) 99.

33. Freud, *Jokes* 98.

34. Weston J. Naef, *Counterparts: Form and Emotion in Photographs* (New York: E. P. Dutton and the Metropolitan Museum of Art, 1982) 48–49.

35. Naef 48–49.

36. Michel Foucault, *The History of Sexuality,* Vol. I: *An Introduction,* trans. Robert Hurley (New York: Pantheon, 1978).

CHAPTER TWO

1. *Screen* 23.3–4 (Sept./Oct.1982): 74–87. The essay is reprinted in this collection. See Chapter One.

2. Doane 82.

3. Joan Riviere, "Womanliness as a Masquerade," *Psychoanalysis and Female Sexuality,* ed. Hendrick M. Ruitenbeek (New Haven: College and UP, 1966) 213, hereafter cited in the text. The essay was originally published in *The International Journal of Psychoanalysis* 10 (1929).

4. Sigmund Freud, "On Narcissism: An Introduction," *General Psychological Theory,* ed. Philip Rieff (New York: Macmillan, 1963) 70.

5. Jacques Lacan, "The Meaning of the Phallus," *Feminine Sexuality: Jacques Lacan and the École Freudienne,* ed. Juliet Mitchell and Jacqueline Rose (New York: Norton, 1982) 85.

6. Tania Modleski, *The Women Who Knew Too Much: Hitchcock and Feminist Theory* (New York: Methuen, 1988) 8, hereafter cited in the text.

7. I should add that the phrase, the "ideals of semiotic systems," was not invoked without a certain amount of irony in the first place (at least with respect to its articulation with sexual difference).

8. Lacan, "Guiding Remarks for a Congress on Feminine Sexuality," *Feminine Sexuality* 97.

9. More accurately, Saussure uses the term "arbitrary" and the economic metaphor of "value" rather than the spatial metaphors of distance and separation invoked by such theorists as Derrida and Kristeva.

10. See Jacques Derrida, *Of Grammatology,* trans. Gayatri Chakravorty Spivak (Baltimore: Johns Hopkins UP, 1976) especially 101–40.

11. Julia Kristeva, "Women's Time," *Signs: Journal of Women in Culture and Society* 7.1 (Autumn 1981): 23.

12. Claude Lévi-Strauss, *The Elementary Structures of Kinship* (Boston: Beacon, 1969) 496.

13. Patrice Petro, "Modernity and Mass Culture in Weimar: Contours of a Discourse on Sexuality in Early Theories of Perceptions and Representation," *New German Critique* 40 (1987): 122.

14. Lacan, "The Meaning of the Phallus" 84.

15. Stephen Heath, "Joan Riviere and the Masquerade," *Formations of Fantasy,* ed. Victor Burgin, James Donald, and Cora Kaplan (London: Methuen, 1986) 56.

16. Doane 87.

17. Meaghan Morris, "*in any event . . . ,*" *Men in Feminism,* ed. Alice Jardine and Paul Smith (New York: Methuen, 1987) 176.

18. Gertrud Koch, "Ex-Changing the Gaze: Re-Visioning Feminist Film Theory," *New German Critique* 34 (Winter 1985): 151.

19. Heath 56.

CHAPTER THREE

1. Stephen Heath, "Difference," *Screen* 19.3 (1978): 58.

2. Jacques Lacan, *The Four Fundamental Concepts of Psycho-analysis,* ed. Jacques-Alain Miller, trans. Alan Sheridan (Harmondsworth, Eng.: Penguin, 1979) 74.

3. Lacan 77.

4. Jacqueline Rose, "Introduction—II," *Feminine Sexuality: Jacques Lacan and the École Freudienne,* ed. Juliet Mitchell and Jacqueline Rose, trans. Jacqueline Rose (New York: Norton, 1982) 42.

5. My analysis is restricted to the usage of the trope of the veil in Western discourse. It seems to me that a quite different problematic informs, for instance, the relation of the Algerian woman to the veil. See Malek Alloula, *The Colonial Harem,* trans. Myrna Godzich and Wlad Godzich (Minneapolis: U of Minnesota P, 1986), especially ch. 2, "Women from the Outside: Obstacle and Transparency," 7–15. In this context, see also Frantz Fanon, "Algeria Unveiled," *A Dying Colonialism* (New York: Grove, 1965) 35–68.

6. Lillian Gish, in *The Movies, Mr. Griffith and Me* (Englewood Cliffs, NJ: Prentice-Hall, 1970) 59–60, cited in Stephen Heath, "Screen Images, Film Memory," *Edinburgh '76 Magazine* 1: Psychoanalysis/Cinema/Avant-garde (1976): 36.

7. Roland Barthes, *Mythologies,* trans. Annette Lavers (New York: Hill and Wang, 1972) 56.

8. This notion that the face is the most intense manifestation of subjectivity is also proposed in Béla Balázs's analysis of the close-up, and here it is tinged with essentialism: "Facial expression is the most subjective manifestation of man, more subjective even than speech, for vocabulary and grammar are subject to more or less universally valid rules and conventions, while the play of features, as has already been said, is a manifestation not governed by objective canons, even though it is largely a matter of imitation. This most subjective and individual of human manifestations is rendered objective in the close-up." *Theory of the Film: Character and Growth of a New Art,* trans. Edith Bone (New York: Dover, 1970) 60.

9. Susan Stewart, *On Longing: Narratives of the Miniature, the Gigantic, the Souvenir, the Collection* (Baltimore: Johns Hopkins UP, 1984) 127.

10. Stewart 125.

11. Lacan, *The Four Fundamental Concepts* 81.

12. Sigmund Freud, *Three Essays on the Theory of Sexuality,* trans. James Strachey (New York: Basic, 1975) 17. The original is: "Die Bedeutung des Moments der Sexualüberschätzung lässt sich am ehesten beim Manne studieren, dessen Liebesleben allein der Erforschung zugänglich geworden ist, während das des Weibes zum Teil infolge der Kulturverkümmerung, zum anderen Teil durch die konventionelle Verschwiegenheit und Unaufrichtigkeit der Frauen in ein noch undurchdringliches Dunkel gehüllt ist" (*Gesammelte Werke* [London: Imago, 1942] vol. 5, 50).

13. Friedrich Nietzsche, *The Gay Science,* trans. Walter Kaufmann (New York: Vintage, 1974) 38, hereafter cited in the text.

14. *Works of Frederick Schiller* (New York: John D. Williams, n.d.) vol. 5, 197–99. Although the celebrated temple of Isis (or Neith, who is often confused with Isis) at Saïs no longer stands, Plutarch writes that it contained this inscription:

"I am all that has been, that is, and that will be. No mortal has yet been able to lift the veil which covers me." See *New Larousse Encyclopedia of Mythology,* trans. Richard Aldington and Delano Ames (New York: Prometheus, 1968) 37.

15. Eric Blondel, "Nietzsche: Life as Metaphor," in *The New Nietzsche: Contemporary Styles of Interpretation,* ed. David B. Allison (New York: Dell, 1977) 157.

16. Nietzsche, *Beyond Good and Evil,* trans. Walter Kaufmann (New York: Vintage, 1966) 163. I should point out that Nietzsche prefaces these—and other even more disparaging—remarks about women in section 232 of *Beyond Good and Evil* with what might be interpreted as a disclaimer at the end of section 231: "After this abundant civility that I have just evidenced in relation to myself I shall perhaps be permitted more readily to state a few truths about 'women as such'—assuming that it is now known from the outset how very much these are after all only—*my* truths" (162). It is not clear, however, to what extent this statement really does function as a disclaimer since truth, for Nietzsche, is certainly not generalizable in any event. The will to knowledge is a form of the will to power and to state that something is simply "*my* truth" is a way of staking out a territory (and a "perspective") in relation to this willing. The text on woman is not necessarily undermined thereby.

17. Luce Irigaray, "Veiled Lips," trans. Sara Speidel, *Mississippi Review* 11.3 (1983): 98, 118.

18. Jacques Derrida, *Spurs: Nietzsche's Styles,* trans. Barbara Harlow (Chicago: U of Chicago P, 1979) 51, hereafter cited in the text.

19. Friedrich Nietzsche, *The Will to Power,* ed. Walter Kaufmann, trans. Walter Kaufmann and R. J. Hollingdale (New York: Vintage, 1968) 425.

20. Nietzsche, *The Gay Science* 125. Despite this access to a knowing subjectivity, the old woman is, like the young one, often treated by Nietzsche as a metaphor for truth; she no longer knows it but represents it (and "truth" here is Nietzsche's despised truth of the metaphysicians). Two examples from *The Gay Science:* "Humanity! Has there ever been a more hideous old woman among all old women—(unless it were 'truth': a question for philosophers)?" (339) and the verse "Up north—embarrassing to tell—/I loved a creepy ancient belle:/The name of this old hag was Truth" (357).

21. Derrida does insist that he is dealing with the question of the woman rather than her figure—"It is not the figure of the woman precisely because we shall bear witness here to her *abduction,* because the question of the figure is at once opened and closed by what is called woman" (41). Still, I would argue that the woman in Derrida's text serves to figure a question—whether it is the question of truth or the question of the figure. Her function is clearly tropological.

22. Irigaray 105.

23. Lacan, *The Four Fundamental Concepts* 111–12, hereafter cited in the text.

24. It should be noted that Lacan does not annihilate the "beyond" of appearance (as Nietzsche often seems to want to do) but dematerializes or desubstantializes it

by locating the gaze there: "I shall take up here the dialectic of appearance and its beyond, in saying that, if beyond appearance there is nothing in itself, there is the gaze" (*The Four Fundamental Concepts* 103).

25. Rose 42.

26. Jane Gallop, *Reading Lacan* (Ithaca: Cornell UP, 1985) 131.

27. Gallop 140.

28. Lacan, "The Meaning of the Phallus," *Feminine Sexuality* 82.

29. Peter Wollen, "Baubo," *subjects/objects* 2 (1984) : 121, 123.

30. Sarah Kofman, "Baubô: Perversion théologique et fétichisme," *Nietzsche et la scène philosophique* (Paris: Union Générale d'Éditions, 1979) 297. Although I agree with much of Kofman's specific analysis of Baubo, that analysis takes place within the context of a more extended investigation of Nietzsche's use of the figure of the woman (and the question of his misogyny) with which I would take issue. In a reading inspired by Derrida, Kofman makes what is essentially an apology for Nietzsche hinge almost entirely on the figure of Baubo as she is linked to Dionysus (clearly a valorized name in Nietzsche's text).

31. In an extremely short text, "A Mythological Parallel to a Visual Obsession," Freud also invokes the myth of Baubo, but the specificity of the feminine gesture of unveiling the genitals and the inscription upon the female body are lost. Freud's male patient is obsessed with an image of his father's body, minus chest and head, but with the facial features represented on the abdomen. Freud recognizes the parallel with the myth of Baubo, but his analysis centers on the son's anal eroticism and his resistance to and caricature of the father (the *Vaterarsch-Patriarch*). See Freud, "A Mythological Parallel to a Visual Obsession," *Collected Papers,* vol. 4, trans. Joan Riviere (New York: Basic, 1959) 345–46.

32. Anamorphosis, although it does point to that which escapes geometral vision, remains within the problematic of that vision, for it is still a question of rays of light—the straight line and the mapping of space rather than sight. Specific to vision, as far as Lacan is concerned, is light as refracted, distorted, diffused—he often uses words such as "pulsatile," "irradiation," "the play of light, fire," "dazzling," etc. In this sense, he sometimes seems to divorce the gaze from the phallic function: "But it is further still that we must seek the function of vision. We shall then see emerging on the basis of vision, not the phallic symbol, the anamorphic ghost, but the gaze as such, in its pulsatile, dazzling and spread out function, as it is in this picture [*The Ambassadors*]" (89). At other times the gaze, in its operation as lack or as *objet a,* clearly plays the role of the veiled phallus.

33. Rose 40.

34. Lacan, "God and the *Jouissance* of the Woman," *Feminine Sexuality* 147. Stephen Heath is quite critical of the immediacy of the image in this passage as well as the use of a photograph of Bernini's statue of Saint Theresa on the cover of the seminar volume from which the passage is taken—*Encore:* "It might be added, moreover, as a kind of working rule, that where a discourse appeals directly to an

image, to an immediacy of seeing, as a point of its argument or demonstration, one can be sure that all difference is being elided, that the unity of some accepted vision is being reproduced" ("Difference" 53).

35. Heath 53.

36. Lacan, "God and the *Jouissance* of the Woman" 144, 145, "A Love Letter," *Feminine Sexuality* 159. Lacan's generalizations about *the* woman are qualified by his insistence upon crossing the definite article: "*The* woman can only be written with *The* crossed through. There is no such thing as *The* woman since of her essence—having already risked the term, why think twice about it?—of her essence, she is not all" (144). It is a strange qualification of generalization, however, which qualifies by imposing another generalization. It only *seems* less totalizing because of its negative formulation ("not all").

37. Lacan, *The Four Fundamental Concepts* 116.

38. For a similar argument see Michèle le Doeuff, "Cheveux longs, idées courtes," in *L'imaginaire philosophique* (Paris: Payot, 1980) 135–66.

CHAPTER FOUR

1. This paper was initially presented at a conference sponsored by the Australian Screen Studies Association, Sydney, December 1986. I would like to thank Liz Gross, Joan Copjec, Meaghan Morris, and Phil Rosen for their valuable comments on the manuscript.

2. This is a particularly persistent representation in Hollywood films of the 1940s where the female protagonist, suffering from an amnesia usually caused by mental depression or neurosis, is given an injection (labeled "narcosynthesis") instigating the memories which are the basis of the narrative. See my *The Desire to Desire: The Woman's Film of the 1940s* (Bloomington: Indiana UP, 1987) 54.

3. *La Signora di tutti* is an extremely complex film and this brief analysis hardly exhausts its interest for the feminist critic. Indeed, there is a sense in which its delineation of the abstraction of Woman through the look and the voice is subjected to a critique within the same film. See my more extensive analysis of the film in Chapter Six.

4. See, for instance, Judith Mayne, "Feminist Film Theory and Criticism," *Signs: Journal of Women in Culture and Society* 11.1 (1985): 81–100; and Mary Ann Doane, Patricia Mellencamp, and Linda Williams, "Feminist Film Criticism: An Introduction," in *Re-vision: Essays in Feminist Film Criticism* (Frederick, MD: U Publications of America and The American Film Institute, 1984) 1–17.

5. Teresa de Lauretis, *Alice Doesn't: Feminism, Semiotics, Cinema* (Bloomington: Indiana UP, 1984) 186.

6. See E. Ann Kaplan, "Feminist Film Criticism: Current Issues and Problems," *Studies in the Literary Imagination* 19.1 (Spring 1986): 7–20; and Annette Kuhn,

Women's Pictures: Feminism and Cinema (London, Routledge & Kegan Paul, 1982).

7. Jean-Louis Baudry, "The Apparatus ," trans. Jean Andrews and Bertrand Augst, *Camera Obscura* 1 (Fall 1976): 104–26; "Ideological Effects of the Basic Cinematographic Apparatus," trans. Alan Williams, *Film Quarterly* 28.2 (Winter 1974–75): 39–47. These two essays are also anthologized in Philip Rosen, *Narrative, Apparatus, Ideology* (New York: Columbia UP, 1986) 286–318.

8. J. Laplanche and J.-B. Pontalis, *The Language of Psychoanalysis,* trans. Donald Nicholson-Smith (New York: Norton, 1974) 358.

9. *The Standard Edition of the Complete Psychological Works of Sigmund Freud,* vol. 5, ed. and trans. James Strachey (London: Hogarth and the Institute of Psychoanalysis, 1973) 536–7. In the continuation of this quotation Freud considers the possibility that the hypothesis of *spatial* order is unnecessary (and could be replaced by that of a *temporal* order). But the appeal of the spatial ordering is evident in the analogies which he invokes.

10. Jean Laplanche, *Life and Death in Psycho-analysis,* trans. Jeffrey Mehlman (Baltimore: Johns Hopkins UP, 1976) 61.

11. Jean-Louis Baudry, "The Apparatus," Rosen 300.

12. See Christian Metz, "The Imaginary Signifier," *Screen* 16.2 (Summer 1975): 14–76; and Jean-Louis Comolli, "Technique and Ideology: Camera, Perspective, Depth of Field" (Parts 3 and 4), Rosen 421–43.

13. Baudry, "Ideological Effects of the Basic Cinematographic Apparatus," Rosen 295.

14. Joan Copjec, "The Delirium of Clinical Perfection," *The Oxford Literary Review* 8.1–2 (1986): 61, 63. It is only fair to point out that Copjec develops this argument (whose substance I agree with) as a counterargument to a position presented in the introduction of a book I coedited—*Revision: Essays in Feminist Film Criticism.* Copjec criticizes our invocation of Foucault's panopticon as an analogy with the position of the woman (in relation to visibility and the gaze) in a patriarchal society. The reference in *Re-vision* is quite brief and not at all fully developed and I believe that Copjec's criticism is at some level quite justified. However, the paragraph she cites does not claim that the panopticon *perfectly* describes the woman's condition but, instead, *seems* to perfectly describe it. In the obsessive search for perfection, this is an important qualification. I find it much more difficult, as stated below in this essay, to see how Lacan's gaze can shed light on the analysis of sexual difference. In Foucault's description of the panopticon, it is not so important to claim that the gaze is fixed at a certain point, or that it *belongs* to someone who is in power, but that the inmate/woman incessantly feels herself to be the potential object of such a gaze.

15. Jacques Lacan, *The Four Fundamental Concepts of Psycho-analysis,* ed. Jacques-Alain Miller, trans. Alan Sheridan (Harmondsworth, Eng.: Penguin, 1979) 106.

16. Lacan 103.

17. Lacan 73.

18. Roger Caillois, "Mimcry and Legendary Psychasthenia," trans. John Shepley, *October* 31 (Winter 1984): 28.

19. Caillois 28.

20. Lacan 75.

21. Freud, *The Standard Edition,* vol. 5, 511.

22. Samuel Weber, *The Legend of Freud* (Minneapolis: U of Minnesota P, 1982) xvi.

23. Weber 13–14.

24. François Roustang, *Psychoanalysis Never Lets Go,* trans. Ned Lukacher (Baltimore: Johns Hopkins UP, 1980) 25.

25. Roustang 17.

26. Roustang, *Dire Mastery: Discipleship from Freud to Lacan,* trans. Ned Lukacher (Baltimore: Johns Hopkins UP, 1982) 70.

27. Roustang, *Dire Mastery* 69.

28. Freud, *The Origins of Psychoanalysis: Letters to Wilhelm Fliess,* trans. Eric Mosbacher and James Strachey (New York: Basic, 1954) 173.

29. Something of what Freud meant by the term "memory" can be gleaned from the way in which he used the term "forgetting." What is lost in forgetting is not an empirical event but a coherent discourse linking events. Freud frequently emphasizes the fact that forgetting involves the loss of connections *between* events. In this sense, it has similarities with Jakobson's "contiguity disorder" in aphasia. This is not necessarily to deny that there are events. Memory's relation to them is, however, tangential rather than direct, instigated rather than determined.

30. Freud, "A Note upon the 'Mystic Writing-Pad,' " *The Standard Edition,* vol. 19, 231.

31. For a discussion of the various ways of distinguishing between memory and history see David Lowenthal, *The Past is a Foreign Country* (Cambridge: Cambridge UP, 1985) 185–259.

32. Michel de Certeau, *Heterologies: Discourse on the Other,* trans. Brian Massumi (Minneapolis: U of Minnesota P, 1986) 4–5.

33. de Certeau 4.

34. de Certeau 4.

35. Freud, "Constructions in Analysis," *The Standard Edition,* vol. 23, 258–9.

36. Freud, "Constructions in Analysis" 265–6.

37. Roustang, *Psychoanalysis Never Lets Go* 36–7.

38. Freud, "Further Recommendations in the Technique of Psychoanalysis: Observations on Transference-Love," *The Standard Edition,* vol. 12, 166–7.

39. *The Gold Diggers* is, perhaps, an overly optimistic discourse with respect to its treatment of the relation between the white woman and the black woman. That relation is one of pure comradeship and alliance against the common enemy—man. There is no sense of the historical alienation which might haunt such a relationship. This absence is particularly telling in the ballroom scenes which invoke the iconography of the Southern plantation and the Southern belle, without overt commentary on the racial hierarchy which subtended this social structure. For a more extensive discussion of some of the vicissitudes of this relation, see Chapter Eleven.

CHAPTER FIVE

1. *Gilda*, dir. Charles Vidor, Columbia, 1946. A short plot summary will facilitate a reading of this analysis: Johnny (Glenn Ford), in the process of being robbed of his gambling earnings on the docks of Buenos Aires, is saved by Ballen (George Macready) who threatens the thief with his cane-knife. Johnny subsequently becomes Ballen's right-hand man in his illegal casino although Uncle Pio, the friendly washroom attendant, continues to call him a "peasant." Ballen leaves on a short trip and returns, married to Gilda. It is apparent from Johnny and Gilda's first meeting that they have had a relationship sometime in the past. From that point on, Gilda, attempting to make Johnny jealous, pretends to have numerous affairs behind Ballen's back. Johnny's friendship with Ballen necessitates that he try to conceal Gilda's promiscuity. Meanwhile, Johnny discovers that Ballen is continually being hounded by two Germans who claim that Ballen has unethically stolen an international cartel with a tungsten monopoly from them. At a masquerade party, one of the Germans is killed and Ballen is forced to stage his own "death" and go into hiding in order to escape the law (represented by a detective who continually haunts the casino.) Johnny marries Gilda, thus guaranteeing his control over the international cartel. But he refuses to see her and keeps her a prisoner in Buenos Aires, isolating her from other men. Gilda flees Buenos Aires and meets and falls in love with a lawyer who convinces her to return to Argentina to get an annulment. Upon returning, Gilda finds that the lawyer is really one of Johnny's hired hands and that she is once again a prisoner. In revolt, she does a modified striptease number to "Put the Blame on Mame" in Johnny's casino. Johnny begins to "break into little pieces" (as the detective puts it) and finally gives the detective the names of the members of the international cartel so that he can go away with Gilda. Yet, just as Johnny and Gilda are about to be reconciled, Ballen returns and attempts to kill both of them. Uncle Pio, however, kills Ballen with his own cane-knife and Johnny and Gilda are finally free to "go home."

2. Gilda is the *only* woman who has a significant role in the film. In fact, the only other woman who speaks in the entire film is Gilda's maid.

3. Laura Mulvey, "Visual Pleasure and Narrative Cinema," *Screen* 16.3 (Autumn 1975): 17. The essay is also reprinted in Mulvey, *Visual and Other Pleasures*

(Bloomington: Indiana UP, 1989) 14–28 and in *Feminism and Film Theory,* ed. Constance Penley (New York and London: Routledge and British Film Institute, 1988) 57–68.

4. See Sigmund Freud, *Beyond the Pleasure Principle,* trans. James Strachey (New York: Norton, 1961) 8–11.

5. Christine Gledhill, *"Klute," Women in Film Noir,* ed. E. Ann Kaplan (London: British Film Institute, 1978) 13.

6. Combinations of the two—for example, *Mildred Pierce*—are particularly informative. See Pam Cook's article in *Women in Film Noir* 68–82.

7. Michèle Montrelay, "Inquiry into Femininity," *m/f* 1 (1978): 89.

8. See "The 'Uncanny,' " Sigmund Freud, *On Creativity and the Unconscious* (New York: Harper, 1958) 122–61.

9. Roland Barthes, *Mythologies,* trans. Annette Lavers (New York: Hill and Wang, 1972) 84–5.

10. See Gledhill 17.

11. See Christian Metz, "The Imaginary Signifier," *Screen* 16.2 (Summer 1975): 14–76.

12. The term "his" is used deliberately here. It is doubtful whether either spectatorship in the classical cinema or the identity proffered by the mirror are accessible to the female in the same way.

13. Jacqueline Rose, "Paranoia and the Film System," *Screen* 17.4 (Winter 1976/7): 85–104.

14. Anika Lemaire, *Jacques Lacan,* trans. David Macey (London: Routledge and Kegan Paul, 1977) 179.

15. See Colin MacCabe, "Realism and the Cinema: Notes on some Brechtian Theses," *Screen* 15.2 (Summer 1974): 7–27.

CHAPTER SIX

1. Max Ophuls, "Thoughts on Film," in *Ophuls,* ed. Paul Willemen (London: British Film Institute, 1978) 43, 44.

2. Ophuls 45.

3. See Andreas Huyssen, *After the Great Divide: Modernism, Mass Culture, Postmodernism* (Bloomington: Indiana UP, 1986) 3–15.

4. Claude Beylie, *Max Ophuls* (Paris: Editions Pierre Lherminier, 1984) 6. (My translation)

5. *La Signora di tutti (Everybody's Lady),* dir. Max Ophuls, 1934. Production Company: Novella Films (Milan); Producer: Emilio Rizzoli; Screenplay: Curt Alexander, Hans Wilhelm, and Max Ophuls, adapted from the novel by Salvator Gotta; Cinematography: Ubaldo Arata; Music: Danièle Amfitheatrof. Cast: Isa Miranda

(Gaby Doriot), Memo Benassi (Leonardo Nanni), Tatiana Pavlova (Alma Nanni), Frederico Benfer (Roberto Nanni), Nelly Corradi (Anna). Filmed at Cines Studios, Rome. The film is not widely available in the United States but may be purchased/rented on videotape from Festival Films, 2841 Irving Ave. South, Minneapolis, Minnesota 55408.

6. See Maurizia Natali, "Il Fantasma dell'Opera, o a proposito di alcune signore reticenti," *Filmcritica* 34 (October 1983): 425–30. I am grateful to Gloria Monti for her translation of sections of this article.

7. At this time, the Cines Studio, where the film was shot, was relatively free of fascist regulation or censorship in its feature productions. See Elaine Mancini, *Struggles of the Italian Film Industry during Fascism, 1930–1935* (Ann Arbor: UMI Research Press, 1985) esp. ch. 3, "The Cines Studio" 57–98.

8. Mancini 85.

9. Jorge Luis Borges, "Funes the Memorious," in *Labyrinths: Selected Stories and Other Writings*, ed. Donald A. Yates and James E. Irby (Norfolk, CT: New Directions, 1962) 66.

10. Willeman, ed. *Ophuls* 44.

11. Quoted in Pierre Leprohon, *The Italian Cinema*, trans. Roger Greaves and Oliver Stallybrass (New York: Praeger, 1972) 34.

12. Quoted in Leprohron 35.

13. Vernon Jarratt, *The Italian Cinema* (New York: Macmillan, 1951) 23.

14. Leprohon 35.

15. Leprohon 37.

16. The similarity between Isa Miranda as Gaby in *La Signora* and the *diva* of the silent cinema has not gone unnoticed. Mancini, for instance, describes Isa Miranda in this way: "In her film acting, she appeared beautiful but bland, passive but powerful in her beauty, a dreamy-eyed creature suffering the pangs of human existence. The combinations of those qualities struck another spark. With *La Signora di tutti*, Isa Miranda was launched as the grand diva of the decade, similar in popularity to the silent stars like Lyda Borelli and Francesca Bertini, similar in looks to Marlene Dietrich, and similar in character portrayals to Greta Garbo" (*Struggles of the Italian Film Industry* 82). Mira Liehm also refers to Miranda as "the diva of the thirties, a perfect femme fatale, and a dignified successor to Francesca Bertini . . ." (*Passion and Defiance: Film in Italy from 1942 to the Present* [Berkeley: U of California P, 1984] 22).

17. Tony Tanner, *Adultery in the Novel: Contract and Transgression* (Baltimore: Johns Hopkins UP, 1979) 179.

18. "Family Plots," *Comparative Criticism* vol. 5 (New York: Cambridge UP, 1983) 318.

19. Tanner 14.

20. "The Transfiguration of History: Ophuls, Vienna, and *Letter from an Un-*

known Woman," in *Letter from an Unknown Woman,* ed. Virginia Wright Wexman (New Brunswick, NJ: Rutgers UP, 1986) 10–11.

21. "Visual Pleasure and Narrative Cinema," *Screen* 16.3 (Autumn 1975): 10.

22. *"La Signora di tutti," Monthly Film Bulletin* 49 (September 1982): 212.

23. Beylie 130. (My translation)

24. There may be some influence here from the films of French Impressionism, which also use the dissolve in aberrant ways. However, their activation of the dissolve is more frequently associated with a symbolic or graphic motivation, making the dissolves more easily readable. As David Bordwell points out, on the whole, "the transitional functions of such optical effects remain standard" (Bordwell, *French Impressionist Cinema: Film Culture, Film Theory, and Film Style* [New York: Arno, 1980] 174. For the full discussion see 172–84).

25. Of all of Ophuls's films, *La Signora di tutti* is perhaps most intriguing in its use of sound—voice-off, voice-over, and music. Ophuls worked in radio from the early 1920s on, developing a form that orchestrated extracts from novels and poetry with commentaries, sounds, and music effects. In an interview, Ophuls referred to radio as his "secret penchant" (Willemen, ed. *Ophuls* 3, 29). For a more extensive discussion of sound in *La Signora,* see Susan M. White's provocative chapter, "To Hear is to Obey: Sound and Image in the Genealogy of Guilt in *La Signora di tutti,"* in "The Cinema of Max Ophuls: Marginality, Magisterial Vision and the Figure of Woman," diss., Johns Hopkins U, 1987, 367–400.

26. I have not yet been able to identify the opera in *La Signora.* It is quite possible that it is not a citation of an actual opera but a fictional construct.

27. For a discussion of the ambiguous nature of Alma's death, see Andrew Sarris, "La Signora di Tutti," *Film Comment* 10.6 (Nov-Dec 1974): 44–46.

28. Walter Benjamin, "The Storyteller: Reflections on the Works of Nikolai Leskov," *Illuminations,* ed. Hannah Arendt, trans. Harry Zohn (New York: Schocken, 1969) 84.

29. Benjamin 92.

30. Benjamin 91.

31. It is interesting to note that Roland Barthes, who also associates narrative with spinning and weaving, does so from the point of view of production rather than reception, as Benjamin would have it (Barthes, *S/Z: An Essay,* trans. Richard Miller [New York: Hill and Wang, 1974] 160).

32. Benjamin 93.

33. Quoted in Brian Henderson, *A Critique of Film Theory* (New York: Dutton, 1980) 51.

CHAPTER SEVEN

1. This paper has a somewhat convoluted history. It is a revised and expanded version of work I did on *Pandora's Box* in the context of a seminar on Weimar

cinema at the University of Iowa during the spring of 1978. That work was cited and rebutted by Thomas Elsaesser in his extremely provocative essay, "Lulu and the Meter Man" (*Screen* 24.4–5 [July–October 1983]: 4–36), which I, in turn, cite and criticize here. Since my ideas about the film and also about the process of film criticism have changed significantly in the last ten years, I have chosen not to respond directly to Elsaesser's critique (which I believe is a misrepresentation of my earlier work in any event). Instead, I concentrate on clarifying the distinctions between my current view of the film and his often compelling arguments in the Screen essay.

2. *Die Büchse der Pandora,* dir. G.W. Pabst, 1929. Producer: Seymour Nebenzahl; Production Company: Nero-Film A.G.; Director of Photography: Günther Krampf; Screenplay: Ladislaus Vajda from two plays by Frank Wedekind, *Erdgeist* and *Die Büchse der Pandora.* Cast: Louise Brooks (Lulu), Fritz Kortner (Dr. Peter Schön), Franz Lederer (Alwa Schön), Carl Goetz (Schigolch), Alice Roberts (Countess Anna Geschwitz), Daisy d'Ora (Marie de Zarniko), Kraft Raschig (Rodrigo Quast), Michael von Newlusky (Marquis Casti-Pianti), Siegfried Arno (The Stage Manager), Gustav Diessl (Jack the Ripper). For more detailed filmographic information, see Eric Rentschler, ed. *The Films of G.W. Pabst* (New Brunswick: Rutgers UP, 1990) 275.

3. This is the title in the English version of the film distributed in the United States. The English translation of the script represents the title as, "My Lord, I have given the court a brief description of some terrible events . . ." (G.W. Pabst, *Pandora's Box [Lulu],* trans. Christopher Holme [New York: Simon and Schuster, 1971] 69). The French intertitle is similar: "Votre Honneur, je vous ai décrit brièvement une destinée terrible" (*L'Avant-Scène Cinéma* 257 [1980]: 44). The significance, however, lies more in the placement of this statement than in its exact vocabulary. Immediately following Schön's death scene, the reference to a description of "terrible events" clearly refers back to the filmic presentation the spectator has just witnessed.

4. Stefan Zweig, *Die Welt von Gestern,* 287, cited in Peter Gay, *Weimar Culture: The Outsider as Insider* (New York: Harper and Row, 1968) 129–30.

5. Louise Brooks, "Pabst and Lulu," in Pabst, *Pandora's Box* 8.

6. Peter Sloterdijk, *Critique of Cynical Reason,* trans. Michael Eldred (Minneapolis: U of Minnesota P, 1987) 389.

7. Sloterdijk 516.

8. Sol Gittleman, *Frank Wedekind* (New York: Twayne, 1969) 53.

9. Brooks 5.

10. Siegfried Kracauer, *From Caligari to Hitler: A Psychological History of the German Film* (Princeton: Princeton U P, 1947) 168.

11. Kracauer 179.

12. Harry Alan Potamkin, "Die Dreigroschenoper," *The Compound Cinema:*

The Film Writings of Harry Alan Potamkin, ed. Lewis Jacobs (New York: Teachers College, 1977) 490. Originally published in *Creative Art,* July 1931.

13. Potamkin, "Pabst and the Social Film," *The Compound Cinema,* 414. Originally published in *Hound and Horn,* January 1933.

14. Potamkin 412.

15. Lotte H. Eisner, "Pabst and the Miracle of Louise Brooks," Pabst, *Pandora's Box* 16.

16. Frank Wedekind, foreward to *Pandora's Box,* in *Five Tragedies of Sex by Frank Wedekind,* trans. Frances Fawcett and Stephen Spender (London: Vision, 1952) 213. See Elsaesser, footnote 24, page 12, for an argument that Wedekind declared Geschwitz to be the central figure only in order to deflect legal objections to the play.

17. Kenneth Macpherson, *"Die Liebe der Jeanne Ney," Close Up* (December 1927): 26. Cited in Anne Friedberg, "Writing about Cinema: 'Close Up' 1927–1933," diss., New York U, 1983, 257.

18. In the original script, the father is referred to as the Prime Minister. In the English version of the film, he is described as Minister of the Interior.

19. See Elsaesser 17–18.

20. Elsaesser 27.

21. The first three quotations are cited in *L'Avant-Scène Cinéma* 257 (1980): 57. The Lotte Eisner citation is from *The Haunted Screen,* trans. Roger Greaves (Berkeley: U of California P, 1973) 298–9. The quotation from Henri Langlois is from James Card, "The Intense Isolation of Louise Brooks," *Sight and Sound* 47.3 (Summer 1958): 241, cited by Elsaesser 4.

22. Elsaesser 15.

23. Elsaesser 15.

24. Elsaesser 25.

25. Wedekind, *Pandora's Box* 225. Alwa says much more than this, presenting an entire philosophy of literature: "That's the curse that weighs on literature today, that it's much too literary. We know nothing about any problems save those that arise among artists and scholars. Our horizon doesn't extend beyond the interests of our profession. To bring about a rebirth of a genuine vigorous art we should go as much as possible among men who have never read a book in their lives, whose actions are dictated by the simplest animal instincts. In my play *Earth-Spirit* I did my utmost to work on these principles."

26. Wedekind, foreward to *Pandora's Box* 214.

27. See Elsaesser 20.

28. Kracauer 99, 122, 171.

29. Walter Benjamin, "Some Motifs in Baudelaire," *Charles Baudelaire: A Lyric Poet in the Era of High Capitalism,* trans. Harry Zohn (London: New Left, 1973) 134.

30. Benjamin 136.

31. Elsaesser 24.

32. Sloterdijk 402.

33. According to Sloterdijk, Weimar society evinced an extraordinary public interest in hypnotism and autosuggestion: "One bibliography lists for the period of the Weimar Republic alone around seven hundred scientific or popular publications on the themes of Couéism, hypnosis, autohypnosis, and suggestion" (490).

34. See Sloterdijk 485.

35. Here I would disagree strongly with Elsaesser's reading of this scene (31). Contrary to his claims, the scene is quite legible and it is always possible to distinguish between Schön and his mirror image. The mirror sequence is clearly localized within the scene as a whole.

36. Wedekind, *Earth-Spirit* 199.

37. Cited in Stuart Ewen, *Captains of Consciousness* (New York: McGraw-Hill, 1977) 48.

38. It is interesting to note that Wedekind acted in at least two performances of the play—first taking on the role of Schön, then that of Jack the Ripper. See *L'Avant-Scène Cinéma* 257 (1980): 6.

39. In certain feminist accounts, the tabloid reporting of Jack the Ripper's crimes is interpreted as a warning to women about the dangers of urban spaces. Judith R. Walkowitz's description evokes—in some respects—the mise-en-scène of the film: "The Ripper's London was represented as a city of 'light' and of 'darkness,' of pockets of civility surrounded by a menacing obscurity. A seasoned urban traveler, the Ripper could move effortlessly and invisibly through these spaces, transgressing all boundaries; committing his murderous acts in the open, under the cover of darkness; exposing the private parts of women to public view. These themes helped to construct the Ripper story as a cautionary tale for women: a warning that the city was a dangerous place when they transgressed the narrow boundaries of hearth and home and entered public space" ("Science and the Seance: Transgressions of Gender and Genre in Late Victorian London," *Representations* 22 [Spring 1988]: 3).

40. Elsaesser 20.

41. Wedekind 242. In the play, this line is presented with some anxiety on Lulu's part. Louise Brooks, who seems to know the Wedekind play well, changes the affect attached to it by describing the final scene of the film as follows: "It is Christmas Eve and she [Lulu] is about to receive the gift which has been her dream since childhood. Death by a sexual maniac" ("Pabst and Lulu" 13). The low-key, gentle quality of the scene, in contrast to the frantic chaos of Wedekind's rendition of the murder, seems to corroborate Brooks's reading. If this is so, the single moment when Lulu is allowed the expression of desire and subjectivity would be simultaneous with her own death. However, in my reading I feel it is more important to stress the accidental quality, the contingent character of her death, which is more

consistent with the filmic representation of her life as lived moment by moment, without the directionality and historicity implied by dreams and desires.

42. Elsaesser 36.

CHAPTER EIGHT

1. Peter Gidal, transcription of a discussion following "Technology and Ideology in/through/and Avant-Garde Film: An Instance," *The Cinematic Apparatus,* ed. Teresa de Lauretis and Stephen Heath (New York: St. Martin's, 1980) 169.

2. This calls for a more thorough dissection and analysis of the assumption underlying the cliché that male models are "effeminate."

3. Stephen Heath, "Difference," *Screen* 19.3 (Autumn 1978): 73.

4. Jean Laplanche, *Life and Death in Psychoanalysis,* trans. Jeffrey Mehlman (Baltimore: Johns Hopkins, 1976) 20.

5. See, for example, "The Denial of the Vagina," *Psychoanalysis and Female Sexuality,* ed. Hendrick M. Ruitenbeek (New Haven: College and UP, 1966) 73–87; and *Feminine Psychology,* ed. Harold Kelman (New York: Norton, 1967).

6. Jacques Lacan, *Écrits: A Selection,* trans. Alan Sheridan (New York: Norton, 1977) 287. Lacan does go on to say, "All these propositions merely conceal the fact that it [the phallus] can play its role only when veiled, that is to say, as itself a sign of the latency with which any signifiable is struck, when it is raised (*aufgehoben*) to the function of signifier" (288). Nevertheless, it is highly significant that Lacan uses the more biologically grounded propositions to prepare the way for the linguistic argument.

7. Parveen Adams, "Representation and Sexuality," *m/f* 1 (1978): 66–67. Even if the phallus is defined as logically prior to the penis, in that it is the phallus which bestows significance on the penis, a *relation* between the two is nevertheless posited, and that is my point.

8. I am grateful to Philip Rosen for this representation of the problem.

9. Michèle Montrelay, "Inquiry into Femininity," *m/f* 1 (1978): 89.

10. Montrelay 89.

11. Montrelay 90.

12. Montrelay 91–92.

13. Montrelay 92.

14. This description is derived from Lacan's conceptualization of masquerade in relation to femininity. See *Écrits: A Selection* 289–90. Lacan, in turn, borrows the notion of masquerade from Joan Riviere; see "Womanliness as Masquerade," *Psychoanalysis and Female Sexuality* 209–20. This analysis of masquerade differs markedly from that offered in Chapter One.

15. Montrelay 91.

16. Montrelay 98. See Chapter Twelve for further discussion of this point.

17. Beverley Brown and Parveen Adams, "The Feminine Body and Feminist Politics," *m/f* 3 (1979): 37.

18. Luce Irigaray, "This Sex Which Is Not One," trans. R. Albury and P. Foss, *Language, Sexuality, Subversion,* ed. Paul Foss and Meaghan Morris (Darlington: Feral Publications, 1978) 161–72. This is a translation of the second essay in *Ce sexe qui n'en est pas un* (Paris: Minuit, 1977) 23–32.

19. Brown and Adams 38.

20. Irigaray, *Ce sexe qui n'en est pas un* 129–30. My translation.

21. The critique of Kristeva is based on *About Chinese Women,* trans. Anita Barrows (New York: Urizen, 1977).

22. Brown and Adams 39.

23. Laplanche 23–24.

24. Roland Barthes, "Introduction to the Structural Analysis of Narratives," *Image-Music-Text,* trans. Stephen Heath (New York: Hill and Wang, 1977) 119.

CHAPTER NINE

1. Roland Barthes, *Empire of Signs,* trans. Richard Howard (New York: Hill and Wang, 1982) xi.

2. Barthes 3.

3. Jonathan Rosenbaum, *Film: The Front Line 1983* (Denver: Arden, 1983) 206.

4. Barthes 9.

5. Quoted in Rosenbaum 206.

6. For an intriguing examination of the relation between feminine and Oriental "otherness" see Lisa Lowe, "The Figuration of the Orient as Woman in Flaubert's *Salammbô, Voyage en Orient,* and *Correspondance," Comparative Literature Studies* 38.2 (Spring 1986).

7. Roland Barthes, *S/Z: An Essay,* trans. Richard Miller (New York: Hill and Wang, 1974) 33.

8. Luce Irigaray, *This Sex Which Is Not One,* trans. Catherine Porter with Carolyn Burke (Ithaca: Cornell UP, 1985) 23–33, 205–18.

9. For a provocative analysis of *Jennifer, Where Are You?* see Su Friedrich's essay in *The Downtown Review* (Fall/Winter/Spring 1981/82).

10. Luce Irigaray, "Is the Subject of Science Sexed?," *Cultural Critique* 1 (Fall 1985) 76.

CHAPTER TEN

1. This essay is a rewritten version of a paper delivered at the conference "Cinema Histories, Cinema Practices II," sponsored by The Center for Twentieth Century Studies, University of Wisconsin-Milwaukee, November 9–12, 1982. I am particularly grateful for specific comments and suggestions made by Peter Brunette, Linda Williams, Robert Scholes, and Peter Wollen.

2. The compatability of cinematic perception and that of railway travel is perhaps most effectively represented in a phenomenon of the primitive cinema— *Hale's Tours and Scenes of the World,* a show which "took the form of an artificial railway car whose operation combined auditory, tactile, visual, and ambulatory sensations to provide a remarkably convincing illusion of railway travel." Spectators were seated in a stationary train car as motion pictures which had been filmed from a cowcatcher of a moving train were projected onto a screen at the front of a car. Sound effects simulating the clickety-clack of railway wheels were provided as well as an artificially produced rush of air and a mechanism whereby the car could be swayed from side to side. The movies projected depicted popular American tourist sites—e.g. Pike's Peak, Niagara Falls, Chicago, the Black Hills—as well as foreign scenes from Argentina, Switzerland, Ireland, etc. The shows ran in the U.S. from approximately 1904–1906, internationally until about 1912. See Raymond Fielding, "Hale's Tours: Ultrarealism in the Pre–1910 Motion Picture," *Cinema Journal* 10.1 (Fall 1970): 34–47.

3. Wolfgang Schivelbusch, *The Railway Journey: Trains and Travel in the 19th Century,* trans. Anselm Hollo (New York: Urizen, 1977) 44, 48.

4. See Walter Benjamin, "The Work of Art in the Age of Mechanical Reproduction," *Illuminations,* ed. Hannah Arendt, trans. Harry Zohn (New York: Schocken, 1969) 217–52.

5. Schivelbusch 65. Schivelbusch's claim about the institution of a "panoramic perception" is buttressed by the names given to two film attractions exhibited at the 1900 Paris Exposition—*Cinéorama* and *Maréorama*—which depicted, respectively, views from a balloon and views of the sea one might have from the bridge of a ship. See Fielding 36–37.

6. Schivelbusch 66. Although Schivelbusch's analysis might appear to involve a form of technological determinism, his discourse does not represent the train as the result of a purely neutral scientific discovery which is subsequently measured by its effects. Rather, "panoramic perception of objects, panoramic ways of relating to objects, make their appearance in connection with, and based upon, the accelerated circulation of commodities" of a capitalist society (186). Ultimately, the train's reorganization of perception cannot be separated from that of glass architecture or the department store.

7. The quotations are from *The Interpretation of Dreams,* trans. James Strachey (New York: Avon, 1965) 461–63.

8. *On Creativity and the Unconscious,* ed. Benjamin Nelson (New York: Harper & Row, 1958) 156. It would seem appropriate here to note also that Freud suffered from a persistant phobia of traveling by train. See Ernest Jones, *The Life and Work of Sigmund Freud,* ed. and abr. Lionel Trilling and Steven Marcus (New York: Basic, 1961) 11, 198–99.

9. Ernst Mach was professor of physics and the philosophy of science, first in Prague (1865–95) and subsequently in Vienna (1895–1902). "He criticized the crude positivism of his day from a sophisticated neo-Kantian position. Thus mechanistic and materialist theories were attacked by denying their underlying assumptions of the existence of matter and 'substance.' This eventually led him towards philosophical subjectivism . . ." (from "Notes to the English Edition" of George Lukács, *History and Class Consciousness,* trans. Rodney Livingstone [Cambridge: MIT P, 1971] 351). Mach, quoted only sporadically by Freud, criticized by Lenin (in *Materialism and Empirico-criticism*), and resuscitated by experimental psychology, is a pivotal figure of intellectual history. See also H. Stuart Hughes, *Consciousness and Society: The Reorientation of European Social Thought 1890–1930* (New York: Vintage, 1958) 105–9.

10. See "Perception of the Upright When the Direction of the Force Acting on the Body is Changed," *Journal of Experimental Psychology* 40 (1950): 93–106. I am grateful to David Tafler and Philip Rosen and, in a different context, Anne Fausto-Sterling, for alerting me to the existence of these studies by H. A. Witkin on perception and sexual difference.

11. Jean-Louis Comolli, "Technique and Ideology: Camera, Perspective, Depth of Field," *Film Reader* 2 (1977): 136. See also *Movies and Methods* vol. 2, ed. Bill Nichols (Berkeley: U of Caliornia P, 1985) 52.

12. Comolli 136.

13. M.L. d'Otrange Mastai, *Illusion in Art: Trompe l'Oeil, A History of Pictorial Illusionism* (London: Martin Secker & Warburg, 1976) 8, 13. Although art critics frequently maintain that the use of the term "trompe l'oeil" should be limited to the art form it was coined to identify—a kind of precisionistic still-life painting first popular in the seventeenth century (Mastai 8)—art critics themselves frequently overstep this boundary, applying it to such diverse practices as Ancient Greek painting, "magic realism," and a contemporary hyperrealism. See also Martin Battersby, *Trompe l'Oeil: The Eye Deceived* (London: Academy Editions, 1974).

14. Battersby 20.

15. Battersby 20. See also Mastai 19.

16. This delineation of the spectatorial effects of trompe l'oeil goes some way toward explaining André Bazin's construction of an opposition between trompe l'oeil and realism wherein the first is a lie, the second truth. While trompe l'oeil aims fully to deceive the subject, if only momentarily, realism depends upon the simultaneity of knowledge and belief and eschews this full deception. See *What is Cinema?,* vol. 1, trans. Hugh Gray (Berkeley: U of California P, 1967) 19.

17. *The Four Fundamental Concepts of Psycho-analysis,* trans. Alan Sheridan (Hammondsworth, Eng.: Penguin, 1979) 109.

18. While the trompe l'oeil undermines the power of one epistemologically central organ—the eye, the image of the woman as castrated threatens the potency of another—the phallus.

19. *The Four Fundamental Concepts of Psycho-analysis* 93.

20. *Roland Barthes by Roland Barthes,* trans. Richard Howard (New York: Hill and Wang, 1977) 105.

21. *The Four Fundamental Concepts of Psycho-analysis* 111–12. Lacan is explicit in distinguishing between the human and animal relations to the imaginary: "Only the subject—the human subject, the subject of the desire that is the essence of man—is not, unlike the animal, entirely caught up in this imaginary capture. He maps himself in it. How? In so far as he isolates the function of the screen and plays with it" (107).

22. "The Avant-Garde and Its Imaginary," *Camera Obscura* 2 (1977): 25.

23. "The Field of Language in Film," *October* 17 (Summer 1981): 54.

24. Quoted in Comolli 136.

25. Nevertheless, at this particular historical conjuncture, there is a sense in which experimental psychology has more ideological currency as a theoretical discourse on subjectivity than psychoanalysis. Hence it would seem even more crucial to submit it to a symptomatic reading, particularly insofar as it attempts to articulate the relations between vision, space, the body, and sexual difference.

26. Witkin, "Perception of the Upright When the Direction of the Force Acting on the Body is Changed" 93.

27. Witkin, "Further Studies of Perception of the Upright When the Direction of the Force Acting on the Body is Changed," *Journal of Experimental Psychology* 43 (1952): 17.

28. Witkin, "Sex Differences in Perception," *New York Academy of Sciences— Transactions,* ser. 2, vol. 12 (1949–50) 23.

29. Witkin 24.

30. Anne Fausto-Sterling, "Biological Constructions of the Female: Scientific Fantasies, Political Facts," unpublished manuscript. Since the time I wrote this essay, Fausto-Sterling has published a book extending this research. See *Myths of Gender: Biological Theories About Women and Men* (New York: Basic, 1985), especially 30–36.

31. Fausto-Sterling, "Biological Constructions."

32. Michèle Le Doeuff, "Pierre Roussel's Chiasmas: from imaginary knowledge to the learned imagination," trans. Colin Gordon, *Ideology and Consciousness* 9 (Winter 1981/82): 50.

33. Le Doeuff 59–60.

34. Parveen Adams, "Representation and Sexuality," *m/f* 1 (1978): 66.

35. *Questions of Cinema* (London: Macmillan, 1981) 37.

36. *Desire in Language,* trans. Leon S. Roudiez (New York: Columbia UP, 1980) 283, 287.

CHAPTER ELEVEN

I would like to thank a number of people who read an earlier version of this manuscript: Ann du Cille, Manthia Diawara, Neil Lazarus, Elizabeth Weed, Maureen Turim, and the members of a feminist reading group at Brown. I am grateful for their encouragement as well as their comments, suggestions, and criticisms.

1. Patrick Brantlinger, "Victorians and Africans: The Genealogy of the Myth of the Dark Continent," *Critical Inquiry* 12.1 (Autumn 1985): 166.

2. Jane Gallop, *Reading Lacan* (Ithaca: Cornell UP, 1985) 127.

3. Sigmund Freud, "The Question of Lay Analysis: Conversations with an Impartial Person," *The Standard Edition of the Complete Psychological Works of Sigmund Freud*, vol. 20, trans. and ed. James Strachey (London: Hogarth, 1953) 212.

4. Freud 212.

5. Freud 217. Although Freud does not use the specific term for "race" here (*die Rasse*), his use of the term *Völkern* clearly suggests a subset of peoples who can be distinguished from others and which the English term "race" closely approximates. *Cassell's German Dictionary* lists both *Volk* and the earlier invoked *der Stamm* as first-level translations for "race." See Freud, "Die Frage der Laienanalyse," *Gesammelte Werke*, vol. 14 (London: Imago, 1948) 241, 247.

6. G.W.F. Hegel, *The Phenomenology of Mind*, trans. J.B. Baillie (New York: Harper and Row, 1967) 496.

7. Class difference may well be added to these categories since Freud compares "races at a low level of civilization" with "the lower strata of civilized races." See the above quotations.

8. Nicolas Monti, ed., *Africa Then: Photographs 1840–1918* (New York: Knopf, 1987) 56.

9. See also Malek Alloula, *The Colonial Harem*, trans. Myrna Godzich and Wlad Godzich (Minneapolis: U of Minnesota P, 1986).

10. Sander L. Gilman, "Black Bodies, White Bodies: Toward an Iconography of Female Sexuality in Late Nineteenth-Century Art, Medicine, and Literature," *Critical Inquiry* 12.1 (Autumn 1985) 229.

11. Gilman 232.

12. Gilman 235.

13. For an extremely provocative reading of *Blonde Venus* and, in particular,

this scene, from a somewhat different angle, see Maurizia Boscagli, "The Eye on The Flesh: Gender, Ideology and the Modernist Body," diss., Brown University, 1990, 56–64. She analyzes *Blonde Venus* as a transformation of the image of the blonde beast in its articulation of nationalism/racism with consumer capitalism.

14. There is also a form of commodification of black female sexuality as the exemplification of the exotic. Josephine Baker, the black ex-patriate American who performed on stage and in films during the 1920s and 1930s in Europe, came to incarnate this representation of black female sexuality, particularly in the film *Princess Tam-Tam* (1935), where she is the personification of life, energy, a heightened sexuality, and primitiveness. However, this type of commodification was much more local and restricted in its effects than the commodification of white female sexuality.

15. See, for instance, Jane Gaines, "White Privilege and Looking Relations: Race and Gender in Feminist Film Theory," *Cultural Critique* 4 (Fall 1986): 59–79. A revised version of this essay appeared in *Screen* 29.4 (Autumn 1988): 12–27.

16. See also O. Mannoni, *Prospero and Caliban: The Psychology of Colonization*, trans. Pamela Powesland (New York: Praeger, 1964). Fanon is highly critical of Mannoni's approach. For an analysis of Fanon's confrontation with Mannoni, see Jock McCulloch, *Black soul white artifact: Fanon's clinical psychology and social theory* (Cambridge: Cambridge UP, 1983) 213–21.

17. While I am aware of the danger of reductiveness in relation to the wide diversity of racial and ethnic differences, I want to focus in this essay on the polarity of whiteness and blackness as it functions to structure the white imagination of sexuality and race. Although there is a sense in which racial relations are always infused with sexuality—that is, the Other, whether black, Asian, Native American, Chicano/a, etc., always carries a sexual threat—sexual fears and desires seem to be played out in the most extreme way in relation to the white imagination of blackness. In fact, Winthrop D. Jordan claims that Native Americans were not perceived in the same highly sexualized terms as blacks by the English colonists and "the entire interracial sexual complex did not pertain to the Indian." See Jordan, *White Over Black: American Attitudes Toward the Negro 1550–1812* (Baltimore: Penguin, 1969) 162–63.

18. Frantz Fanon, *Black Skin, White Masks*, trans. Charles Lam Markmann (New York: Grove, 1967) 23, hereafter cited in the text.

19. Fanon's attitude toward the negritude movement changes over the course of his writings. For an incisive analysis of these changes, see McCulloch 35–62.

20. McCulloch criticizes Fanon for confining his analysis to the petty bourgeoisie of the Antilles (in *Masks*) and claims that he "ignores completely the relationship between social class and alienation" (60).

21. McCulloch 74–75.

22. Fanon is also, quite rightly, suspicious of negritude because it posits an

essential connection between blackness and emotion/rhythm/the body—divorcing the black from the realm of the rational associated with the white European.

23. See Jacquelyn Dowd Hall, " 'The Mind That Burns in Each Body': Women, Rape, and Racial Violence," *Powers of Desire: The Politics of Sexuality*, ed. Ann Snitow, Christine Stansell, and Sharon Thompson (New York: Monthly Review, 1983) 328–49.

24. Hazel Carby, *Reconstructing Womanhood: The Emergence of the Afro-American Woman Novelist* (New York: Oxford UP, 1987) 109–15.

25. Carby 111; Hall 334.

26. In *Masks* (132–40), Fanon is highly critical of the argument about negritude Sartre presents in this introduction.

27. Jean-Paul Sartre, *Black Orpheus*, trans. S. W. Allen (Paris: Présence Africaine, 1963) 7–8.

28. Jordan 17–19.

29. "Since the racial drama is played out in the open, the black man has no time to 'make it unconscious.' The white man, on the other hand, succeeds in doing so to a certain extent, because a new element appears: guilt. The Negro's inferiority or superiority complex or his feeling of equality is *conscious*" (150).

30. Homi K. Bhabha, "The other question: difference, discrimination and the discourse of colonialism," *Literature, Politics, and Theory: Papers from the Essex Conference, 1976–84*, ed. Francis Barker, Peter Hulme, Margaret Iversen, and Diana Loxley (London: Methuen, 1986) 165–66.

31. Castration has also been a punishment meted out to Jews, but I believe the general import of Fanon's distinction still stands. The threat of Jewishness to the anti-Semite is less a physical than an intellectual threat. It is important to keep in mind how strongly Fanon was influenced by Sartre's work on anti-Semitism.

32. Sigmund Freud, "The 'Uncanny,' " *On Creativity and the Unconscious*, ed. Benjamin Nelson (New York: Harper and Row, 1958) 122–61.

33. Brantlinger 199.

34. Cited in Brantlinger 199.

35. Fanon is especially interested in *Home of the Brave* (Mark Robson, 1949) which he claims is a particularly corrupt attempt to apply psychoanalysis to the black (151, see also 139, 140). *Home of the Brave* fits extremely well into a subgenre I have elsewhere labeled the "medical discourse." In it, a black soldier is subjected to a procedure for prompting memory (and narrative)—"narcosynthesis"—which is usually reserved for the white woman within the subgenre. Not only is his position revealed as that of extreme cultural marginalization but he is also feminized in his relation to the doctor who applies the technique. See Doane, *The Desire to Desire* (Bloomington: Indiana UP, 1987) 38–69 and 190n.

36. In the 1910s and 1920s, a very small number of black production companies also concentrated on the melodramatic form. For an analysis of one of the most

available of these films, *Scar of Shame* (1927), see Jane Gaines, "*The Scar of Shame*: Skin Color and Caste in Black Silent Melodrama," *Cinema Journal* 26.4 (Summer 1987) 3–21.

37. Michael Rogin, *Ronald Reagan, The Movie and Other Episodes in Political Demonology* (Berkeley: U of California P, 1987) 213.

38. Rogin 226.

39. Jordan 165–78.

40. Hazel V. Carby, "White woman listen! Black feminism and the boundaries of sisterhood," *The Empire Strikes Back: Race and racism in 70s Britain* (London: Hutchinson and the Centre for Contemporary Cultural Studies, University of Birmingham, 1982) 213.

41. Bell Hooks, *Ain't I A Woman: Black Women and Feminism* (Boston: South End, 1981) 138. See also Elizabeth V. Spelman, *Inessential Woman: Problems of Exclusion in Feminist Thought* (Boston: Beacon, 1988).

42. For other analyses of Sirk's *Imitation of Life* from a feminist point of view, see Marina Heung, "'What's the Matter with Sara Jane?': Daughters and Mothers in Douglas Sirk's *Imitation of Life*," *Cinema Journal* 26.3 (Spring 1987): 21–43; Sandy Flitterman-Lewis, "*Imitation(s) of Life*: The Black Woman's Double Determination As Troubling 'Other,'" *Literature and Psychology* 34.4 (1988): 44–57; Lauren Berlant, "National Brands/National Body: *Imitation of Life*," in "Comparative American Identities: Race, Sex, and Nationality in the Modern Text," *Selected Papers from the English Institute*, ed. Hortense J. Spillers (Routledge, Chapman and Hall, forthcoming). Flitterman-Lewis compares the Stahl version and the Sirk version while Berlant deals with the Hurst novel and the two film versions in a provocative analysis of the imbrication of racial issues with the development of capitalist consumerism and commodity fetishism.

43. As a number of black scholars (Hazel Carby, Cornel West) have pointed out, an overemphasis upon the concept of a "Harlem Renaissance" can serve to make that period and place falsely paradigmatic of African-American cultural history, thus effacing other movements and schools. It is not my intention to reinforce this tendency, but it is important to delineate Fannie Hurst's relation to writers associated with the period known as the Harlem Renaissance.

44. Cary D. Wintz, *Black Culture and the Harlem Renaissance* (Houston: Rice UP, 1988) 179; see also John Lowe, "Hurston, Humor, and the Harlem Renaissance," *The Harlem Renaissance Re-examined*, ed. Victor A. Kramer (New York: AMS, 1987) 287; Virgina M. Burke, "Zora Neale Hurston and Fannie Hurst As They Saw Each Other," *CLA Journal* 20.4 (June 1977): 435–47; Robert E. Hemenway, *Zora Neale Hurston: A Literary Biography* (Urbana: U of Illinois P, 1977) 20–21, 24–25. According to Hemenway, privately Hurston "expressed doubts about why Hurst was so interested in their appearing in public together; she told at least one friend that she thought it was because Hurst liked the way Zora's dark skin highlighted her own lily-like complexion" (21).

45. Gaines, "White Privilege and Looking Relations," 24.

46. Cheryl A. Wall, "Passing for What? Aspects of Identity in Nella Larsen's Novels," *Black American Literature Forum* 20 (Spring/Summer 1986): 109.

47. Claudia Tate, "Nella Larsen's *Passing*: A Problem of Interpretation," *Black American Literature Forum* 14 (Winter 1980): 142. See also Barbara Christian, *Black Women Novelists: The Development of a Tradition, 1892–1976* (Westport, CT: Greenwood, 1980) 16, 44–45.

48. Carby, *Reconstructing Womanhood*, 89.

49. Nella Larsen, *"Quicksand" and "Passing,"* ed. Deborah E. McDowell (New Brunswick, N.J.: Rutgers UP, 1986) 150.

50. Robert E. Fleming, "*Kingsblood Royal* and the Black 'Passing' Novel," *Critical Essays on Sinclair Lewis*, ed. Martin Bucco (Boston: G.K. Hall, 1986) 217.

51. See Tate and Wall.

52. Donald Bogle, *Toms, Coons, Mulattoes, Mammies, & Bucks: An Interpretive History of Blacks in American Films* (New York: Continuum, 1989) 150.

53. This desire is clearly overdetermined since it also activates conventions stipulating the hypersexualization of the black woman.

54. Thomas Elsaesser, "Tales of Sound and Fury: Observations on the Family Melodrama," *Home is Where the Heart Is: Studies in Melodrama and the Woman's Film*, ed. Christine Gledhill (London: British Film Institute, 1987) 61–62.

55. See Jordan 171.

56. Rainer Werner Fassbinder, "Six Films by Douglas Sirk," trans. Thomas Elsaesser, *Douglas Sirk*, ed. Laura Mulvey and Jon Halliday (Edinburgh: Edinburgh Film Festival, 1972) 106.

57. Christine Gledhill, "The Melodramatic Field: An Investigation," *Home is Where the Heart Is*, 12.

58. Christian 18.

59. Richard Dyer, "White," *Screen* 29.4 (Autumn 1988): 44.

60. Carby, *Reconstructing Womanhood*, 115.

61. See Barbara Johnson, "Psychoanalysis and Normative Whiteness," Div. on Psychological Approaches to Literature, MLA Convention, Washington, D.C., 28 Dec. 1989.

62. This is beginning to change but the most profound effects of this change can be seen not in the American cinema but in the movement referred to as Black British Cinema. See, for instance, *Dreaming Rivers*, dir. Martina Attile, Sankofa, 1988 and *The Passion of Remembrance*, dir. Maureen Blackwood and Isaac Julien, Sankofa, 1986. Important independent films in the United States have been made by Julie Dash (*Illusions*, 1982) and Alile Sharon Larkin (*A Different Image*, 1982).

63. Henry Louis Gates, Jr., "Editor's Introduction: Writing 'Race' and the Difference It Makes," *Critical Inquiry* 12.1 (1985): 4.

64. Gates 5.

65. Jacques Derrida, "Structure, Sign, and Play in the Discourse of the Human Sciences," *Writing and Difference* (Chicago: U of Chicago P, 1978) 278–93.

66. This is, perhaps, most true in the United States and totally inapplicable to certain other countries.

67. Gayatri Chakravorty Spivak with Ellen Rooney, "In a Word. *Interview*," *Differences* 1.2 (Summer 1989): 153.

68. Brantlinger 199.

CHAPTER TWELVE

1. Jean Laplanche, *Problématiques III: La sublimation* (Paris: Presses Universitaires de France, 1980) 119. My translation.

2. Sigmund Freud, "The origin and development of psychoanalysis," *A General Selection from the Works of Sigmund Freud* (New York: Doubleday, 1957) 35.

3. J. Laplanche and J.-B. Pontalis, *The Language of Psychoanalysis*, trans. Donald Nicholson-Smith (New York: Norton, 1974) 433.

4. Luce Irigaray, *Speculum of the Other Woman*, trans. Gillian C. Gill (Ithaca: Cornell UP, 1985) 124.

5. Irigaray 125.

6. John Frow, "Spectacle Binding: On Character," *Poetics Today* 7.2 (1986): 227.

7. Frow 228.

8. Frow 227.

9. See, for instance, Constance Penley, "Feminism, Film Theory and the Bachelor Machines," *m/f* 10 (1985): 53–54; and Elizabeth Cowie, "Fantasia," *m/f* 9 (1984): 71–104.

10. J. Laplanche and J.-B. Pontalis, "Fantasy and the Origins of Sexuality," *Formations of Fantasy*, ed. Victor Burgin, James Donald, and Cora Kaplan (London: Methuen, 1986) 26.

11. Laplanche and Pontalis, *Language* 318.

12. Laplanche and Pontalis, "Fantasy" 14–15.

13. Laplanche and Pontalis, "Fantasy" 26.

14. Sigmund Freud, "The Ego and the Id," *General Selection* 227.

15. Jean Laplanche, "To Situate Sublimation," trans. Richard Miller, *October* 28 (Spring 1984): 24.

16. Laplanche, "To Situate Sublimation," 19.

17. Laplanche refers to sublimation as "a sort of *plaiting, from the origin,*

between the nonsexual and that permanent source of the sexual." Problématiques
III 249. My translation.

18. Jacques Lacan, *The Four Fundamental Concepts of Psycho-analysis*, ed.
Jacques-Alain Miller, trans. Alan Sheridan (Harmondsworth, Eng.: Penguin, 1979)
165.

19. Lacan, *Four Fundamental Concepts* 165–66.

20. Jacques Lacan, *Le séminaire livre VII: L'éthique de la psychanalyse* (Paris:
Éditions du seuil) 155. All translations from this source are mine.

21. Lacan, *L'éthique* 145. Lacan goes on to claim that in precisely the same way
speech (*parole*) and discourse can be empty or full.

22. Lacan, *L'éthique* 133.

23. Lacan, *L'éthique* 179.

24. Lacan, *L'éthique* 133.

25. Michèle Montrelay, "Inquiry Into Femininity," *m/f* 1 (1978): 96.

26. Montrelay 98.

27. Montrelay 98.

28. See Frances Ferguson, "The Nuclear Sublime," *Diacritics* 14.2 (Summer
1984): 4–10.

29. Sigmund Freud, "Leonardo da Vinci and a Memory of His Childhood," *The
Standard Edition of The Complete Psychological Works of Sigmund Freud*, vol.
11, ed. James Strachey (London: Hogarth, 1957) 59–137.

30. Freud, "Civilization and Its Discontents," *The Standard Edition*, vol. 21,
80n.

31. Freud, "Civilization," 80n.

32. Freud, "Three Essays on the Theory of Sexuality," *The Standard Edition*,
vol. 7, 238.

33. Freud, " 'Civilized' Sexual Morality and Modern Nervousness," *Collected
Papers*, vol. 2 (New York: Basic, 1959) 83.

34. Freud, "The 'Uncanny,' " *The Standard Edition*, vol. 17, 237.

35. See, for instance, "Femininity," *Standard Edition*, vol. 22, 121, where Freud
addresses the reader: "I have no doubt you are ready to suspect that this portrayal
of the abundance and strength of a little girl's sexual relations with her mother is
very much overdrawn."

36. In "Three Essays on the Theory of Sexuality," Freud refers to "the immense
number of women who are prostitutes or who must be supposed to have an aptitude
for prostitution without becoming engaged in it" (191).

37. Christine Buci-Glucksmann, "Catastrophic Utopia: The Feminine as Allegory of the Modern," *Representations* 14 (Spring 1986): 226.

38. Freud, "Three Essays," 238.

39. Freud, "Three Essays," 191. For a more extensive discussion of Freud's

attitude toward prostitution and its relation to prevalent ideas about the seductive child and the lower-class female, see Sander L. Gilman, "Freud and the Prostitute: Male Stereotypes of Female Sexuality in *fin-de-siècle* Vienna," *Journal of the American Academy of Psychoanalysis*, 9.3 (1981): 337–60.

40. See Alain Corbin, *Women for Hire: Prostitution and Sexuality in France after 1850*, trans. Alan Sheridan (Cambridge, MA: Harvard UP, 1990) and Charles Bernheimer, *Figures of Ill Repute: Representing Prostitution in Nineteenth-Century France* (Cambridge, MA: Harvard UP, 1989).

41. Corbin xv.

42. Corbin 6.

43. Corbin 10.

44. Corbin 336.

45. Corbin 337.

46. T.J. Clark, *The Painting of Modern Life: Paris in the Art of Manet and His Followers* (Princeton: Princeton UP, 1984) 103.

47. Cited in Susan Buck-Morss, "The Flaneur, the Sandwichman and the Whore: The Politics of Loitering," *New German Critique* 39 (Fall 1986): 121.

48. Buci-Glucksmann 224.

49. Ferguson 6.

50. According to Benjamin, "The commodity attempts to look itself in the face. It celebrates its becoming human in the whore." "Central Park," *New German Critique* 34 (Winter 1985): 42. Also, for a somewhat different analysis of the relation between the prostitute and the commodity, which emphasizes a historical parallel between prostitution and the fad of collecting, see Emily Apter, "Cabinet Secrets: Fetishism, Prostitution, and the Fin de Siècle Interior," *Assemblage: A Critical Journal of Architecture and Design Culture* 9 (June 1989): 7–19.

51. Cited in Walter Benjamin, *Charles Baudelaire: A Lyric Poet in the Era of High Capitalism*, trans. Harry Zohn (London: New Left, 1973) 56.

52. Both Laplanche and Leo Bersani believe that the relation between sexuality and the aesthetic work can be more precisely defined through the concept of sublimation. This involves, however, fully accepting the viability of this concept and neglecting the difficulties which have been delineated here. One of the consequences in Laplanche's reading is to limit the definition of the art work to a quite classical one involving a unity and harmony which could be analogous to the notion of genital primacy. See Laplanche, "To Situate Sublimation," 25. Bersani's argument also involves an enormous expansion of the notion of sexuality which, while it is certainly not inconsistent with Freudian strategy, weakens the specificity of the term. See Bersani, "Sexuality and Aesthetics," *October* 28 (Spring 1984): 27–42.

53. As long as the symptoms are attributed not to characters but to texts.

54. Montrelay 96.

Index

Absence: in *La Signora di tutti*, 121, 134, 141; and sublimation, 256

Abstraction: the cinema and, 122; in *La Signora di tutti*, 124, 140–41

Achebe, Chinua, 248

Acting: in *Imitation of Life* (1959), 236–37

Adams, Parveen, 170, 173–75

Adams Rib, 24–25

Adynata, 13, 178–87

Aesthetics: in Freudian psychoanalysis, 265–66

Affirmation: woman as, 61–62; 68–69

Affron, Charles, 20

Africa: as the dark continent, 209, 210

Aggressivity: and the imaginary relation, 110–11

Akerman, Chantal, 176

Althusser, Louis, 7

Ambassadors, The: Lacan's analysis of, 66–67, 84

Anaclisis (propping), 169, 254–55

Anamorphosis: Lacan on, 66–67, 84, 277n.32

Androgyny: in *Pandora's Box*, 153

Anti-essentialism, 12–13, 168–75; and Nietzsche, 58; and race, 9

Anti-Semitism, 295n.31

Apparatus: Freud on the, 80–81; theory of the, 78, 80, 86

Apparatus, cinematic: and feminist film theory, 94–95; relation between the woman and the, 77–78, 122–24; theory of the, 82–86, 165–66

Apter, Emily, 300n.50

Art: and sublimation, 250–51, 256

Art criticism: and Doisneau, 30–31

Astruc, Alexandre, 139

Avant-garde cinema, 190; as interrogation of the image, 196–200; and psychoanalysis, 192; and the trompe l'oeil, 195–200

Baker, Josephine, 294n.14

Balázs, Béla, 275n.8

Barthes, Roland: analysis of Garbo, 47; on beauty, 182–83; *Empire of Signs*, 178–80; on the grain of the voice, 187; on narrative, 176–77, 284n.31; on photography, 178; on striptease, 106

Baubo, 65–67

Baudelaire, Charles, 266

Baudry, Jean-Louis, 80–86, 88, 89

Bazin, André, 291n.16

Benjamin, Walter: on the commodity, 300n.50; on gambling, 156–57; on prostitution, 263–64; on storytelling, 138–39

Berg, Alban, 159, 161

Berlant, Lauren, 296n.42

Bersani, Leo, 300n.52